Last of the Lancasters

Last of the Lancasters

Martin W. Bowman

Pen & Sword
AVIATION

First Published in Great Britain in 2014 by
Pen & Sword Aviation
an imprint of
Pen & Sword Books Ltd
47 Church Street, Barnsley, South Yorkshire S70 2AS

A CIP catalogue record for this book is
available from the British Library.

Typeset in 10/12pt Palatino
by GMS Enterprises

Printed and bound in England by
CPI Group (UK) Ltd, Croydon, CR0 4YY

Pen & Sword Books Ltd incorporates the Imprints of Pen & Sword
Aviation, Pen & Sword Family History, Pen & Sword Maritime, Pen & Sword
Military, Pen & Sword Discovery, Wharncliffe Local History, Wharncliffe
True Crime, Wharncliffe Transport, Pen & Sword Select, Pen & Sword
Military Classics, Leo Cooper, The Praetorian Press, Remember When,
Seaforth Publishing and Frontline Publishing.

For a complete list of Pen & Sword titles please contact
PEN & SWORD BOOKS LIMITED

47 Church Street, Barnsley, South Yorkshire, S70 2AS, England
E-mail: enquiries@pen-and-sword.co.uk
Website: www.pen-and-sword.co.uk

Contents

Acknowledgements

I am indebted to all the contributors for their words and photographs. Thanks also go to my fellow author, friend and colleague, Graham Simons, for getting the book to press ready standard and for his detailed work on the photographs; to Pen & Sword and in particular, Laura Hirst; and to Jon Wilkinson, for his unique jacket design once again. Equally, I am most grateful to Sam Mealing-Mills of the Mildenhall Register for kindly allowing me to quote from his taped interview with Norman Gregory and to Nigel Clarke for putting me in touch with this fine gentleman in the first instance. Thanks also are due to Philip Swan, author of *Diary of a Bomb Aimer: Training in America and Flying With 12 Squadron in WWII*, for kindly allowing me to quote passages concerning Campbell Muirhead; and to my old friend and fellow author, Ian McLachlan for kindly permitting me to quote passages from the story of Harry Church in Ian's book, Flights Into History which was published in 2007. *Memorial Flight 2000; Journal of the Linconshire Lancaster Association;* No.33 spring 2000 and No.34, autumn 2000. Special mention too must be made of the contributions made by Hugh Trevor, for his research into the activities of Major Tony Cotterell and for the photographs used in this story; 49 Squadron Association; Nigel McTeer; The Norfolk & Suffolk Aviation Museum; the Second Air Division Memorial Library, Norwich; *Aeroplane* and *Flypast* magazines and the City Of Norwich Aviation Museum.

Prologue
S. D. Clewer

My journey was the path of many airmen via 81 OTU Whitleys, then to 1662 HCU Lancasters and our posting to103 Squadron at Elsham Wolds. We arrived there in June 1943 by crew bus to book in at the Guard Room. At that moment a Queen Mary transport was leaving loaded with kit bags. I quickly realised they were missing and deceased airmens' kit. A sad welcome to a great Squadron. I found myself saying out loud 'My kit won't go that way.' Someone replied, 'Famous last words.' The first two weeks on squadron were a complete disaster. We had four operational take offs, three of these being aborted, mainly for mechanical reasons. A mine-laying trip was no better I saw the ground twice in just over six hours flying both times - once at take off and on landing. Our skipper was carpeted for not pressing on regardless and was posted away. So there were six odd bods, one was posted to a nearby squadron. Within a month only Johnny Sheedy, flight engineer and myself remained. Johnny crewed up with Warrant Officer Kenneth Reuben Lee DFC. I flew with three crews and each time I was replaced they went missing. On one occasion my name was taken from the war order list and a Pilot Officer Deakins was substituted as he had that day returned from a Gunnery Leaders course. Fate played another card in my survival when Bob Edie's rear gunner was classed as LMF. I took his place. Johnny Sheedy and I had been together for almost a year, I had a lot to thank him for. He rescued me from drowning in a dinghy drill accident. He also suffered freezing conditions when he attended to my frozen oxygen supply. He had completed 25 trips when they also failed to return, on Kassel on 22/23 October 1943. This was a shock to me as Johnny Sheedy was without doubt a brave and intelligent flight engineer. So five months and one week had elapsed when I passed the Guard Room with my kit and with my first tour completed. I have every cause to believe I was fated to survive.

Flight Lieutenant S. D. Clewer, rear gunner, 103 Squadron at Elsham Wolds, 1943.

Chapter 1

The First 'Daylights'

It had been my ambition tonight to tell you the story of the daylight raid on Augsburg in the way it deserves to be told - to weld into words this great flying epic of all time which will rank - not merely in air history but in war history - more highly as the years go by and its glory takes on the legendary lustre of the great deeds of the past. As I sat down pen in hand, a sorry Tennyson with the story of this greater 'Light Brigade of the Air' still dormant in the inkpot, I could see those twelve thirty-ton monsters on which they rode their charge. I had a memoried vision of trees blurring past the leading edge of a wing - of cannon shells rocketing into a little white-washed village - of the tense steely eyes of the pilot looking forward, never more than a field or two ahead - hour after hour. And then I'm sorry to say I gave it up - the brush was too shaky - the canvas too small. But I can at any rate try to re-tell you the story somehow - and re-tell it I will. They were called in for briefing at twelve noon on 17 April - eighty young men, mostly in their early twenties. They weren't specially picked, trained or doped with Benzedrine on the German model - they were just normally interested to find out what all the excitement was about and when they were told that they were to take on the sort of job which the Luftwaffe had given up two years ago as impossible, they seemed chiefly concerned with the contours of that last wooded hill before Augsburg over which in a few hours time some of them were to get their first glimpse of the deadly breeding ground of the submarine Diesel. Then, later in the afternoon the hunt started - a hunt for a thousand miles at fifty feet over hedges and ditches which has made every airman in the world who has ever tree-hopped for half a mile see in imagination a picture of the most fantastic chase that probably the history of pursuit has ever known - a hunt to the tally-ho of roaring engines which would have made Jorrocks turn in his grave.
**Group Captain W. Helmore 'April 30th' one of his monthly commentaries
on the BBC after the 9 o'clock news.**

In the afternoon of 17 April 1942, a few days before the four-night attack on Rostock, a very different method was used by 5 Group, Bomber Command to attack an objective as small as, or even smaller than, the Heinkel assembly shed at Marienehe outside the town. This was the dispatch of twelve Lancaster bombers in daylight to the submarine Diesel engine assembly shed in the M.A.N. factory at Augsburg, far down in southern Germany. The Lancasters were to be back by midnight. The whole plan of this attack was worked out at Headquarters at least a week before, but the crews were told about it only on the day of the attack. They knew, however, that something was in the wind, because they had been taken off all other work and told to practise low flying in formation across country and, in particular, navigation at such a low level. When they were briefed, they were told of the great importance of the target. Half the Diesel engines for ocean-going U-boats were made in the M.A.N. factory. To reduce the supply of diesel engines would throw the whole submarine-building programme out of gear. At a time when the U-boats in the Atlantic were becoming a most serious menace it would be hard to imagine any more important single target than this assembly shed at Augsburg. It would be worth serious losses to hit this target.

On 11 April 44 Squadron was ordered to fly long distance flights in formation to obtain endurance data on the Lancaster. At the same time 97 Squadron began flying low in groups of three in 'vee' formation to Selsey Bill, then up to Lanark, across to Falkirk and up to Inverness to a point just outside the town, where they feigned an attack and then back to Woodhall Spa. Crews in both the squadrons knew that the real reason was that they were training for a special operation and speculation as to the target was rife.

'Despite frequent groundings', recalls David Penman, a pilot on 97 Squadron.'Training continued and early in April rumours of some special task for the Lancasters were confirmed when eight crews were selected to practice low level formation flying and bombing. The final practice was a cross-country at 250 feet for two sections of three led by Squadron Leader John S. Sherwood DFC* with myself leading the second section.[1] We took off from Woodhall Spa and were to rendezvous with 44 Squadron near Grantham but because of unserviceability they did not take off. We flew down to Selsey Bill and then turned round and headed for Inverness. Due to compass errors the lead section got off track and they were heading into an area of masts and balloons. With no communication allowed I eventually parted company with the lead section and we did not see them again until we were bombing the target in the Wash at Wainfleet. Our low-level flight up valleys to Edinburgh was exciting, but over the higher ground in the North we climbed to a reasonable altitude over cloud, descending in the clear at Inverness for a low-level run. Once beyond Edinburgh, on the way back, we descended again to low level and, full of confidence, really got down to hedge hopping. Flying Officer Deverill on the left and Warrant Officer Thomas Mycock DFC.[2] on the right maintained very tight formation and my only regret was the stampeding cattle when we could not avoid flying over them. Greater satisfaction came as we roared across familiar airfields a few feet from the hangar roofs and Waddington got the full blast of our slip stream as we rubbed in our success whilst they were stuck on the ground. A perfect formation bombing run with Sherwood's section running in behind completed a very successful day.

'A few days later I went to HQ 5 Group in Grantham with the Station Commander from Coningsby and Squadron Leader Sherwood. At 5 Group when the target was revealed, we were shattered and suicide was common thought. However, the briefing was thorough with an excellent scale model of the target area and emphasis on low level to avoid detection, massive diversionary raids and little ack-ack or opposition at Augsburg. This briefing was only a day or two before the 17th and no one else was to be informed until the briefing on the day of the raid when take-off was to be 1515 hours. On

Friday the 17th briefing was immediately after lunch with crew kitted ready to go. The scale model of the target was on display and the gasps as crews entered the room and saw the target were noticeable.'

At Waddington Wing Commander Roderick A. B. 'Babe' Learoyd VC the 44 Squadron CO, began his address to the crews with 'Bomber Command have come up with a real beauty this time' and added 'I shan't be coming with you. I've got my VC already. I've no desire to get another.'[3] At Woodhall Spa when the curtain was drawn back at the briefing there was a roar of laughter instead of the gasp of horror. Before the laughter had died down, the 97 Squadron commander, Wing Commander Collier, entered and walked quietly forward to the front of the briefing room and mounted the dais. The crews came to order at once, listening intently. 'Well gentlemen', smiled the wing commander, 'now you know what the target is'.

The target was the diesel engine manufacturing workshop at the MAN[4] factory at Augsburg but no one in the room believed that the RAF would be so stupid as to send twelve of its newest four-engined bombers all that distance inside Germany in daylight. Crews sat back and waited calmly for someone to say, 'Now the real target is this' but Augsburg was the real target. Air Marshal Harris wanted the plant raided by a small force of Lancasters flying at low level (500 feet) and in daylight despite some opposition from the Ministry of Economic Warfare, who wanted the ball-bearing plant at Schweinfurt attacked instead. Crews were ordered to take their steel helmets on this raid. Sixteen Lancaster crews, eight each from 44 (Rhodesia) and 97 Squadrons (including four first and second reserve) were specially selected. Squadron Leader John Dering Nettleton, still on his first tour in 44 Squadron, was chosen to lead the operation. The 24-year old South African, who had been born at Nongoma in Natal and educated in Cape Town, had spent eighteen months at sea in the merchant service before coming to England to join the RAF in 1938 to train as a pilot. Dark haired but fair-skinned, tall and reticent, grandson of an admiral, he was an inspired choice as leader.

Pilot Officer Patrick Dorehill, Nettleton's 20-year-old second pilot wrote: 'There was certainly some surprise on entering the briefing room to see the pink tape leading all the way into the heart of Germany. I can't say I felt anxious. I had an extraordinary faith in the power of the Lancaster to defend itself. And then flying at low level seemed to me to be the perfect way to outwit the enemy. I thought the only danger might be over the target and, even there, believed we would be in and away before there was much response.'

Flying Officer Eric E. 'Rod' Rodley, the reserve pilot, who was known for his whimsical sense of humour, found nothing to smile about. He was appalled when the target was named but he and his crew of 'F-Freddie' had clung to the hope that they were only the reserve. Rodley had been 'one of the lucky ones', joining the RAFVR in 1937 and he already had instructing experience when war broke out. Consequently, he graced the first 'War Instructors Course' at CFS in October, 1939, after which he spent an exhausting and unrewarding year and a half in Training Command. Hence, by June 1941, he had over 1,000 hours in his logbook but he was 'quite unprepared for any wider aspects of the art.' A strange set of circumstances rescued him from the thralldom of instructing when 97

Squadron was re-formed and equipped with the Avro Manchester when all pilots had to have at least 1,000 hours under their belts. One of his contemporaries in 97 Squadron, Norfolk-man Flying Officer Brian Roger Wakefield 'Darkie' Hallows, who after flying three days of long formation cross-countries was set to fly 'B-Baker'.[5] Like Rodley, Hallows had been an instructor before becoming a Manchester and then a Lancaster pilot.[6] It was his reputation for the use of R/T language 'which caused some watch tower WAAFs to giggle, some to blush'[7] and not for his jet black hair and full moustache that earned him his nickname 'Darkie'. When he had got lost and invoked the R/T get-you-home service of those early days: 'Darkie, Darkie', receiving no response, he had tried again, but still no reply. Once more he had transmitted to the void: 'Darkie, Darkie - where are you, you little black bastard?'

Hallows recalls.

'Plenty was said about how important it [Augsburg] was and all that stuff. So we were obviously not intended to come back in any strength. Fighter Command had been on the job for several days, hounding the German fighters and when we were on the job we saw no fighters at all, all the way...' Just before the Lancasters took off thirty Bostons bombed targets in France in a planned attempt to force hundreds of German fighters up over the Pas de Calais, Cherbourg and Rouen areas. This was designed to draw the enemy fighters into combat so that the passage of the Lancasters would coincide with their refuelling and re-arming. Unfortunately it had the opposite effect and the incursion put the Luftwaffe on the alert. David Penman continues.

'Take-off was to be at 1515 hours with the two reserve aircraft taking off and dropping out when the two Vics of three set course.[8] We were to meet 44 Squadron near Grantham and then on to Selsey Bill, across the Channel, then down south of Paris before turning left and heading for Lake Constance. Take-off was on time, singly, with full fuel [2,134 gallons] and four 1,000lb RDX bombs with 11-second delay fuses to be dropped from 250 feet. Weather forecast was perfect with clear skies and good visibility all the way. I took off and soon had Deverill on my left and Mycock on my right. We joined the lead section of Squadron Leader Sherwood, Flying Officer Hallows and Flying Officer Rodley. [As they had watched the other six aircraft starting up some of Rodley's crew had begun to have mixed feelings and almost wished now that they had got this far that they were going. Then 'A-Apple' had a mag drop on No.1 engine and Rodley's crew had fallen silent. Rodley thought of his wife in Woodhall Spa. She would probably guess what had happened. He took off with the others and moved into the No.3 position, tucked in to port of Sherwood.[9]] Once again there was no sign of 44 Squadron near Grantham and we were never to meet. We maintained 250 feet to Selsey Bill and then got down as close to the sea as possible for the Channel crossing. As we approached the French coast my rear gunner informed me his turret was U/S and I told him it was too late to do anything about it and he would just have to do what he could with it. Crossing the French coast was an anti-climax as not a shot was fired and we flew on at tree top height to Lake Constance. We saw the odd aircraft in the distance but otherwise it was a very pleasant trip.'

Penman's Australian navigator, Pilot Officer E. Lister 'Ding' Ifould who had joined the RAAF in 1940 and went to England in July 1941, saw frightened bullocks scampering across the furrows with their ploughs bumping along behind them. He saw French workers wave to them but usually only when they were working in secluded parts where their greeting would be unobserved. One greeting came from two or three workers deep in a quarry, down which Ifould had a momentary glimpse as their Lancaster flew over almost at tree-top height; and again, in a wood, some charcoal burners stopped to give them a secret wave. The Lancs passed over no fewer than twenty-seven German airfields almost at ground level and saw nothing except a few parked aircraft. This hedgehopping was a severe test of skill and endurance. Ifould's captain, Penman, had blisters on both hands when the job was done.[10]

44 Squadron meanwhile had not been as fortunate as 97 Squadron. Nettleton took his formation flying in Vics of three down to just 50 feet over the waves of the Channel as the French coast came into view. Five minutes later, Nettleton's first two sections were intercepted by fighters and a running fight lasted an hour. The Lancasters tightened formation, flying wingtip to wingtip to give mutual protection with their guns as they skimmed low over villages and rising and falling countryside. The Bf 109s of II./JG2 were forced to attack from above. Nettleton's No.3, 'H-Harry', flown by Sergeant G. T. 'Dusty' Rhodes, was first to go down, a victim of Spanish Civil War veteran Major Walter 'Gulle' Oesau, Kommodore, JG 2.[11] None of the crew stood a chance at such a low altitude in an aircraft travelling at 200 mph. Nettleton recalled. 'I saw two or three fighters about 1,000 feet above us. The next thing I knew, there were German fighters all round us. The first casualty I saw was Sergeant Rhodes' aircraft. Smoke poured from his cockpit and his port wing caught fire. He came straight for me out of control and I thought we were going to collide. We missed by a matter of feet and he crashed beneath me. Two others went down almost at once and I saw a fourth on fire. At the time I was too much occupied to feel very much. I remember a bullet chipped a piece of perspex, which hit my second pilot in the back of the neck. I could hear him say 'What the hell.' I laughed at that.'

The whole of 44 Squadron's second 'Vee' were shot out of the sky. 'T-Tommy' was being flown by Warrant Officer Herbert V. Crum DFM, a wily bird, old in years and experience by comparison with most of the others. Sergeant Bert Dowty the nineteen-year old front gunner recalled sea spray from the aircraft hitting the front turret and remembered Crum lifting the nose of their Lancaster to clear the French cliffs at Le Havre. About 70 miles inland, they flew over an airfield where three Bf 109s were landing. Next thing the crew heard the sound of cannon fire as Warrant Officer J. F. 'Joe' Beckett DFM, flying 'V-Victor' the starboard Lancaster, said over the intercom: 'Fighters 11 o'clock high'. Beckett's rear turret was out of action and he had attracted most of the enemy fighters. There were about 30 of them at around 5,000 feet and the order came to 'close up and keep tight'. That was the last Dowty heard for the intercom went dead. He saw tracers flashing by and was surprised to see more 109s below as he tried to pick them off. At this point, they saw Beckett's aircraft crash in a ball of flame. Hauptmann Heine Greisert of II./JG2 was later credited with shooting the Lancaster down. It crashed into a tree and disintegrated. The crew never stood a chance.

Unteroffizier Pohl of II./JG2 singled out 'T-Tommy' and he set two engines on fire. Dowty noticed that the ground was getting uncomfortably close and he was unable to hear what was happening. He instinctively ducked as the Lancaster flew under a high tension cable. Bert Crum had reacted splendidly to avoid a tree and make a wheels-up belly landing in a reasonably flat wheat field at Folleville. Dowty avoided injury by keeping his feet fixed in the frame above the bomb sight. However, he was only too aware that they had taken off with four 1,000lb bombs and these had only 11 second delay fuses. He was to learn later that the bombs had been jettisoned by the second pilot, Sergeant Alan Dedman before the aircraft crash-landed, but with the absence of any intercom Dowty was unaware of this. Removing the left-hand gun from its mounting he was feverishly trying to smash the perspex of his turret when an axe blade suddenly appeared on the left hand side. Wielding the axe was Bert Crum, who smashed a hole in the perspex and dragged Dowty out on to terra firma. Crum then turned his attention to the fuel tanks and Crum split the petrol tanks with his axe and tried to set fire to the escaping petrol using a Very pistol but it would not ignite. Sergeant Birkett the navigator endeavoured to set the fuel alight with incendiary canisters but this equally proved fruitless. But then Dowty remembered that he kept a 4oz 'Tom Long' tobacco tin in his turret and in the tin were ten cigarettes and a box of matches. Returning to the turret he recovered the matches, lit two and threw them on the fuel. Nothing happened. He struck another pair of matches and this time the fuel went up, singeing his hair and eyebrows. About 500 yards away another Lancaster was ablaze. This was not, as they had supposed, Beckett's aircraft but that of their Flight Leader Flight Lieutenant Nicky Sandford DFC, the last aircraft of the second Vic to be hit. Crum, armed with the axe, left his crew and went off to see if he could help this other stricken Lancaster.

Sandford had faced the milling enemy fighters alone and forced his aircraft down even lower in a desperate attempt to shake off his pursuers. Suddenly ahead of him he saw a line of telephone wires. He held the nose down and flew underneath them but the FW 190s followed firing all the time. 'A little fellow with a pleasing personality, who was keen on music and who bought all the records for the Officers' Mess, he always wore his pyjamas under his flying suit for luck. This time Sandford was all out of luck. He finally fell victim to the guns of Feldwebel Bosseckert. With all four engines on fire his Lancaster crashed into the ground in an inferno of flame.

Meanwhile the remaining six members on Crum's crew took stock. The time of the attack was evident as the wireless operator's watch had stopped at 1712 hours. Sergeant Miller's face was covered in blood caused by a cannon shell which had passed through his turret grazing his scalp en route. They bandaged him up as best they could using the aircraft first aid pack. To add to their problems, Sergeant Cobb the rear gunner had damaged his knee and was unable to walk properly. The six of them then made for a wood about half a mile away and here they decided to split up. The two wounded men were to lie low in the woods while Dedman, Birkett, Saunderson and Dowty took a compass reading and headed due south. Around 20.30 hours, after walking about ten kilometres, they came across a woodman burning brushwood. Birkett had a smattering of French and told them who they were. They were directed to a farm some 400 yards away where the lady took them in, gave them food and coffee and let them stay the night. The events of the day meant that sleep was not easy to come by and at 5a.m. not wanting to present any problems to the lady, they left the house and took refuge in a small copse in the centre of a nearby field where they hid all day. Several truckloads of troops went by and in the evening they returned to the farm for food and water. They were told that the Germans had been searching the area all day looking for airmen so to save further embarrassment to the lady they headed south and entered a forest. Negotiating this forest was not without incident. Startled at first by what they thought were lights - these turned out to be fireflies - they then encountered a wild boar which made a ferocious noise and succeeded in 'scaring the living daylights out of all of them.' Walking through the middle of a forest at night with only occasional moonlight through the tops of the trees, it was easy for the four to believe they had stumbled on a carefully hidden Panzer tank division. In a large clearing were tanks covered in tarpaulins with 88mm guns pointing wickedly towards them. A figure moved about in a look-out sentry post up in the trees. They spent some time crawling flat on their stomachs before they realised the truth. It was a forestry clearing and the 'tanks' were pit-props covered in tarpaulins. The look-out post was indeed a fire look-out post but the 'movement' had been caused by branches silhouetted by the moon, swaying in the wind. This forest, as they discovered later, was 17 kilometres across and it had taken them a night and a day negotiating it. Around 2300 hours on the second night they emerged to a clear moonlit night and saw a cottage only a few yards away. The door opened in response to Birkett's knock and a lady invited them in and gave them food and coffee. Taking pity on the airmen, she went out into the yard and killed one of her chickens, plucked and boiled it in a pot before presenting it to them as they resumed their journey. Dowty carried the chicken until eventually hunger overcame them all and they gratefully quelled their appetites.

As they proceeded south, they were overtaken by an elderly lady on a bicycle who looked at them curiously. Accordingly the four airmen hid up in a wood and did not pay too much attention the sound of a vehicle pull nearby. They were startled by a blast on a whistle and found themselves surrounded by a posse of gendarmes. The old lady had alerted the French that there were four 'bandits' in the area and they had come out to search for them. Somewhat nonplussed, the chief gendarme took a chance that none of his men were collaborators and suggested that the four airmen, who thinking the game was up were now eating their escape ration chocolates, should move out of the area. This they did to the 'Bon chance' from the gendarmes. They had now been evading the enemy for nine days, during which time they had received no material assistance other than food.

In their escape kit, they little French money, a silk compass and a few escape rations. It was at this point that they made a decision to change their direction and head west for the coast. Approaching a railway line they followed it until they came upon a station cafe where Birkett used some of his French money to buy some cigarettes. However, being observed by two doubtful looking characters they decided once again to seek the shelter of a wood. On reaching the far side they saw a farmer ploughing his field and Birkett explained who they were. The farmer told them to lie low and he would return in the evening. Staying there on tenterhooks, not knowing whether the farmer would hand them over, they were relieved to see him return and take him to his farmhouse. There they were fed by the farmer's wife and introduced to a 15-year-old lad, who was to take them to the farmer's father-in-law's farm some 17 kilometres further. Apparently it was a larger farm situated in a cul-de-sac and afforded better cover. He swore the lad to secrecy saying that the four were Spanish woodcutters seeking employment. They left at midnight and arrived at the farm at 6am. During the journey, Birkett told the lad they were in fact RAF airmen. After being given a hot drink and food they were taken to the granary where they were able to sleep in the hay. After two nights they were then taken two at a time, in a pony and trap driven by a lady they had not seen before. They lay in the trap beneath two bales of straw and after about 5 kilometres they drew into a lay-by alongside a wood. Awaiting them was a pick-up truck which presented an unusual sight inasmuch as it was fitted out with a gas-bag - the only means of propulsion. Both straw and airmen were then transferred into the truck and driven to a 'safe' house 20 kilometres away. Here they met a Frenchman who had been a pilot in the French Air Force in 1921 and after checking back that they were genuine evaders he made arrangements to take them, again two at a time, in the pick-up truck to the cafe of a hotel in Alençon. It was here that they first encountered German troops in strength. They also met their first English speaking person. He had been a captain in the Royal Navy during the First World War before settling in France. He explained that the plan was to get them into Vichy France. They would first go by train, tickets were provided, to Le Mans. After spending two nights there, the four airmen with their guide duly boarded the train for Le Mans amid a crowd of German troops. Luck was with the evaders. They changed trains at Le Mans and boarded a train to Tours. Fifteen kilometres south of Tours they alighted and boarded a bus. By this time they had managed to change their RAF trousers for ones provided by their be-frienders although they still carried their battle-dress tops in sacks in case they were arrested.

It was a somewhat bemused Sergeant Dowty who found himself clad in decorator's trousers, sitting in a bus facing two German officers.When their guide alighted, so the airmen followed suit. Their guide entered a cafe and emerged with another man. This, in 1942 was an early form of resistance line and the two explained that once they crossed the field ahead and made for the church, they would be in Vichy France. As they were about to make the run. two German guards appeared complete with dog and they were obliged to take cover in a ditch. It was early morning and dew from the kale in the banks of the ditch trickled down the backs of their necks. A miserable sensation! When the guards had passed, they broke cover and ran for the church. It was with a feeling of elation that they had at last escaped from enemy-occupied France. Now their journey continued to Châteauroux where there was a single track railway. While sitting in the local park where they were supplied with bread and sausage by the guide they were told that they would be catching a train for Limoges shortly after midnight. To avoid suspicion their guide took them to a cinema where they sat through two performances of the same film before leaving for the station. Boarding the train with the tickets their guide had bought, they split up and sat in different compartments. It was about 2.30 am when things started to go wrong. Unbeknown to them, the secret police had boarded the train ostensibly looking for refugees making for Spain.

The first airman to be picked up was Flight Sergeant Saunderson who, of course, was unable to produce an identity card. Seeing this, Dowty attempted to open the carriage door only to find that all the doors had been locked on the outside. He then moved to another carriage and sat down between two nuns. This did not save him, however and one by one the crew were picked up and herded into the guard's van. They were joined by the guide and a heated argument resulted during which he remonstrated with the police that they were picking up the wrong people and these were men who were trying to liberate Europe. The argument ended abruptly when one of the policemen drew his revolver and levelled it at the guide. They were taken off the train at Limoges with the guide bidding them farewell and apologising for the behaviour of his countrymen before he hastened away. As Dowty was to remark later, with the Germans and Italians you knew that they were the enemy, but with the French you were never quite sure which side some of them were on.

After a night in the police cells they were taken under escort back to Châteauroux. Here they were taken to the town hospital and to their surprise were rejoined with the two wounded members of their crew, Sergeants J Miller and A Cobb, who had been caught the previous night. The crew numbered six again and the following evening they were taken by train to Toulouse1 and then transferred by tram to what is now Toulouse airport. Here they were questioned and it was apparent that the questioners were anxious to know what would become of Vichy France when the invasion started. They were then taken back to Toulouse station and transported to Nice. Here they disembarked and with a posse of guards, complete with outriders, they were driven along the Grand Corniche until they arrived at a fortress complete with moat and drawbridge. The fortress was to be their prison camp.[12]

'...It was only sheer bad luck' wrote Patrick Dorehill 'that we flew past an enemy airfield to which their fighters were returning from the diversionary raids our fighters and Boston bombers had laid on to the North. 'Up they came and I shall never forget those terrible moments. I do not think there were as many fighters as our gunners reported; it was just that each made several attacks which made it seem like more. Being on the jump seat I stood up and saw quite a bit of the action. Maybe there were a dozen. At any rate I looked back through the astrodome to see Nick Sandford's plane in flames. He always wore his pyjamas on ops under his uniform. He thought it would bring him good luck. This was followed by Dusty Rhodes' plane on our starboard catching fire. The rest went down except Garwell on our port side. There was nothing for it really but to press on. A passing thought was given to turning south and then out to the Bay of Biscay but we reckoned that as we had come so far we might as well see it through. By this time I can tell you I didn't give much for our chances. On we went and I marvelled at the peaceful countryside, sheep, cattle and fields of daisies or buttercups. Along came the Alps on our right, wonderful sight, Lake Constance looking peaceful. We had climbed up a bit by then, it being pretty hilly and then down we came again getting close to the target. My recollection may be faulty but I thought we approached Augsburg from the south, following a canal or railway, factory chimneys appeared on the low horizon and then we came to the town. Large sheds were right in our path, Des Sands, the navigator and McClure the bomb aimer had done a pretty good job of map reading.

'Bombs away at about a hundred feet.

'The flak zipped past and as we crossed the town to begin a left turn for home a small fire was apparent, gradually gaining strength, in Garwell's plane. Our gunners saw it make a crash landing, which seemed to go relatively well.

Nettleton and Flying Officer John 'Ginger' Garwell DFM piloting 'A-Apple' continued to the target alone, flying low in the afternoon sun across southern Germany until the South African sighted the River Lech, which he followed to the target. Over France Nettleton had noticed people working in the fields and cows and sheep grazing and a fat woman wearing a blue blouse and a white skirt and horses bolting at the roar of his engines, with the ploughs to which they were attached bumping behind them. But once in Germany nothing was to be seen. 'The fields appeared untenanted by man or beast and there was no traffic on the roads. But when we got near the target they started to shoot at us, but the heavy flak soon stopped - I think because the gunners could not depress their guns low enough to hit us. The light flak, however, was terrific. We could see the target so well that we went straight in and dropped all our bombs in one salvo.' Coming over the brow of a hill on to the target the two Lancasters were met with heavy fire from quick-firing guns. The bomb aimers could not miss at chimney-top height on a factory covering an area of 626 by 293 feet. Nettleton and 'Ginger' Garwell went in and dropped their bomb loads but Flight Sergeant R. J. Flux DFM his wireless operator, yelled in Garwell's ear.

'We're on fire!'

Flux kept pointing over his shoulder and Garwell took a quick look behind him. The armour-plated door leading into the fuselage was open and he could see that the interior was a mass of flames. Garwell ordered 'Shut the door' and saw Nettleton and some of his crew staring at his burning Lancaster. Garwell stuck his fingers up in a V-sign before turning to port into wind and putting 'A-Apple' down in a field two miles west of the town. By now all five men crowded into the front cabin were coughing violently from the blinding and choking smoke and Flux opened the escape hatch over the navigator's table to try to get some air. A sudden down draught from the hatch cleared the smoke for a fraction of a second and Garwell could see a line of tall trees straight ahead. He opened up the engines and pulled back on the stick and flew into the ground at 80 mph. The Lancaster slid on its belly for about fifty yards and the fuselage broke at the mid-turret. Garwell and Sergeants J. Watson and L. L. Dando scrambled from the hatch but outside they found Flux lying dead under the starboard inner engine. He had been thrown out on impact. His quick action had probably saved their lives. Sergeants F. S. Kirke

DFM RNZAF, I. Edwards and Flight Sergeant D H McAlpine RCAF also perished. [13]

The second formation of six Lancasters on 97 Squadron had flown a slightly different route and had avoided the fighters in France. All they saw was a single German Army Co-operation aircraft, which approached them and then made off quickly. Just inside Germany Flying Officer Ernie Deverill DFM at the controls of 'Y-Yorker' noticed a man in the uniform of the SS who took in the situation at a glance and ran to a nearby post office where there was a telephone. Brian Hallows' crew in 'B-Baker' shot up a passenger train in a large station and saw an aerodrome crowded with Ju 90s. South of Paris Flying Officer 'Rod' Rodley flying 'F-Freddie' saw only the second aircraft he saw during the whole war. It was probably a courier, a Heinkel 111. It approached and recognizing them, did a 90-degree bank and turn back towards Paris. Rodley continued on flying at 100-feet. Occasionally he would see some Frenchmen take a second look and wave their berets or their shovels. A bunch of German soldiers doing PT in their singlets broke hurriedly for their shelters as the Lancs roared over. Their physical exercises were enlivened by a burst of fire from one of the rear gunners and 'the speed with which they took cover did great credit to their instructor.' At a frontier post on the Swiss-German border an SS man in black uniform, black boots and black cap shook his fist at the low flying Lancasters. Crossing Lake Constance a German officer standing on the stern of one of the white ferry boat steamers fired his revolver at the bombers. Rodley could see him quite clearly, 'defending the ladies with his Luger against 48 Browning machine guns.' At Lake Ammer, the last turning point ten miles south of the target, an old bearded Bavarian standing on the shores of the lake took pot shots at them with a duck-gun. One of the gunners asked his pilot if he could 'tickle' him.

'No leave him alone' was the reply.

Accurate map reading, notably by Flight Lieutenant McClure and Pilot Officer D. O. Sands, Nettleton's navigator, in the first flight and Flying Officer Hepburn in the second, brought them to their destination. [14]

David Penman continues.

'Rising ground then forced us to fly a little higher and eventually we spotted our final turning point, a small lake. I had dropped back a little from Sherwood's section at this stage and mindful of the delay fuses on the bombs, made one orbit before turning to run in on the target. The river was a very good guide and the run in was exactly as shown in the scale model at briefing. A column of smoke beyond the target, presumably came from Garwell's aircraft and it was soon joined by another...'

Brian Hallows continues. 'The target was easily picked out - the situation of the factory in a fork made by the River Wertach and an Autobahn made it easy to identify - and we bombed the hell out of it. The gunners were ready for us and it was as hot as hell for a few minutes.' 'Rod' Rodley recalled. 'We were belting at full throttle at about 100 feet towards the targets. I dropped the bombs along the side wall. We flashed across the target and won the other side to about 50 feet because flak was quite heavy. As we went away I could see light flak shells overtaking us, green balls flowing away on our right and hitting the ground ahead of us. Leaving the target I looked down at our leader's aircraft [15] and saw that there was a little wisp of steam trailing back from it. The white steam turned to black smoke with fire in the wing. I was slightly above him. In the top of the Lancaster there was a little wooden hatch for getting out if you had to land at sea. I realised that this wooden hatch had burned away and I could look down into the fuselage. It looked like a blow lamp with the petrol swilling around the wings and the centre section, igniting the fuselage and the slipstream blowing it down. I asked our gunner to keep an eye on him. Suddenly he said, 'Oh God, skip, he's gone. He looks like a chrysanthemum of fire.'

David Penman watched as 'K-King' flown by Sherwood, also aged 23, received a shell through the port tank just behind the inboard engine and it crashed and blew up about ten miles north of the town. 'Escaping vapour caught fire and as he turned left on leaving the target with rising ground, the port wing struck the ground and the aircraft exploded in a ball of flame. (I was sure that no one had survived and said so, on return to Woodhall Spa but Mrs. Sherwood would not believe it and she proved to be right.[16] I met Sherwood after the war and he had been thrown out of the aircraft, still strapped in his seat, up the hill and had been the sole survivor). As we ran in at 250 feet, tracer shells from light anti-aircraft guns on the roof of the factory produced a hail of fire and all aircraft were hit. Mycock's aircraft on the right received a shell in the front turret, which set fire to the hydraulic oil and in seconds the aircraft was a sheet of flame. It went into a climb and swinging left passed over my head with bomb doors open and finally burning from end to end was seen by my rear gunner to plunge into the ground.' [17]

As soon as Ifould had let the bombs go, he heard Penman say: 'He's on fire!' Ifould looked over the side and saw flames streaming ten to fifteen feet behind Sherwood's Lancaster. Then he looked to starboard and saw that the other Lancaster (Mycock's) too was on fire. A second or two later the starboard side Lancaster dropped its bombs and dived like a stone to earth. Ifould learned later that it had been hit and set on fire when the Vee first got to the edge of the town, yet Mycock had carried on to the target and bombed. Penman's Lancaster, Ifould having dropped its bombs from about 300 feet, dived again to the safer level of the housetops and cleared the town safely. Seconds later they were overtaken by the port Lancaster in the vee, in which the mid-upper gunner and wireless operator had gallantly succeeded in putting out the fire Ifould had seen streaming from it earlier. On only three engines, it seemed to overtake literally like a flash. As it passed Ifould caught a glimpse of a hole six feet by four feet wide in the metal of the fuselage, were the fire had burned through. The two men who had put the fire out later received the DFM for their bravery, which brought their aircraft safely home with no one hurt. [18]

A shell ripped the cowling of Penman's port inner engine and at the same time Deverill received a hit near the mid-upper turret and a fire started. Deverill told the mid-upper gunner to put it out. The starboard inner engine was pouring smoke and flame and Deverill fought to hold his position. Ron Irons, Deverill's wireless operator, left his set to help put out the fire. The oil recuperators had been punctured and burning oil was trickling down the fuselage into the well of the aircraft. 'Despite the distractions' recalls Penman, 'we held course and the front gunner did his best to reduce the opposition. My navigator was then passing instructions on the bombing run and finally called, 'Bombs gone.' We passed over the factory. I increased power and dived to ground level just as Deverill passed me with one engine feathered and the other three on full power. His navigator, Pilot Officer Butler had managed to put out the fire near the mid-upper. I called Deverill and he asked if I would cover his rear as his turrets were U/S. However, as my turrets were also U/S and Ifould had no wish to relinquish the lead, I told him to resume his position. Our attack had been close to the planned time of 2020 hours and as darkness took over we climbed to 20,000 feet for a straight run over Germany. It says a lot for Deverill's skill that he remained in formation until we reached the English coast and eventually landed at Woodhall Spa just before midnight.' [19]

It was close fighting; one rear-gunner spotted a German behind a machine gun on the roof and saw him collapse under his return fire. As the survivors turned westward, the light failed and the aircraft, led by Darkie Hallows flew back without any opposition under cover of darkness. Hallows noted, 'The quintessence of loneliness is to be 500 miles inside Occupied Europe with one serviceable turret! Time 8.15 hours.'

Hallows returned safely and was one of eight officers to be awarded the DFC for his part in the raid. Winston Churchill sent the following message to Arthur T. Harris, 'We must plainly regard the attack of the Lancasters on the U-boat engine factory at Augsburg as an outstanding achievement of the Royal Air Force. Undeterred by heavy losses at the outset, the bombers pierced in broad daylight into the heart of Germany and struck a vital point with deadly precision. Pray convey my thanks of His Majesty's Government to the officers and men who accomplished this memorable feat of arms in which no life was lost in vain.' [20]

Several days later Sir Dudley Pound, the Chief of Naval Staff having waited for confirmation that the raid had been successful, wrote, 'I have now seen the photographs and assessment. I am sure this attack will have greatly helped in achieving our object. I much deplore the comparatively heavy causalities but I feel sure their loss was not in vain.'

Later, Hallows wrote in his diary:

'One event sticks in my mind. Over half the bombs dropped failed to explode!' Five of the seventeen bombs dropped did not explode and although the others devastated four machine shops, only 3 per cent of the machine tools in the entire plant were wrecked. 'A bad way to spend an afternoon!'

'The trip home' said Patrick Dorehill 'was uneventful, thank goodness ... Nettleton did a brisk circuit and down we came to be almost out of fuel. Golly, I can tell you I was glad to feel those wheels touch the grass.' [21]

Squadron Leader John Dering Nettleton, who landed his badly damaged Lancaster at Squires Gate, Blackpool ten hours after leaving Waddington, was awarded the VC for his efforts. David Penman adds. 'Nettleton, it would appear, having increased speed to avoid fighters, bombed early and unable to cross Germany alone in daylight, turned back the way he had come. Due to navigational errors he eventually reached the Irish Channel and landed at Squires Gate. All surviving crews were grounded until a press conference, which I attended, was held at the Ministry of Information in London, when awards were announced.' [22]

Oblique photographs taken some distance from the factory would not show much actual damage. But a careful reconnaissance was made later and photographs taken then showed that the whole roof of the main Diesel engine assembly shed, covering an area of 626 by 293 feet, was wrecked by high-explosive and fire. The largest hole is eighty feet across and, quite apart from the holes, the main structure of the roof is a wreck. The building has several storeys and it is certain that the top storey is devastated. How many bombs penetrated farther down can only be guesswork, but there can be no doubt that, with such damage visible in the aerial photograph, the interior of the building and its machinery have been most severely damaged if not entirely wrecked. Repairs to the roof had begun, but had not got very far, when the photograph was taken.

Close beside the main assembly shop are two crank-grinding shops. They are smaller buildings, but of great importance both to the factory as a whole and in the production of diesel engines. One of these shops was entirely demolished and the other, together with some sheds beside it, was severely damaged. Other buildings in the factory, including a shed 373 by 186 feet, the roof of which was destroyed, also incurred heavy damage.

Exactly six months later, despite the failure of the Augsburg raid, when seven out of the twelve Lancasters dispatched were shot down, AVM Alec Coryton at 5 Group received word that another daylight raid was in the offing. Sergeant Roy Gould, a pilot on 49 Squadron at Scampton, recalls.

'We were all summoned to the Briefing Room quite early one morning so we knew that 'something was on' of particular note. But we were wrong. We were told we would practice low level formation flying over the sea for a future raid but on no account were we to mention this inside or outside of the Camp for our own safety and that of our fellow crews. This was a new experience for us, one we were previously forbidden to do. It was quite enjoyable, but one day I was on the starboard wing of a Vic formation of three and the lead pilot decided to do sharp turns to right and left. He obviously did not realise the problem it gave to his wing pilots when flying at less than fifty feet over the sea. When you are on the wing of a formation on the inside of a turn you have to bank, throttle back slightly and drop lower to keep your wings in the same line as the leader's. One day we were doing this and I watched my starboard wing tip only just skim over the crest of the waves of a very cold sea. In the end I could not contain myself and said over the R/T, 'If you go any lower you will have to pick me out of the drink.'

As a navigator, Roy Gould had flown ops on 83 Squadron before qualifying as a pilot. After his posting to 49 Squadron he flew four Hampden ops in April 1942 followed by 24 on Lancasters. 'By now I was approaching the end of my tour of operations and I expect I was getting a bit nervous and wondering if I would 'make it' after all. I had in fact been on 33 trips already, but if you had been recalled before reaching the target or returned in a like manner with only two or three engines or radio failure, they did not count!

'The seven members of our crew were a mixed bag. The front gunner was an Australian, Sergeant Acker by name. He was in the Australian Air Force operating with the Royal Air Force. He was a quiet chap and to try to keep warm he would have been wearing the issue long sleeved vest and underpants (we knew them as passion killers), his battle dress, a thick long sleeved pullover and then fur lined jacket and trousers - and he still felt cold. The flight engineer was a little Cockney by the name of Sergeant Brown. I took my hat off to him for he was a bundle of nerves when we were briefed for our target and he continued like that right up to when we were on board and he had to deal with all his switches, valves and dials for the four Rolls Royce engines. Then he felt all right. We all had butterflies during this period but he seemed to suffer more than most of us. The engineer sat in the co-pilot's seat in the cockpit where we had some heating and, other than the heavy underwear, battledress and pullover, we normally only used the fur-lined jackets. Just behind the cockpit sat the navigator. Pilot Officer Ridley, a Canadian. He had a curtain all round his compartment so that he could use his Terry lamp on his charts and things without disturbing us in the driving seats. On the ground, technically, I had to salute him, for he was a pilot officer and I was only a flight sergeant, but as soon as we entered the plane he did as I said, for I was the captain. Later I climbed the ladder to flight lieutenant, but that is another story. The next down the line was the wireless operator, Sergeant Seaman, who was also surrounded with curtains so that he could twist his dials with his light on. He was also in charge of the two carrier pigeons that we always took lest we had to ditch in the sea. Sergeant Grey, another Australian, manned the mid-upper gun turret; a big lively chap whose father had a fruit farm and he frequently handed out prunes from home which proved very beneficial to the whole of the crew.

'We were told to attend a very early briefing at last on the morning of 17 October and then we found we would be on something new and very big. The whole of 5 Group would be involved in attacking armament and engineering works at Le Creusot right in the middle of occupied France.'

After a favourable weather report was received, 94 Lancasters were detailed to attack the Schneider armaments factory at Le Creusot 90 miles from Geneva and less than twelve miles north of the frontier. The factory, 200 miles southeast of Paris and more than 300 miles inside France, on the eastern side of the Massif Central, was adjacent to that area whose place names - Gevrey-Chambertin, Nuits-St-Georges, Beaune, Meursault, Mâcon - read like a melodious passage of a favourite wine list. But it was a long way, not far from the Swiss frontier; only Lancasters would have the necessary performance.[23] Le Creusot was regarded as the French equivalent to Krupps and produced heavy guns, railway engines and, it was believed, tanks and armoured cars. A large workers' housing estate was situated at one end of the factory. Bomber Command had been given this as the highest priority target in France for a night attack but only in the most favourable of conditions. To maintain secrecy the code name Operation 'Robinson' was chosen; a rather allusive name if the popular mispronunciation of Creusot is considered. Eighty-eight Lancasters would be led by Wing Commander Leonard Cain 'Slosher' Slee DFC the 49 Squadron CO at Scampton who were to bomb the Schneider factory and the other six were to attack a nearby transformer station at Montchanin which supplied the factory with electricity.

'The navigators were briefed on the route we would take although all the Squadron would go as one massive formation!' recalls Roy Gould. 'We were also given the position that all the pilots would have to take up behind the leader who would be 49 Squadron's Wing Commander Slee [who Roy Gould refers to as 'Slasher']. Unfortunately he considered his Squadron to be an elite one and he appeared to have no time for non-commissioned pilots. There were three of us, Sergeant Mart, Flight Sergeant Webster and myself, also a Flight Sergeant by that time, and actually we were probably more experienced than many of the newly acquired Pilot Officer pilots. His apathy towards NCOs, however, became a talking point in the Squadron when it was noted that Flight Sergeant Webster was to be on his right flank and I was on his left, the two most vulnerable positions in an attack by fighters!

Tom Bennett, navigator on Flight Sergeant Gerry Webster's crew recalls.

'Slosher' Slee sprang a surprise with a final announcement to hushed crews before they left the crew room. It had been decided that all eleven of 49 Squadron's aircraft would take off in formation! This was typical of the morale-boosting, almost 'spur-of-the-moment' innovations that 5 Group Squadrons introduced at Station level. I like to think that this inspiration originated from the alert and impish mind of Charlie Whitworth, truly an 'aircrews' Station Commander.'

'After we had been briefed, we went to the crew room' recalls Roy Gould. 'There we would go to our lockers, collect our parachute, helmet, oxygen mask and the like and gather to wait for transport. This was usually a light canvas covered van driven by a young but very 'worldly' WAAF. She took two crews at a time and when we arrived at the hard standing for our plane she would call out 'Q-Queen' and our crew would scramble out. We would dump all our things near the steps up into our aircraft. We then ceremoniously gathered round the tail wheel of 'Q-Queen'. A moment of quiet would descend over us whilst we all, I expect, said our own silent prayer for a safe return. Then at a nod from me we would all pee over that tail wheel and woe betide anyone who missed. (On reflection we did some silly things to keep up our morale.) Having completed the ritual, the crew scrambled up into the aircraft whilst I looked all round it to check that the ground crew had done everything they should. Then in I went and we all had plenty to do to check everything inside was OK for take-off. All the 'blues' were gone and we had left the remaining butterflies in our stomach on that tail wheel.

'We took off at about mid-day and formed up behind 'Slasher' with the nine Lancs in our squadron. To be honest, my recollections of the trip are very scant. I was too busy keeping my station with the leader of this whole assembly and making sure that a mere NCO could do the job as well as anyone else!'

Tom Bennett continues:

'The eleven Lancasters trundled and bounced their way across the grass airfield, to take up their appointed places, along the far north east boundary. They were hardly visible to the ground-crew, who had taken-up vantage points to observe this unique and historic take-off. At 12.08 hours the Squadron

Commander's aircraft rolled forward, to be followed at precise intervals by the rest of the formation: We were airborne at 12.09 hours and were to hear next day the graphic accounts of the watching ground-crew as 'Webby' manoeuvred his aircraft adroitly between the dispersals and hangars!'

'Slosher' flew at reduced speed until all aircraft had assumed the requisite vic-formations; with two of the NCO pilots tucked in behind the leading vic. Airspeed was then increased to normal cruising, heading for Upper Heyford. This Oxfordshire airfield was reached at precisely 12.45 hours, with 61 and 9 Squadrons positioned to join formation while near Swindon a similar smooth procedure was followed by 97, 50 and 57, with 106, 44 and 207 completing the mass formation near Frome. I was to learn from Sergeant Mortimer, mid-upper gunner on Pilot Officer Ayres' crew on 49, that during the leg from Frome to Start Point, he had flown directly over his Somerset home. 'I looked down one side and could see the back-garden, whilst down the other I could see the front door! I was convinced that this was my last operation ... that I had been allowed to see my home for the last time!' So much for portents and premonitions!

'Cloud-base was 1,000 feet on the leg to Start Point and 'Slosher' had dropped to 800 feet, with the formations behind him stepped down to 600 and 400 feet respectively. Between Start Point and the Lizard, we approached a small formation of tugs towing lighters, heading for Plymouth, escorted by what appeared to be an armed trawler. I was amused when the escort pugnaciously flashed the challenge letter of the period at the approaching 'air armada'... it struck me that the combined slipstreams could have turned the whole lot over! Nevertheless, quite solemnly Gerry Fawke answered with the reply letter that Paul Fortin, our French-Canadian wireless operator, had readily to hand and the 'danger' was averted. South westwards from the Lizard and the whole loose formation dropped down to 300 feet. Some 400 miles of featureless sea legs lay ahead until we crossed the coast of France. I reverted to 'Gee' navigation and was delighted with the strength and reception of the Southern Chain signals. Soon the w/vs and ground speeds were buttoned-up and confirmed.

'There was the opportunity to have some sandwiches and beverage in the warm autumn sunshine that was now bathing the canopy from cloudless blue skies. I was able to ensure a supply of fruit drops on my table for the mouth - during land sequence ahead. I stood up and looked around...no sign of any shipping...so peaceful it was almost a time out of the war ... but what lay ahead?

'At the turn at 0500W, I returned to the 'Gee' set to check ... and re-check ... the forward ground-speed. Satisfied, I completed the preparation of my topographical maps. I switched off 'Gee' and stood up behind the flight engineer when I knew we were in the lee of the Ile d'Yeu fifty miles south of St. Nazaire, with my maps ready I glanced out to port to confirm my assumption and was shaken to see the dim outline of a small boat two miles away, between us and the island. Was a transmitter already pouring forth some fateful warning? No time to worry, for here was the French coast! I shall always believe that if 5 Group had raised a pole on the west coast of France at the required crossing, Pilot Officer A. S. Grant, Slee's Australian navigator, would have guided Slee immaculately over it! The landfall was superb!

'Airspeed climbed to 180 mph and unexpectedly 'Slosher' dropped his height to around 60 feet and we followed suit. The application required performing map-reading correctly at this height and speed was quite demanding but the days of training were paying off. There was no time to take much notice of the novelty of flying over France in daylight. One appreciated the quiet beauty of the sun-bathed landscape but clear non-operational details of that flight are just a kaleidoscope of memory ... rolling fields, rivers and streams ... I remember an open carriage pulled by two horses, jogging gently along a tow-path with what appeared to be an old lady and gent enjoying an afternoon spin. God knows how the horses reacted when the en masse thunder of those low-flying exultant Merlins hit them!

'Across an internment camp at Chinan, with an incredulous German-uniformed guard, too amazed to un-sling his rifle! I felt that I would have no opportunity to man that Vickers gun by the exit door! Montrichard and the turn westwards to Sancerre... No enemy reaction yet, in the air or from the ground but that was just a fleeting thought before the new track was embraced and the demands of map-reading met. As we approached Sancerre 'Slosher' pulled to port to allow the formation to come round over the town on course for Nevers. A river wound its way from Sancerre to Nevers, looking so peaceful in the warm sunshine...but I did not notice if there was any boating or swimming activity. If there was, the majesty of this Lancaster formation must have left them deafened and speechless!

'Just before Nevers Slee again pulled wide, this time to starboard and the formation came round to port, easily committed to this leg, the run-in to the targets. Green Very Signals erupted from the lead aircraft to indicate the commencement of the climb to 6,000 feet and the assumption of the 'bombing arc'. The seven aircraft detailed to attack the transformers at Montchanin stayed low and moved to starboard of the climbing Lancasters. Two of these aircraft were drawn from 61 Squadron, three from 97 and the other two from 106.

'We reached 6,000 feet and flew straight and level. I calculated the data for the automatic bombsight and passed it to Sergeant Erwin Osler our Canadian bomb-aimer. We always used this sight as a fixed sight. We found that trying to manipulate it in the automatic role often caused the bombs to fall early, if the wheel control on this bomb-sight was used clumsily. Then I noticed that 'Slosher's aircraft was pumping out red Very signals agitatedly. I looked to starboard and saw that part of the arc formed by 9, 57 and 207 Squadrons was threatening to take over the run-in! I smiled inwardly, as I could imagine those bods saying 'Why should bloody 49 be the first in?' Slee abandoned the disciplinary attempt and poked his speed up to something approaching 195 mph. We followed suit, naturally and I rapidly re-calculated the bomb-sight data from scratch, warning Oz to scrub all the current settings. Soon the sight was re-aligned. Gerry opened the bomb-doors and the bombing run was on. I looked out of the starboard blister. Opposition from the ground was negligible... certainly nothing came our way. Gerry held the Lancaster level and steady at the indicated airspeed required. 'Bombs gone!' came confidently from the nose of the aircraft.

'Dusk was gathering as I continued to survey the ground from the blister. Suddenly, my heart stopped in unbelieving horror, as black smoke and lurid flames belched from the thirty pound incendiaries as they burst amid a cluster of attractive French villas. I knew we were the first aircraft in with a part-load of HE and these bombs. It was the very first time that I had personally observed the impact of bombs we had dropped. I thought 'So much for the assurance that the incendiaries are timed to drop into the damage caused by the HE!' My feelings were a mix of anger and horror ... to think we had done this to French homes! Sickening!

'But there were things to do ... I had set the course out on the pilot's repeater during the bombing run and Gerry was now coming round to starboard on to it, ensuring that he was well away from the bombers still approaching Le Creusot. The darkness had thickened considerably and Gerry decided to climb to 8,000 feet for the whole route home. On ETA we turned northwards for Bayeux and soon 'Gee' was giving us its assurance and assistance.

'We reached Bayeux without incident or interference and crossed to Worthing, to find the weather beginning to close in. Paul reported that Group was warning that weather at bases was deteriorating but Gerry decided to make for Scampton anyway, for diversion 'dromes could be so very uncomfortable and there was no place like home after an op like this! After crossing the English coast, 5 Group aircraft were required to contact base on W/T and ask for a 'turn to land'. On receipt of this figure, the pilot would adjust his ETA so that he would more-or-less go 'straight in' at Base, rather than be prey to possible enemy intruders. At the appropriate time, I asked Paul to get a 'turn to land'. After some interval, he came back on the intercom very puzzled. 'Everybody is getting 'Q', which means wait,' he reported. [24] Eventually, Paul came up with the information sought and we duly arrived at Scampton to touch down at 21.57 hours. All 49 Squadron aircraft landed safely at Scampton with Squadron Leader Couch last down at 22.24 hours, having lost an engine with a glycol leak at the south coast. It transpired afterwards that of the 94 aircraft that had originally set course on Operation 'Robinson', five had returned early and another had lost an engine just before the French coast and had abandoned, leaving a final attack total of 88 Lancasters. Of these, one was unable to open its bomb doors on the bombing run. Eighty Lancasters attacked the primary. The attack on the transformers was a great success but the one aircraft lost went down on this target.

'Forty-one aircraft landed at their 'home' base in Lincolnshire but 45 'dropped-in' at 23 airfields south and south west of Lincolnshire, one as far west as Exeter. It is a fact that 'diversion offers' were sometimes welcomed by crews, as it occasionally gave them the opportunity for a 'gash' night at home!

'Sergeant Ronald Wilson, pilot of the 207 Squadron aircraft that lost an engine and returned just before crossing the French coast had an interesting story to tell. Fifty miles west of Brest on the return, at a height of forty feet above the sea, his aircraft was attacked by three Arado Ar 196A-3 two-seater seaplanes. These aircraft were armed with two 20mm cannon and one 7.9mm machine-gun, all forward-firing, plus a rear-mounted machine-gun. The first

Arado came in astern and opened fire at 300 yards. The rear gunner replied with four short bursts. The Arado flipped over on to its back, emitting black smoke and crashed into the sea. The second Arado attacked from the port beam. Wilson turned into this attack, with the mid-upper gunner firing two short bursts but this encounter proved indecisive. Arado No.3 crossed from port to starboard of the Lancaster and attacked from the starboard beam, a bullet killing Sergeant Kenneth Chalmers the flight engineer. The front gunner gave a long burst, which struck the enemy aircraft. It plunged straight into the sea. The second Arado made a renewed attack from the port quarter. The mid-upper gunner gave two short bursts and the rear gunner managed a long sustained burst whilst it was within his compass. The enemy aircraft sheered-off towards the French coast, claimed heavily damaged. The Lancaster reached Langar, Nottinghamshire safely. This NCO crew received immediate awards of the DFM. It is ironic that they were the only crew to go missing on the night of 7/8 November 1942 during a raid on Genoa; one of the relaxing 'milk run' targets that were available to 5 Group crews during the support raids for the land offensive in North Africa. [25]

'Bombing results on Le Creusot were good but should have been better in the circumstances. The main section of the transformers at Montchanin was put out of commission by the low-level bombing and subsequent strafing by the six attacking Lancasters. [A Lancaster on 106 Squadron captained by Flight Lieutenant John Vere Hopgood DFC was damaged by the blast of its own bombs. After dropping their bombs the aircraft then flew round the target while the gunners fired at the transformer; each time a bullet hit a vital spot there was a brilliant blue flash. It was on this attack on Montchanin that the single aircraft missing from the whole force of 94 Lancasters was lost, but not by enemy action; Squadron Leader William Duncan Corr DFC on 61 Squadron was seen to hit a building during the attack and all except one of the crew perished. In the light conditions prevailing, the cause of the crash was not observed by the other six crews attacking this target.] This was one of the most vital points in the whole electric power system in France and was considered to be out of action for two years. Jim Davis' ploy worked. We obtained the only photograph with bombing. It showed our HE bursting on the locomotive machine shop. Charlie Whitworth was delighted but shared my reservations about the support timing for the incendiaries. He waived aside the graphs that the bombing leader produced to justify his calculations and sent a personal letter to 5 Group Headquarters, strongly recommending that immediate steps be taken to check the efficacy of the trials carried out with this weapon.

'Keith 'Aspro' Astbury, 'Slosher' Slee's uncompromising Australian bomb aimer was having a mug of tea after debriefing when a young, eager news-hawk approached him. Apparently fit, military-aged Poms never cut much ice with 'Aspro'! 'Did the French civilians wave at you?' enquired the man invitingly. 'Aspro' looked at him speculatively. 'Mate, at the height and speed at which we were flying it was difficult to decide if they were waving or shaking their fists' he observed. The news-hawk disappeared in search of more amenable 'copy', leaving 'Aspro' grimly satisfied!'

Sergeant N. J. Waddington RAAF, who was bomb aimer in a leading

Lancaster, remembers that even over England the Lancasters flew so low so that they were below German radar that the trailing aerial of his aircraft was taken off by a rock on the coast. Four aircraft were damaged by bird strikes. The flight engineer in one aircraft was injured when a bird came through the perspex; in another aircraft the pilot was temporarily blinded when a bird smashed his windscreen; 'K for King' collected a bird in the starboard inner radiator shutter over England causing overheating and a drop in pressure; later three French partridges came bouncing through the bomb-aimer's perspex and another bird lodged in the camera; in yet another the perspex in both front and the mid-upper turrets was smashed.

Going over France, the Lancasters hurdled telephone wires and houses, while people opened their doors and windows and waved. A horse with a plough burst its way helter-skelter through hedges and ditches while the ploughman stood and waved. 'K-King's Australian navigator on 50 Squadron, Flying Officer Percy William 'Paddy' Rowling, was exhilarated by it all. 'I'd never seen so many bolting horses and oxen. Everything stampeded as we crossed France on the deck; some of the people stood and waved - others just stood and others, like one farmer, dived for cover or lay flat. This particular farmer had the quietest of horses and he was playing ostriches under his drag, head down and arse up, with the arse very much in sight.'

'In retrospect' concludes Tom Bennett, 'it is amazing how many of the aircrew engaged that day on the Le Creusot operation were to serve later on 617 Squadron. Guy Gibson, 'Hoppy' Hopgood, Dave Shannon (all of 106) and Les Knight with 'Spam' Spafford (50 Squadron) were all to form part of the original Squadron. [26]'Aspro', Gerry Fawke and myself (49 Squadron) together with Drew Wyness (50 Squadron) and Trevor Muhl (207) were to serve later.[27] Sergeant L. J. King, a flight engineer badly injured in a bird strike over France in a 57 Squadron aircraft was to serve as Flying Officer King in Leonard Cheshire's crew in 1944. Ray Ellwood (97 Squadron), also a participant in the Augsburg raid, joined 617 in early 1944 and the same is probably true of other aircrew engaged on this memorable 1942 'daylight'!'

The 5 Group crews claimed a successful attack on the Schneider factory but photographs taken later showed that much of the bombing had fallen short and had struck the workers' housing estate near the factory. Some bombs had fallen into the factory area but damage there was not extensive.[28] Flight Sergeant J. E. Taylor DFM the pilot of 'R for Robert' on 50 Squadron arrived over the target to find the bomb doors would not open and had to carry his 4,000lb load back to Upper Heyford where he arrived dangerously low on fuel. The ten hour flight was, according to 'Paddy' Rowling 'a wizard trip and the whole world is talking about it today.'

The *Daily Express* claimed that the Lancasters had done a 'Grand National' over hedges to blast French Krupps'.

'Once we were home' recalled Roy Gould 'we filled in our log books showing that we had just completed a trip lasting ten hours and ten minutes and this was done this time in green ink because it was in daylight. Strangely enough, what was to prove to be my last operation on 24 October was also a 'green ink' and a low level trip as before but very different from the previous one. In retrospect it seems as though it must have been an exercise to wave the Union Jack under the noses of Hitler and Mussolini for we were to go all the way to the railway junction at Milan in Italy.

This time a fighter escort of Spitfires would accompany the force across the Channel to the Normandy coast. The aircraft would fly on independently over France close together and very low, hedgehopping in the manner in which the Augsburg and Le Creusot raids had been made possible and using partial cloud cover, to a rendezvous at Lake Annecy and the Alps would then be crossed.

'There must have been about eighty Lancasters [29] recalled Roy Gould, 'which set off whilst there was a cold weather front over the French coastal defences. It was thick cloud up to a great height and so we flew in or above it as far as we could and when it fizzled out we dropped down to tree top height. It had then turned into a lovely morning. The navigator had previously worked out all the courses we should take to avoid large towns and so he stood behind me in the cockpit map reading. The front gunner sat in his turret and warned me, 'Wires ahead' or, 'Steeple on our starboard bow' so that we would not knock anything over. Thus we went along mile after mile. A gendarme shook his fist at us and some nuns, after getting over their surprise, waved up at us furiously. Another gendarme un-slung his rifle and pointed it at us but a quick burst from the rear gunner made him change his mind!

'Thus we all made our way right over France and when we came to the Alps we rose up to 15,000 feet with the intention of meeting over Lake Annecy. I was a little early so I diverted a little and did a trip round Mont Blanc after going a bit higher. It was a wonderful sight in the brilliant afternoon sunlight. So back to Lake Annecy, over the Alps and on to Milan with the other Lancs. When we got there everything was covered with a thick layer of cloud. We had come all this way and there was no clear target, but I was not going to take all those bombs back. The bomb aimer thought he could see some railway junction through a hole in the cloud so we let them have our load.

At four minutes after 5 o'clock in the afternoon, the first Lancaster nosed down through the heavy clouds and unloaded. They came in rapidly, pinpointing their targets and wheeling round. Mixed in the general delivery of HEs and incendiaries were a goodly proportion of 4,000-pounders. Some of the Lancasters went down to fifty feet to bomb their targets. The raiders caught Milan by surprise and the bombing was accurate with 135 tons of bombs being dropped in 18 minutes. Only when they were well on their homeward run did darkness come down and afford them any protection. 'With our job done' concludes Roy Gould 'we set course for the long journey home which was accomplished without any serious trouble. I was back again for my last green ink entry of a ten hour trip to Milan. I had now done 35 operations to my calculations but unfortunately, the Air Force did not count ones where we had had to return to base because the trip had been aborted for one reason or another.' [30]

Three Lancasters that failed to return were all presumed lost over the sea. Returning aircraft low on fuel and with wounded on board lobbed down at the first available airfield on England's south coast. A fourth Lancaster piloted by Flight Lieutenant Dorian Dick Bonnett DFC on 49 Squadron at Scampton crashed on approach to Ford airfield 'an aerodrome that left little to be desired' with good approaches from east and west and flanked by the Sussex Downs to the north and the English Channel to the south'. Sometimes the bombers would go out over Ford and often the bombers would land back there. Their arrival, unannounced and out of the gloom on a dark night were quite a sight for the night fighter boys, accustomed to being, as they thought, in the centre of the stage. Bonnett and five crew members died - three of them Australians - and two men were injured; one of whom died six days later.

There were no more 'daylights' to Italian targets. Trips over the snow-capped Alps to Genoa and Milan on several nights throughout late October became a regular run and on November nights it was the Fiat Works in Turin in North West Italy. Increasing numbers of Lancasters - 86 of them on the night of 20/21 November as part of a force of 232 aircraft and 117 Lancasters on the night of 28/29th November, when 228 aircraft were dispatched. Italian targets were not considered worthy of a bomb symbol painted on the nose of a bomber - ice-cream cones were used instead - but crews still had to fight their way through France and beyond - a distance of 1,350 miles there and back. With their coming, the sky was soon strewn with night-fighters. One Lancaster crew sighted as many as twenty-three in Northern France and had a running fight with eight, sending one FW 190 down in flames.

'Targets were not often in Italy and not all got off so lightly, even in those days' wrote Wing Commander Roderick Aeneas Chisholm DFC, who in June had taken command of the Fighter Interception Unit at Ford. [31] 'The bomber crews were going hard at it, several times a week, whenever the weather allowed, plugging away, making trips of six, eight or more hours, getting shot up and limping back with dead men on board, engines out or with no hydraulics, scrambling in, say to Ford, to feed and sleep and then to return to their station in Lincolnshire or Yorkshire to prepare for it all over again. It was not uncommon for twenty or thirty of the four-engined weight-lifting bombers to come in, diverted from their own bases because of bad weather. Amongst them were always some lame ducks scrambling in somehow and ending up through a hedge with no brakes, or prone with an undercarriage that collapsed or would not come down, or by good fortune on their wheels and neatly parked near the perimeter track awaiting the repair squads. Sometimes there was a disaster and a machine, already home, crashed for reasons unknown and without survivors.

'At Ford it was more than just the news of casualties that made one want to have a go at the enemy fighters. The casualties and the battle damage were often there. Unforgettable was a Lancaster from whose mid-upper turret the headless corpse of the gunner had been removed the night before. It was gory and shocking; a cannon-shell had hit and burst in the turret and the rest of the aircraft was riddled with jagged holes. Those chaps had had little chance. I was not alone in feeling a worm when I thought of the relative safety of our job.[32]

'A November night and the following morning in 1942 were, to me, significant... It was at about eleven o'clock when I heard several aircraft going overhead; the noise soon increased to a thunder and then died away to the spasmodic outbreaks of the stragglers. A raid was going out in weather I had readily denounced as unfit for our trials. Local weather was then clear and needing to restore our self-respect we reinstituted our programme and flew, but unsuccessfully.

'I was lying in bed next morning half awake, feeling satisfied that we had in the end done all we could the night before. Suddenly I was jerked into full consciousness. There was an aircraft close and it sounded as if it was coming over the mess. I looked out of the window at a grey wall of drizzle and cloud at 200 or 300 hundred feet. This was what our forecaster had seen ahead and had mistimed. It looked impossible for a stranger to land at Ford. The machine passed very close and the noise of its four Merlins gave way momentarily to a swishing sound; it was very low.

'The noise faded away. I suspected that he had had a shot at getting in and had given up, but I felt helplessly anxious, because I knew that a returning bomber could not have much petrol left and that a desperate effort to get down - an overwhelming tendency springing from more than a desire to save an aeroplane - could lead to disaster to the north where the Downs would certainly be in cloud. It came over again and now I felt sure that it must be in difficulties. The noise died away and, as is often the case when one is powerless to help, I thought of other things for a bit, turned over and went to sleep again. I had ample excuse for being late. Had I not flown the night before?

'At breakfast there was a stranger and I sat down next to him and asked where he came from. He mentioned an airfield in Lincolnshire.

'Lancs?' I asked.

'Yes.'

'When did you arrive here?'

'This morning.'

'What was it like?'

'Not so easy. We were on instruments most of the way across France.'

'Did you have any difficulty getting in here? I heard you come over the mess twice.'

'No, not really. We made two bosh shots at it, but got in OK the third.'

'Where did you go?'

'Turin.'

'How long did it take?'

'About eight hours.'

'What were the defences like?'

'They've increased. There are two guns now and they must be manned by Germans because they went on firing after the bombs began to fall.'

Footnotes Chapter 1

1   Squadron Leader 'Flap' Sherwood, fair-haired and aesthetic looking, only just 23. In his desire to infuse his crews with his own fanatical keenness he often tried to panic them into a sense of urgency, hence the nickname, 'Flap'. *Strike Hard, Strike Sure; Epics of the Bombers* by Ralph Barker (Chatto & Windus 1963/Pen & Sword Military Classics 2003).

2   Deverill was 26, an ex-apprentice with eleven years' service, recently commissioned and a veteran of over 100 operational flights. Mycock, slight and ginger-haired, had been awarded the DFC for a daylight raid on the *Scharnhorst* and *Gneisenau* in Brest. *Strike Hard, Strike Sure; Epics of the Bombers* by Ralph Barker (Chatto & Windus 1963/Pen & Sword Military Classics 2003).

3   Learoyd was awarded Bomber Command's first VC of the war for his determined attack on the Dortmund-Ems Canal in a 49 Squadron Hampden on 12/13 August 1940.

4   Maschinenfabrik Augsburg-Nurnberg Aktiengesellschaft.

5   Hallows was 11 years at Gresham's School, Holt, where his father was proprietor of the old market town's Steam Laundry. Hallows later passed through Sandhurst and took a commission in the King's Liverpool Regiment, which he later relinquished to take up flying. In June 1938 he joined the RAFVR when he felt that a war was inevitable, so it was no surprise when all Reservists were called to report to their units around the end of August 1939. Then followed a wait until October, when he begun a 'Wings' course at No.9 FTS, Hullavington. They were an unruly lot and finally the station commander got them all together and said that he was going to award them their wings and commission all Sergeant Pilots to acting Pilot Officers. He added that they were not fit to be senior NCO pilots - how right he was! Then it was off to Central Flying School, to become a RAF flying instructor, which had been Hallows' profession prior to August 1939. At CFS he won a trophy for 'Best all-round Cadet'.

6   At Hullavington he had been a Qualified Flying Instructor until in June 1941 he had seen a 'rather odd' notice asking for experienced twin-engined pilots to join Bomber Command, to fly Manchester bombers. Little did any of them know what a killer the Manchester was. Anyway, it was off to Finningley, with not a Manchester to be seen - they were all grounded with engine trouble. Eventually, in September 1941, Hallows got to 97 Squadron at Coningsby, where he actually flew a Manchester.

7   *The Augsburg Raid* by Jack Currie DFC (Goodall Publications, 1987).

8   All 16 had taxied out so the second reserve cut their engines and watched the others leave and over Selsey Bill the first reserves swung round and returned to Lincolnshire, leaving 12 Lancasters flying low over the water.

9   *Strike Hard, Strike Sure; Epics of the Bombers* by Ralph Barker (Chatto & Windus 1963/Pen & Sword Military Classics 2003).

10   *Royal Australian Air Force Overseas* (Eyre & Spottiswoode London 1946).

11   Oesau had shot down ten aircraft in Spain and was the 3rd German pilot to reach 100 victories, on 26 October 1941. He was shot down and killed in air combat with P-38 Lightnings SW of St. Vith, Belgium on 11 May 1944 in his Bf 109G-6. At the time of his death, his score stood at 127 aerial victories, including 14 four engined bombers.

12   *The Augsburg raid - a survivor's story* by Bob Nelson, Research Officer. Bomber Command Association, writing in *Bomber Command News*, 1993.

13   All four men who were taken prisoner, were decorated, Garwell being awarded the DFC, Kirke a bar to his DFM and DFMs for Watson and Dando.

14   Sands, McClure and Pilot Officer Patrick Dorehill were awarded the DFC and the four sergeants on the crew each received the DFM.

15   L7573 flown by Squadron Leader J. S. Sherwood DFC *.

16   She shook her head and told Penman 'I would have known if he'd died. I'm convinced he's all right. Don't worry' she said. He had suffered no more than minor burns.

17   R5513 was on fire over a mile from the target but Mycock continued on to drop his bombs on the factory and became enveloped in flames and crashed. There were no survivors. Mycock's navigator was an old school friend from his home town.

18   *Australian Air Force Overseas* (Eyre & Spottiswoode London 1946).

19   The aircraft was a complete write-off. Squadron Leader E. A. Deverill DFC AFC DFM and five of his were killed when his Lancaster crashed near Graveley, Hunts returning from Berlin on the night of 16/17 December 1943.

20   Of the seven crews lost, 37 men were killed and 12 men survived to be made PoW. 36 men returned.

21   *Lancaster: The Biography* by Squadron Leader Tony Iveson DFC and Brian Milton (André Deutsch 2009). Patrick Dorehill was awarded the DFC.

22   Although also recommended for a VC by Air Marshal Harris, Sherwood was awarded the DSO After a brief spell instructing with 1661 HCU and being promoted to Wing Commander, Nettleton returned to 44 Squadron as OC in January 1943. He FTR from a raid on Turin on 12/13 July 1943. In addition to the awards already mentioned, Penman was awarded the DSO and Lester Ifould, Darkie Hallows, Ernie Deverill and Rod Rodley and Pilot Officer Hooey, Penman's second pilot, the DFC. Six sergeants on 97 Squadron each received the DFM.

23   *The Right of the Line: The Royal Air Force in the European War 1939-1945* by John Terraine (Hodder & Stoughton 1985).

24   'The 'Q' mystery was solved soon after landing at Scampton. 'Slosher' had been behind at the south coast. His WOp had heard aircraft beginning to call up for landing instructions and decided that the 'Wingco' should not be too far down the queue, so, off his own bat, he had been transmitting 'Q' to interrogating aircraft until he himself had been specifically asked to get a turn to land!'

25   Over France Lancaster I L7546 'G-for George' and Pilot Officer Ronald Sydney Wilson DFM's crew were lost with no survivors.

26   Flying Officer Frederick Michael 'Spam' Spafford DFC DFM RAAF, who was the bomb aimer on Guy Gibson's crew in the attack on the Möhne dam on16/17 May 1943 and Pilot Officer Les Knight DSO RAAF, who also flew the Dams' raid, were both KIA on 15/16 September 1943 on the operation to Ladbergen. Flight Lieutenant John Vere 'Hoppy' Hopgood DFC* was KIA on the Dams raid on 16/17 May 1943.

27   Squadron Leader D. R. C, 'Duke' Wyness DFC a six-footer, slim, with blue eyes, a somewhat classical nose and really golden, curly hair, had a reputation as a 'press-on' type. The Dam Busters by Paul Brickhill (Evans Bros 1951). Wyness (23) FTR from the operation by 617 Squadron on the Kembs Dam on the Rhine just north of Basle on 7 October 1944. He and three of his crew were shot in cold blood and three gunners who bailed out were never seen again. The Lancaster piloted by Flight Lieutenant C. J. G. 'Kit' Howard was also lost with all the crew killed.

28   See *The Bomber Command War Diaries: An Operational reference book 1939-1945* by Martin Middlebrook and Chris Everitt. (Midland Publishing 1985). Wing Commander Slee was awarded the DSO for his leadership of the formation and Pilot Officer A. S. Grant received an immediate DSO for his navigation on the raid. Later in the war he added a DFC and bar to his decorations.

29   There were 88.

30   *Memories of My Life in The RAF* by Roy Gould, The 4T9er, August 2013.

31   Chisholm had destroyed seven German bombers flying Beaufighters on 604 Squadron in 1941 and he would add two more victories in 1943 flying Mosquitoes on the FIU.

32   *Cover of Darkness* by Roderick Chisholm (Chatto & Windus 1953).

33   *Cover of Darkness* by Roderick Chisholm (Chatto & Windus 1953).

Chapter 2

Lady Luck

Pilot Officer 'Chad' Chadwick

Pilot Officer Richard Hubert 'Chad' Chadwick, navigator, Lancaster PB522
AR-G2, 460 Squadron RAAF, raid on Essen, 25/26 July 1943 when 705 aircraft
were dispatched. 26 aircraft were lost. For their attack on the target and for bringing
the entire crew safely home Flight Sergeant Michael Christensen was awarded the
DFM and Pilot Officer R. H. Chadwick received the DFC.

At the start of the Battle of the Ruhr 'Bomber' Harris had been able to call
upon almost 600 heavies for Main Force operations and at the pinnacle of
the Battle, near the end of May, more than 800 aircraft took part.
Innovations such as Path Finders to find and mark targets with their TIs
and wizardry such as Oboe, which enabled crews to find them, were
instrumental in the mounting levels of death and destruction. Little it
seemed could be done to assuage the bomber losses, which by the end of
the campaign had reached high proportions. There was however, a simple
but brilliant device, which at a stroke could render German radar defences
almost ineffective. On 24/25 July when Harris launched the first of four
raids, code-named Gomorrah, on the port of Hamburg, each Station
Commander was authorised to tell the crews that, 'Tonight you are going
to use a new and simple counter-measure called 'Window' to protect
yourselves against the German defence system. 'Window' consists of
packets of metal strips, which when dropped in bundles of a thousand at a
time at one-minute intervals produce almost the same reactions on RDF
equipment as do aircraft and you should stand a good chance of getting
through unscathed'. Strips of black paper with aluminium foil stuck to
one side and cut to a length (30cm by 1.5cm) were equivalent to half the
wavelength of the Würzburg ground and Lichtenstein airborne
interception, radar. Although 'Window' had been devised in 1942 its use
had been forbidden until now for fear that the Luftwaffe would use it in a
new Blitz on Great Britain. It was carried on the 791 aircraft (347
Lancasters, 246 Halifaxes, 125 Stirlings and 73 Wellingtons) which set out
for Hamburg. (During the Battle of Hamburg 24/25 July-2/3 August 1943
'Window' prevented about 100-130 potential Bomber Command losses). In
his message of good luck to his crews Harris said that 'The Battle of

Hamburg cannot be won in a single night. It is estimated that at least 10,000 tons of bombs will have to be dropped to complete the process of elimination. To achieve the maximum effect of air bombardment this city should be subjected to sustained attack. On the first attack a large number of incendiaries are to be carried in order to saturate the Fire Services.' Led by H2S PFF aircraft, 740 out of 791 bombers dispatched rained down 2,284 tons of high explosive and incendiary bombs in two and a half hours upon the suburb of Barmbeck, on both banks of the Alster, on the suburbs of Hoheluft, Eirnsbüttel and Altona and on the inner city. The advantages enjoyed by Kammhuber's Himmelbett system, dependent as it was on radar, had been removed at a stroke by the use of 'Window'. The German fighter pilots and their Bordfunkers were blind. Twelve bombers were lost in action; four Halifaxes and four Lancasters, a Wellington and three Stirlings. Brigadier General Fred L Anderson commanding VIIIth Bomber Command flew as an observer on the next raid, on the night of 25/26 July when bad weather over north Germany prevented all but a handful of Mosquitoes bombing Hamburg but 'Window' was still effective and so 705 heavies were dispatched to Essen.

'The afternoon of 25 July 1943 was one of those that made one forget the vagaries of the English summer. However, Flight Sergeant Mick Christensen, pilot of Lancaster Mk.3 PB522 AR-G2 and the crew were not really appreciating either the weather or the views across the splendid Lincolnshire countryside. We stood outside No.2 hangar at RAF Binbrook, 460 Royal Australian Air Force Squadron's base, discussing the previous night's raid and wondering about the one to come. 'Ops' were 'on' again. The night before we had bombed Hamburg and the new technique of dropping 'Window' anti-radar tapes had been used. Also we had followed a new instruction not to weave the aircraft whilst over enemy territory, a manoeuvre carried out in the belief that it distracted fighters, radar and flak, but to fly straight and level. I was arguing that the new idea worked as the force had only lost seventeen bombers from a fairly large raid and those were very light losses for that period of the war, but the skipper was not impressed. He believed in throwing his aircraft around the sky, certain that this was a good tactic. I on the other hand, found my more precise work interfered with by the pitching of the aircraft.

The crew was fairly typical of those in Bomber Command. Five of us, Mick, me, Peter Moore the bomb aimer, Cliff Hart the wireless operator and John Patrick Francis O'Shaugnnessy, known simply as 'Jack', the rear gunner, had been together since the previous October, when we had teamed up on Wellingtons at OTU. George Moyes the mid upper gunner had joined us soon after we arrived at the Squadron in April.

The discussion about the use of 'Window' raged on. We all agreed that it had obviously upset the German radar because we hadn't seen a single aircraft 'coned' by searchlights over the target and the flak had been somewhat haphazard. Mick still stuck to his own ideas though, 'If we're weaving, a fighter is bound to have a harder job lining up on us,' he said. And on that note we each went off to our own section to check equipment and get ready for the night's work ahead.

Nav briefing came first so I was the first to learn that, yet again, it was the Ruhr, universally known throughout Bomber Command as 'Happy Valley', with Essen being the actual target. On our 17 ops so far, 15 of them had been to the Ruhr or close by, so we had a healthy respect for the massive anti-aircraft defences the Germans had concentrated around there. The route was straightforward. Across the Dutch coast at Ijmuiden; a very familiar spot to RAF navigators, to a point about ten miles north of Essen. Then right turn and run due south across the city aiming for the red TIs (target indicators) laid by Mosquitoes and the Lancasters of the Path Finder Force, then right turn out and it was 'balls out for home.'

Peter, the bomb aimer, joined me about halfway through the Navigators' briefing and drew the tracks on his maps in case, from his vantage point in the Lancaster's nose, he could pick up any pinpoints along their route to help the navigator.

With briefing completed the boys and me went off to the traditional pre-op meal of bacon and eggs. Then we got together in the operations room for main briefing. Squadron Leader 'Leathers' Leatherdale, the Senior Intelligence Officer, went over the main details of the route and the target and provided what special information he was able to give on the German ground and night fighter defences. He also commented on the effectiveness of the 'Window' dropping of the night before and confirmed that it had thrown the German radar system into complete chaos. A few words of advice followed from Wing Commander C 'Chad' Martin, the Commanding Officer, plus some instructions on times to start engines, the order for taxi and take-off from the senior Air Traffic Control officer. Martin became the first airman product of the Empire Air Training scheme of any nationality to command a heavy bomber squadron. He was appointed to 460 squadron with instructions to do as many operations as possible. He had done his first tour in 1941, as a member of 57 squadron, RAF, and seldom did the citation to an award sum up a man's personality and character as Chad Martin's did when he was awarded the DFC. It read: 'On 24th July, 1941 this officer as Captain of an aircraft participated in a daylight attack on Gneisenau at Brest. Flight Lieutenant Martin kept in tight formation and with his leader, presented such a determined front that the numerous enemy fighters did not dare to attack. One night last Autumn, whilst flying to Berlin he failed to receive a general recall signal and went on to his target. He penetrated into the center of the city and bombed his target. On his return to this country, he made a successful landing in thick fog.'

Out at the aircraft 'Bluey' Russell, the corporal engine fitter for Lancaster AR-G2, had a cheerful greeting for the crew. 'You're alright tonight Mick', he said 'I got the bloke on the fuel bowser to slip an extra 60 gallons in'.

There was a bit more cheerful banter with 'Bluey' and two other ground crew. Then a ceremonial 'watering' of the tail wheel by Cliff, who must have drunk too much tea with his bacon and eggs and the seven of us climbed on board to sort out equipment and carry out pre-start up drills.

When all four Merlin engines had started and were up to running temperature, the aircraft taxied out to the end of the runway on time. Our turn came, Mick turned onto the runway, a quick 'green' from the runway controller and we were off. After a smooth take-off we climbed over base until I instructed Mick to set course for the rendezvous point, Mablethorpe, on the Lincolnshire coast, so as to arrive at the correct time to set off on the main route. A great deal of emphasis was placed on timing, the aim being to keep all the bomber force concentrated in a small area to prevent German radar picking up stragglers and homing Luftwaffe night-fighters in on us. In addition the effect of several hundred bombers delivering their load in the space of only 10 minutes was reckoned to have a demoralizing effect on the recipients.

The North Sea was crossed without incident and about 20 miles before crossing the Dutch coast, Cliff, the wireless operator, moved to the flare chute and started his task of dropping the bundles of 'Window'. The flight across Holland and into Germany continued quiet - maybe 'Window' was having the right effect. However, there was one small snag, Cliff, ever an observant person, noticed that Peter's odd comments about the crossing point of the Dutch coast sounded rather strained, so he asked 'Are you alright Peter?'

'No, I'm not' was the reply. 'I think that tea I had before we left has upset my stomach, it feels terrible.'

'Better get him up on the rest bed', said Mick and without any argument, Peter crawled up and was helped onto the bed and his oxygen supply reconnected.

Lancaster AR-G2 was in the First Phase, which meant it was scheduled to bomb between H and H plus two minutes. At H minus 5, just as we were coming up to the final turning point north of the target, the first TIs went down. Giving Mick the time to turn on course for the final run in, I left my navigator's position, slipped down into the nose and, standing in for the ailing Peter who was still on the rest bed, prepared to drop the bombs. As always over Essen the flak was fierce, but the run up to the aiming point was smooth. The bomb doors opened and the Lancaster shuddered a little, but, as the red target indicator flare moved down into the centre of the bomb sight, my thumb pressed the button and the heavy bomb load started to cascade into the night. Just at that moment I felt a bump and shards of perspex from the front turret over my head fell around me. I was just about to say, 'We've been hit,' but was beaten to it by similar cries from George in the mid upper turret and Ken the flight engineer who added that the starboard inner engine was on fire and that he was shutting it down, feathering the propeller.

Just then Mick called over the intercom, 'I think you'll all have to bail out'.

I looked down on the fires starting to blaze in Essen and suddenly the aircraft seemed a warm, comfortable and familiar place. I couldn't see the fire in the starboard wing from my position in the nose or my reaction may have been different, but I called, 'For Christ's sake Mick what d'you mean, are you sure we have to go?'

'Hold on,' said Mick, then a few moments later, 'I think we'll hang on a bit. Come up and give me a course.

'I scrambled up from the nose and, as I slid into my seat, I noticed the feathered starboard inner with very little sign of fire. I was not aware that only a few moments before the flames had stretched back beyond the tail!

Miraculously, during that time we had not been 'coned' by searchlights or picked up by a prowling night fighter. I sorted out the course, revised his navigation calculations on the basis of our much-reduced speed, due to having lost one engine, completely and another giving only half power and then popped out from my navigation position to talk over the position with the pilot. Meanwhile Mick had discovered that he had lost his main elevator controls, which had prompted his initial reaction to bail out, but he regained control with the trim wheel and, using this, he was flying the aircraft successfully.

First thoughts were to get away from the target area and then bail out, but the aircraft continued to fly reasonably well on its remaining two-and-a-half engines. The starboard outer was only giving half power so most of the 'urge' was coming from the port side. Even so, Mick was making a good job of flying what he had and so the next thought was to get over Holland and then bail out, with the idea of, perhaps, being able to contact the Dutch resistance.

Over Holland the aircraft stopped its gradual descent and Mick managed to hold height at roughly 13,000 feet; again plans were revised and the crew unanimously agreed to have a go at getting across the North Sea and then baling out over home territory.

By the time the English coast slid underneath, we were getting cocky. 'Let's land it,' 'You can make it Mick!' 'Have a go.' A few more comments like this and Mick agreed to 'have a go' at putting it down on the runway at Binbrook.

When he called Binbrook tower and told them the condition of the aircraft and what he intended to try, the ATC officer wasted no time and quickly had both fire engines and the ambulance waiting at the end of the duty runway. After telling Mick 'You can make it,' we showed our confidence by jettisoning all escape hatches and with the exception of Mick and Ken, got into crash positions. The two gunners stayed braced in their turrets. Jack in the rear having swung his fully round to port and opened the doors so that he had an immediate exit available. Peter, who was feeling much better now that the aircraft was at low altitude, stayed on the rest bed, just under the centre escape hatch, his feet braced against the armoured door which was closed across the aircraft just aft of the radio position. Cliff and I joined him, sitting on the floor with our backs to the armoured door. I plugged into the adjacent intercom position to keep in contact with my skipper on whom everything depended. Through my earphones, I could hear Mick and Ken going through the pre-landing checks. Then the aircraft banked and settled on final approach. All seemed to be going well. Then suddenly I heard Mick's voice; 'More power Ken! All you've got and that's not enough!'

There was an increased roar from the engines, the aircraft suddenly lurched upwards and then appeared to drop. There was an almighty bang and through the escape hatch in the roof I saw a great sheet of flame.

We three crewmen in the centre went out of the escape hatch like jack rabbits, out onto the starboard wing - the port one was blazing furiously - and straight onto the ground. This required no athletic jumping as the main undercarriage had collapsed and the wing was resting on the ground. We raced round to the front of the aircraft, being joined by Jack and suddenly saw Ken catapult out through the front escape hatch, closely followed by Mick. He got to his feet, but Ken seemed dazed so the others grabbed him and, fearing the aircraft would explode, tried to run towards the ambulance which could be seen by the light of the flames. Ken showed no enthusiasm for running, so he was dragged along, his mates shouting 'Run Ken, run!' Next morning, we discovered he had a fractured skull, so it was not surprising that he found it hard to perform like an Olympic athlete.

We reached the ambulance at last and by now the two fire engines had got a good layer of foam over the fire and it was virtually out. There was no sign of George, until, in the distance, coming down the runway a figure appeared, who turned out to be the missing air-gunner. He had scrambled out through the main door and run so fast away from the wreck that no one had seen him!

Next morning I went up to Sick Quarters where he found the Wing Commander and Group Captain with Mick who thought he had been hit by flak and that this was due to flying straight and level instead of weaving as he used to do. In no way put off by their rank, he was just giving the two senior officers a piece of his mind on that subject, which we took in the best of good humour.

When we had gone Mick told me what had happened in the last few moments before the crash. Apparently the approach was quite good until, at about 200 feet, AR-G2 started to steepen its dive. With no normal elevator controls, he had to turn the trim wheel fully back but, as we seemed to elicit no response, called for all the power Ken could give. Then the trim suddenly took effect; the nose came up sharply. The aircraft stalled and fell in on its port wing. Ken had struggled to get out but had forgotten to remove his helmet, so he got mixed up and held back by his intercom and oxygen connections. Mick, spurred on by the sight of the fire, seized his legs and gave him an enormous heave, which explained why Ken had suddenly shot out like a cork from a bottle and had fractured his skull falling to the runway. Mick had got away with only superficial burns, but had suffered cracked bones in each arm from his fall to the runway.

After my visit to the patients, I met 'Bluey' Russell the engine fitter and together we went out to inspect the wreckage. The whole of the rear of the fuselage was still intact and, on entering it, we found an unexploded 4lb incendiary bomb lying just below the place where a 2-foot length of the elevator control rod had been broken off. This, then, was the cause of the trouble. We had not been hit by enemy flak but had collected several incendiaries from another Lancaster just above us. Obviously one had hit and smashed the front turret, but had not entered the aircraft. Another had started the fire in the starboard inner Merlin but must have burned through the cowling and fallen away without causing the fuel tank to explode. A third had entered the port side of the fuselage, severed the elevator control rod, but had not gone off. Lady Luck had been on our side that night!'

Chapter 3

The Bomber Boys

Martha Gellhorn[34]

*Sleep evaded me that night. As I glanced round the ward of the RAF hospital at Ely
I noted that I was the only patient awake. Worse still, the sergeant air-gunner
opposite was snoring fiercely. The Night Sister brought me a drink and stayed to
chat. She told me I was to have a new neighbour in the next bed. The only survivor
of a plane crash was being rushed to the hospital. Half an hour later the slight creak
of a trolley disturbed my half-conscious sleep and I knew that my new neighbour had
arrived. Speedily and gently the night staff lifted the Sergeant-pilot into bed and as I
looked a chill ran through me. Instead of a face, I saw what appeared to be a charred
mass of flesh, with two sunken eyes gazing helplessly around. I dozed off and when I
awoke a cheery 'Hallo!' greeted me from the burned face. I responded gladly,
admiring the courage that lay behind his spirit. We started to chat and he told me
that his plane had been hit while returning from a Berlin air-raid. He had managed
to get the machine as far as the English coast before the engines finally packed in and
they crashed. We talked quite a while. Yes, he was married, but only for a month. His
wife, he said, was a Red Cross nurse and as he described her there was love and
tenderness in his voice. I began to realize that his main fear was for her, not for
himself. I understood why: he dreaded that she should see his face as it was. Shortly
afterwards the Senior Medical Officer began his morning inspection. He told my
new acquaintance that he was sending for his wife to come down and see him. The
pilot began pleading with him not to do so. 'I'm afraid it's regulations,' replied the
doctor, 'but don't worry; your wife is a nurse and is used to such things. Besides,
her company will do you a lot of good.' All day my friend kept expressing his fears of
the reaction his appearance would have on his bride. I tried in vain to reassure him
and so did the Staff Sister. Then she told him that his wife would arrive the next
afternoon. I began to share the vague fears of my bed-fellow about the shock his
appearance would have on his wife and as the hours passed the tension seemed to
grow. Then the Day Sister came to the door of the ward with the loveliest girl I had
ever seen. She had the face of an angel, tender and kind. She walked over to her
husband's bedside and with a sweet smile, gently clasped the bandaged hands. Then,
pressing her head to his chest, she said with sincerity and conviction: 'Darling, how
lovely to be together again!'*
Reunion by Jack Winter

They were very quiet. There was enough noise going on around them, but they had no part in it. A truck clanked past with a string of bomb trolleys behind it. The ground crew was still loading the thousand-pound high-explosive bombs that look like huge rust-coloured sausages. A WAAF's clear high English voice, relaying orders, mixed with the metal noises. A light on the open bomb bay made the darkness around the plane even darker. The moon was skimmed over with cloud and around the field the great black Lancasters waited and men finished the final job of getting them ready. But the crews who were going to fly seemed to have nothing to do with this action and haste. Enormous and top-heavy in their Mae Wests or their electrically heated flying suits, these men seemed over-life-size statues. They stood together near their planes.

The Group Captain had been driving fast around the perimeter track of the field in a beetle of a car, checking up. He appeared the way people seem to, suddenly out of the flat black emptiness of the airdrome and said, 'Come and meet the boys.' The pilot of this crew was twenty-one and tall and thin, with a face far too sensitive for this business. He said, 'I was in Texas for nine months. Smashing place.' This would mean that Texas was wonderful. The others said how do you do. They were polite and kind and far away. Talk was nonsense now. Every man went tight and concentrated into himself, waiting and ready for the job ahead and the seven of them who were going together made a solid unit; and anyone who had not done what they did and would never go where they were going could not understand and had no right to intrude. One could only stand in the cold darkness and feel how hard we were at waiting.

We drove to the control station, which looks like a trailer painted in yellow and black checks and though there was no wind the cold ate into you. The motors were warming up, humming and heavy. Now the big black planes wheeled out and one by one rolled around the perimeter and got into position on the runway. A green light blinked and there was a roar of four motors that beat back in an echo from the sky. Then the first plane was gone into the blackness, not seeming to move very fast and we saw the tail-light lifting and presently the thirteen planes that were taking off from this field floated against the sky as if the sky were water. Then they changed into distant, slow-moving stars. That was that. The chaps were off. They would be gone all this night. They were going to fly over France, over known and loved cities, cities they would not see and that did not now concern them. They were going south to bomb marshalling yards, to destroy if possible and however briefly one of the two rail connections between France and Italy. If they succeeded, the infantry in southern Italy would have an easier job for a little while.

Several hundreds of planes, thousands of bomber boys, were taking off into the wavering moon from different fields all over this part of England. They were out for the night with the defended coast of France ahead and the mountain ranges where the peaks go up to ten thousand feet and the winter weather is never a gift; and then of course there would be the target. This trip, however, came under the heading of 'a piece of cake,' which means in the wonderful RAF language a pushover. If you were taking a pessimistic view of this raid you might have called it 'a long stooge,' which means simply a dreary, unsatisfactory bore. No one would have given the mission more importance than that. Still they were very quiet and the airdrome felt bleak when they were gone and the waiting had simply changed its shape. First you wait for them to go and then you wait for them to get back.

Perhaps this is a typical bomber station; I do not know. Perhaps every station is different as every man is different.

This was an RAF station and the crews flying tonight were English and Canadian, except for one South African and two Australians and an American pilot from Chicago. The youngest pilot was twenty-one and the oldest thirty-two and before the war they had been various things: a commercial artist, a schoolteacher, a detective, a civil servant, a contractor. None of this tells you anything about them. They look tired and they look older than they are. They fly by night and sleep somewhat during the day and when they are not flying there is work to do and probably it is exhausting to wait to fly, knowing what the flying is. So they look tired and do not speak of this and if you mention it they say they get plenty of rest and everyone feels very well.

The land where they live is as flat as Kansas and cold now and dun-colored. The land seems unused and almost not lived in, but the air is always busy. At sunset you see a squadron of Spitfires flying back to their station against a tan evening sky, looking like little rowboats and flying home, neat and close. In the thin morning, the day bombers roar over toward the Channel. The air is loud and occupied and the airdrome is noisy too. But the home life of the men is quiet.

They say that if you find all the chaps in the mess reading at teatime, you know there are operations scheduled for that night. This afternoon they sat in the big living room of the country house that has become their mess and they looked like good tidy children doing their homework. If you read hard enough you can get away from yourself and everyone else and from thinking about the night ahead. That morning they would have made a night flying test, taking the planes up to see that everything was okay. Between the test and the afternoon briefing is the rumor period, during which someone finds out how much gasoline is being loaded on the planes and everyone starts guessing about the target, basing guesses on miles per gallon. The briefing (the instructions about the trip and the target) would normally be finished by late afternoon and then there is an operational meal and then the few bad hours to kill 'before take-off time. It is a routine they all know and have learned to handle; they have taken on this orderly unshaken quietness as a way of living.

Of course there is relaxation in the nearest village on free nights - the village dance hall and the local girls to dance with, the pubs where you can drink weak war beer and the movies where you can see the old films. At eleven o'clock all such gaieties stop and the village shuts firmly. No one could say this is a flashing romantic existence; it is somewhere between a boarding school and a monastery. They have their job to do and they take this sort of life as it comes and do not think too much about it or about anything. There is only one clear universal thought and that is: finish it. Win the war and get it over with. There's been enough; there's been too much. The thing to do is win now soon, as fast as possible.

The old life that perhaps seemed flat when they had it becomes beautiful and rare when they remember it. No one who flies could make any detailed plans; there is no sense in counting your bridges as well and safely crossed when you know how many tough bridges are ahead. But vaguely each man thinks of that not-so-distant almost incredible past, when no one did anything much, nothing spectacular, nothing fatal, when a day was quite long and there was an amazing number of agreeable ways to spend it. They want that again, though they want a life that has grown lovelier in their memories. They want a future that is as good as they now imagine the past to have been.

It is a long night when you are waiting for the planes from Europe to come back and it is cold, but it has to end. At four o'clock or around then, the duty officers go to the control tower. The operations officers walk about a certain amount and smoke pipes and say casual things to each other and the waiting gets to be a thing you can touch. Then the first plane calls in to the control tower switchboard. Two WAAFs, who have been up all night and are still looking wide-awake, wonderfully pink-cheeked, perfectly collected and not frozen stiff, begin to direct the planes in. The girls' voices that sound so remarkable to us (it is hard to decide why, perhaps because they seem so poised, so neat) begin: 'Hello George pancake over.' In the glassed-in room you hear the pilots answer. Then the girl again: 'Hello Queen airdrome one thousand over.' The night suddenly becomes weird, with the moon still up and the bright stars and the great searchlights like leaning trees over the runway and the wing lights of the plane far off and then nearer, the noise of the motors circling the field, the ambulances rolling out and the girls' voices going on and on, cool, efficient, unchanging. 'Hello Uncle airdrome twelve fifty over.' This means that a plane, 'U for Uncle', is to circle the field at twelve hundred and fifty feet until told to 'pancake' or land. The planes come in slowly at first and then there will be four of them circling and landing. The more planes that come in and are marked up on the blackboard, the worse the waiting gets. None of this shows. No voice changes, no one makes a movement that is in any way unusual, the routine proceeds as normally as if people were waiting in line to buy theater tickets. Nothing shows and nothing is said and it is all there.

Finally all the planes were in except 'P for Peter' and 'J for Jig'. They were late. The job was a piece of cake. They should be in. They would of course be in. Obviously. Any minute now. No one mentioned the delay. We started to go down to the interrogation room and the Group Captain remarked without emphasis that he would stay up here for a bit until the chaps got in.

The crews of the eleven planes that had returned were coming into the basement operations room for questioning. They all had mugs of tea, white china shaving mugs filled with a sweetish ghastly lukewarm drink that seems to mean something to them. They looked tireder around their eyelids and mouths and slanting lines under their eyes were deeply marked. The interrogation again gives the curious impression of being in school. The crews sit on a wooden bench in front of a wooden table and the intelligence officer, behind the table, asks questions. Both questions and answers are made in such low ordinary voices that the group seems to be discussing something dull and insignificant. No one liked this trip much. It was very long and the weather was terrible; the target was small; there was a lot of smoke; they couldn't see the results well.

The Group Captain in command sat on a table and spoke to the crew members by name, saying, 'Have a good trip?'

'Fairly good, sir.'

'Have a good trip?'

'Not bad, sir.'

'Have a good trip?'

'Quite good, sir.'

That was all there was to that. Then he said, 'Anyone get angry with you?'

'No sir,' they said, smiling, 'didn't see a thing.'

This is the way they talk and behave and this is the way it is. When it was known that all the planes were back and all undamaged and no one hurt, there was a visible added jovialness. But everyone was tired, anxious to get through the questioning and back to the mess, back to the famous operational fried egg and fried potatoes, the margarine and the marmalade and the bread that seems to be partially made of sand and then to sleep.

The bomber crews were standing at the mess bar, which is a closet in the wall, drinking beer and waiting for breakfast. They were talking a little now, making private jokes and laughing easily at them. It was after seven in the morning, a dark cold unfriendly hour. Some of the men had saved their raid rations, a can of American orange juice and a chocolate bar, to eat now. They value them highly. The orange juice is fine; the chocolate bar is a treat. There are those who drink the orange juice and eat the chocolate early on, not wanting to be done out of them at least, no matter what happens.

The Lancasters looked like enormous deadly black birds going off into the night; somehow they looked different when they came back. The planes carried from this field 117,000 pounds of high explosive and the crews flew all night to drop the load as ordered. Now the trains would not run between France and Italy for a while, not on those bombed tracks anyhow.[35]

Here are the men who did it, with mussed hair and weary faces, dirty sweaters under their flying suits, sleep-bright eyes, making humble comradely little jokes and eating their saved-up chocolate bars.

Footnotes Chapter 3

34   One of a series of articles written for *Collier's Magazine* in New York and included later in *The Face of War* (1959). Martha Gellhorn was born in St Louis, Missouri. Leaving Bryn Mawr College, in a hurry to get started, she arrived in Paris less than a year later after two jobs, on the New Republic and the Hearst Times Union. She decided to pay her way around the world as a reporter and to write about it in fiction. Returning to the US in 1934, she was hired by Harry Hopkins to report on the way the Federal Emergency Relief program really worked. The result was, in 1936, a widely acclaimed book of four linked novellas about Americans in the Depression, called The Trouble I've Seen. In 1937 she went to Spain and then in the midst of war and sent to *Colliers* in New York an unsolicited article on daily life in besieged Madrid. So began her career as a war correspondent and for the next nine years she reported on war in Spain, Finland, China, Europe in World War II and Java. She had married Ernest Hemingway in November 1940; they had both covered the Spanish Civil War. Between assignments, she wrote two novels and a book of short stories. Hemingway and Martha Gellhorn divorced early in 1945. Martha Gellhorn settled in London after the war, re-married and after 1946 her journalism became occasional and freelance, a means to see for herself whatever absorbed her interest and concern, from the Nuremberg and Eichmann Trials to the war in Vietnam, the Arab-Israeli conflict and wars in El Salvador and Nicaragua and the US invasion of Panama. All her life she was both fascinated and repelled by war. She died aged 89 in 1998.

35   On 10/11 November 313 Lancasters of 5 and 8 Groups attacked the railway yards at Modane in Southern France on the main line to Italy. One Lancaster crashed on take-off. All the aircraft returned safely.

Chapter 4

The Seven Survivors

Flight Lieutenant Jack Gowan DFC

*On a Bomber Command station everyone's work directly or indirectly helps towards the
take-off time. Perhaps that is why when the first engines break the evening silence we
move to the windows, or look up from our desks, or pause in our walk, or lean on our
cycles, to watch the great aircraft swinging 'off the deck.' There they go, free of the
daylong fuss and flutter of fitters and riggers, bowsers, bomb trailers and section vans,
no longer bearing all patiently, but alive now with personalities of their own, churning
stubbornly away through the air to face what we can only imagine.*

*There were those take-offs in the spring, when the dusk was warm and full of sweet
scents and bird song, when the first 'kites' could be seen as they went, black and sinister,
but the last ones tumbled away invisible save for their red and green navigation lights
darting across the airfield.*

*There were take-offs when we rode round to the caravan and propped our bicycles against
it and lay on the grass so that the wings swung almost above us when the Lancasters
taxied down the perimeter and turned on to the runway. A moment of horrible pause
then, before the engines roared up so loudly that the turf shook and we held on waiting
for a 'green' from the controller. When it came they were off at once, seeming to move so
much more slowly than by day, looking so much bigger than by day, climbing
ponderously across the tranquil sky. When the last one had gone we would listen for a
while as they all gained height over base, making the country hum as though a swarm of
giant bees had been disturbed from their hive.*

*There were midsummer take-offs, before the sun set, when we would watch from the roof
of flying control and see the camouflaged tops of the aircraft rolling away like chameleons
beneath us. On one side the engines of the ambulance and fire tender would be ticking
over, on the other knots of people standing in their overalls or shirtsleeves. On the
veranda some air crew would be sitting, watching also and knowing more than the rest
of us the thoughts of the hidden men who looked down as they went at the evening light
lying over the calm countryside. Not yet dark when the last one had climbed away, but
the sunset painting the west, pale pink and green and purple.*

*At tea-time in November, when the air was crisp with frost a group of MT girls were
digging outside their hut, making a patch of garden, as a crew walked by to their machine
and laughingly suggested changing places. When the engines began to run up the girls
turned with glowing faces to lean on their spades and waved to the gunners as they taxied
by and called out the letters, M-Mother; P-Peter; E-Easy; Y-Yorker. When the last had
thundered away, it was cold and nearly dark. Everyone joined the long trail of hungry
men and WAAFs hurrying down the road to tea and a new moon began to show.*

48

There were late take-offs on winter nights, when jerkined men would stand about in the dispersal hut, pinpricks of sidelights showing on the vans parked outside and within only the glow of the stove in the middle of the floor lighting their faces and outlining ghostly moving shapes. No curtains over the windows, which showed the black wispy sky, the lines of flares along the runway and the blue perimeter glims winking in the wind. Through the windows the first aircraft taking off, seeming to come straight at the hut then swinging up, closing their wheels in slowly, so calm and methodical and black. Men stamping and warming their hands by the fire, then the roaring growing faint as no more come and it is over.
Spring burst into summer, summer fades to autumn which hardens into winter and the seasons slip by again. The trees become graceful and green, then grow thick branches into shady tunnels, then whirl away their leaves again to show bare tracery against the hard sky and still the aircraft take off and still we who are earthbound stay a moment to look as they go. As we stand and watch their flight they leave us and unconsciously we are staring up at the stars.
Take-off by Leading Aircraftwoman P. Whitlock.

We had completed our OTU training and selected our crew of six. The engineer to join us at Conversion Unit, which was the Bomber Command drill. I remember vividly when the Flight Sergeant was marching us from the station to Cottesmore. Some 300 yards from the entrance he gave the command 'Eyes left'. We observed a cemetery - a Royal Air Force cemetery. As we marched, left, left, right, left, the flight sergeant called out 'There lie 144 of you poor bastards killed in training and live too far to be sent home.' He meant Commonwealth countries - sending us deep into thought as he gave the order 'Eyes front,' which we automatically did while our minds were elsewhere. We were posted eventually from Conversion Unit to our first ever squadron at Woodhall Spa, 619 Squadron. The pilot of my first crew, Sergeant Frank Shirley, an Irishman from Dublin, had become very friendly with a Scots pilot. It so happened that Frank's crew and the Scots pilot's crew, fourteen of us, were posted to Woodhall Spa. We had become so friendly that no one really knew which crew we were in. On arrival at Woodhall Spa we in Frank Shirley's crew were given a virgin Lancaster, 'L for Love'. The Scots' pilot was given a virgin Lancaster, 'K-King'.

We carried out all our details without snags. Not so the Scot's crew. They could not get their Lanc airborne. With my sixth sense hard at work, unconsciously I said: 'You know, we shall be detailed to air test your kite.' This became a fact. As fate would have it, the order did not reach my ears. On this fateful day [9 June 1943] I do not recall having my breakfast - a routine happening - and I did not see any of the crews in question. I found myself outside the Squadron stores. I was there to draw some rags 'for the use of'. We were to go on our first operation the following day, so I was going out to our beautiful 'L-Love' to give my rear turret a final polish for reasons taught in training. A spot of oil could look like a fighter at night.

Unbeknown to me, my crew less myself had assembled with the Scotsman's crew out at 'K-King's dispersal - thirteen crew members instead of fourteen. As I did not show up they decided to pick a crew from the thirteen - unlucky for some but not for me - I was born in 1913. The two pilots being so friendly decided that they would both go, one in the capacity of flight engineer and so letting off the two engineers. Our navigator went also (being Irish from Dublin) and therefore very close to Frank Shirley our pilot. Our wireless operator said to theirs, 'No point in my going to check your equipment,' so the 'K' WOP went. The two mid-upper gunners went, one in the rear turret taking my place. Our bomb aimer gave way to their bomb aimer. Off they went, happy on a beautiful day for flying with not a cloud in the sky. The remaining crew members on the ground - the lucky ones - waved them goodbye. They headed out over the Wash and were never seen or heard of again. This was the story given to me when I returned from dispersal to my quarters. Yet another of my deaths from which I walked away. [36]

Inside 24 hours the 'survivors' were posted back to Conversion Unit to re-crew up. I found myself billeted with Jimmy Stewart, 'K-King's engineer. What happened to the other survivors I have never heard. I was detailed a new crew. Each evening I returned to my billet after flying exercises, I expressed my displeasure with my new crew. 'Jimmy,' I said, 'I cannot see myself getting through ops with this new crew.' I was, of course, comparing them with the excellent crew I had lost. We got round to the last but one exercise before returning to a squadron. On return, Jimmy would say, 'Well, how did it go tonight?' 'I am not happy with the way they fly or their discipline, Jimmy.' The reply was like sweet music to my ears. My guardian angel was taking over. The man with the lucky charm. Jimmy said quite casually, without taking his eyes off the book he was always reading, 'We are going to change our rear gunner. He has an impediment in his speech.' My reply was electric. I said, 'I will be at the Wing Commander's office twenty minutes before he arrives in the morning.' which I was. It was all arranged and he told me that my new crew was on a cross country that morning and when they landed they were going on a 48 hour pass and I was to join them when they returned. 'Thank you sir'. Once again a happy crew member. I immediately saw the possibility of a 48 hour pass for myself. 'Why not a surprise for my family at Weston-super-Mare? I arranged the same immediately. When I arrived at the guard room the flight sergeant pointed out that I needed an early pass to get away at that time of the morning. I suggested he rang the duty flight sergeant who would allow me to proceed, as he referred to me as 'the methodical man' because of the way I always laid my gear out. He phoned and my luck was in. He was at the other end of the line. OK, I could go. I departed in a flash.

I was to learn later that when the flight sergeant put the phone down he remembered that he should have told me to 'fly' on that last long seven hour flight all round England and then join my new crew. I was gone. The following morning a telegram arrived from the Adjutant. I was to phone him at once, which I did. He said, 'Name and number', 'Gowan, 1335839.' 'Repeat it' he said, which I did in service fashion. 'Repeat it again' he demanded. I did so. His response: 'I am not satisfied. Return at once,' which I did. I reported to the guardroom. The same flight sergeant was on duty. He went white when he saw me. He said, 'I don't believe it. You were killed last night. Report to the Adjutant at once.' I knocked on Ad's door, 'Come in.' In I went, saluted. He sat staring at me for some minutes and then passed me a telegram to read. It was to my wife reporting that I had been killed in action. I then learned that the crew I should have flown with the previous evening on that last exercise had crashed into the Welsh mountains and their bodies were spread over five acres.

I further learned that this crew of whom I had made reference about their lack of discipline, at briefing before take off when my name was called someone answered 'Here Sir.' My name was entered into the authorisation book as a member of that crew flying. The only reason for so doing, I believe, was, it was the last exercise of one's extensive training. When one was more than ready for the real thing, they did not want to be held back. They were more than ready for a squadron. They would have put the mid upper gunner in the R/T, resulting in a valuable pair of eyes missing from the mid upper turret. Once again my guardian angel pulls me from death, knowingly in a quest for six more survivors to join me.

I join my new crew. Pilot Australian Bill Marshall, Jimmy Stewart and Maurice Colvin, Scotsmen, Albert Youdan, Ginger Hallam, Curly Bates, Jack Gowan (self) all English. Our first Operation, Milan 12 August 1943.

You may well wonder why I, the grandfather of the crew at 30 years of age, was so long on reaching my first operation. When the war broke out in 1939 I held a luxurious appointment in the SS *Strathnaver*. We were on a millionaires cruise to South America. We turned round. They fitted her with a 6 inch gun and anti-aircraft gun and we were on our way to China, the Merchant Navy at war, all 25,000 tons of us. We followed a zigzag course. Because of our speed we travelled out of convoy. I made three trips to China. We were the first of 26 ships to get through the magnetic minefield; twenty-six went down ahead of us. They did not have a guardian angel and a lucky charm (yours truly) aboard. I did not sign for a fourth voyage to China because of my 200 per cent fitness. I felt I could be more use to the Royal Air Force, without any disrespect to the wonderful Merchant Navy. Sadly the superb *Viceroy of India*, a P&O directors' dream ship to which I had been transferred shortly before the war started was torpedoed and sunk before she reached Gibraltar. Again I have to say the lucky charm and his guardian angel were not aboard. The next fly in the ointment holding me back from starting my aircrew training was a bottleneck with aircrew training, so I became an auxiliary ambulance driver until they sent for me 17 months later in May 1942.

Back to our first operation to Milan which turned out to be virtually a Cook's tour. Nothing happened. When we passed Turin the searchlights were straight up in the air, the guns were not firing and there was no sign of a fighter. A lovely clear night, beautiful flying over the Alps and safely back to base.[37]

The next night we were off, so I said to Jimmy 'How about a ballroom dance in Grantham?' which was fairly close by. 'Yes' said Jimmy in his fairly broad accent, confirming from whence he came 'I'll have some of that. So we set off on our bikes - for the use of - happy as sand boys. We had quickly forgotten that there was a war on as we cycled along the country roads. The beautiful birds serenaded us with their operatic vocal chords. We had a great evening at the ball. Unfortunately, when we left it rained cats and dogs. I noticed Jimmy had his forage cap in his belt, a habit of his. I reminded him that it would be a good idea if he put it on his head. He simply said: 'My head is soaking wet now, so no point.' However, I had mine on with the strap fixed under my chin. By the time we reached the Squadron guardroom, the flight sergeant said: 'Drowned rats round the corner,' I don't know what happened to Jimmy, but I went for a very hot shower, followed by a cold one, a good rub down and into bed. The following morning poor Jimmy was hospitalised with a shocking cold and grounded. One was never allowed to fly with a cold - sinus could develop.

We were on Ops again this night [14/15 August, when 140 Lancasters of 1, 5 and 8 Groups carried out another attack on Milan]; another beautiful clear night but not so quiet. It developed into the longest ever Op - five weeks from dispersal back to base. It started with a fighter attack crossing the French coast. We were hit by a '109' and we lost an engine. The skipper said: 'We have a choice. We are on three engines. We have a full bomb load up, which we could jettison in the sea and boomerang back to base, or we can press on and drop the load of fruit bang on the target.'

Our second trip, dead keen, operationally inexperienced; one hundred per cent unanimous. 'Press on.' Press on we did. I had stoppages in three of my guns. I would be working on those over the Alps. We were losing height as a result of the cutting of one engine. We had to maintain at least 14,000 feet to clear Mont Blanc. By the time we crossed the Alps I had three of my guns working. As we passed Turin all hell was breaking loose. Jerry must be taking a hand. Searchlights spraying the sky, anti-aircraft was thick and heavy, fighter activity, combats a-plenty. We press on. We were falling behind the bomber stream, still losing height. Bomb aimer sights the target. We are dispatching our window cover, hopefully fogging their radar. We are now down to about 8,000 feet. We are now in the target area. We enter our first ever corkscrew evasive action. Alone, a sitting duck at 8,000 feet. We make our bombing run - a good one. Bombs gone. Skipper to navigator. 'Give me a course to North Africa.' The navigator came back with the course immediately. He knew we were not going to get back home that night. We survived seven fighter attacks around and over the target area. Now on course for North Africa I take a wind drift for the navigator. Our wireless operator was sending out distress signals, May Day! May Day! Petrol could be the problem, maybe others. Ron North, our spare engineer, was doing a good job on his first trip. Our bomb aimer, cool calm and collected on his bombing run, as if we were on a mere cross country. We gunners spitting venom at the enemy at each and every burst. Quiet reigned. No casualties as yet.

A very clear moonlit night, each of us with our own very private thoughts, yet ready to spring into action. Our wireless operator concentrating on his key board, probably speaking to it saying: 'Come on, there must be someone out there that can hear my distress signal.' Then it happened. An RAF Corporal, who used his little two valve set as a hobby, would listen out at night, 'just in case'. He was satisfied with his reports and we were more than satisfied. He took us some 200 miles inland until petrol ran out and we crashed 75 kilometres inside the Sahara Desert. We were collected and taken to the Transatlantic Hotel, Biskra. After a few weeks we acquired a cast-off army truck, overhauled it and drove across the desert to Constantine US aerodrome and discovered a Lanc to come back to UK. Inside a couple of days we left for UK. The only problem was that in the Middle East they did not have de-icing paste for the trailing edges of our wings, so when we hit the Bay of Biscay at 11,000 feet the mid-upper gunner called up the skipper and reported ice building up on our wings. We heard the skipper say 'Right we will climb over it. Keep me posted if it gets worse.'

We climbed to our maximum height. 'Mid upper to Skipper. We have about two tons of icing on our wings' Suddenly all engines cut. We start to drop. 'Skipper to engineer. Grab hold of the stick with me.' Crew's mental picture - pilot and engineer struggling to keep the aircraft straight and level. (I guess my guardian angel was there also). My immediate impression was like being in a hydraulic lift and the cable had been severed and we were tearing down into the sea. I did my drill, beamed my turret, seat belt undone, turret door open and ready to be thrown out. Everything was happening so quickly as we descended through the different temperatures, icing must have started breaking away, one engine coughed and started firing, then another and so on. By the time we had dropped from 18,000 feet to 4,000 feet in record time all engines were throbbing beautifully. Now we were completely lost presumably still over the Bay - at least over water. Some instruments were 'up the spout'. Our WOp was bashing out 'May Day', 'May Day' hoping for yet another 'Corporal'. No such luck.

To cut a more detailed story short, we were at a point where we did not know if we were over water or land, so our pilot and skipper gave the order, 'Prepare to bail out.' My drill, centralise my turret, lock it, get into the fuselage, for my chute and receive two members of crew whom I observe coming along the fuselage. It was then my responsibility to plug in my intercom by the Elsan, see the two crew members out of the rear door, report to the skipper that they had gone and I was ready to jump. Being a very positive thinker, I could not believe for one moment that this would happen. My astute sixth sense was working twenty to the dozen. Suddenly I was aware that this Lanc was one of the earlier type and had these small blinds held by small screw studs. They had removed them all from UK Lancs for safety reasons. I opened the blind by the Elsan and looked out and saw what I believed to be Drem lighting. I immediately called the skipper, reporting I thought that a drome was below us on the port quarter.

'Right,' was his response, 'We will come round and have a look.' The next thing we knew our skipper - now confirmed again and again since - had landed our Lanc on a fighter drome at Warmwell, Dorset. We piled out.

This wonderful little Aussie pilot and skipper Bill Marshall were walking round in large circles, the top of his trunk bent over, endeavouring to keep his balance and get his adrenaline going again. He was determined not to go down and he did not. What a responsibility, what personal strain and stress. Remember this was only his second operation as they say in Cockney-land 'You ain't 'eard nuffin yet.'

We became the only crew at the time who carried two photographers on clear nights. After bombing at 18,000 feet we came down to 8,000 feet into the blazing inferno, right among the 'dirt'. I politely say, to take pictures for the brass hats back at base. I the lucky charm with the guardian angel, volunteered for a second and third tour. Ron North our spare engineer passed his test with my guardian angel; he was the seventh survivor all the way even though we were at the top of the 'chop' list at 467 Squadron. Seven survivors without injury regardless of the punishment to our beloved 'Q-Queenie.'[38]

Footnotes Chapter 4

36 Altogether, nine crew including Sergeant Francis William Shirley and Sergeant John James Wemyss died on board Lancaster III EE113. All the names appear on the Runnymede Memorial.

37 The night of Thursday 12th/Friday 13th of August was a long one for 321 Lancasters and 183 Halifaxes to Milan, while 152 aircraft of 3 and 8 Groups were detailed to bomb Turin. Two Halifaxes and a Lancaster were lost on the operation on Milan. Another Lancaster was written off when it crashed into a Beaufighter at Ford. A 207 Squadron Lancaster which collided with a 619 Squadron Lancaster was abandoned at Plaidstow, Sussex. Two Stirlings were lost on Turin.

38 Adapted from an article by Flight Lieutenant Jack Gowan DFC in *Bomber Command News*, 1992.

Chapter 5

Night Of No Return

Where the hell have those bombers gone?' This, no doubt, must have been the thought which flashed across the minds of the Luftwaffe night fighter pilots sent up to intercept an RAF bomber raid on the night of 20/21 June 1943. The bombers, 56 Lancasters from 5 Group led by four Pathfinder aircraft of 97 Squadron, 8 (Pathfinder) Group, had roared overhead and disappeared in a south-easterly direction earlier in the evening and the night fighters eagerly waited for their prey to start the homeward trek. But, the bombers did not return ... And as far as the baffled Luftwaffe knew they had just vanished into the void. What Reichmarschall Hermann Goering's pilots did not know was that after the bombers had completed their raid on the old Zeppelin sheds at Friedrichshafen where Würzburg radar sets were being manufactured in quantity they did not set course for their home base at Scampton. England, but flew southwards, climbing high over the Alps heading for Algeria which had recently been taken over by the Allied armies where they landed safely. The decision not to return home but carry on to North Africa was not a hasty move made after the attack, but a brilliant tactical plan which completely thwarted the Luftwaffe and I for one am thankful that it was devised as it certainly saved my own and countless numbers of other lives which would obviously have been lost had we returned to face the waiting Me 110 and Ju 88 night fighters. This unusual raid began for me on 16 June.
Pathfinder pilot, Pilot Officer D. I. Jones DFC on 97 Squadron.

On the night of 19/20 June 1943 290 aircraft of 3, 4, 6 and 8 Groups took off to bomb the Breuil steelworks and the Schneider armaments factory at Le Creusot and the electrical-transformer station at Montchanin, which had been bombed in daylight by Lancasters in October 1942. Twenty-six H_2S-equipped Path Finders who released flares at Le Creusot flew on to drop flares over Montchanin, which was bombed by the light of these flares by a further 26 Lancasters of 8 Group who made two runs from between 5,000 and 10,000 feet, dropping a short stick of bombs each time. The smoke from the many flares that were dropped however obscured the targets and most mistook a small metals factory for the transformer station and bombed that target instead. Many bombs fell in residential areas. At Le Creusot all crews bombed the target but only about one fifth managed to hit the factories with many bombs falling on nearby residential property. Two Halifaxes failed to return from the raid on Le Creusot.

The following night 56 Lancasters of 5 Group and four Path Finder crews on 97 Squadron in 8 Group in Operation 'Bellicose' were detailed to fly the first shuttle raid to North Africa with an attack on the Zeppelin Works at

Friedrichshafen on the North shore of the Bodensee (Lake Constance), the south shore of which is in Switzerland. Zeppelins were no longer being built or housed at the factory, bombed by Royal Naval Air Service Avro 504s in November 1914 but was now turning out Würzburg radar, which was used to locate RAF bombers approaching the night-fighter zones on the continent.

Pilot Officer D. I. Jones, Flight Lieutenants Johnny Sauvage and Eric E 'Rod' Rodley, a survivor of the Augsburg low level raid and Pilot Officer Jimmy Munro of 97 Squadron at Bourn were the four Path Finder crews detailed to fly to Scampton to join 5 Group. Jones recalled: 'We lost no time in taking off and heading northwards. When we arrived at our destination I noticed that Scampton airfield was completely grass covered and this caused me some anxiety during our stay there. Group Captain Leonard 'Slosher' Slee DFC who had led the Le Creusot daylight operation on 17 October 1942 welcomed us. He told us we had been chosen to lead the main force to Friedrichshafen on the shores of Lake Constance. Attacking the Friedrichshafen works, however, would be no easy task. Intelligence insisted that the raid must be carried out before the end of June. But, the distance involved made a return night flight impossible during the few dark hours of early summer. To be caught over France at dawn would be suicidal, while heavy concentrations of flak plus swarms of fighters ruled out the possibility of a daylight operation. In addition to these problems the factory was small, necessitating pinpoint target marking and bombing under the worst possible conditions. Group Captain Slee was cheerful as he outlined the difficulties, but at the time we found no reason to share his good humour. Not that is, until his carefully thought-out plan was unfolded In addition to these problems the factory was small, necessitating pinpoint target marking and bombing under the worst possible conditions. I can tell you there were a few gasps of surprise as it was revealed to us that instead of having to run the gauntlet of night fighters we were going to try for North Africa. He told us that to achieve his aim - the target badly battered at a minimum cost to aircraft and lives - there was no other way and, he said, he hoped this ruse would fool the Luftwaffe. It was a bold, ingenious plan, but how right he was to be. Intensive bombing and tactical exercises occupied the next two days, during which time we theoretically left our target a mass of smoking ruins!'

The raid employed two new bombing procedures. The first was the appointment of a Master Bomber, Group Captain Leonard Slee, to control the Main Force in the target area sending instruction by radiotelephone over the target. This was introduced following Guy Gibson's successful use of VHF on the dams' raid a month earlier. The second was to fly to Allied bases at Blida and Maison Blanche in North Africa after the raid to confuse the German night fighter defences in France. Group Captain Slee's deputy flying 'Y-Yankee' was Australian Wing Commander Cosme Lockwood Gomm on 467 Squadron, one of two controllers, either of whom could take charge of the proceedings in the event of an emergency. Born in 1913 in Curitiba, an industrial town in Panama State, Brazil, Gomm flew his first tour on 77 Squadron and he had also flown Beaufighters on operations on 604 Squadron.

'An order was issued on 19 June confining all personnel to camp' recalled

D. I Jones 'and on the following day aircrews were called to general briefing. Here we were told that the operation was to be carried out that night by the Lancasters of 5 Group led by our four Pathfinder aircraft.

'The stuttering roar of more than 100 Merlin engines shattered the peace of that summer evening around our airfield. From my cockpit of 'T-Tommy' I glanced over at the Lancasters of Rod Rodley, Johnny Sauvage and Jimmy Munro. I wondered if they were thinking as I was of the grass covered runways as we were getting ready for take-off. Our Pathfinder aircraft carried a maximum load of 2.154 gallons of petrol - plus a heavy consignment of flares and target markers, so you will understand why I crossed my fingers as I taxied away for take-off. The reason for my apprehension and no doubt that of the other members of my little group was that the aircraft was overloaded by 2,000lbs! This meant that, although taking off from concrete runways under such conditions could prove a little uncomfortable, using an uneven grass airfield in these circumstances was definitely dangerous. Luckily the take-off was uneventful and soon I was setting course for the English Channel. Once across the Channel I pushed the nose of my aircraft down and like the others hugged the ground so as to escape radar detection. This proved very successful.'

Over France the force progressively lost height down to 10,000 feet as they passed Orléans and then lower still to between 2,500 and 3,000 feet. After crossing the Rhine they began to climb to their attack altitude.

'We were now flying in total blackness' continues Jones. 'A shapeless mass down in the nose of my Lancaster could be identified as Flying Officer Tommy Hodkinson, a bomb aimer with remarkably good night vision. He was searching for the narrow ribbon of the Rhine, and it was not long before he found it.

'A steady climb was made to the pre-arranged bombing height of 5,000 feet. I knew that 5 Group aircraft would continue up to 10,000 feet so as to provide an effective cover over the target while we did our job of marking.

'Tommy announced the approach of Lake Constance and looking down I could see its water gleaming in the darkness. Jimmy Munro and I were to drop a line of flares stretching from Friedrichshafen down to the old Zeppelin works, so that Rod Rodley and Johnny Sauvage could place green and red target markers on the sheds which sheltered thousands of partly built radar sets. Jimmy Munro and I would then drop more target markers as required. I turned to port over the lake at zero hour minus three minutes, heading for the dark shape of the town and hoping that Jimmy Munro was on schedule; accurate timing was essential for this operation.

'Tommy Hodkinson ordered 'bomb doors open' just as a string of yellow balls blossomed over to starboard. I realised Jimmy Munro was there doing his job. After our flares were released we swung away, waiting for Rod Rodley and Johnny Sauvage to do their stuff. The defences had taken note of our arrival and the whole of the target area, besides being brightly illuminated by our flares, was alive with probing searchlight beams and angry pin points of flak.

'Suddenly over the R/T' continues Jones 'came the voice of Wing

Commander G. L Gomm who took over as Master of Ceremonies when Group Captain Slee developed engine trouble'.

Aboard Slee's aircraft was Major Mullock MC the 5 Group flak liaison officer who had previously flown with Guy Gibson to Italy and had participated in raids over the Ruhr to observe the German defences first hand.

'Approaching the French coast at 19,000 feet we encountered heavy cloud and electric storms up to 24,000 feet. We therefore decided to come down below the front and lost height to 5,000 feet. We were suddenly engaged by the defences of Caen or the outer defences of Le Havre - owing to technical difficulties with navigation instruments we were uncertain of our exact position. Four 4-gun heavy flak positions engaged us for about four minutes. During the time we altered course by about 30 degrees every eight seconds, alternatively losing and gaining height by 1,000 feet. The flak bursts were mainly 300-500 feet behind and about the same distance above us. It was noticed that the rate of fire of the guns was extremely high! We flew on below cloud at 2,500-3,000 feet across France and encountered no further opposition.

'About 45 minutes from the target area by which time we had increased our height to 6,000 feet, we had to feather our port inner engine, which had been emitting sparks. And so we continued on three engines until we sighted Lake Constance. As the port inner engine is essential for the Mk.XIV bombsight it was un-feathered and allowed to windmill but shortly after the engine caught fire. We were unable to feather it or extinguish the fire, which grew in intensity. We jettisoned our bombs and the order to prepare to abandon the aircraft was given, first diving across the lake into Switzerland and subsequently turning the aircraft towards Germany. We were about to bail out, expecting the petrol tanks to explode, when the engine seized up and the fire went out. By this time we were at 4,000 feet but were able to maintain height.'

The weather at the target was clear, with Lake Constance and surrounding area bathed in bright moonlight, which enabled The Path Finders to place their markers very close to the target. Circling Friedrichshafen the crews awaited instructions from the deputy leader. Both attacking elements had been briefed to bomb visually from a height of 5,000 feet. There were approximately sixteen to twenty heavy flak guns and 18-20 light flak guns and about 25 searchlights, all within a radius of about six to eight miles of the target. They were more active than expected so Gomm ordered the bombers to climb to a safer height before attacking. 'However', adds Pilot Officer Jones 'the visual markings of our target would be almost impossible to see from 10,000 feet and I decided to stay at 5,000 feet as did the three other Pathfinders. Unfortunately, this meant that our four aircraft stood out alone in the dark sky and because of this we received a heavy hammering from the defences.

'Rod Rodley turned over Lake Constance, headed directly between our rows of flares and strained every nerve to drop a target marker before Johnny Sauvage could make it. The factory was plainly visible when Rod opened his bomb doors. His bomb aimer released a target marker only to see a green cascade burst slightly ahead of the shed roofs. Johnny Sauvage had beaten him to it after all. Rod Rodley then became aware for the first time of the intensity of the flak, but still managed to swing back to release more target markers. I followed suit. [Jones and Jimmy Munro released a string of flares parallel to and on either side of the Zeppelin sheds]. Within seconds high explosive bombs from the aircraft of 5 Group high above came crashing down on our markers. Concussions from the resulting explosions added to our discomfort, and I was forced to abandon one run in to the target because it was impossible to hold my aircraft on an even keel.'

The first wave of bombers dropped their bombs on the Target Indicators laid down by the Pathfinders and the second wave was briefed to make a time and distance run from a prominent point on the shore of the Lake to the estimated position of the factory. Stronger winds at the higher altitudes caused problems but around ten per cent of the bombs hit the relatively small target. Slee's Lancaster remained over Lake Constance for thirteen minutes and the crew had an excellent view of the attack, as Major Mullock recalls. 'Several aircraft were coned but not for any length of time. Leaving the target area, we continued to fly over the Alps. By skirting the peaks we eventually crossed, gradually gaining height to above about 14,000 feet. The 600-mile flight over the Mediterranean was slow, as we were limited to 140mph to prevent overheating. Eventually we sighted the Algerian coast and landed safely at Maison Blanche at 0752 hours, after a flight of ten hours and thirteen minutes.'

'One of my most anxious moments of the whole raid' continues Pilot Officer Jones 'was when, during one of my five successful runs over the target, 'T-Tommy' was caught in a cone of searchlights. I fought desperately to lose those probing beams of light which had caught my aircraft in their web. Shrapnel rattled along the fuselage like hailstones until, by diving at near maximum speed, I escaped into the friendly darkness. Poor Jack Hannah, my W/Op stationed at the astrodome on the lookout for enemy fighters, protested in vigorous terms as he was tossed about like a pea in a pod.

'Soon our target markers were obscured by smoke which covered the factory. No 5 Group then adopted their alternative method of attack, making timed runs from a prominent landmark on Lake Constance which we had illuminated with flares. The subsequent bombing was remarkably accurate.

'Eventually it was time to leave the smouldering ruins of our target and a course to steer was given to me by Pilot Officer Jimmy Silk, my dour and utterly reliable Scots navigator.

'All the Lancasters except one had an uneventful journey before landing at either Maison Blanche or Blida airfields. The odd one out was Rod Rodley's aircraft. For him and his crew it was a far from peaceful flight to North Africa. As he slowly descended over the Mediterranean, a lurid red glow suddenly blossomed below his Lancaster. Cursing violently Rod took evasive action, obviously thinking that a night fighter or a convoy had spotted him. His flight engineer Sergeant J. Duffy set off on a tour of inspection and found the bomb bay a mass of flames. The damage, however, had not been caused by a night fighter or flak from a convoy but from a target marker which had failed to drop over the target and had ignited when its barometric pressure fuse operated at a pre-set height. Rod pulled the jettison toggle and was vastly relieved to see the deadly ball of fire drop away into the sea below.'

Six of the Lancasters were damaged by flak, one beyond repair but the new bombing procedures tried during Operation 'Bellicose' were deemed successful. When reconnaissance photographs were examined they showed that 10% of the bombs hit the target factory and many of the near misses destroyed other industrial premises. By flying on to North Africa after the raid the bomber force confused the German night fighters that were waiting in the Florennes-Juvincourt area for them to return directly to England and as a result there were no Lancaster losses during either part of this operation.

'The next three days' says Pilot Officer Jones 'were spent sightseeing in Algiers before returning home to England'.

On 23 June, fifty-two of the Lancasters that had bombed Friedrichshafen were bombed up and the aircrews were briefed to attack the oil depot at the northern Italian port of La Spezia. After completing the operation the crews were instructed to return to their home bases in England. Eight of the aircraft that bombed Friedrichshafen remained in North Africa for maintenance as D. I Jones recalls:

'Jimmy Munro and I were the only Pathfinders available to mark the target as Johnny Sauvage's aircraft was damaged beyond repair by flak, while Rod Rodley's extensively scorched Lancaster needed a great deal of repairs. Their two crews stayed on at Maison Blanche, eventually flying home in Rod Rodley's machine via Gibraltar. Of my three colleagues who took part in this raid, Canadian Jimmy Munro was killed later in 1943 [39] while my navigator, Jimmy Silk, also lost his life with Munro. As for Rod Rodley he rose to command a Squadron of Mosquitoes and after the war he became a captain with BOAC, flying jets across the Atlantic. He lived at Esher, Surrey. Johnny Sauvage served with Transport Command after leaving 97 Squadron and post-war became an executive with Cunard Eagle Airways.'

Wing Commander Gomm DSO DFC was killed on 15/16 August 1943 on the operation to Milan, on his 24th sortie of his second tour of operations. 'Y-Yankee' exploded near the village of Beaumont scattering debris over two square miles. The only the survivor was 20-year old Sergeant James Lee, the flight engineer and youngest crewmember on board, who badly burned, had the luck to parachute down onto a hayrick and was taken prisoner. When the Lancasters of 467 Squadron RAAF landed back at Bottesford and entered debriefing, the news was broken to a distraught Section Officer Paula Fisher, a WAAF in the Intelligence Section who had formed a relationship with the highly regarded pilot. Gomm's parents, who lived at Sao Paulo in Brazil, were notified of his death.

Footnotes Chapter 5

39 Flight Lieutenant James Francis Munro DFC RCAF was KIA on the operation on Berlin on 22/23 November 1943.

Chapter 6

Night Trip To Munich

D. W. Pye

Where are they now, those young men of all nations,
Who flew through they knew not what might lie ahead
And those who returned with their mission accomplished
And next night would beat up the Saracen's Head?
Lancasters Audrey Grealy

The time was the latter end of 1943, when my squadron belonging to Bomber Command was based on a 'drome in Lincolnshire.

The crew of which I was Wireless Operator Air-gunner were on the programme for that might's operation [40] and the usual rumours were going the rounds in the mess as to where they were going. We knew that we had on board our Lancaster a 2,200 gallon petrol load and so the trip must be in the region of a ten-hour 'Op' - quite a long one. We reported to the Briefing Room at 17.00 hours. This was it. Now we would know the worst. We learned that our target was Munich, a tough one, with about eleven hundred ack-ack guns, 300 searchlights and on top of that a good chance of heavy night-fighter defence on the way in and out.

'We [41] are routed-in over France, across the Alps skirting the Swiss border and down south; a nasty way if one got engine trouble and had to climb the 16,000 feet to clear such peaks as Mont Blanc.

We are now out in our usual plane, 'Q-for-Queenie', a grand job, tuned up to perfection. We do our last pre-flight checks. All is OK so we climb out again for a last natter, a cup of tea, a smoke and a joke or two with our ground crew. The Commanding Officer comes up in his jeep, asks if all is well and wishes us all the best. Then he is on to the next dispersal point and crew. A hard job the CO has; he knows for sure that a number of the boys he is talking to will not come back and tomorrow he will have the task of writing to their mothers, wives and sweethearts.

The Skipper checks the time and, seeing that we were the first off, we switched on, revved up and taxied out on to the runway. The 'green' comes from the Airfield Controller and we are off, tearing down the runway and up into the night, circling, climbing and eventually setting course on the first leg of our route to Munich.

'It is a dark night, with cloud above us and cloud below. One feels very lonely in a world of one's own with a population of only seven, each with a job to do and each dependent upon the other doing his job and doing it right if all are to survive. But one knows that one is with the best and most reliable chaps in the world.

'So the trip went on with no real incident. The night was clear and moonlit and the mountains below looked beautiful and even peaceful. Little could we guess what a menace they would be upon our return. I should mention at this time that my crew, along with three others, had a special job to do over Munich. We were to fly over the target five minutes before the main force of 250 planes and find the wind's speed and direction, which I had then to radio back to ensure accurate bombing.

This added considerably to the danger of the 'Op' for us, as it meant that the full force of Munich's defence would be thrown at just four aircraft until the main force arrived.

Anyhow, on to the target we ran and then all hell burst loose. In the twenty trips I had done before never had I seen such a density of ack-ack fire. It seemed to cover the whole town. We were picked up with searchlights within seconds of entering the target area.

Having to find the wind direction necessitated the Skipper keeping our plane on a straight and level course for a while, which meant that if we were to do our duty we could not take evasive action. We were right in the midst of the flak now and still we had not been hit.

Then we got it, a direct hit on the outer starboard engine. It packed up like a light gone out and the whole of that side of the aircraft became a mass of holes from shrapnel. But we were lucky: not one of us was wounded. Just before the hit we had completed getting the wind, so I got cracking in sending it back. I repeated it three times to make sure of its reception and then informed the Skipper of what I had done. That was the main part of our job completed. We have only to run out and come in again with the main force to bomb - and then for home. That is going to be a difficult job, though, for I see on looking round again that one engine was finished altogether and another was only working on half power. The Skipper came on to the intercom to the whole crew and asked if we were still all OK. We were, except for the bomb-aimer's flying-suit that had been cut right across the chest by a piece of flying shrapnel: a lucky miss.

The Skipper asks us if we feel that we would be justified in ditching the bombs and getting out as quickly as possible but we are all in full agreement that we have to run in again and finish the bombing.

By this time the main force has arrived and we turn towards the target to commence our bombing run. Our height is now down to 8,000 feet and we cannot climb any higher, though we can maintain this height with care. The flares have gone down and the target area is bathed in a brilliant white light. The markers are exploding and the Master Bomber has commenced his instructions over the wireless. He tells us that the markers are not quite on target and that we must not bomb until he had been down to assess how we must aim in relation to the red marker-bombs.

'We can see the Master Bomber's Lancaster far below us and going lower all the time. The light anti-aircraft guns are all after him now but his words come through quite clear and confident: 'Bomb in such and such an area away from the markers.' Then we see his plane burst into flames. It is going down afire from nose to tail but his instructions still come through. He passes all the information we need and then: 'Cheerio, lads, this is it,' he calls and dives to the ground in a mass of flames. [42]

'By this time we have got quite a way over the target and our bomb-aimer informs the Skipper that if we are to bomb accurately we shall have to run round again. So we turn round out of the target area and make a half-circle to get back on to a new bombing run. We manage this without further mishap and start on our third run over the target. If we keep this up much longer, old Queenie will know Munich pretty well.

Our bomb-aimer's instructions to the pilot are now coming over the intercom.: 'Left, left, right, left, left, steady, steady, on aiming point, steady, bombs, gone.' We feel the plane give its customary jump after being freed of the seven-ton weight of HE and we have started on the long flight home.[43]

We run into more flak but a few more holes won't make much difference for the plane is more like a sieve than anything else. There are still no wounded aboard and the rear and mid-upper gunners are getting a bit of their own back with shooting out searchlights. They finish a couple of them and that cheers us up considerably.

We know that we have a very tough job to get back. As we can only just maintain a height of 8,000 feet, it means we have to work our way through the Alps, flying down the passes and keeping a sharp look-out for any unexpected peaks. It is rather nerve-racking to see the mountains towering up above the plane but we get through, thanks to the brilliant flying of our Skipper. We carry on over France and now another big snag appears. The engineer says that we have barely enough petrol to reach the coast of England. The problem is whether to land in France and try to avoid capture or to carry on and possibly have to ditch in the sea.

We decide to keep going and to help us maintain height we throw out all the equipment we can manage without. This helps a little and we go limping on. One good thing about this trip was that so far we have not met up with any German fighter planes.

We are now over the sea, the tanks were very nearly empty and I am trying to contact a wireless station to inform them of our plight and position. I get in touch with Manston (Kent), which is an emergency-landing 'drome and they tell me we are to try to reach them, when they will have everything ready for a crash landing.

We go in a direct line for Manston. We are all tense, praying and hoping for just an extra bit of luck to pull us through. The coast comes into sight and then the lights of the 'drome. We get fastened down but when the Skipper checks the flaps and undercarriage he finds that the latter will not come down. It must be badly damaged, so we inform Control that we shall have to make a belly-landing. The Skipper asks us if we would like to bail out while he brings the aircraft in alone. We all tell him that he has brought us all this way back and we would rather take our chance with him than otherwise.

We were now in line with the runway and losing height rapidly when the port outer engine starts coughing and spluttering, then cuts out altogether.

The other engines follow suit in quick succession but now we are nearly on the deck. We go tearing up the runway and what happens next is difficult to describe because the plane does everything but loop-the-loop.

There is a dreadful racket of tearing metal, banging and crashing but we eventually come to a stop. The wings have been torn from the fuselage, the tail we have left halfway down the runway and the nose of the plane is crumpled in like a broken egg-shell. But the thing that matters really is that, except for a goodly number of minor cuts, abrasions and bruises, we are quite all right.

The fire-tender comes up with the ambulance in close attendance and the next thing we know is that we are in bed in hospital, quite fit but according to the MO, suffering from 'severe strain and operational shock.'

We are only 'invalids' for one night and then back to base.' [44]

Footnotes Chapter 6

40   2/3 October.

41   Around 290 Lancasters and two B-17s.

42   Possibly Squadron Leader G. B. F. Cousens on 61 Squadron whose Lancaster came under a sustained attack from a night fighter while south of Munich. A fierce fire broke out as the Lancaster dived and at about 6,000 feet the bomber exploded, throwing Cousens and his rear gunner clear. The other five members of his crew were killed. *RAF Bomber Command Losses of the Second World War, Vol.4 1943* by W. R. Chorley (Midland 1996).

43   Visibility over the target was clear but the initial marking was scattered. A record was established when almost four tons of bombs per minute were dropped on the city in a 25-minute period between 2230 and 2255 hours. Heavy bombing developed over the southern and south-eastern districts of Munich but later stages of the raid fell up to 15 miles back along the approach route. Most of this inaccurate bombing was carried out by 5 Group Lancasters, which were again attempting their 'time-and-distance' bombing method independently of the Path Finder marking. The 5 Group crews were unable to pick out the Wurmsee Lake, which was the starting-point for their timed run.

44   Adapted from *Night Trip To Munich* by D. W. Pye in *70 True Stories of the Second World War*, (Odhams Press).

Chapter 7

No Particular Courage

Harry Church

When the target was announced by the wing commander as Düsseldorf, there were hearty groans
Sergeant Harry D. Church, navigator on Lancaster III JB305, 'E-Easy' on 49 Squadron at Fiskerton - Düsseldorf operation, 3/4 November 1943. 589 aircraft - 344 Lancasters, 233 Halifaxes, 12 Mosquitoes were dispatched; one aircraft crashed on take-off at the start of the operation. 18 aircraft - 11 Lancasters and 7 Halifaxes - were lost. Five other bombers crashed or were written off on the return and a further 37 bombers were damaged.

'We did not know, we could not know, that within two hours some of us would die, violently. Statistically, we were aware that there was at least a 5 per cent chance we would not return that night, or any other such night, but we refused to admit it, even to ourselves. A one in twenty chance tonight did not necessarily mean a certainty by twenty such nights. It happened to others, so we persuaded ourselves; we believed, or pretended to believe, we were immune, even though, privately, most of us were scared of what lay ahead. Even if we had known, there was little anyone of us could do, except report sick and it was too late for that now. It would be unthinkable to desert comrades with whom work and pleasure had been shared. Besides, any action deliberately taken to avoid participation would result in disgrace. Last month, one friend, a flight sergeant, suffering from extreme stress, had asked to be relieved of any more operational flying. The letters LMF (lack of moral fibre) had been duly entered in his service book and he had been reduced to the ranks and sent elsewhere and was now probably cleaning lavatories or whitewashing coal. It was harsh treatment for such a person, a volunteer, as we all were, who was genuinely at the end of his tether, but possibly advisable in order to attempt to ensure that expensive training was not wasted. Fortunately such action was necessary only for a few. It is surprising how much value is attached to self-esteem. What was it that Shakespeare wrote, in Hamlet? 'This above all: to thine own self be true. And it must follow, as the night the day, Thou canst not then be false to any man.' If we had opted out, we would remember and be ashamed of ourselves for the rest of our lives.

Fourteen colleagues had failed to return one night last week. We had raised our glasses and toasted 'Absent Friends' and then those friends had been replaced almost immediately by new crews, who would soon become friends, even if only for a short time. Such was life - and death - in the autumn of 1943 on a Lancaster bomber base. 49 Squadron, based at Fiskerton, a few miles east of Lincoln, was one of many in 5 Group, regarded by many and certainly by the crews themselves, as the elite of Bomber Command. Their isolated bases were scattered over the flat Lincolnshire countryside. 49 Squadron's brick buildings, Nissen huts, control tower, three hangars, bomb dumps and all the other necessities had been erected hastily and three concrete runways laid down in the usual 'A' pattern. Over a thousand airmen and members of the Women's Auxiliary Air Force (WAAFs), of all ranks from lowly aircraftmen to group captain, had moved in some months ago from their previous base at Scampton, an established pre-war aerodrome. The grass runways at Scampton were unsuitable for heavy bombers, particularly when they were fully loaded on take-off. The people adapted quickly to their new base. Even though they missed Scampton's many facilities and complained endlessly about the war, Adolf Hitler, the rations, the basic accommodation and the mud, they still set to work and cheerfully got on with their jobs. The squadron consisted of sixteen aircraft divided between two flights, A and B, usually with a few spares, both in men and machines.

Unlike most bomber squadrons, here painted emblems of blondes or bombs on the fuselages were scorned. This squadron was above such fripperies; the Lancasters flew unadorned, their crews proud of their individuality. Only the RAF roundels, the squadron identification letters (EA) and the individual aircraft letters were displayed. Nothing else was necessary. If questioned, though, they would have had to admit that the lack of emblems was based on pure superstition. Earlier in the war a few crews on the squadron had had their aircraft decorated with emblems and it so happened that they were the ones that failed to return. So the commanding officer, or someone else in authority, had decreed that such adornments were not welcome. Many airmen were superstitious and a large number of them carried mascots on their operations.

Our crew of seven stood by the undercarriage of Lancaster, 'E-Easy', our flies open, ready for the ritual urination before climbing into the aircraft's dark and narrow interior. As well as fulfilling a superstitious need, this was a very practical thing to do, as there would be no other reasonable opportunity for several hours. True, there was the Elsan (the chemical urinal) but there was little time to use that.

The stars twinkled brightly in the early November sky; mist lay like a silver carpet on the damp grass; the dope on the wings and fuselage contributed to the unmistakable and evocative smell of a wartime airfield at night, one that cannot be described to those who have not experienced it. The heightened awareness of the senses augmented the sights, sounds and smells to produce a feeling of excitement and adventure. This feeling was a natural one for young men. Some of our crew were still teenagers: one of us was 18 and another 23. (His friends sometimes called the latter 'granddad') Older men (over 30 years of age) were often considered unsuitable for the job and they usually had more sense than to volunteer for flying duties, even though they did get paid an extra shilling or so a day as flying pay. Was it by reason of their youth or their hairstyle that RAF air-crews were nicknamed the 'Brylcreem Boys' by some in the other armed services?

Norman Carfoot was our pilot. A flight lieutenant by the age of 21, he had already completed almost 2,000 hours' flying, most of them on Sunderlands patrolling the Atlantic, searching for enemy submarines. He had become bored with this comparatively mundane life and had requested a transfer to Bomber

Command. A burly young man, he had the confidence and deep respect of his crew, who would willingly accompany him to hell and back - and often did. The aircraft he piloted did not just land; they floated down on to the runway and kissed the ground lightly. Norman's magnificent moustache was the envy of many air-crews. Why did they still have mere down on their upper lips when they had tried so hard to grow something to twirl? All they could do to be different was to leave undone the top button of their tunic or battle-dress. This method of 'cocking a snook' at authority became a tradition in Bomber Command. Sergeant 'Jock' Mason, the flight engineer, was a typical Scot, dour, down-to-earth, good at his job and reliable. He had reached the ripe old age of 22. He had been an engineer with a reputable British motor manufacturer before volunteering for aircrew and spent many of his non-duty hours fussing around the aircraft's engines with the mechanics.

I, Harold Church (Harry to all my RAF friends), was the navigator; aged 21, I was born and bred in Hemsby, Norfolk. I was able to boast, quite modestly of course, that I had never been lost in the air. I neglected to mention that on one occasion I had got lost in Lincoln after drinking a few pints!

The bomb-aimer, Flight Sergeant Steve Putnam, aged 21, was a Canadian from Winnipeg, who had almost completed his pilot's training in Canada when he was advised to transfer to a bomb-aimers' course. He spent most of his time in the nose of the aircraft and always carried an empty milk bottle, in case he needed to urinate. That particular part of his anatomy which relieved the need became stuck in it on one occasion, during a long flight, much to the glee of the rest of the crew.

Sergeant Hank Wood, a Londoner, was the wireless operator. He was 20 and dated a different girl every night of the week when he was not flying and wrote letters to several others. His line-shooting to his colleagues consisted of boasting about his many conquests. His line-shooting to some of his conquests followed a different pattern. He would sit in the Mess, writing to one of his 'popsies', as airmen usually called their girlfriends, pretending to be flying over Germany while he wrote and professing his undying love and hopes to see her in the not-too-distant future, should he survive the current operation! Hank could send and receive Morse code messages at well over twenty words per minute.

Flight Sergeant Steve List, the rear gunner, aged 21, came from Newcastle. He didn't have a 'Geordie' accent, though, as his home town was the Newcastle in Australia. He had volunteered to travel halfway round the world for the purpose of sitting, cramped and cold, despite the electrically heated suit, in the most exposed, most lonely and most dangerous part of the aeroplane. He called himself a fatalist, taking the view that, if his time was up, he would not survive. While maintaining there was little purpose in searching the skies for enemy aircraft for his own sake, he assured the rest of the crew that he would keep a keen look-out in case he could save their lives! Was he serious, or was he indulging in an Aussie leg-pull? On the assumption that the latter was the case, the rest of the crew had made a point of thanking him effusively when he announced that generous concession! Steve was an excellent gunner, having qualified with high marks on his particular course, which included instant aircraft recognition as well as gunnery.

Sergeant Wilf Marson, the mid-upper gunner, was the baby of the crew at just 18 years old, having falsified his age in order to volunteer at the age of 17. Amused by the initials of his position in the aircraft, he told his friends that he must be a

MUG to sit there for hours, searching the skies for something to shoot at. His home was only a few miles north of Lincoln. He always carried an old Home Guard helmet with him on operations, which he carefully tied around his groin. Many aircrew members particularly feared two fates: burning to death and suffering damage to the 'family jewels'. Wilf was determined to avoid the latter if at all possible. He was the joker of the crew. Small and wiry, he smoked an enormous pipe and had an imaginary dog, a figment of his fertile imagination. He 'walked' it around the perimeter, to the pub and even took it on the train to Lincoln, talking to it and praising or scolding its behaviour. Many a spectator was puzzled, to say the least. Wilf called this 'dog' 'Fido', named after the fog dispersal system recently installed on either side of the main runway. FIDO - an acronym for Fog, Intensive, Dispersal Operation - consisted of a system, of pipes along which petrol, mixed with methane, was pumped in foggy weather. When ignited, the flames from the regularly spaced holes in the pipes helped to clear the fog over and near the runway, so that planes from the squadron and others in the vicinity, or even those based in Yorkshire or Norfolk could land reasonably safely. However, it was only 'reasonably safe', because the glare from the flames and the turbulence they caused provided considerable problems for pilots who were already tired from an operation over enemy territory. Our squadron was the first to have the FIDO system and the crew of 'E-Easy' were the first to test it, late one afternoon in October. This honour, if so it could be called, was a source of great pride to Wilf, although we were almost certainly chosen because Norman was the most experienced pilot on the squadron. On the first night testing, fire engines raced over from Lincoln, thinking the buildings were on fire. No one had told them about the practice burn. FIDO was very expensive on fuel; nearly 200,000 gallons of petrol could be consumed in one burn and petrol was generally in very short supply. Nevertheless, the system undoubtedly saved many aircraft and the lives of their crews from the Lincolnshire fogs. War is an expensive business!

This was the seventeenth 'op' for most of the crew, although the great majority of them had been undertaken with another squadron, before being posted to this special one. 'Op', short for operation, sounded more casual, less ostentatious, than the American 'mission'. They had only thirteen more to do after this one to complete their tour. Completing a tour was not a simple exercise; towards the end of 1943 few crews managed to complete thirty operations over enemy territory. However, they did have the privilege of a week's leave every month or so. If they were lucky and the weather was suitable, the tour could be completed in four to six months. Then they would be entitled to a long rest, probably as instructors, before beginning another tour. Needless to say, the completion of those thirty operations provided a reason for great celebration, both by and for the fortunate crew. Unfortunately many crews did not complete a tour at the same time; some individuals missed operations for one reason or another and then had to function as a replacement with another crew.

'E-Easy' was an almost new Lancaster, only weeks old. It had been delivered to the squadron by a young female pilot. Many aircraft were flown to the operating squadrons by young women of the Air Transport Auxiliary, who, by reason of their sex, were not allowed to fly on operations. I for one felt envious and quite inadequate when seeing these slips of girls piloting huge aircraft so competently. At Elementary

Flying Training School, more than a year before, I had learned to fly a Tiger Moth. I was allowed to go solo after 10 hours of instruction, but after that memorable flight, which lasted about 15 minutes, I tried to land about 6 feet above the ground! The Tiger Moth had inelegantly bounced and bounced again, before coming to rest close to a hedge on the perimeter fence with a damaged undercarriage. I was not particularly popular with the instructor. I liked to think that I was chosen for the navigators' course because of my good examination marks and ability in that occupation, rather than because of any lack of promise as a trainee pilot. After all, I had managed to fly once without the help and advice of an instructor.

The commanding officer, Wing Commander A. A. Adams DFC, inevitably known as 'Triple A', enjoyed flying 'E-Easy' and usually did so when he selected himself for operations. When 'Wingco' was not flying, Norman welcomed the opportunity to take over what he liked to think of as his 'own' aircraft, for night-flying exercises as well as operations. Our previous regular Lancaster, 'F-Freddie', had been written off, full of bullet and shrapnel holes and with one engine damaged beyond repair, on a previous op. [45]

Even with the aircraft in that condition, Norman had landed with his usual skill and aplomb. Lancasters were marvellous aircraft, but they did differ in performance. While 'F-Freddie' had been a bit of a beast, slow to climb and slow to turn, 'E-Easy' was a delight, with a ceiling of 22,000 feet fully loaded and a top speed of almost 200 knots unloaded. The average life of a Lancaster on operations was, in those days, about forty hours.

The briefing had been held that afternoon and was attended by all fourteen crews nominated for the operation. The number of aircraft involved depended on the demands of Group Headquarters, the number of serviceable aircraft and the number of crews available.

Therefore it was only on rare occasions that all the squadron's Lancasters were involved in a particular operation. When the target was announced by the wing commander as Düsseldorf, there were hearty groans. The Rhine / Ruhr Valley, known by air-crew as 'Happy Valley', was not a popular destination, being well guarded by anti-aircraft batteries, searchlights and fighters. 'Short, sharp and shitty' was the pithy description given to these trips by the aircrews. Together with all the other information necessary, we were given tracks to follow, expected wind velocities and known searchlight and flak sites and were advised of predicted cloud cover. The briefings always ended with 'Synchronise your watches, gentlemen; the time is now.'

After the briefing the navigators stayed to complete their plotting of tracks and establish the first course to follow, based on the predicted wind velocity supplied by the met officer. Later, they would need to obtain fixes on their actual position over the ground, calculate the actual wind speed and direction and work out the new compass course to take. This information would then be passed to the pilot over the intercom. Individual preparations were made by all other members of the air-crew. It was ironic that many of the ground staff would already have a good idea of the target area for tonight; the amount of petrol put in the tanks to ensure that the maximum bomb-load was carried gave them a vital clue. Just 500-600 gallons, with a consumption rate of about a gallon a mile, meant a short trip and there was only one realistic destination: 'Happy Valley'.

Many of the ops recently had been concentrated in that area and they were the most dreaded targets, along with the 'Big City', as Berlin was known. Then came the kitting-out; helmet, oxygen mask, flying boots, jackets, parachute harnesses and 'Mae Wests' were donned and parachutes issued. Valuables and all form of identification were handed in or put in lockers.

We were then ready for transport to the dispersed hard-standings. We were usually driven out by a pretty young blonde WAAF called Vi, who was always very quiet on such occasions, though usually happy and talkative, particularly when she collected us on our return. Climbing the steps behind the wing on the starboard side, we made our way along the narrow fuselage, made clumsy by our accoutrements. We who were stationed at the fore climbed laboriously over the main spar, while the rear and mid-upper gunners settled themselves for an uncomfortable journey. The four mighty Merlin engines were started; one by one they coughed, spluttered and roared into life. The necessary checks were made to ensure all was well. At a signal the aircraft taxied out of its dispersal bay, leading the rest of the squadron aircraft towards the main runway. When we reached the runway, we waited for the 'take-off' signal and then the engines howled at full throttle as 'E-Easy' sped towards the far hedge. Becoming airborne was always a tricky business with a full load of bombs and with only two or three minutes between each aircraft taking off. Three weeks ago one Lanc had failed to lift off, with disastrous consequences for all the crew as well as the plane itself. Fortunately the bombs had not exploded. Tonight we had about 14,000lbs of bombs slung under the Lanc, consisting of two 'cookies' and several smaller bombs and incendiaries. No doubt the ground crew had inscribed the cookies with short and impolite messages addressed to Mr A. Hitler.

Once airborne, the usual drills were followed. The undercarriage was retracted and a course set. We climbed steadily, westwards first to gain height, then eastwards, for the rendezvous over Skegness. 589 bombers, mainly Lancasters and Halifaxes, were operational that evening, all on the same course, flying without exterior lights along a corridor twenty miles long, two miles wide and at heights between 16,000 and 22,000 feet. On previous operations there had been many near-misses and some had no doubt collided, but it was a calculated risk; certainly it was preferable to the use of navigation lights or straying from the main stream, where a ponderous bomber could be easily picked off by an enemy fighter. There was safety in numbers; the enemy could not attack all the aircraft at once! It was a grim fact that those singled out for special attention seldom returned to base and those that did return usually bore scars. Landings with only three engines functioning were not unusual, while shell holes in the wings were commonplace.

After crossing the coast, the air-gunners tested their Brownings with a short burst, to ensure efficiency and readiness. The following exchange would be typical: 'Navigator to pilot - course 097 - airspeed 185 knots - on track.' 'Pilot to navigator - thank-you - changing course, now, to 097, at 185 knots.'

'Enemy coast ahead' announced the bomb-aimer over the intercom and then we were over hostile territory, not that we had been particularly safe from fighter attention over the North Sea. Now we would have searchlights and flak to deal with too. We were becoming used to this, gaining more and more confidence with each op, but we knew we could not afford to become over-confident or careless. I remembered the first one; after the target had been confirmed and the time of take-off approached, I had felt very unwell and had almost persuaded myself that I was unfit to fly, that I would be a danger to the rest of the crew and ought really to report sick. It had taken a great deal of will-power to convince myself that I was not really ill, just scared stiff. After that, it had been a bit easier. The waiting was the problem; once in the aircraft, all the crew members had their specific tasks to perform and involvement with the job in hand left little time to think of other things.

At a pre-arranged point, a further change of course was made; the track to the target usually entailed at least two such manoeuvres in an attempt to confuse the enemy as to the target. A further minor course correction was necessary, arising from a glance at the H_2S and my subsequent calculations of wind speed and direction. The H_2S was a blessing; this navigational aid had been developed quite recently and our squadron, often known as the 'try it out squadron', was one of the first to use it. Pulses from the transmitter beneath the aircraft were reflected back to the aircraft from the surface below, whether or not there was cloud. The nature of those surfaces was displayed on a cathode ray tube above the navigator's table; towns and water below could be distinguished by the difference in shades from light grey to black. Dead reckoning, using the Mercator's chart, was still essential, but this new aid was very valuable in obtaining a fix. However, we and the boffins did not then know that German fighters could home in on the H_2S, having already salvaged and painstakingly reconstructed one from a crashed bomber. Had it been known, or suspected, aircrew would not have been at all keen to use it anywhere near the target! On later raids the navigators would make sure it was switched off before the bombing run began. The 'Gee' set, its predecessor, was still installed and could be useful, but it was limited in range because it relied on synchronised radio signals from England, which could be jammed by the Germans, while astro-navigation, using major stars to obtain bearings, could not give an accurate fix. The wireless operator, too, had to maintain silence, except in case of dire emergency, as Morse-code signals would be picked up and homed in on by the enemy.

Then came the first attack. 'Enemy fighter to port,' called Steve and his Browning guns began to chatter spitefully at the intruder in their air space. Wilf joined in and the enemy broke off to choose another target. The two gunners had sent a twin-engined German fighter, a Ju 88, spiralling down in flames on one trip, much to their delight and the relief of all. Most operations were like this. Enemy fighters were often spotted, but there was no point in attracting attention unless they attacked. Some did attack and were either driven off or broke off the engagement for some reason. Such attacks had sometimes resulted in minor damage to the aircraft, but so far none of the members of our crew had been injured and Wilf's helmet had been superfluous. On two or three occasions anti-aircraft fire had torn jagged holes in the wings, but the overworked, dedicated and efficient ground-crew were adept at such repairs, so that the damaged aeroplane was quickly made serviceable again.

'Window', the aluminium strips that confounded enemy radar were ejected and then, spot on the ETA, the target loomed ahead. It could hardly be missed. Myriad searchlights probed the night sky and occasionally an aircraft was caught in the interlocking beams. A blazing bomber spiralled down in flames, while another suddenly exploded. The crew of that one did not have time to suffer. Innocuous-looking but deadly white puffs, like balls of cotton-wool, blossomed around us: as expected in 'Happy Valley', the flak was heavy tonight. The cotton- wool puffs were close now and 'E-Easy' rocked, as if in protesting at the intrusion. Then began the run-in, straight and level. Now came the really hairy half-minute or so.

After the bomb-aimer had released the load, the aircraft would leap, owing to the sudden loss of weight, but it would be necessary for the pilot to stay as straight and level as possible until the camera had done its job. The resultant photographs would indicate the accuracy of the bombing and also give valuable information as to probable damage when they were analysed by the experts. For that reason Bomber Command pilots had been recently instructed that they must not weave over the target.

'Bomb-aimer to pilot, left, left - steady, right, - steady ... steady ... bombs gone.'

Simultaneously and before I could enter that fact and the time in my log-book, we were coned by searchlights. The interior of 'E-Easy' was starkly illuminated. All air-crews dreaded being caught by the lights as the operators rarely allowed their victims to elude them. Anti-aircraft shells or a night-fighter's bullets would soon target them and all too few returned to base to tell the tale. Norman threw the aircraft into a dive, turning violently to port at the same time. The searchlights pursued 'E-Easy' relentlessly and the flak increased in intensity. The aircraft shuddered like a wounded beast as the anti-aircraft shells exploded; in the harsh light it was obvious that the starboard wing had been damaged. The flak stopped suddenly, but the crew knew the likely consequence. Sure enough, Steve announced, almost conversationally, 'Ju 88 to starboard - dive, dive'. The gunners' Brownings burst into action. But they were already diving. Norman fought for control. Then came disaster; our gunners' fire had no effect on this occasion. I escaped death by inches as tracer bullets appeared lazily across my vision from left to right. This illusion of laziness was caused by the fact that tracers were regularly spaced among the equally deadly other bullets in order to help the gunner direct and correct his fire.

The port wing burst into flames. Jock made valiant efforts to divert the fuel supply to a different wing-tank. Norman's calm voice was heard over the intercom, checking the well-being of the crew. No reply came from the wireless operator, but we others reported in, one by one. Seconds only had passed, but already it was obvious there would be no bacon and egg tonight after landing and debriefing. As the op was an early evening one, that treasured meal in wartime Britain, always keenly anticipated, was due on our return, rather than before the trip. Often on a long operation, perhaps of eight hours in duration, crews were served with a meal beforehand. Some aircrew were unkind enough to suggest that by serving the meal after the operation, a saving of rations was very likely. [46]

Inevitably, the dreaded 'Abracadabra, Jump, Jump' order was issued, calmly, by the pilot. 'Skipper, I can't get out,' called Steve from the rear turret. 'The navigator will come to help you,' said Norman reassuringly, as if such a minor problem would soon be solved. I drew the blackout curtain behind me and was about to move when Steve announced, 'I'm OK now, skipper'. I could not help my vast relief that I would not now have to struggle to the rear of the blazing aircraft. Relief turned to shock as I looked to my left and saw the wireless operator, or what remained of him. The bullets that had passed across the navigator's table had not missed Hank, who was now quite unrecognisable. The shock was even greater in that I had never before seen a dead body, even one that had passed away peacefully. By this time Norman had managed to pull the Lanc out of its steep dive in order to enable his crew to bail out. Had he been unable to do so, our evacuation would have been almost impossible. I quickly reported Hank's fate, clipped on my parachute, removed my oxygen mask and moved to the escape hatch in the nose. As I passed Norman, still fighting the controls in order to keep the aircraft as steady as possible, my pilot, skipper, friend and colleague briefly took one hand from the controls and waved goodbye. 'Greater love has no man...' We both knew that Norman had no chance of survival. If he relinquished the controls, 'E-Easy' would spin violently. The hundreds of gallons in the tanks would probably cause a major explosion at any second. Even if, by some miracle, he managed to reach the hatch, it would not have provided him with a means of escape; he had often joked about it: 'I've tried out the hatch for size and I'm far too fat for it to be any use to me', or words to that effect.

Reaching the nose, I saw that the hatch had been removed and Steve and Jock had gone.

Now it was my turn. 'E-Easy' was now burning fiercely. I dived out. At that height the temperature was far below freezing point and my oxygen supply was non-existent. It was inadvisable to use the ripcord on the chest parachute too soon, in case the aircraft exploded immediately and it was necessary to fall towards breathable air and a warmer temperature as quickly as possible, but it was also important to avoid blacking out before pulling the D-ring. The few seconds' delay in my doing so was certainly not from force of habit. I had not had this experience previously and sincerely hoped I would never repeat it. As the chute opened several seconds later, I saw our aircraft, below and in front, plunging earthwards in a ball of flame. A minute or two earlier I had escaped death by inches; now I had survived by seconds, but I had thoughts only for Norman, Hank and any others of those close friends who could not escape the inferno.

I drifted down. The quietness now was almost unbelievable, entirely free from the barely perceptible sounds that are not even registered in the brain in what is thought of as total silence, on a quiet night in the countryside or on a deserted mountain. Not only was it an enormous contrast from what had just happened, but it was also a silence I had never before experienced. It was all so peaceful and, in spite of my predicament, almost relaxing. The fall seemed unending; it must have taken at least 30 minutes. Then I saw clouds below and suddenly, with no warning, I just stopped, standing upright! The chute collapsed around and on me.

'Now I know where I am' came the thought. 'I am at the Pearly Gates and at any moment St. Peter will greet me.' However, as I came to my senses, which no doubt had been partly befuddled by lack of oxygen, I realised what had happened. The cloud was actually a ground mist, the same type of mist we had left behind such a short time ago. I had landed gently in a ploughed field. So much for the warning that landing by parachute was similar to jumping off a high wall. As I gathered up my parachute I also gathered my wits, deciding what to do next. Fortunately I was wearing the new type of flying boots, with laced shoes on the feet to which the legs were attached; so many others had lost the old type while baling out. In order to avoid attracting attention I cut off the tops with the knife provided, then tore off my navigator's brevet and insignia of rank. A nearby straw-stack offered a hiding place for the parachute, harness and Mae West; I ripped the chute into several pieces and pushed them under the straw, retaining one small piece. I knew that I had torn the parachute so that it could not be used by the enemy, but had no idea why I kept a piece of it. This was no time to think of mementoes and I wasn't a sentimental type! Then I sat by the stack for a few minutes, deciding what to do.

Orientating myself by the Pole star, I trudged south, hoping to find a copse or wood to hide in until any probable search had been called off. However, after a few hundred paces I climbed over a low bank and found myself on a narrow road, along which I walked. By now the moon was shining brightly and I was able to identify what looked like a village ahead. Deciding to bypass it, I prepared to take to the fields again, but before I could do so, heard footfalls and a man's voice called 'Gute nacht'. Although a few German phrases were posted in the Mess for such an eventuality, I now wished I had learned to speak the language better. However, the meaning was obvious, so I returned the greeting as best I could. One small hurdle had been surmounted. Jumping another bank, I crossed another field and - my luck was in - saw trees ahead. Approaching, I found it was indeed a small wood in the corner of the field. I entered, pushing my way through bracken and bushes and sat down. I would wait until midnight, when all should be fairly quiet, before resuming the journey. Looking at my navigator's Omega watch, I could see well enough that the time was 21:25. 'What a lot has happened in a few hours,' I muttered to myself. A favourite quip among air-crew was 'Join the Navy and see the world; join the Air Force and see the next'. Well, I hadn't done that - not yet, but I thought again of my friends, who had so recently died. Hank was dead and Norman could not possibly have survived; of the other four, how many had been as fortunate as I?' [47]

Harry Church was soon captured. After interrogation at Dulag Luft, Frankfurt he was taken into captivity and placed in Stalag 4B. Christmas 1943 came and went, a tunnel was dug the following spring but in June it was discovered. Camp life was monotonous and their captors remained arrogant but during the summer months of 1944 the attitude of the German officers and guards began to change. Fewer rifle butts were viciously used by the younger guards who had previously been only too willing to vent their spite on those had dared to oppose Hitler. St. George's Day, 23 April 1945 was a date to be remembered for the rest of the prisoners' lives. The whole camp appeared to be deserted. Then the outer gates were flung open and a troop of Cossacks rode through, armed to the teeth with revolvers, rifles and swords festooned around them and with hand-grenades on their belts. Liberation, of a sort, had arrived.

Footnotes Chapter 7

45 Lancaster III ED452 which was damaged in action on 14 May 1943 on the raid on Pilzen when it was flown by another crew and overshot on landing at Fiskerton.

46 Research into the Abschussliste (Claims listings) indicates that the Lancaster was most likely hit by Oberfeldwebel Erich Becher of 2./NJG6, who claimed four victories before his own death in aerial combat on 24 February 1944.

47 Sergeant J. S. 'Jock' Mason and Flight Sergeant Steve G. Putnam RCAF survived and were taken into captivity. Norman Carfoot, Sergeant Henry Leonard 'Hank' Wood, Sergeant Wilfred H. Marson and Flight Sergeant Steven McCarthy List RAAF are buried in the Reichswald Forest Cemetery.

Chapter 8

Abracadabra, Jump! Jump!

Geoff Taylor RAAF

On the night of 18/19 October 1943 one of the 360 Lancasters that were detailed to bomb Hannover was 'Z-Zebra' on 207 Squadron, which was piloted by Flight Sergeant Geoff Taylor RAAF and his crew who had taken off from Spilsby at 1716 hours. The Lancaster was attacked by Hauptmann Friedrich Karl Müller, a 'Wilde Sau' pilot of Stab JG 300, an ex-bomber pilot and pre-war Lufthansa captain. Müller, who was nicknamed 'Felix' or 'Nasen' ('Nose' on account of his aristocratic proboscis) shot 'Z-Zebra' down near Reinerbeck for his 19th victory. All the crew were taken prisoner.

The sky was empty as we began to orbit Mablethorpe. We could have been the only aircraft flying in the length and breadth of England. Then I saw them - little black specks at first, crawling out of a layer of low cloud; then circling like black birds of prey, breeding incredibly quickly, too fast to count, until they were all about us; a vast, smothering cloud of hundreds of Lancasters, Halifaxes and Stirlings that seemed to overflow the once-empty confines of the sky.

The bomber country of East Anglia had once more sprung to life on that autumn evening of 18/19 October 1943. There seemed no end to the bombers which joined our own Lancaster, 'Z-Zebra,' at the rendezvous. They banked and climbed, the last of daylight glinted on their wings and on the bright perspex of turrets and cockpits, until, as if appalled at the sight, the sun slipped abruptly over the horizon.

The clouds, the sea and the horizon deserted us as we flew east into the rising night towards the target - Hanover. The ghosts of those who had flown this way before would have had to come close to see our silent figures - Don J. Duff, our flight engineer, standing motionless before his engine panel on the starboard side, myself hunched over the controls, Bill [W. Worthington], the newly married mid-upper gunner, spinning in his turret on top of the fuselage and Mac's [Flight Sergeant W. J. McCarthy RAAF] four Brownings in the tail following his restless search of the treacherous sky behind us. Jock [A. G. McLeod], the navigator, bowed in monk-like contemplation of chart and computer, Joe [A. R. Burton], the wireless op and Smithy [C. R. Smith], our Canadian bomb-aimer, in the nose, completed the almost immobile tableau moving steadily towards its destiny. Time seemed to be our only dimension.

The intercom was silent, the way we all liked it. Not a single switch, for once, had been left on to rasp in our ears as the forgetful one's breathing was magnified by his microphone. Peace, perfect peace.

I knew, as we approached the enemy coast in silence, that Mac and Bill were at their unending vigil, for always the aircraft was yawing steadily as they swung their turrets in the buffeting slipstream.

A flurry of white sparks suddenly jumped up and twinkled in the darkness ahead. 'Looks like Texel, Skipper,' called Smithy from the nose.

Texel, in the Frisian Islands off the coast of Holland, was an outpost of German flak and a regular, unfailing signpost for incoming British bombers.

We crossed the coast and flew on in silence. Every one of us, except Jock, who was still bowed over his chart, was staring out into the night, searching, always searching, for the dark, lurking shape which could be another Lancaster or a German night-fighter.

Every few minutes I rolled 'Z-Zebra' from side to side while Bill from his turret on top of the fuselage scanned the level flight blind spot behind us.

Quite suddenly Mac's voice rasped over the intercom from the rear turret. 'Jerry! Jerry! Corkscrew port, corkscrew!'

Startled and without thinking I rolled 'Z-Zebra' over and down into the corkscrewing evasive action we had rehearsed so often in training. The intercom was silent except for the roar of my laboured breathing as I hauled back on the stick to lift 'Z-Zebra,' 63,000lb all-up weight, out of the diving turn, controls stiffening as the airspeed flickered round violently to 300 mph. Then she was vibrating to the harsh chatter of Mac's four Brownings.

Dive port, climb port, roll, climb starboard, dive starboard, roll and then dive port all over again.

'OK' came Mack's reedy voice. 'Resume course. I think I hit him, but he didn't burn. Just dived away.'

I steadied everything back to normal. No one was hurt and nothing damaged, thanks to Mac. Staring into the dark side of the sky, where the moon would soon be rising, I suddenly strained forward in my seat to get my eyes a few inches nearer where a black shape was looming ahead of us. One of ours? One of theirs?

I never did find out.

A string of balls of fire floated out prettily and gracefully from the dark stranger and hurtled themselves in streaks of colour straight towards us.

There was only time for a startled 'Christ!' and I was wrenching 'Z-Zebra' over in a diving corkscrew towards the attacker.

Cannon shells banged and exploded their way into the fuselage. Instinctively I ducked. In my mouth the familiar insipid taste of chewing gum and bottled oxygen suddenly acquired the sharper tang of cordite stench and the acrid reek of scorched metal.

We had corkscrewed into our evasive action really fast and this time I thought we'd never pull out. Heavy with her bomb load, 'Z-Zebra' had her nose well down.

I grabbed the stick with both hands and applied sheer brute force. She was really wound up. Slowly at first, as I strained and then almost too suddenly, the nose came up.

For an eternity of time, as the stars swung crazily above the cockpit canopy,

I coaxed and pushed and kicked the Lancaster on a spiralling, twisting path through the night: listening only for the gunner's urgent 'Jerry! Jerry!' heralding another attack; taking comfort from the rattle of our own guns.

The corkscrewing was sheer physical labour and the sweat ran down my fingers, moistening the leather of my gloves. My shirt was wet against my belly. The flavour of chewed-out gum and the stink of cordite seemed to have been with me all my life.

This wasn't happening to me. It couldn't be. It was a nightmare, and in the full terror of it I was consoling myself with the thought that I should be awake soon.

Time ceased to exist until a far-away voice was talking in my earphones.

'OK. He's broken off the attack. Resume course.' It was young Bill in the mid-upper-turret.

Thankfully, because of the aching pains across my shoulders, I straightened out. Over the intercom I counted heads. None of the crew, thank God, had been hit. 'Z-Zebra' herself was not so lucky. Mac could rotate his rear turret but couldn't fire his guns. Another burst of cannon fire had cut the oxygen supply to Bill's turret. A burst of cannon-shell had exploded in the fuselage between my feet and Smithy's prostrate form in the nose. The back of the instrument panel seemed to be a shambles. Airspeed indicator, altimeter, artificial horizon, directional gyro and DR compass were dead.

From the astrodome, Joe mentioned that another cannon shell had ripped through the fuselage below Jock's navigation table.

There was no answer from Jock when I called him. I tried again and to my relief and surprise he came back heartily on the intercom.

'Hullo, Skip,' he called cheerily, 'what's your trouble? What can I do for you? How're things out there?'

I couldn't appreciate Jock's light-heartedness.

'How are things out here?' I repeated. 'They'd be a bloody sight better when I know how things are in there. What time do we turn on course for the target?'

'That's all right, Skipper,' he said gaily. 'There's lots of time. Lots and lots of time.' He giggled foolishly over the intercom.

In sheer exasperation I turned in my seat and peered back down the fuselage. Jock was standing there, his helmet bunched fantastically on the top of his head, his face gleaming whitely in the dark.

Turning back to check the sky again, I thought, 'That's funny - Jock's face!' Suddenly, I realised his oxygen mask was dangling under his chin. Jesus! No oxygen at 23,000 feet!

Hastily I called to Joe. 'Jock's got no oxygen. He's off his rocker. Shove his helmet and mask back on, quick.

'OK Skip.' Joe's quiet, precise voice was oil on troubled waters.

I settled back in my seat and sighed gustily into the intercom, too tired to switch my mike off. The task of reaching the target dead on time and course was difficult enough with a fit navigator and a full panel of instruments. And now here we were, the blind flying Sperry panel practically in my lap, literally nothing on the clock and my navigator dancing around on his charts talking gibberish, while somewhere ahead in the darkness lay our target.

We flew on east, waiting for the glow of fire-lit clouds or the vivid reds and greens of Pathfinder flares. Except for the intermittent pipping of 'Monica' - an audible warning of enemy fighters - we flew in complete silence, searching, scanning the sky for trouble.

Jock called up. It was good to hear his normal voice on the intercom again. He'd had a hectic few minutes. He said we'd be turning to the target in two minutes.

By the time we turned and began our run-up on Hanover it was getting lighter in the cockpit from the glow of the fires. Below and around us a sea of glowing, wriggling maggots of fire squirmed and flared through gaps in the overcast - a cauldron varied only by the red bubble-burst of an exploding blockbuster bomb.

A sudden blinding flash jolted me round, staring up to starboard. Hanging in the sky was a mass of fire spurting rivulets of coloured Very lights and trailing streamers of blazing petrol. The Lancaster that had been riding with us had got as far as he would ever get.

I had seen no flak, no fighters.

Then Smithy was calling from the nose.

'OK Skipper. Bomb doors open.'

Sitting there with sweat running down my neck and time standing still, I listened to Smithy calling the bomb-run.

'Left, left. Right. Steady. Steady.'

'Don't you send us round again, Smithy,' I thought. 'I'll break your bloody neck if you do.'

Tensed at his bomb sight, Smithy was whispering into the intercom.

'Steady, Skip, steady.' Time was a fingernail in your flesh.

'Bombs going, bombs going. Bombs gone! Bombs gone!' The aircraft and our hearts, lifted as the bombs fell.

I shouted with satisfaction and relief, 'Good boy, Smithy!'

Bomb doors closed over empty bays. I pushed the nose down for the friendly gloom ahead and the long run home.

'Corkscrew port!' It was Joe shouting from the astrodome. I swore as I rolled over and in under the attack. Once again I ceased to think and became a sweating, labouring, aching part of the aircraft. Tears of sheer, choking, frustrated rage smarted in my eyes. Like a small boy singled out for punishment after a mass misbehaviour, I wanted to hit back. Then I could hear and feel strikes drumming into the fuselage and wings. For a splintered second I thought of Mac perched away in the rear turret, crouched over his dead guns. Without warning, the revs of both port motors simultaneously went off the clock. The scream of the racing airscrews and engines was like a needle in your brains; an animal screech of pain and protest.

I wrenched back the pitch controls for the port motors, slammed the throttles closed and reached out for the feathering buttons and called Don, the flight engineer, trying to keep the panic out of my voice. The windmilling port airscrews had not feathered and were dragging the nose down and away from the course home.

I kicked on the right rudder to bring her back again, right leg braced ready for the strain of holding the rudder against the thrust of the two good starboard motors. There was no strain. The rudder pedals slammed back and forth easily.

It was like back-pedalling on a freewheeling bicycle.

Then it was that the nightmare became reality; something which you prayed would end soon but against the end of which you fought with everything you knew. Desperately you try all you have been taught and anything you can improvise to keep 'Z-Zebra' flying.

As the dark horizon of Germany rapidly climbs higher round you and 'Z-Zebra' drops bumping into low-cloud, rage grips you again, this time at the thought of the six men, six friends they are, riding with you and waiting for you to do something, hoping for an act of wizardry.

Like a stab in the back the starboard inner engine suddenly screams and spews flame. Don reaches for the feathering and fire buttons. He might as well have sat back and sung the Lord's Prayer.

Aching with the sheer muscular effort of holding up the plunging port wing, you feel the elevators tighten as the nose goes down with a lurch.

Too tired to think, you hear your voice giving the queer little order they taught you one drowsy day at the operational training unit in pastoral Oxfordshire: the absurd jingle you never thought you would really use.

'Abracadabra, Jump, Jump. Abracadabra, Jump, Jump.'

Repeating it, you think how damn silly it sounds.

But it leaves no room for doubt or confusion.

Over the intercom you hear Bill shouting to Mac. Don, after several fumbling tries in the dark, has clipped the parachute pack to your chest harness. Then he is gone, sliding down under the instrument panel into the nose, which Smithy has already left.

Mac calls up from somewhere in the dark shambles of the fuselage, his voice tense. He can't find his parachute pack. You feel like telling him to jump without it. Instead, you urge him, For Christ's sake hurry, Mac, she's going.' Somehow he finds it and then he is gone' too. You check if anyone is left in the aircraft. You are quite alone. The intercom is silent except for the slipstream roaring through a microphone where someone has left their helmet plugged in...

Suddenly you are conscious of feeling tired.

The main responsibility of the whole night, the crew, is off your shoulders. You can't do any more for them now.

Then, at once, frantic to live, you rip off your helmet, slide out of the seat with the stick held hard over until the last possible second; hurl yourself down into the nose. There's a jerk as your parachute harness fouls something. God Almighty! Mentally stunned, hanging head down over the open escape hatch, there's nothing left in the world but the slipstream howling past.

The inevitable fact that in, maybe, less than sixty seconds you are going to be killed, relaxes you into a mental torpor. Then the thought of being face down in the nose when 'Z-Zebra' hits the ground revolts you into frenzied action.

'I will get out!' you shout. 'I will get out!' God knows why. There's nobody to hear you.

Wrenching and tugging at your fouled harness, you feel something cold and hard hit you. It punches the air out of your lungs and pins your eyelids closed. You can't even think straight, but it's air. Lovely night air and somehow you've hurtled right out into the middle of it at Lord only knows what speed. You reach for the shiny metal handle of the parachute rip cord.

It's not there.

The pack must have been ripped off when you tugged the harness free from the aircraft. Whatever did happen just doesn't matter now.
Once again you accept the fact that in a few seconds you will be dead. You are no longer frightened. It's not courage. There's no point in being scared. There's no point in anything now.

Mainly you feel rather sorry for yourself in a quite impersonal sort of way. It seems a lonely way to end what has so far been a good life. Just a bag of flesh and bones falling unseen out of the sky, not even a dog barking.

It's an anti-climax.

Thinking these thoughts, you suddenly realise that your body is fighting for life again, its hands are clutching at the air, trying to grasp the parachute pack, which may be falling through the darkness close to it.

Something wraps itself round your neck with a not unpleasant jerk and from up above you comes the inexplicable sound of an invisible sail flapping in the dark.

It's your parachute canopy. It has opened and you are hanging from it. You don't know how or why; you don't remember grabbing anything. You don't care. Life with all its unhappened sorrow and laughter stretches beautifully before you.

The parachute spins slowly, you with it. Fantastic in the darkness, the fires of Hanover rotate slowly past your line of vision. Below, in the greater darkness that is Germany, a glowing cancer of fire festers, its proportions swelling magically as you fall towards it. It's 'Z-Zebra' cremated in a funeral pyre of savage beauty. Then fear grips you lest you land sprawling in the burning wreckage.

The flaming, spewed-out wreck rotates behind you.

The parachute is swinging you back and forth and you can see something dark underneath.

Even while you are wondering whether it's a lake or wood a thousand feet below you, your left leg suddenly doubles up under your body and you yell involuntarily as something hits you right on the back of the neck, slugging you so hard you feel dizzy.

It is the solid, ploughed earth of Germany.

You are completely, utterly and finally shot down.

You are also thankfully and undeniably alive.[48]

Eighteen Lancasters were lost Müller, who received the 'Ritterkreuz' in July 1944, destroyed 29 'Viermots' and a Mosquito in just 52 sorties, making him the most successful Wild Boar pilot of all. Geoff Taylor was taken prisoner. He made one daring attempt at escape which failed and was eventually liberated by the Russians in 1945. After the war he lived in Melbourne and he worked as an executive for an advertising agency.

Footnotes Chapter 8

48 *RAF Flying Review, January 1957* extracted from *Piece of Cake* by Geoff Taylor (George Mann, 1956).

Chapter 9

Fire Over Frankfurt

'Once I was lucky. I was flying one night and we were told the target may be Cologne. I was climbing up to 8500 metres, about 25,000 feet and then I saw under me, near Cologne the searchlights going into the clouds. Then we could see from above all the planes moving along on the clouds. At night I always came up on the enemy aircraft from underneath, so as to come from the dark. Usually I only had two successes in one night and then I landed - but that night I really was in the middle of the bomber stream and I looked to the left and I looked to the right suddenly I was in the middle. I was flying through the wind stream and my plane was shaking and so I dived and I saw the first plane in front, the next to the right, the next to the left. Then I tried to attack and on the first attack I did something I feel was wrong. I was shooting between the two motors - it was a Lancaster - and to the left another Lancaster. I shot again between the two motors, only a short time, though sometimes I needed only four to eight bullets until the plane was burning. I shot between the motors, I tell you this because the first plane I attacked that night I shot in the body and that one exploded - but I never did that again. I knew the planes were flying now with bombs to a town, maybe Cologne, it may be Frankfurt and I just had to do that. I saw the next plane was shooting and I was naturally proud I brought them down with bombs. I was sure they could jump out, the crew from the planes, because when the plane burns they could still jump out because I didn't touch the body I had another success with a bomber to Frankfurt and now on the way back I found another three. The last one was the hardest, because there was also a Lancaster and the Lancaster saw me. I knew how they had seen me because I came from Frankfurt that was all burning; it was a huge fire. So I want to the right, overtook and then I came from the right underneath, but again I was shooting the plane in the body because I knew they had seen me, so for their own defence - and please forgive me - again I was shooting at the whole body and the plane exploded and burned until it crashed into the earth. It was terrible, but it was self defence.

33-year old Major Wilhelm Herget, I./NJG4 who on the night of 20/21 December 1943 destroyed five Halifaxes and three Lancasters in 45 minutes. For one kill Herget latched onto a Lancaster and manoeuvred his Bf 110 below the bomber and using its engine glow as an aiming point, he fired four cannon rounds into the Lancaster which fell away on fire. Known as 'The Little Kadi' or Der Kleine (the small one) Herget scored twelve victories in the Battle of Britain flying Bf 110Gs in ZG76 before he transitioned to night fighting in mid-1941 and by the end of the war 58 of his 73 Abschüsse had been gained at night which earned him the award of the Ritterkreuz with Oak Leaves.

Robert 'Bob' Edgar Knights was born in January 1921 in London. He volunteered for service as a pilot in the RAF and eventually he was called up in March 1941, aged 20. Having completed his flying training in America under the Arnold Scheme, flying Stearman PT-17s, Vultee BT-13s and AT-6A Texans, in May 1942 he returned to England to complete his training, whereupon he crashed in an Airspeed Oxford twin-engine aircraft, badly injuring his hand in the accident and keeping him off flying for six months. When the time came to crew-up, in a hangar on 14 OTU at Cottesmore, Peter Derham, a 29 year old rear gunner, approached John Bell, a bomb aimer who was chatting with Harry Rhude, a Canadian navigator and asked them if they had got a pilot. They said 'no'. Derham, or 'Dad' as he was known because he was much older than the rest of the crew, had a wife and a small child and was absolutely determined to survive the war. He said: 'Well, I've found this chap who I think will be all right, he crashed an aircraft in training so I think he'll be a bloody sight more careful in future!' John Bell recalls, 'He took us over to Bob Knights and said 'I've found you a bomb-aimer and a navigator, so all we need is a wireless operator to make five'. So we found 'Jock' Rowan. Then when we moved to 1660 Heavy Conversion Unit at Swinderby we found a mid-upper gunner and a flight engineer, Bill Hobbs and Ernie Twells respectively.[49]

With 474 hours' flying under his belt, Pilot Officer Bob Knights and his crew joined 619 Squadron at Woodhall Spa in June 1943 to fly Lancasters on bombing operations. Before he could fly operationally with his own crew, Bob Knights had to complete the traditional 'second dickey op' with an experienced crew to learn the ropes. He flew on an operation on Cologne with Flight Lieutenant Ted' Dampier-Crossley DFC, a New Zealander in the Royal Australian Air Force. Dampier-Crossley's aircraft was Lancaster EE112 PG-T. Normally T was for 'Tommy' but the crew had named it T for *Thumper* and painted the Walt Disney rabbit character, from the 1942 Walt Disney film Bambi on the nose. Dampier-Crossley was an experienced operational bomber pilot and he taught Bob Knights some useful tricks and tactics, which Bob Knight's crew subsequently credited with helping to keep them alive later when they got shot at by a fighter but not shot down, as John Bell recalls: 'Dampier-Crossley taught Bob never to fly in a straight line, always to keep weaving from side to side. Bob was pretty switched on. I think it took a lot of effort to haul around a very heavy aircraft loaded up with bombs and fuel, but it paid off.'

A couple of months later, on the night of 10/11 August 1943, Dampier-Crossley and his entire crew were killed during a raid on Nuremburg. A replacement Lancaster coded PG-T arrived on the squadron and was allocated to Knights and his crew, who decided to name it *Thumper Mk.II* in honour of Ted Dampier-Crossley.

As a Lancaster had only a single pilot, Bob Knights decided that he would train his bomb-aimer to fly the aircraft in case he was killed or incapacitated. He felt that the bomb-aimer could most easily be spared from his other duties in such an eventuality. John Bell had applied to join the RAF in June 1941 when he was just over 18, the minimum age for volunteering and expressed his wish to be trained as a pilot. Being 6 feet 4 inches tall, his leg length was deemed too long for rapid evacuation of the cockpit in an emergency and he was offered navigator training. He later discovered that taller men who were pilots but his disappointment passed and he was called up three months' later. After navigation, bombing and air gunnery training in South Africa he returned to England in 1942 and was selected as a bomb aimer. He spent several hours in all at the controls of a Lancaster with Bob Knights standing beside him advising him. He always seemed to over-control the aircraft, finding it difficult to keep it steady. When he was flying it, he said: 'The rest of the crew were not best pleased!'[50]

The Battle of Berlin began shortly afterwards and the Bob Knights crew made eight attacks against the 'Big City'; raids in which Bomber Command's losses were particularly high. 'During our first week of operations on 619 Squadron there were four trips to Hamburg' recalls John Bell 'and we were on three of them. The first was on 24 July and was the first time 'Window' was used to confuse the German radar. 'Window' was the codename for 17cm strips of metal foil which the flight engineer dropped in bundles down the flare chute behind the bomb-bay. As Ernie Twells opened the chute he saw flames - an engine was on fire. Bob operated the fire extinguisher, stopped the engine and feathered the propeller. Luckily the fire went out, so Bob then asked us what we wanted to do, as we couldn't maintain height at 20,000 feet with a full bomb load. We decided to carry on and bomb at 10,000 feet, reasoning that we were below the height of the flak. Unfortunately we were also below where all the bombs were coming from! It was a bit hairy crossing the fires of Hamburg at 10,000 feet.

'Flying with the Bomber Command Main Force, we were part of anything from 400 to 700 aircraft going in waves over the target. There were markers dropped for us to aim at, but by the time we bombed there were usually fires burning everywhere. It was difficult to confine bombs to the target in the industrial area; inevitably bombs got dropped on to houses as well. It wasn't a very pleasant thing to be doing, but we thought: 'Well this is war and this is what we've been trained for'. I'd also experienced mass bombing by the Luftwaffe in London, as had others in the crew.

'In the early part of the war bombing wasn't very accurate. We used 'Gee' as a radio navigation system, but its range didn't extend far into Germany and it could also be jammed. However, bombing accuracy did improve with the introduction of the Pathfinder Force, who dropped Target Indicator flares at which you aimed.

'We were pretty lucky, we got flak holes in the aircraft now and then, but nobody got injured and we lost an engine on one or two occasions. Indeed on a trip to Leipzig we were in thick cloud the whole way and lost two engines due to icing up, so we had to jettison our bombs and turn back. With the loss of power we also lost height and eventually got the engines restarted.'[51]

Towards the end of 1943 the crew was approaching the required 30 ops of a full operational tour on 619 Squadron. On the night of Monday 20 December they were on the Battle Order for the raid on Frankfurt by 650 bombers - 390 Lancasters, 257 Halifaxes and three Mosquitoes - which was going ahead after a lull in operations following the raid on Berlin on 16/17 December. Knights' crew discovered that they would be carrying Major J. Anthony Cotterell, an Army Bureau of Current Affairs Staff Writer, which issued fortnightly 'WAR' bulletins to soldiers. Cotterell wrote a first-hand account of the briefing and the raid, which later featured in WAR pamphlet No.62 on 22 January 1944 entitled   'Did I ever tell you about my operation?'

'The fact that there is going to be an operation is generally known to the crews about 10 am of the morning of the operation. They don't know where it will be until the briefing later in the day. In the case of the RAF Bomber Station visited [Woodhall Spa], transport left the officers' mess, a requisitioned hotel, [Petwood] two miles from the aerodrome, at 9 am. The pilots report to their Squadron Leader in his office. Three mornings a week there is PT for aircrews at 9.30 am to 9.45 am. But the general impression is of them waiting around for the decision which is the focal point of their day. The point is that though they may not have operated for more than a week, they never know each morning whether or not they will be doing so. Of course, extreme weather conditions are a pretty good guide when they get up in the morning. But the weather overhead may have no particular bearing on the weather over Germany that night.

About 10 o'clock the telephone rings to say whether or not there will be operations. Every morning, whether or not they are operating, each aircraft must be tested. If there is no operation they probably make a practice flight. They may do some practice bombing with small practice bombs. If, on the other hand, they are going to be operating that night they will probably do their night flying test - 'NFTS' as the morning tests are called - on the ground. This takes up most of the morning. In the afternoon there are probably lectures. There is a school for each operational job in the air crew.' For instance, the navigators have lectures, inquests and discussions of their own. So do the wireless operators and the gunners and the bomb aimers. They finish about tea-time and the rest of the day is their own.

On this particular day the crews had been flying in the morning and, at the point when I was introduced, the members of the particular crew to which I had been allotted were on their way to spend Sunday afternoon cleaning their Lancaster, 'T for Tommy'. There were seven in the crew: pilot, flight engineer, navigator, air bomber (or bomb-aimer), wireless operator, mid-upper gunner and rear-gunner. The Lancaster didn't look sensationally large despite its sensationally large bomb load. Knights showed me round it and indicated where I would stand for the operation; while the rest of the crew cleaned it. Apparently a pilot had to pay a half-crown fine if the Squadron Leader found any uncleaned portion of the aircraft. We weren't there for long, as we had to be back at 4 pm for a post-mortem discussion on the last Berlin raid, which had taken place a few days before [on the night of 16/17 December]. It was held in the briefing room, which was about the size of a small church hall, with a table and forms for each crew.

The Group Captain conducted the meeting. Apparently it was the first of the kind held on this station. He explained that after each operation the report and photographs brought back by each crew were individually considered. He hoped that if the post-mortems were held in the presence of all concerned very useful lessons might be learned. It might help to counteract the tendency to think you knew a thing when you weren't really sure. But criticism was to be constructive, not destructive. 'When I ask why were you 20 miles off track, I don't mean why the hell were you 20 miles off track; I just mean why were you 20 miles off track?'

The various specialist officers, Intelligence, Radio, Ordnance etc and the two Squadron Leaders and the Wing Commander sat on each side of him. The Group Captain sat alone at a small table raised on a shallow platform. He had a pile of dossiers before him, one relating to each crew. He took these in turn.

'Tomlin [52] came back with two engines U/S and a third likely to go. Very good performance. Now, the point is this - he asked for radio priority and he couldn't get it because another aircraft already had priority. Now, was it really necessary for the other aircraft to have priority and why was it necessary?' The navigator of the crew [53] concerned stood up and said that they had become uncertain of their whereabouts because he, the navigator, had been attending to another member of the crew who was unconscious through oxygen failure. The Group Captain went into the question of why there had been an oxygen failure. He prescribed a revised and tightened up arrangement for inspecting each man's oxygen mask before taking off.

One crew had complained that the door of the aircraft had blown open. The room became divided into two schools. Those who maintained the official view that it was mechanically impossible for the door to blow open. And those with experience of doors inclined to blow open.

'T for Tommy' was the last aircraft to be considered. There was laughter in the post-mortem when the Group Captain read out that Knights had bombed on the reciprocal. That is to say, he had been unsatisfied with his first bombing run and hadn't dropped his bombs, but had turned and made another run. To do this he had to fly in the opposite direction to the general traffic path for aircraft over Berlin. It was considered very funny. 'I don't know what to say to you,' said the Group Captain. 'Don't know quite what to say.'

'It would have taken too long to circle the town and come in again in the ordinary way, sir,' said Knights.

Yes, couldn't do that over Berlin. Quite hopeless. Yes, I think you were justified. After all, you achieved your primary object. Dropped the bombs on the target. Yes, I think you were justified. Very creditable.'

The rest of the day was our own.

Next morning the pilots were hanging round the Squadron Leader's office in the same way as yesterday.

Nothing definite had come in by 10 o'clock when we went out to the aircraft, though the weather was considered ominously suitable. Accumulators were being changed out in the aircraft, the radio was being tested. A girl's voice said,   'I hear you strong and clear. I hear you strong and clear.'

Discipline was informal but definite. Or rather, there didn't have to be any.

The sense of interdependence between various members of the crew was complete. They all looked to the pilot for guidance. Each one was conscious of his vital part in the crew. Apart from the pilot, the outstanding character was the tail-gunner who was referred to as 'the old man' or 'Dad' because of his pessimistic and hypochondriac tendencies. Apparently Dad was inclined to be an alarmist, to see fighters in a clear sky. But this increased the general confidence in him as a tail-gunner. They were convinced that no fighter could possibly catch Dad napping.

'Look at this, that's ominous,' said Knights. A 4,000lb bomb was being towed up to the aircraft on a ground level buggy. The engines were given a ground run. There was a sense of pleasurable excitement as they started up one by one. The compartment warmed up very quickly. A new zest was detectable as it became evident that there was going to be an operation tonight. The sense of adventure is infectious. You feel that you are taking life by the throat and shaking it.

After a cup of tea at the YMCA mobile van we drove back to the mess for lunch at noon. My room-mate was changing. He put a small German dictionary in his pocket. 'Come in handy in the Stalag,' he said.

There was an atmosphere of quietly mounting excitement at lunch. People's minds were obviously slightly ahead of the current meal. Certainly mine was. Pilots were to be briefed at 1 pm. We sat around on wicker chairs and forms in a small room just off the main briefing room. The windows looked out over the airfield, but the aircraft were too dispersed to be visible. This room was the Intelligence Library. It was covered with training pamphlets, intelligence reports, not to mention the ABCA pamphlets. We were still waiting at 1.35 pm.

The pilots were discussing possible destinations.

Eventually the target map was brought in and unveiled. Coloured cords and pins marked the route to and from the target. It was Frankfurt, in South-west Germany. 'I hate that name,' said Knights. 'Biggest concentration of searchlights you ever saw.'

Roll call was then taken. The Group Captain came in and sat up on a table. 'Met, will you give your story?' said the Wing Commander. The Meteorological Officer started his technical monologue, illustrated by a large and complicated cloud diagram. 'No fronts definitely affecting your route... bases should be OK to land all night...' and so on. The Intelligence Officer described Frankfurt. Population about 570,000, a very important town; a commercial and financial centre; with very vital railway ramifications, also of considerable importance as an industrial centre. The docks had been badly damaged in October of this year.

The pilots had each been issued with a map of the target area set in a map-case, on the back of which there was a space marked off under various headings for them to make notes. The Wing Commander said that there would be several hundred aircraft on the raid (he gave the exact figure). The attack would be in waves. He read out which aircraft would be in the various waves. He went on to give particulars of the petrol load, the bomb load and the overall or all-up weight of the aircraft. One of these aircraft weighs as much as a small convoy of motor lorries. 'You'll set course over base at 17.50 hours. Must be comfortable at your height - 20,000 feet - shortly before crossing the enemy coast. Remain at maximum height all the way to the target. You can climb up afterwards but not above 23,000, as the wind increases at that point.'

There was to be a spoof attack on Mannheim [by 44 Lancasters and ten Mosquitoes of 1 and 8 Groups], to divert the enemy defences; this would go in earlier. There would be coffee and sandwiches in the crew-room at 3 pm, transport at 3.35 pm. We were to be at the aircraft by 4 pm. First take-off at 5 pm. Zero hour would be 7.35 pm. Zero hour for the last wave would be between 14 and 17 minutes later.

We moved into the neighbouring room for the main briefing. Here the crews were sitting, each of them on their separate tables. Ours was in the middle of the room. Knights started telling them what had gone on in the pilots' briefing. When all the pilots had finished telling their crews the Group Captain stood up on the platform at the end of the room and read out one of the Prime Minister's messages of congratulation to Sir Arthur Harris. The Group Captain said he was sure they would all be glad to hear that Sir Arthur had sent a message expressing their appreciation of the Prime Minister's thoughtfulness. 'And I'm sure you will join me in congratulating our late Wing Commander - Wing Commander Abercromby - on his very well deserved bar to the DFC. I wired him congratulations from us all.'

He went on to say that Frankfurt had often been scheduled as a target, but bad weather had often interfered. Tonight was perfect. 'The Met merchant won't dare to show his face if anything goes wrong.

'Now let's have 14 first-class aiming-point photographs for the Wing Commander's first trip. Have a good trip - 14 aiming-points, remember and 14 back.'

We went to dress ourselves. I put on the whole rigmarole; flying suit, fleece-lined boots, sweater, parachute harness and Mae West. We were driven out to the aircraft and stood around warming ourselves at the ground crew's fire which was burning outside their little shack. It was pretty cold. Things were very quiet. No sensation of being surrounded by an air armada waiting to take off. Just a small party in a corner of a big, windy field. It was about twenty to five when Knights said: 'Well, better be getting in.'

The engines were started at 4.50 pm. The pilot and the engineer started going through their checking and testing rigmarole. I stood just behind them in the gangway which leads past the pilot's chair from the nose where the bomb aimer was reclining to the navigator's position just behind me. The navigator was a rubicund country boy. He sat at a table which grew out from the wall of the aircraft and worked at his maps.[54] I had a very good view out of the right-hand side of the aircraft which consisted mostly of glass. I could see out of the left-hand side, but only a limited range of vision owing to the high back of the pilot's seat and the blackout curtain which partitioned off the navigator's compartment. Outside the ground crew were shivering with their hands in their pockets.

'Is the door shut, Bill?' asked the pilot over the intercom. On hearing that it was he began to start the engines, one by one, from right to left, until the four of them were roaring. Almost immediately the cabin began to get noticeably warmer. The aircraft edged out on to the taxi track. Other aircraft were lumbering in the same direction. Presently we wheeled into the runway past the little group of blue figures standing to watch the take-off and wave good-bye.

The sense of adventure was further enhanced by the gathering darkness into which the aircraft ahead was just disappearing, followed at about 30-

second intervals by our own. The pilot and the engineer were meanwhile carrying on their technical dialogue. 'Undercarriage' said the pilot.

'Undercarriage up,' said the engineer.

We flew over a river. 'Let me know when I'm right over the drome' said the pilot. 'OK' said the navigator. 'OK, that'll do.' 'OK, navigator.'

There was a band of olive green, orange and scarlet across the general greyness of the sky: it was like marzipan. Turning round I could look down the length of the aircraft; it looked much bigger in the air than on the ground. There was a slightly sinister red glow from each of the four engines.

The navigator asked the pilot to give him the air speed and height. '170; 11,200,' intoned Knights. We started passing large formations of aircraft flying in the opposite direction and distinguishable by their navigation lights. Sometimes they flashed past, seeming to be dangerously near. All this time we were climbing. At ten to six I noted that the stars were looking down.

'OK. Turn right now,' said the navigator and we started wheeling round.

I noticed that Knights always looked behind before turning. In the Squadron Leader's office there was a list of instructions for pilots headed 'Experientia Docet,' in which one of the rules was 'Always look behind before taking off. Also before doing a turn in the air. The machine you are flying isn't the only one in existence. Neither are you the only fool. Make a habit of this, but not the habit that makes you screw your head round without seeing anything.'

There were other rules. 'A good pilot when travelling by train or car should subconsciously be seeing the passing country in the light of a forced landing ground.' 'Always regard the other man as a fool. Then if he turns out to be one, you won't be surprised. Do everything in the air smoothly - one might almost say with rhythm. Treat the machine as you would a lady.' The one which I hoped Pilot Officer Knights had taken most to heart was: 'A steady, consistent pilot is of far more use than a brilliant, erratic one.'

'Is that the coast?' the rear-gunner's voice suddenly asked, over the intercom. I looked down and just made out the division between land and water.

'Yep, Norfolk,' said Knights.

'There's a convoy off Great Yarmouth,' announced the navigator.

At 6.25 someone asked if we could have the heat lowered. I couldn't identify the inter-com. voice, but he said he was getting fairly sweating. The rear-gunner excitedly announced the approach of an aircraft and then said, 'OK, Lancaster.'

'Keep a good look round, Dad,' said the pilot.

Distant flashes and searchlight cones began to be visible. The aircraft broke into an odd swaying motion. As we drew nearer Europe the whole horizon was punctuated by signs of strife. These activities were forbiddingly widespread.

'Coast coming up,' said Knights presently.

'You're heading straight for flak,' said the bomb aimer.

'That's right, run right into it,' said the engineer sarcastically.

Knights was suddenly concerned that his windscreen was icing up. The engineer bent up forward and rubbed the rag round it.

'Two searchlights on the starboard bow,' said the tail-gunner.

'OK,' said Knights.

The aircraft started weaving slightly. The two searchlights were creeping with sinister purposefulness around the sky; every now and then executing a dart as if to demonstrate their reserves of mobility. They seemed to stroke the sky all round us, playing cat and mouse. It seemed unlastably good luck that they didn't find us. There would be no trouble about the morale of searchlight detachments if the men could be taken for a ride in a bomber and experience the attention and respect induced by the weapons they wield.

I looked at my watch, which I could read quite plainly in the reflected light of the searchlights. It was 6.45 pm. We seemed to be passing through a belt of searchlights, which in the way of searchlights switched on and off without much apparent logic. There seemed to be no telling where they would spring up next and this was horrifying.

There seemed to be a lot of gunfire, but nothing came near us. Our relative position to most of the clusters of searchlights took a long time to change, which meant, I suppose, that they were much farther away than I imagined. Quite suddenly, after flying in this atmosphere of action and enemy protest for some time, we were in the clear again. We were in fact clear of the coast, or in the fighters' parlour, according to how you felt. Incidentally, there isn't much you can feel.

'I think everybody's early, Bob. There's no searchlights at the back now,' said the tail-gunner after a little while. The tail-gunner seemed to be easily the best-informed commentator on the social scene. He seemed to know the most and talked the most.[55] Perhaps his isolation stimulated his appetite for sociability. Presently he said, 'There's one going down in flames. Right behind us.' I looked back and couldn't see anything until the engineer pointed it out. I could distinguish a faint, shapeless glow of flames. It served to emphasise that admission to these quarters was not free. The gate was shut behind. The house was haunted. Europe was all around us and we were all alone. Looking down on the ground you could see odd, inexplicable, unaggressive looking lights from time to time. They had no apparent operational significance and may even have been blackout infringements of the grosser kind. But they served to emphasise our sense of being cut off. I need hardly say, because it has been said so often already, that this gives one a tremendous sense of comradeship with the other members of the crew. Your companionship with each other knows no inhibitions of temperament or prejudice. Friendship is perfect and complete. The idea of carrying an irritation or a resentment against one of them into the air seems quite out of the question.

'Fighter flares in front,' said Knights. 'Keep a good look out, Dad.'

I began keeping a good look out immediately. I saw a row of orange flares hanging pendant in the sky. They seemed to be quite a distance away, but I distrusted them none the less for that. Having already underestimated the distance of some searchlights, there seems no reason why I shouldn't be overestimating the distance of these flares.

Back in the rear-turret, Dad seemed to be having a whale of a time. He kept asking Knights to switch the aircraft in different directions so that he could get a better view of points where he thought he saw a fighter. (Incidentally, though he had nearly finished his operational tour and been on many of the severest recent raids, he had never yet been opened fire on by a fighter.)

The Ruhr ('Happy Valley') was now pointed out to me. I looked and saw nothing but distant cones of searchlights. 'I think that's Cologne,' said the engineer, pointing at nothing in particular. It wasn't really a very satisfactory view of the Ruhr. But I felt glad to have seen it. It felt very grand to be able to look out of the window and say to oneself: 'Oh yes, of course, the Ruhr.'

'That's Mannheim. Looks as if they're going in early,' said Knights.[56]

You could see it quite plainly ahead of us to the right, though it must have been about a hundred miles away. You could see the clusters of searchlights, the flares, the fires and the flashes. Mannheim is about fifty miles from Frankfurt and it was about this time that we began to come in sight of our target. There were the same flashes and searchlights, but much more clearly defined. It was quite unlike what I expected. Everything was so neatly beautiful.

'Hello, Bob; Junkers 88 coming up, starboard,' said Dad in a sudden urgent voice. Knights threw the aircraft over to allow the gunners to get a better view. 'No, OK, sorry, it's a Lanc,' said Dad. I looked up and saw that it was indeed a Lanc, coming towards us in what seemed like a sideways motion. One second a vague shape, it alarmingly materialised and defined its outline. There just seemed no possibility of avoiding collision. It was all over in a second, but it seemed quite a time. It passed just to the rear and slightly high. I looked up and saw its underbelly skim over us. 'Jesus, did you see that?' said Knights. 'I thought we'd had it that time,' said the engineer. The aircraft was still rocking from the impact with the other aircraft's slipstream.

We were now coming up to Frankfurt proper. You could see what looked like hundreds of thousands of electric light bulbs carpeting the ground. It took me some little time to realise that these were incendiaries. They looked so regular and artificial, so naively pretty, that you couldn't associate them with any work of destruction. There was a large, long area of them shaped like the lobes of a gigantic liver.

The sky was suddenly filled with the regular grey puffs of a flak barrage. These barrages seemed to me extraordinarily consistent in their strength. They don't just throw up a few hundred rounds and stop. They continue with what seems like unlimited regularity.

With the flares dropped by the pathfinders, the flares dropped by the enemy fighters, the waving searchlights, the bead-like pattern of incendiary fires on the ground and the flashes of gunfire, there is a sense of supreme experience and excitement.[57] Knights was working to keep us out of the clutches of some peculiarly inquisitive searchlights and away to the right another aircraft had failed to keep out of the way. You could see it wriggling in the cone of searchlights doing their best to hold it there while the guns concentrated on this one aircraft. The cruel thing is that one's only sensation is one of relief that the searchlights are temporarily diverted elsewhere. You feel no urge to go to the assistance of the unfortunate aircraft that is cornered. Of course, obviously it would be senseless to do so, but it seems extraordinary that one 'doesn't feel any urge to do so. I noticed the same indifference to the

Top: Lancaster B1 L7578 with John Nettleton at the controls, on either 14 or 15 April 1942; the last two days he spent practising for the Augsburg raid. Nettleton actually flew 'B-Baker' R5508 on the famous daylight raid.

Above: Squadron Leader John Dering Nettleton VC with Squadron Leader Whitehead DFC.

Left: Flight Lieutenant R. R. 'Nick' Sandford with his pet dog at Waddington.

Above: Some of the survivors of the Augsburg raid. From left: Squadron Leader David J. Penman DSO DFC; Sergeant D. N. Huntley DFM; Pilot Officer D. Sands DFC; Brendan Bracken (Minister of Information); Flight Lieutenant Brian R. W. 'Darkie' Hallows DFC; Sergeant R. P. Irons DFM; Squadron Leader John Dering Nettleton VC.

Left: French mass grave for members of Sandford's and Becket's crews lost on the Augsburg raid.

Below: On the afternoon of 17 October 1942 Wing Commander Leonard C. Slee DFC of 49 Squadron led a force of 94 Lancasters to the Schneider armaments factory at Le Creusot on the eastern side of the Massif Central, 200 miles southeast of Paris. On 20/21 June 1943 Group Captain Leonard Slee DSO DFC was the Master Bomber for Operation Bellicose when 56 Lancasters and four Pathfinders of 97 Squadron made a precision attack on the Zeppelin works at Friedrichshafen.

777646 SGT. B. D. MOSS. R.A.F
R.64340 F.SGT. A. E. ROSS.R.C.A.F
918988 SGT. 8. G. SEAGOE. R.A.F
1199025 SGT. J. H. HACKETT. R.A.F
1268146 SGT. R. L. TRUSTAM. R.A.F
42580 F.LT. R.R. SANDFORD. R.A.F
80067 P.O. H. A. P. PEALL. R.A.F
932122 SGT.G.W. J.HADGRAFT. R.A.F
777701 SGT. P. J. VENTNER. R.A.F
962127 SGT. R. E. WING. R.A.F
17 . 4 . 42

Lancaster I EM-O L7580 'O-Orange' on 207 Squadron on display in Trafalgar Square during London's 'Wings For Victory Week' in March 1943. L7580 went on to serve on 5 Lancaster Finishing School before being SOC in November 1945.

Flight Sergeant Keith Tasker, skipper of 'H-Harry' on 460 Squadron RAAF at RAF Binbrook in the late summer and autumn of 1943.

A Lancaster illuminated by fires and pyrotechnics during the raid on Hamburg on 30/31 January 1943. (IWM)

Hamburg burning on 24/25 July 1943 when 'Bomber' Harris launched the first of four raids code-named Gomorrah. (IWM)

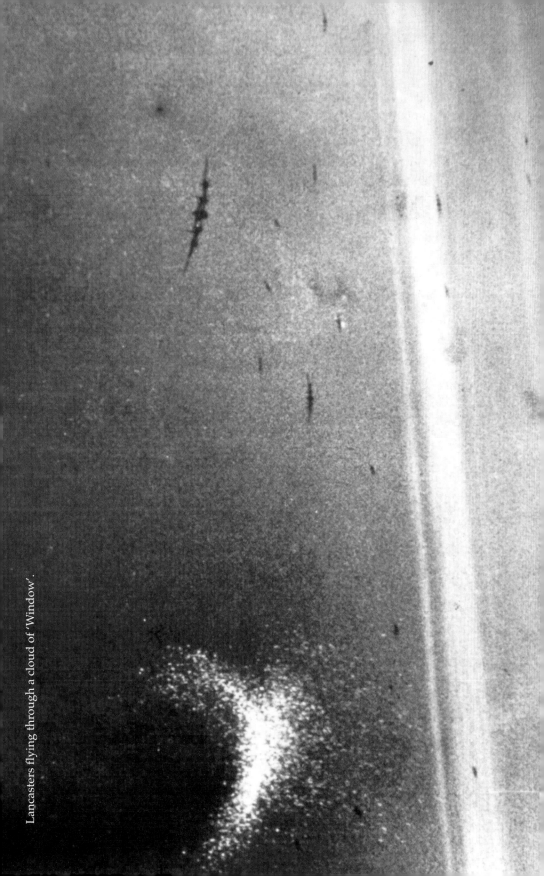

Lancasters flying through a cloud of 'Window'.

Above: Briefing for Berlin at RAF Binbrook on 26 November 1943.

Right: Martha Gellhorn.

Below: Lancaster IIs of 6 Group RCAF await the Green signal of the airfield controller's Aldis lamp, which will start them on their way to Berlin. (Canadian Forces)

Pilot Officer D. I. Jones who retired at the end of the war with the rank of flight lieutenant. Living at Grappenhall, Warrington, he began work in the design office of a large engineering works in the district.

FIDO (Fog Investigation and Dispersal Operation) in action. Burning petrol and allied fuels, this apparatus successfully cleared fog from runways and was responsible for the safe landing of many bombers, particularly in the winter of 1944-45 when 15 airfields were then equipped with FIDO.

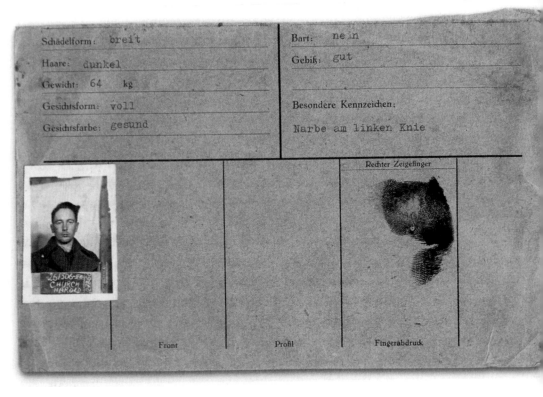

Schädelform: breit	Bart: nein
Haare: dunkel	Gebiß: gut
Gewicht: 64 kg	
Gesichtsform: voll	Besondere Kennzeichen:
Gesichtsfarbe: gesund	Narbe am linken Knie

Rechter Zeigefinger

Front   Profil   Fingerabdruck

Above: Harold Church's PoW record card which he liberated after the departure of his captors. (Harold Church via Ian McLachlan)

Left: Harold D. Church. (Harold Church via Ian McLachlan)

Opposite page: Lancasters on 49 Squadron prepare to taxi out. EA-T L7453 served on 97 Squadron as OF-X and then Nos. 83, 49 and 44 Squadrons before being transferred to 1661 CU where it was wrecked on 1 May 1943.

Lancaster III LM326 EM-Z Z-Zebra of 207 Squadron on a local flight over countryside east of Grantham and Barkston Heath airfield. 207 Squadron suffered the highest percentage losses in 5 Group and in Nissen-hut rumour was a 'chop' squadron. 'Z-Zebra' lasted four months before failing to return on 18/19 October 1943 on Hanover with Flight Sergeant Geoff Taylor RAAF and his crew after taking off from Spilsby at 17.16 hours. Hauptmann Friedrich Karl 'Nose' Müller, a Wilde Sau pilot of Stab JG300 [Inset], shot down 'Z-Zebra'. LM326 crashed at 2030 hours onto a road near Reinerbeck, 4 km WSW of Aerzen. Taylor, Sergeant's Don J. Duff, A. G. McLeod, C. R. Smith RCAF, A. R. Burton, W. Worthington and Flight Sergeant W. J. McCarthy RAAF were taken prisoner.

Pilot Officer Bob Knights and his crew on 619 Squadron at Woodhall Spa. L-R: Peter 'Dad' Derham, rear gunner; Bill Hobbs, mid upper gunner; Bob Knights; Major Cotterell; Ernie Twells, flight engineer; Jack Rowan; John Bell, bomb aimer and stand-in navigator (?) for Harry Rhude, their Canadian navigator. On the night of Monday 20 December 1943 they were on the Battle Order for the raid on Frankfurt when Knights' crew discovered that they would be carrying Major J. Anthony Cotterell, an Army Bureau of Current Affairs Staff Writer, which issued fortnightly 'WAR' bulletins to soldiers. Cotterell wrote a first-hand account of the briefing and the raid, which later featured in WAR pamphlet No.62 on 22 January 1944 entitled 'Did I ever tell you about my operation?' (via Hugh Trevor)

Lancaster DV385 *Thumper Mk.III* on 617 Squadron which was flown by Bob Knights and crew in 1944. The aircraft eventually flew 36 successful operations before it was retired from service in March 1945. (via Hugh Trevor)

Left: Pilot Officer Bob Knights (right) and Major Cotterell (centre). (via Hugh Trevor)

Below: Pilot Officer Bob Knights and crew on 619 Squadron and Major Cotterell and ground crew at Woodhall Spa on Monday 20 December 1943 before the raid on Frankfurt. (via Hugh Trevor)

Three members of the crew of Lancaster II DS686 OW-D on 426 'Thunderbird' Squadron RCAF at Linton-on-Ouse examining the damage inflicted by night-fighters on the way to Leipzig on 21/22 October 1943. This aircraft and Flight Lieutenant Thomas Robert Shaw RCAF's crew were lost on Berlin on 27/28 January 1944. (Canadian Forces)

'Our Mary II' on 408 'Goose' Squadron RCAF saw action in the Battle of Berlin and also bombed targets in Western Europe in preparation for the D-Day landings. (Canadian Forces)

Above left: Air Vice Marshal The Honourable Sir Ralph A. Cochrane KBE CB AFC the Air Officer Commanding (AOC) 5 Group. Above right: In the USA on 3 December 1943 radio listeners tuned in to hear their favourite foreign correspondent Edward R. Murrow, head of CBS European Bureau in London, begin his broadcast, *This Is London*. Murrow, proceeded to regale his listeners with a gripping account of his experience over Berlin in a Lancaster the night before. (CBS) Below left: Wing Commander Kenneth Holstead 'Bobby' Burns DSO DFC*, who was taken prisoner on 31 August 1943 when his Lancaster exploded and crashed in the target area on the raid on Berlin. Burns lost a hand and he and four crew were taken prisoner. Two men were killed. Burns resumed his flying career after he was repatriated in 1944.(IWM) Below right: 30. Pilot Officer Hubert C. 'Nick' Knilans USAAF spent eighteen months on operations on 619 Squadron at Woodhall Spa before joining 617 'Dam Busters' Squadron The American finished the war with both the DSO and DFC.

Flight Lieutenant Joseph Charles 'Big Joe' McCarthy DFC RCAF and his crew on 617 'Dam Busters' Squadron. McCarthy was a burly 23-year-old, 6-foot 3-inch Irish-American from New York City. He was awarded the DSO for his part in the Dam's raid.

Flight Lieutenant (later Squadron Leader) Harold 'Mick' Martin DSO* DFC* meets the King after the Dam Busters raid in May 1943. Guy Gibson is pictured (right).

Dave Shannon RAAF;
Hugh Trevor-Roper
and George Holden
(right) on 617 'Dam
Busters' Squadron.
Guy Gibson (Inset).

Guy Gibson and crews on 617 'Dam Busters' Squadron who
took part in the famous Dam's raid in May 1943. Far right is
Flight Lieutenant 'Big Joe' McCarthy DFC RCAF.

troubles of others when flying, with the Americans. There is complete unity within the individual aircraft, but for some reason that seems to be the limit of one's horizon. Nor is it simply the expression of my own individual idiosyncrasy. It was obviously a general state of mind.

All this time the pilot and the navigator were keeping up a running dialogue on how the time was going for the approach to the target. Apparently we were a minute or two early, so we had to lose that amount of time. It was pretty impressive, if the word isn't too banal, to hear the young men talking about losing a minute or two while passing through this firework display. I hadn't much idea of what was going on. I didn't know whether we were running up to the target or still cruising round and I didn't want to disturb the crew in any way. It hardly seemed in my best interest to do so. I was anxious that they should give of their best and concentrate closely on the work in hand, i.e., my safe return to England. But presently I realised that we were running up.

'Get weaving, Skipper, the night's too long,' said someone.

'I can't see that river,' said Knights.

'Bomb-doors open,' said whoever's business it was to open them!

'How're we doing?' said someone. 'Fine,' said someone else.

The first time over the target, conditions weren't apparently satisfactory. They couldn't see the path finding flares which they were supposed to bomb, so we flew across the town, then circled round and approached the target area from almost the diametrically opposite direction to the main stream of bombers. Coming back on to the target, it was like bright daylight.[58]

It is very difficult to describe. Nothing that I have ever read on the subject of bombing gave me anything like the impression which I actually had on the spot. I expected something of the atmosphere of a fire-blitz on the ground, detachment produced by being 20,000 feet high, down there was a town of half a million people, the engineer's shoulder I could see the bomb aimer preparing to press the button which would release another 4,000lbs on to the town. But it seemed quite unreal.

The incendiaries were dropped first and then the 4,000lb cookie. Just beforehand there was an appreciable tenseness of the crew. The pilot, of course, had to keep the aircraft flying as level as possible for the bombing run. He turned and half rose from his seat as if he was willing the aircraft to a supreme effort. I tried to write down the dialogue between pilot and bomb aimer, but it was too fast for my hobbling shorthand. I wrote it down, but now I can't transcribe it.

I did not feel any appreciable lightness of the aircraft when 'bombs away' was announced. All I knew was that the dialogue of 'Steady,' 'Hold her steady,' 'OK Bob,' 'OK bomb-aimer' and the sing-song intonation of members just before the dropping, subsided.

Knights asked the bomb aimer if he thought they had obtained a satisfactory picture; the bomb aimer thought he had. They were all professionally satisfied with the delivery of the bomb. There was a sense of achievement. The engineer pointed out the burning streets of Frankfurt. I could just make them out from an orange streak in the carpet of fairy-like lights produced by the incendiaries. I tried to think of the spectacle in terms of what was going on twenty thousand feet below, but it was just impossible to worry about. Mostly, I suppose, because we had plenty to worry about twenty thousand feet above.

The amount of fun and fury and fighter flares was extraordinary. The sky was simply full of trouble. Yet, oddly enough, it was difficult to think of us in this particular aircraft as actively threatened by sudden death. I don't mean that, speaking for myself, I wasn't afraid. Certainly I was in a state of great alarm. But I didn't really expect that we in this aircraft would buy it.

There seemed to be plenty to buy. The tail-gunner reported that he counted 49 fighter flares. Just afterwards he reported a fight going on behind us to starboard. I looked back and saw the flares and stabs of flame. This and the one we saw just after crossing the coast were the only two aircraft we saw going down, though we later learned that 42 aircraft had been lost that night.

Is there a small defended area on the starboard?' Knights asked the navigator. Two or three of the crew got into an argument as to whether it was Aachen or Brussels. 'That's Antwerp a bit farther up,' said one of them. It was ridiculous to hear the young men talk of the cities of Western Europe in terms of where they were last Friday, no, I'm a liar, that was Tuesday; or knowing their way so matter-of-factly round the Continent in these bizarre circumstances. They knew them not by their cultural monuments, their political significance or their hotels, but simply by their flak and searchlight barrages. They all looked alike to me, but I was told that after only two or three trips you remember the way awfully well.

There was quite a lot of flak going up over Brussels. We crossed the coast in the neighbourhood of Rotterdam. And just before doing so were nearly caught by searchlights. 'Hello, they're having a go,' said Knights, as the light seemed to lift the fuselage. The aircraft started weaving as, amid the incongruously facetious encouragement of the crew; Knights went about the routine of evasion.

When you consider how large the coast of Europe is it seems extraordinary how difficult it is to cross it without coming up against resistance of one kind or another. 'Keep a good look out, Dad. See we're not being followed,' said Knights. 'OK' said Dad.

It seemed a long way back over the North Sea. I was getting very tired of standing. The engineer let me sit on his seat for a spell, but then he had to have it back to go on with his business.

Coffee was now served from Thermos flasks. I opened the paper bag of rations with which we had been issued. There was an orange, a packet of chocolate, some boiled streets and two packets of chewing gum. I ate the chocolate, but with difficulty, as it was frozen hard. I then ate the orange, which was also frozen. In fact, the emotional experience of eating that orange was quite lost. It was painfully cold in the mouth.

We were now down to 10,000 of 11,000 feet and had taken off-our oxygen masks. It wasn't long, but it seemed long, before we were skirting the English coast. There were searchlights here, too, but what a difference in their attitude. These were kindly lights pointing the way to security, not fingers of fate contriving your doom.

It was now something past 10 pm and we were due to land at 11pm. That last hour seemed interminable. I found it odd that I hadn't any particular sense of achievement, such as I had anticipated. All I felt was awfully tired.

The landing grounds were illuminated by circles of tiny light. And over each aerodrome there was a guiding cone of searchlights. The odd thing was at this height they seemed so very close together. It was as if all the landing grounds were in adjoining fields, instead of being many miles apart. I got to the point where I didn't think we were ever going to land, but eventually we did.

We were driven back to be interrogated and then home to the mess for bacon and egg. I got to bed sometime after 2 am.

This crew had been on operations for some time and expected to finish their term in a month or so. The operations weren't at all monotonous, said Knights, but they were all of a kind. After the first few trips you learned your way round. Some crews regarded the business as getting progressively easier with each raid, but this crew made a point of regarding each raid as the first. They thought that was the surest way of getting through.'[59]

Major Cotterell continued to report the war throughout 1944. During the 'Market-Garden' operation in September he was attached to 1 Airborne Division and he went in with the airborne forces at Arnhem. Major John Frost's men took the bridge at Arnhem but were unable to hold on to it without support and when the bridge fell Cotterell joined up with Major Tony Hibbert, Brigade Major of the 1st Parachute Brigade who set about making a plan to break out in the hope of getting as many men as possible back to Oosterbeek. The break out force of approximately 120 was organized into just two platoons, each consisting of five sections, each under the command of an officer. Though exhausted and woefully short of ammunition, almost all of the men made it out and assembled as planned at a convent school 100 yards to the north of the perimeter. One by one the sections set out, but almost everyone involved was captured before making much progress. Hibbert led the last section away a few hours before dawn, but it quickly became apparent that the Germans had a stranglehold on the town and there was no way through. Having advanced no further than the Cathedral, 300 yards north-west of the bridge, Hibbert halted his group and instructed them to hide in the back garden of a house. Most were barricaded by Hibbert inside a bedroom, two more hid inside a tool shed and Hibbert and Major 'Tony' Cotterell installed themselves in a coal shed, 'which' recalled Hibbert 'was so small that we hoped it would seem an unlikely place for anyone to look. Unfortunately someone hiding near us fell asleep and started to snore so loudly that the Germans started ferreting around. Soon Tony and I were hauled out, covered in coal dust, feeling very angry and foolish. They marched us off to the cathedral square where a depressing sight met our eyes. About 20 officers and 130 other ranks were being guarded by a large number of unfriendly SS guards. This probably represented most of the survivors from the bridge. It was a great shock - we'd felt sure some of them would have got away.'

At 1730 on Saturday 23rd, having being held at the temporary PoW camp at Velp, Tony Hibbert, Tony Cotterell and other captured officers were transported in an open lorry towards Munich. Hibbert recalled: 'I was in the last group to leave - our lorry was a three-tonner, open, with sideboards about three feet high and thirty of us, mostly officers, were crammed into it, along with two old Luftwaffe guards armed with pistols and rifles. There was a third guard with a Schmeisser on the front mudguard. The lorry tore off at about 60 mph, which was obviously intended to prevent us hopping off in transit. We continued to give the V sign to the Dutch as well as the odd German and every time we did this, the corporal on the mudguard lost his temper and stopped the lorry to tell us he'd shoot us if we did it again. But we carried on playing the fool, because every time we stopped it took some time for the lorry to build up speed again and this was the opportunity we were waiting for. We stopped for a third time for the usual tirade and I winked to Dennis Munford that we'd make a jump for it when the lorry got going again. I asked Pat Barnett next to me to keep the nearest guard busy and pulled myself over the side as the lorry started, the guard shouting, 'Nein, nein!' I hit the road fairly hard but nothing seemed broken though there seemed a lot of blood flowing. Dennis was caught by the corporal's machine gun as he climbed over a wall, while I made a dash for the nearest side-turning, zigzagging to avoid the bullets and crashing straight through the wooden fence at the end, Donald-Duck style. Then I zipped through half a dozen gardens and decided to go to ground until it got dark. I covered myself with logs in a small garden hut and listened to the weapons still firing in the streets and the shouts of the search party. The noise eventually-died down and, after a long time, I heard the lorry move off. My plan was to get well outside the town [Brummen] and approach a small farmhouse and try to find out where I was, get news of our troops and how to contact the underground.'

Munford set off in the opposite direction but was dragged out form his hiding place under a chicken shed and soon recaptured. The tragedy of this escape attempt was that immediately after they had jumped one of the German guards in the truck panicked and turned his Schmeisser on the other men in the lorry. A German soldier and four airborne men were killed outright, while a further two were mortally wounded. Amongst the dead was Major Tony Cotterell.[60]

On 619 Squadron meanwhile, Bob Knights had completed his tour of 30 operations and was in line for six months 'rest' - instructing at an OTU. John Bell and some other crew members had not completed their 30 sorties, as they had missed a few 'ops' due to illness and would be reassigned to other crews to finish their tours, which would mean the crew being split up. John Bell recalls: 'The crew bond together and become your family. You go out together, virtually live together and trust each other. We felt we didn't want to be separated, so as a crew we volunteered to fly with 617 Squadron. We were interviewed by the CO, Wing Commander Leonard Cheshire and he accepted us as an experienced crew; which we then were. We joined 617 in January 1944. They were engaged in bombing selected targets, mainly in

France - aircraft engine factories, ammunition dumps and so on.'

On the night of 20 January 1944 Flight Lieutenant Thomas Vincent 'Tom' O'Shaughnessy, who had so far been the regular pilot of DV385 on 617 Squadron, took off from Scampton at 1930 hours in ED918 AJ-F, the Lancaster flown on the Dam Buster's raid by Flight Sergeant Brown, in a practise bombing sortie for a proposed raid on an Italian dam but which did not go ahead. Thirty-five minutes later O'Shaughnessy crashed into the sand dunes at the Wash bombing ranges at Snettisham, Norfolk, while. O'Shaughnessy and his navigator Flying Officer Arthur David Holding were killed. The two other crew were injured. After O'Shaughnessy's death, DV385 was allocated to Bob Knights. He and his crew immediately decided that their new aircraft should be named *Thumper Mk.III* and the artwork - the cartoon rabbit holding a foaming pint of beer - was duly painted on the nose. They also started the 'bomb log' under the cockpit with a bomb symbol for each op successfully completed by *Thumper Mk.III*. The aircraft eventually flew 36 successful operations before it was retired from service in March 1945 It also flew an additional 13 sorties on which it reached the target, but circumstances prevented the bombs being dropped and they were brought back, as the Squadron's precision role sometimes demanded.

Bob Knights and his crew first flew *Thumper Mk.III* operationally on the night of 8 February, as part of a force of twelve Lancasters which carried out an outstandingly accurate and successful night bombing raid against the Gnome-Rhône aero engine factory at Limoges. Four nights later, on 12/13 February the crew was one of ten Lancasters on 617 Squadron that took part in the third operation on the Anthéor viaduct 15 miles west of Cannes on the coastal railway line leading from Toulon to Italy. The target was heavily defended and ground fire was intense as the crew dropped their first 12,000lb HC bomb. As on the two previous raids the 90-foot stone arches curving back across the beach at the foot of a ravine resisted all attempts to destroy them. Two low level Lancasters flown by Wing Commander Cheshire and Squadron Leader Mick Martin were damaged by anti aircraft guns, which mortally wounded Flight Lieutenant 'Bob' Hay, the bomb aimer on Martin's aircraft. Martin had headed for Ajaccio in northern Corsica after one of his crew confirmed that the island was in Allied hands - he had read it in the News of the World the Sunday before - but he finally put 'P-Popsie' down at Elmas Field in South Sardinia where a doctor was available. They buried Bob Hay in Sardinia. The other Lancasters landed back at Ford where the weather threatened to prevent them from returning to Woodhall Spa.

'There were a lot of Lancasters lost on the Leipzig raid [44 Lancasters and 34 Halifaxes were lost on 19/20 February] recalls John Bell 'and 'Bob Knights wrote a newspaper article in which he said that Lancasters fitted with Packard Merlins were much more prone to icing up. He thought that many losses were due to icing of the engines, which could have been our fate if we hadn't got the two started again.' In April 1944, having completed 30 operations Bob Knights was awarded the DFC.

On the eve of D-Day, 5/6 June, Knights' crew flew *Thumper Mk.III* on the Top Secret deception raid. Operations 'Taxable' and 'Glimmer', both devised by Wing Commander E. I. Dickie, created 'Phantom Fleets' on enemy radar screens. 'Taxable' involved 16 Lancasters of 617 Squadron and is a joint RN/RAF operation aimed at making the Germans believe that an invasion force was attacking the French coast between Dieppe and Cap d'Antifer. Attacks on enemy radar installations had all but destroyed their effectiveness, but care had been taken to leave enough operational to allow the Germans to deceive themselves that their radars were showing an invasion fleet.[61]

On fifteen occasions, ten of them with Bob Knights at the controls, *Thumper Mk.III* was used to drop the 12,030lb 'Tallboy' deep-penetration, earthquake bombs with 11-second delay developed by Dr. Barnes Wallis. These had been tested successfully at Ashley Walk range in the New Forest and the operational debut for this fearsome weapon was on the night of 8/9 June (D-Day+2) when the target for *Thumper Mk.III* and twenty-four other Lancasters on 617 Squadron was the Saumur railway tunnel near Tours in the Loire region of western France. This had to be destroyed to prevent the 17th (SS) Panzer Grenadier Division's move from south of the River Loire to the Normandy front by train. The Panzer unit had begun leaving the Poitiers area on 7 June. French Resistance attacks had started before they reached the Loire bridges, some of which had already been destroyed on 7 and 8 June. Heavy attacks by Bomber Command during the ensuing three nights on all the rail centres in both eastern Brittany and the Cotentin caused general chaos on those railways, which were being used by the 17th (SS) Panzer Grenadier Division. The Saumur tunnel area was devoid of features that would assist the H$_2$S sets of the four aircraft on 83 Squadron that were to act as the flare force. Their flares were laid too far south and too far east, with only the last two or three flares in each stick being useful to the three Mosquitoes. Leonard Cheshire found the tunnel mouth and laid his spot flares perfectly on the aiming point. During the latter part of the attack Flight Lieutenant Gerry Fawke and his navigator Flying Officer 'Ben' Bennett were to mark the other end of the tunnel where it emerged on to a bridge across the Loire and some Lancasters were to drop 'Tallboys' on these markers while two other Lancasters with full loads of 1,000lb bombs would attack the bridge. As Fawke's Mosquito came round to assess Cheshire's spot flares 'Ben' Bennett felt that they could not have been positioned more accurately than if they had 'been wheeled there in a barrow!'

'Cheshire gave the order to begin bombing and the 21-foot long weapons encased in blue-black steel were dropped from 13,000 feet. 'Ben' Bennett recalled. 'The first 'Tallboy' was so near the markers that the glow of the spot fires was vividly reflected in the debris thrown up. Another pierced the hill through which the tunnel ran and exploded on the track. Other 'Tallboys' were effectively grouped around the aiming point. The bridge was demolished along much of its length. [The blocking of the tunnel came just at the wrong time for five of the trains, which, unable to proceed any further, disgorged their troops with orders to land-march]. The rail access to Normandy was denied the Wehrmacht and their forces arrived piecemeal on the Normandy battlefield, failing to make the impact that their compact arrival might have achieved. The indefatigable Germans set to work to clear the line and this work was completed, only to be abandoned through the rapid advance of Allied forces in strength into the area. The line was not brought into full use until four years after the end of the war.' [62]

To achieve accuracy with these large single bombs, 617 Squadron used a special bombsight - the Stabilising Automatic Bombsight (SABS) Mk.IIA - which, for the first time in the RAF's history, permitted true precision bombing from medium altitude. These special bomb sights were handmade, precision instruments, produced in small numbers and used only in specialist roles. With a well-trained and practiced bomb-aimer, able to keep the SABS aiming graticule exactly over the aiming point during the approach to the target, the sight automatically calculated the aircraft's ground speed and wind drift. These were the principal factors which led to inaccuracies with earlier bomb sights, like the Mk.XTV in use with the rest of Bomber Command.

During a daylight raid against E-boat pens at Le Havre on 14 June *Thumper Mk III* was hit by flak but only lightly damaged. It was flying again the next day, dropping a 'Tallboy' against the E-boat pens at Boulogne. Most of *Thumper's* ops over the next few weeks were 'Tallboy' raids against various V-weapon sites, including a V1 bomb store, various V2 rocket sites and the V3 long-range-gun construction site at Mimoyecques. On 19 June, after standing by for three days waiting for cloud over the Pas-de-Calais to clear, eighteen Lancasters and two Mosquitoes on 617 Squadron, with nine Mosquitoes of 8 Group providing preliminary marking, set out to attack the Blockhaus V2 store in the Fôret d'Eperlecques a mile from the village of Watten. The conditions proved too difficult for accurate marking and the nearest 'Tallboys' to the main building were 75 feet and 100 feet away from it. Next day seventeen Lancasters and three Mosquitoes on 617 Squadron, with escort, were dispatched to the V-2 launching and storage bunker under construction in a quarry near Wizernes in Northern France with 'Tallboys' but they were recalled just before they reached the French coast because of 10/10ths cloud at the target. John Bell remembers the direct hit with 'his' 'Tallboy' on the north-west edge of the concrete dome at the V2 rocket site on 17 July. He watched the bomb all the way down to impact. This attack by 16 Lancasters on 617 Squadron with a Mosquito and a Mustang as marker aircraft caused severe damage to the site. Three 'Tallboy's, including the one dropped from *Thumper*, exploded next to the tunnels. One burst just under the huge concrete dome, 20-feet thick, which lay on the edge of a chalk quarry protecting rocket stores and launching tunnels that led out of the face of the quarry pointing towards London and another burst in the mouth of one tunnel. The dome was knocked askew. Another hit caused part of the chalk cliff to collapse, undermining the dome, with part of the resulting landslide also blocking four tunnel entrances, including the two that were intended for the erected V-2s.

Watten was bombed again on 25 July by sixteen Lancasters on 617 Squadron with a Mosquito and a Mustang marking the target. Ironically, though the construction was not hit the whole area around was so badly 'churned up' that it was unapproachable and the bunker jeopardized from underneath so the Germans abandoned the site and the V-2s were pulled back to The Hague in Holland where, in September they began firing them from mobile launchers. [63]

The last op that Bob Knights flew *Thumper* was on 5 August, dropping a 'Tallboy' on the U-boat submarine pens at Brest. On 7 August he delivered the aircraft to Coningsby for servicing and modifications to be carried out; subsequently Lancaster LM482 KC-Q became his aircraft. On 5 August 1944 John Bell completed his 50th operation and left to instruct at an OTU, on Wellingtons again. [64]

Thumper Mk.III (now coded KC-V) returned to operations on 3 October, piloted by Flying Officer James 'Cas' Castagnola (later Flight Lieutenant Castagnola DSO DFC). On 28 October and 12 November he captained *Thumper* on the final raids against the 45,000 ton German battleship *Tirpitz*, moored at Tromsö, 215 miles inside the Arctic Circle in Norway. The *Tirpitz* was very heavily armoured expressly against air attack. Her horizontal armour was in two layers, the upper layers two inches thick and the lower, twenty feet below the upper, 3.2 inches thick; the armour was even stronger over the gun turrets and magazine. In common with all the Lancasters used on these operations, *Thumper* was modified for long-range flying. The mid-upper turret was removed along with many other internal fittings and ex-Vickers Wellington overload fuel tanks were fitted, along with a Mosquito long-range tank, increasing the fuel capacity from 2,154 to 2,406 gallons, giving a range of 2,250 miles. On the last of these operations, the Castagnola crew reported a direct hit with their 'Tallboy' against the battleship's superstructure. At least two 'Tallboys' hit the ship, which capsized to remain bottom upwards. For *Thumper* Mk.III the war was almost but not quite over and a swastika on the 32nd bomb symbol on the bomb log indicated a German fighter shot down by its gunners - its luck was still holding. *Thumper* flew its last successful op dropping a 'Tallboy' on the Bielefeld viaduct on 22 February 1945 and then, in March 1945, as the war approached its end, *Thumper* was retired.[65]

Bob Knights flew 41 ops with 617 Squadron, 29 of them in *Thumper* and many of them among the unit's most challenging precision bombing operations. He also took part in all three Lancaster raids on the *Tirpitz*. In December 1944, after flying an official total of 67 bombing operations, Bob was rested. In January 1945 he was awarded the DSO. During his ten months on 617 Squadron, eight of the unit's Lancasters had failed to return from ops and another had been lost in an accident. Thirty-two of his fellow squadron aircrew had been killed and more had been injured or become prisoners of war. In April 1945 Bob Knights was seconded to BOAC; he stayed with the airline for 32 years, retiring in 1976 as a Boeing 747 training captain. Bob Knights DSO DFC died in December 2004, aged 83.

Footnotes Chapter 9

49 *The Power of the Pen* by Hugh Trevor writing in *Flypast* magazine, October 2010.

50 See *Dambusters: The Most Daring Raid in the RAF's History* by Clive Rowley MBE (Mortons Media Group Ltd 2013).

51 Interview courtesy Hugh Trevor.

52 Flight Lieutenant A. H. Tomlin DFC crashed on return to base from Berlin at the controls of Lancaster EE150 PH-F. (Tomlin had crashed near Hutton Cranswick, Yorkshire returning from Berlin on 26 November at the controls of Lancaster EE168). There were no injuries to the crew on either occasion.

53 Pilot Officer T. A. Peatfield.

54 Navigators have a separate and elaborate briefing: 'The major responsibility for arriving at the right place at the right time rests with the navigator of each aircraft. He maps out the route and then, using the wind directions and speeds obtained from 'met.' plots the times over the turning-points en route. In flight as often as possible he checks his course by obtaining a ' fix'; then calculates any change there has been in wind speed and direction and revises his flight plan.

55 'He said his main job was keeping warm and seeing the fighter first. Fighters usually approach from astern and below, unless they get an aircraft silhouetted against a cloud, when they approach from above.'

56 The Mannheim diversion did not draw fighters away from the main attack until after the raid was over but the return flight was quieter. Martin Middlebrook & Chris Everitt, *The Bomber Command War Diaries.* An operational reference book, 1939-1945 (Midland 1985).

57 The German control rooms were able to plot the bomber force as soon as it left the English coast and they were able to continue plotting it all the way to Frankfurt so that there were many combats on the route to the target. The Path Finders prepared a ground-marking plan on the basis of a forecast giving clear weather but at Frankfurt they found up to 8/10ths cloud. The Germans lit a decoy fire site five miles south-east of the city and they also used dummy target indicators. In a period of barely 40 minutes, 2,200 tons of HE and incendiary bombs were dropped on Frankfurt. Some of the bombing fell around the decoy but part of the creep back fell on Frankfurt causing more damage than Bomber Command realized at the time. It is believed that the main gasworks in Frankfurt blew up 20 minutes after the attack began. The explosion was clearly perceptible up to an altitude of almost 20,000 feet. Over 460 houses were completely destroyed and 1,948 seriously damaged in Frankfurt and the outlying townships of Sachsenhausen and Offenbach and 23,000 people were bombed out. Some 117 bombs hit various industrial premises and a large number of cultural, historical and public buildings were hit including the cathedral, the city library, the city hospital and no fewer than 69 schools. One squadron ran under the hail of flak and flew over the Hauptbahnhof, or chief train station, at an altitude of 975 feet. They raced along the Kaiserstrasse, which a few minutes later had turned into a single sea of flame. Part of the bombing fell on Mainz 17 miles to the west and many houses along the Rhine waterfront and in southern suburbs were hit. *The Bomber Command War Diaries; An operational reference book, 1939-1945* by Martin Middlebrook & Chris Everitt (Midland 1985).

58 'Approaching the target the bomb-aimer reports every indication of position to the navigator. When the navigator judges the aircraft to be over the target area the bomb-aimer guides the aircraft through the flak until he sees his target in the bomb-sight and releases his bombs. He tries to drop the cookie in the middle of the incendiaries. When the bombs drop the navigator logs the time, heading of the aircraft, speed and height. These particulars enable Intelligence to plot where the bomb has fallen.'

59 Altogether, 41 aircraft failed to return from the raid on Frankfurt. Martin Middlebrook & Chris Everitt, *The Bomber Command War Diaries.* An operational reference book, 1939-1945 (Midland 1985).

60 The other men who died were Captain H. A. Platt, Lieutenants T. V. P. McNabb and K. S. Mills and Privates S. Allen and G. E. McCracken. Rapidly weaving a random path over fences, through gardens and down alleyways, Tony Hibbert successfully evaded recapture. He was hidden by the Dutch for three weeks. Later he commanded forty other ranks and successfully took them across the Rhine to the Allied lines. See *Air War: Market-Garden Vol.4 A Bridge Too Far?* by Martin W. Bowman (Pen & Sword, 2013).

61 1,012 RAF aircraft bombed coastal batteries, 110 aircraft of 100 Group carried out extensive bomber-support operations. 2 Halifaxes and 1 Lancaster were lost. 24 ABC-equipped Lancasters of 101 Squadron patrolled all known night-fighter approaches. (2 Intruders and one ABC Lancaster were

lost). 58 aircraft flew diversion operations. 31 Mosquitoes bombed Osnabrück without loss. In all RAF Bomber Command flew 1,211 sorties. 24 Lancasters on 101 Squadron and five B-17 Flying Fortresses on 214 Squadron carrying 82 radio jammers between them obliterated the German night-fighter frequencies for more than five hours. One Lancaster was shot down.

62   Panzer units moving by rail to Normandy used the main line Toulouse-Limoges-Chateauroux-Tours. Up to 14 June a single track bridge at Port-Boulet near Saumur was used to traverse the Loire but on its destruction the division had to use the only other bridge available, that at Tours-la-Riche. To do so the railway waggons had to be pushed over it one by one, for the bridge had been too heavily damaged to support the weight of a locomotive. The last elements of the division had not arrived in or near the lodgement area until 23 June, having taken 17 days to travel about 450 miles. Had no air assault been made, the movement would have taken about five days. *The Fight Is Won: Royal Air Force 1939-45 Vol.3* by Hilary St. George Saunders (HMSO 1975).

63   The site is now the La Coupole museum.

64   He became an admin (accounts) officer for six years and then he subsequently served as a photographic interpreter for the rest of his career, leaving the RAF on retirement in 1977 as Wing Commander Bell MBE DFC and with two Korean War medals.

65   DV385 ended its life at 46 Maintenance Unit in April 1945 and was eventually struck off charge and scrapped in November 1946.

Chapter 10

'This Is London'

'There's a battle going on, on the starboard beam.'
We couldn't see the aircraft but we could see the jets of red tracer being exchanged.
Suddenly there was a burst of yellow flame and Jock remarked, 'That's a fighter going
down - note the position.'
The whole thing was interesting but remote. Dave the navigator who was sitting
back with his maps charts and compasses said, 'The attack ought to begin in
exactly two minutes.'
We were still over the clouds. But suddenly those dirty grey clouds turned white. We
were over the outer searchlight defences - the clouds below us were white and we were
black. D-Dog seemed like a black bug on a white sheet. The flak began coming up but
none of it close. We were still a long way from Berlin. I didn't realize just how far.
Edward R. Murrow head of CBS European Bureau in London.

'This Is London'.

In the USA on 3 December 1943 radio listeners tuned in to hear their favourite foreign correspondent Edward R. Murrow, head of CBS European Bureau in London, begin his penetrating broadcast. Murrow had become well known in America for his broadcasts during the 'Blitz' when the USA was still neutral.[66]

'Yesterday afternoon the waiting was over. The weather was right; the target was to be the big city. The crew captains walked into the briefing room; looked at the maps and charts and sat down with their big celluloid pads on their knees. The atmosphere was that of a school and a church. The weatherman gave us the weather. The pilots were reminded that Berlin is Germany's greatest centre of war production. The intelligence officer told us how many heavy and light ack-ack guns, how many searchlights we might expect to encounter. Then Jock the wing commander, explained the system of markings, the kind of flare that would be used by the Path Finders. He said that concentration was the secret of success in these raids, that as long as the aircraft stayed well bunched, they would protect each other. The captains of aircraft walked out.'

Murrow boarded Lancaster 'D-Dog' on 619 Squadron RAAF at Woodhall Spa airfield one and a half miles from the Victorian spa town. His pilot was Acting Wing Commander William 'Jock' Abercromby DFC* and his crew[67] of 'D-Dog', one of 458 aircraft taking part in the raid on the Big City, the fifth heavy attack on Berlin within a fortnight.

'I noticed the big Canadian with the slow, easy grin had printed 'Berlin' at the top of his pad and then embellished it with a scroll. The red headed English boy with the two weeks' old moustache was the last to leave the room. Late in the afternoon we went to the locker-room to draw parachutes, Mae West's and all the rest. As we dressed a couple of the Australians were whistling. Walking out to the bus that was to take us to the aircraft I heard the station loud speakers announcing-that that evening all personnel would be able to see a film: *Star Spangled Rhythm*, free!

'We went out and stood around a big, black, four-motored Lancaster, 'D-Dog'. A small station wagon delivered a vacuum flask of coffee, chewing gum, an orange and a bit of chocolate for each man. Up in that part of England the air hums and throbs with the sound of aircraft motors all day. But for half an hour before take-off the skies are dead silent and expectant. A lone hawk hovered over the airfield, absolutely still as he faced into the wind. Jack, the tail gunner, said, 'It would be nice if we could fly like that.'

"D-Dog' eased around the perimeter track to the end of the runway. We sat there for a moment, the green light flashed and we were rolling ten seconds ahead of schedule. The take-off was smooth as silk. The wheels came up and 'D-Dog' started the long climb. As we carne up through the clouds I looked right and a left and counted 14 black Lancasters climbing for the place where men must burn oxygen to live. The sun was going down and its red glow made rivers and lakes of fire on top of the clouds. Down to the southward the clouds piled up to form castles, battlements and whole cities, all tinged with red.

'Soon we were out over the North Sea. Dave, the navigator, asked Jock if he couldn't make a little more speed - we were nearly two minutes late. By this time we were all using oxygen. The talk on the intercom was brief and crisp. Everyone sounded relaxed. For a while the eight of us in our little world in exile moved over the sea. There was a quarter moon on the starboard beam. Jock's quiet voice came through the intercom: 'That'll be flak ahead.' We were approaching the enemy coast. The flak looked like a cigarette lighter in a dark room - one that won't light. Sparks but no flame. The sparks crackling just about level with the cloud tops. We flew steady and straight and soon the flak was directly below us.

D-Dog rocked from right to left but that wasn't caused by the flak. We were in the slipstream of other Lancasters ahead: and we were over the enemy coast.

'And then a strange thing happened. The aircraft seemed to grow smaller. Jack in the rear turret, Wally, the mid-upper gunner and Titch the wireless operator all seemed somehow to draw closer to Jock in the cockpit. It was as though each man's shoulder was against the others. The understanding was complete. The intercom came to life and Jock said; 'Two aircraft on the port beam.'

Jack in the tail said, 'Okay sir; they're Lancs.' The whole crew was a unit and wasn't wasting words.

'The cloud below was ten-tenths. The blue green jet of the exhaust licked back along the leading edge and there were other aircraft all around us. The whole great aerial armada was hurtling towards Berlin. We flew so for 20 minutes, when Jock looked up at a vapour trail curling across above us, remarking in a conversational tone that from the look of it he thought there was a fighter up there. Occasionally the angry red of ack-ack burst through the clouds but it was far away and we took only an academic interest. We were flying in the third wave. Jock asked Wally in the mid-upper turret and Jack in the rear turret if they were cold. They said they were all right and thanked him for asking. Even asked how I was and I said, 'All right so far.' The cloud was beginning to thin out. Up to the north we could see light and the flak began to liven up ahead of it.

'Boz, the bomb-aimer crackled through on the intercom. 'There's a battle going on, on the starboard beam.' We couldn't see the aircraft but we could see the jets of red tracer being exchanged. Suddenly there was a burst of yellow flame and Jock remarked, 'That's a fighter going down - note the position.' The whole thing was interesting but remote. Dave the navigator who was sitting back with his maps charts and compasses said, 'The attack ought to begin in exactly two minutes.' We were still over the clouds. But suddenly those dirty grey clouds turned white. We were over the outer searchlight defences - the clouds below us were white and we were black. 'D-Dog' seemed like a black bug on a white sheet. The flak began coming up but none of it close. We were still a long way from Berlin. I didn't realise just how far.

'Jock observed: 'There's a kite on fire dead ahead.' It was a great golden, slow-moving meteor slanting towards the earth. By this time we were about 30 miles from our target area in Berlin. That 30 miles was the longest flight I have ever made. Dead on time. Boz the bomb-aimer reported, 'Target indicators going down.' The same moment the sky ahead was lit up by brilliant yellow flares. Off to starboard another kite went down in flames. The flares were sprouting all over the sky - reds and greens and yellows; and we were flying straight for the centre of the fireworks. 'D-Dog' seemed to be standing still, the four propellers thrashing the air. But we didn't seem to be closing in. The cloud had cleared and off to starboard a Lanc was caught by at least 14 searchlight beams. We could see him twist and turn and finally break out. But still the whole thing had a quality of unreality about it. No one seemed to be shooting at us but it was getting lighter all the time. Suddenly a tremendous big blob of yellow light appeared dead ahead, another to the right and another to the left. We were flying straight for them.

'Jack pointed out to me the dummy fires and flares to right and left but we kept going in. Dead ahead there was a whole chain of red flares looking like stoplights. Another Lanc coned on our starboard beam; the lights seemed to be supporting it. Again we could see those little bubbles of coloured lead driving at it from two sides. The German fighters were at him.

'And then, with no warning at all, 'D for Dog' was filled with an unhealthy white light; I was standing just behind Jock and could see the seams of the wings. His quiet Scots voice beat into my ears. 'Steady, lads - we've been coned.' His slender body lifted half out of the seat as he jammed the control column forward and to the left. We were going down.

'Jock was wearing woollen gloves with the fingers cut off. I could see his fingernails turn white as he gripped the wheel. And then I was on my knees, flat on the deck, for he had whipped the 'Dog' back into a climbing turn. The knees should have been strong enough to support me but they weren't and the stomach seemed in some danger of letting me down, too. I picked myself up and looked out again. It seemed that one big searchlight, instead of being 20,000 feet below, was mounted right on the wingtip.

'D for Dog' was corkscrewing. As we rolled down on the other side I began to see what was happening to Berlin.

'The clouds were gone and the sticks of incendiaries from yellow and started to flow to the preceding waves made the place look like a badly laid-out city with the street lights on. The small incendiaries were going down like a fistful of white rice thrown on a piece of black velvet. As Jock hauled the Dog up again I was thrown to the other side of the cockpit and there below were more incendiaries glowing white and then turning red. The cookies - the four 1,000lb high explosives - were bursting below, like great sunflowers gone mad. And then as we started down, still held in the lights. I remember that the 'Dog' still had one of those cookies and a whole basket of incendiaries in his belly and the lights still held us. And I was very frightened.

'While Jock was flinging him about in the air he suddenly flung over the intercom, 'Two aircraft on the port. Beam.' I looked astern and saw Wally, the mid-upper gunner, whip his turret round to port and then looked up to see a single-engined fighter slide below us. The other aircraft was one of ours. Finally we were out of the cone, flying level. I looked down and the white fires had turned red; they were beginning to merge and spread. Just like butter does on a hot plate. Jock and Boz, the bomb-aimer, began to discuss the target. The smoke was getting thick down below. Boz said he liked the two green flares on the ground almost dead ahead. He began calling his directions and just then a new bunch of big flares went down on the far side of the sea of flame and flare that seemed to be directly below us. He thought that would be a better aiming point. Jock agreed and we flew on. The bomb doors were open. Boz called his directions: 'Five left...five left.' Then there was a gentle, confident upward thrust under my feet and Boz said, 'Cookie gone.' A few seconds later the incendiaries went and 'D-Dog' seemed lighter and easier to handle.

'I thought I could make out the outline of streets below, this time all those patches of white on black had turned caught us but didn't hold us. Then through the intercom, 'We're still carrying it.' And Jock replied, 'Is it a big one or a little one? I'm not sure - I'll check.' More of those yellow flares came down and hung about us. I hadn't seen so much light since the day war began. Finally, the intercom announced that it was only a small container of incendiaries left and Jock remarked, 'Well, it's hardly worth going back and doing another run-up for that.' If there had been a good fat bundle left he would have gone back through that stuff and done it all again.

'I began to breathe and to reflect again - that all men would be brave if only they could leave their stomachs at home, when there was a tremendous whoomp, an unintelligible shout from the tail-gunner... 'D-Dog' shivered and lost altitude. I looked out the port side and there was a Lancaster that seemed close enough to touch; he had whipped straight under us - missed us by 25-50 feet. No one knew how much.

'The navigator sang out the new course and we were heading for home. Jock was doing what I had heard him tell his pilots to do so often - flying dead on course. He flew straight into a huge green searchlight and as he rammed the throttles home remarked, 'We'll have a little trouble getting away from this one.' And again 'D-Dog' dived, climbed and twisted and was finally free. We flew level then and I looked on the port beam at the target area. There was a red, sullen, obscene glare - the fires seemed to have found each other...and we were heading home.

'For a little while it was smooth sailing - we saw more battles and then another plane in flames but no one could tell whether it was ours or theirs. We were still near the target. Dave, the navigator, said 'Hold her steady skipper. I want to get an astral sight.' And Jock held her steady. And the flak began coming up at us. It seemed to be very close. It was winking off both wings. But the 'Dog' was steady. Finally, Dave said, 'Okay, skipper, thank you very much' and a great orange blob of flak smacked up straight in front of us. Jock said, 'I think they're shooting at us.' (I had thought-so for some time) and he began to throw 'D for Dog' up, around and about again. When we were clear, of the barrage I asked him how close the bursts were and he said, 'Not very close. When they are really near you can smell 'em.' That proved nothing; for I had been holding my breath.

'Jack sang out from the rear turret, said his oxygen was getting low; thought maybe the lead was frozen. Titch, the radio-operator, went scrambling back with a new mask and a bottle of oxygen. Dave, the navigator, said, 'We're crossing the coast.' My mind went back to the time I had crossed that coast in 1938 in a plane that had taken off from Prague. Just ahead of me sat two refugees from Vienna - an old man and his wife. The co-pilot came back and told them that - we were outside German territory. The old man reached out and grasped his wife's hand. The work that was done last night was a massive blow of retribution for all those who have fled from the -sound of shots and blows on that stricken continent.

'We began to lose height over the North Sea. We were over England's shore. The land was dark beneath us. Somewhere down there below American boys were probably bombing up Fortresses and Liberators getting ready-for the day's work.

'We were over the home field; we called the control tower; and the calm, clear voice of an English girl replied, 'Greetings 'D-Dog', you are a diverted to 'Mulebag'.' We swung round, contacted 'Mulebag', came in on the flare path, touched down very gently, ran along to the end of the runway and turned left and Jock, the finest pilot in Bomber Command, said to the control tower, 'D-Dog clear of runway.'

'When we went in for interrogation, I looked on the board and saw that the big slow smiling Canadian and the red headed English boy with the two week-old-moustache hadn't made it. [68] They were missing. There were four reporters on this operation. Two of them didn't come back - two friends of mine, Norman Stockton, of Australian Associated Newspapers and Lowell Bennett, an American representing International News Service. There is something of a tradition amongst reporters that those who are prevented by circumstances from filing their stories will be covered by their colleagues. This has been my effort to do so. In the aircraft in which I flew, the men who flew and fought it poured into my ears their comments on fighters, flak and flares - in the same tones they would have used in reporting a host of daffodils. I have no doubt that Bennett and Stockton would have given you a better report of last night's activities. [69]

'Berlin was a kind of orchestrated hell - a terrible symphony of light and flame. It isn't a pleasant kind of warfare. The men doing it speak of it as a job. Yesterday afternoon, when the tapes were stretched out on the big map all the way to Berlin and back again, a young pilot with old eyes said to me, 'I see were working again tonight.' That's the frame of mind in which the job is being done. The job isn't pleasant - it's terribly tiring - men die in the sky while others are roasted alive in their cellars. Berlin last night wasn't a pretty sight. In about 35 minutes it was hit with about three times the amount of stuff that ever came down on London in a nightlong blitz. This is a calculated, remorseless campaign of destruction. Right now the mechanics are probably working on 'D-Dog', getting him ready to fly again.' [70]

104

Footnotes Chapter 10

66 Millions more digested the column inches graphically written by reporters who were syndicated in many hundreds of newspapers throughout the USA but not all columnists were as enthusiastic as Murrow when it came to championing the British cause. Boake Carter, who was syndicated in 83 newspapers with a combined circulation of more than seven million readers asked, 'Where does the Roosevelt Administration drive the idea that Americans want to go gallivanting forth to play Sir Galahad again?' Walter Winchell, syndicated in 150 newspapers, 8½ million-circulation, struck home; saying, 'The future of American youth is on top of American soil not underneath European dirt.' See *No Need To Die: American Flyers in RAF Bomber Command* by Gordon Thorburn (Haynes Publishing 2009).

67 Abercromby, who had been promoted to Squadron Leader on 19 November, was born in Inverness-shire.

68 Flying Officer J. F. Bowyer RCAF and two of his crew of Lancaster III JA847 PG-C were killed, the aircraft crashed into the Tegel, a heavily wooded area near Berlin. Four of the crew survived and were taken prisoner. Pilot Officer J. F. Ward and 5 of his crew were killed after Lancaster III EE170 PG-N was hit by flak North of Magdeburg and burst into flames. As the crew prepared to bail out the Lancaster exploded. Sergeant G. W. Cross regained consciousness at 5,000 feet and landed safely, albeit with several broken ribs.

69 Murrow's account of the 2/3 December raid, which cost 40 bombers, 37 of them Lancasters, appeared in the morning edition of the *Daily Express* under the banner headline, 'Berlin - Orchestrated Hell of Light and Flame'. Fifty-three aircraft were damaged by flak. The Bomber Command ORS Report (No.481) said: 'Unexpected winds en route blew many aircraft off track and nullified the Pathfinders' efforts to make DR runs from Rathenow. Consequently there were gaps in the cloud covering the city; most of the bombing was scattered over a wide area of open country to the south. At the beginning of the attack, heavy flak was fired in a loose barrage up to 22,000 feet around the marker flares and was predicted at seen targets through gaps in the cloud. Searchlights were active in great numbers and took every opportunity the weather offered for illuminating the bombers. After the raid had been in progress half an hour and soon after the appearance of fighter flares the ceiling of the barrage was lowered and the flak decreased, although individual aircraft were heavily engaged when coned. The running commentary began plotting the bombers from the neighbourhood of the Zuider Zee and announced that Berlin was the main objective at 1947 hours, 19 minutes before zero hour. Many illuminated targets were provided for the fighters over the capital'. At least 32 bombers went down in the main air battle that was concentrated in the target area. It was a one-sided battle; only three Nachtjäger were lost in return fire. 460 Squadron RAAF at Binbrook lost five of its 25 Lancasters on this raid, including two carrying press correspondents. Captain J. M. B. Greig of the Free Norwegian Army representing the *Daily Mail* who flew with Flying Officer Alan Roy Mitchell RAAF and crew on Lancaster III LM316 AR-H2, died; as did all the crew. The Lancaster crashed at Döberitz. A night-fighter attacked Lancaster I W4881 AR-K, which exploded killing Pilot Officer James Herbert John English RAAF a native of New South Wales and three crew and 40-year old Australian, Norman Stockton of the *Sydney Sun*. Three crew survived to be taken prisoner. Stockton is buried in the Berlin War Cemetery. Flight Lieutenant I. D. Bolton on 50 Squadron at Skellingthorpe flying Lancaster I DV325 VN-B was shot down by a night-fighter and crashed in the target area. Two crew died. Lowell L. Bennett, a 24-year old war correspondent employed by the *Daily Express* and Bolton and four of his crew survived and were made PoW. Bennett escaped from captivity and managed to file his story at one point but he was later recaptured and held prisoner until the end of the war. Walter King an Australian war correspondent returned safely.

70 Wing Commander Abercromby and his crew of Lancaster III ND354 OL-A of 83 Squadron, 8 (Pathfinder Force) Group was one of 28 aircraft lost from a force of 421 Lancasters sent to bomb Berlin on the night of 1/2 January 1944. Sergeant L. H. Lewis, flight engineer, was the only survivor. Murrow continued to report on the war from Europe and North Africa throughout WW2. A heavy smoker, he died on 22 April 1965 aged 57.

Chapter 11

Press on Regardless

Keith Parry

I was at this time a sergeant pilot in the Royal Air Force Volunteer Reserve, twenty-one years of age. My crew consisted for five other sergeants and our bomb-aimer who was a Flying Officer in the Royal Canadian Air Force. Our ages ranged from the youngest at eighteen to the oldest at twenty-four. We spent the month of November at 1654 Heavy Conversion Unit at Wigsley, a few miles from Lincoln. Here we converted onto the four-engined bombers in which we were to fight our war. We flew the Halifax for a few hours and then, much to my delight, transferred to the Lancaster. I took to this aircraft like a duck to water. Compared with the Halifax it was light, responsive and, most important of all, with one engine feathered and shut down, it flew like a bird. After one dual flight with a Canadian flying officer instructor named Frankie Falls I went solo and felt completely confident and at home in the cockpit. We successfully completed the course and on 30 November 1943 were posted to 61 Squadron at Skellingthorpe. For us the war had begun and there was no going back.

November 1943 was a cold, dank and misty time. The Lincolnshire Fens lay swathed in fog for days on end and frost gleamed on the fields and hedges, warmed now and again by fitful bursts of sunshine, which made it possible to fly. On these occasions Bomber Command burst into life, for this was the time of the so-called Battle of Berlin, the target known to the bomber crews as the 'Big City'. When the weather forecast predicted not only favourable conditions over the target but acceptable landing conditions for the returning bomber fleet, which usually numbered between four and seven hundred aircraft, Bomber Command would go to war. The vibration from some two thousand Merlin engines running at climbing power (2,850 revs and +9lb boost) would make the glasses dance on the bars of Lincolnshire's pubs, much to the wonder of those whose wartime role was possibly more permanent than that of the aircrew who rode the sky above them.

Royal Air Force Station Skellingthorpe, 'Skelly' to all who were stationed there, was a typical World War II bomber airfield. Situated about four miles southwest of Lincoln, it was an out-station of 5 Bomber Command and home to Nos. 50 and 61 Squadrons, both equipped with Lancaster aircraft. Each squadron consisted of 'A' and 'B' Flights, both with nine aircraft and nine crews. If an aircraft and crew were lost on a night operation they were replaced, usually the next day - such was the efficiency of the British aircraft industry and the Royal Air Force training machine. I never did know who it was we replaced: once gone their names were rubbed off the Flight Commander's board and they were never spoken of again.

On night raids of 'maximum effort' Skelly could therefore, launch thirty-six aircraft. They took off at one-minute intervals and the noise level underneath the climb-out lane must have been considerable. There were no complaints from the noise abatement brigade in those days! The returning aircraft, usually fewer than thirty-six, were landed in the same way at one-minute intervals or less. Most would have 30 to 45 minutes endurance remaining. There was no instrument landing system then which could possibly have coped with this density of traffic. It was all done, as we would say at the time, 'on the eye-ball', with the aid of a circle of lights around the airfield known as the 'Drem'. This circle led into the 'funnel' and the funnel led to the flare-path. If the visibility was less than three thousand yards it was reckoned to be dodgy. The only alternative was to bail out and, on occasions when fog and shortage of fuel prevailed, a number of aircraft were lost in this way.

We were transported from Wigsley to Skelly with our worldly goods and flying kit by Bedford three-ton crew transport and reported to the Adjutant of 61 Squadron. We were allocated to 'B' Flight and, as captain of the crew, I reported to my new Flight Commander, Squadron Leader Jimmy Moss. On entering the office I saw a tall, fresh-faced man, probably in his early thirties - much older than the usual aircrew. His manner was pleasant and friendly and did much to put me at ease in my new surroundings. I was, after all, a fledgling among the aces. I was later to learn that, before the war, Jimmy Moss had been a house master at Radley College, Oxford. He had survived Dunkirk with the Territorial Army before transferring to the RAF for a quiet life! He was popular with his crews, well liked and respected by all who knew him. He was destined to die, with so many others, on the ill-fated Nuremburg raid at the end of March 1944. But this was some months in the future and twenty-four hours was a long time in Bomber Command. [71]

The usual procedure with new crews on the squadron was to do a couple of night cross country flights, drop a few practice bombs on one of the many bombing ranges and then for the pilot to go on an operational flight as second pilot to an experienced captain. We flew our two cross country flights and I managed to find my way around the airfield without too much trouble. (This was not as easy as one might think on a dimly lit wartime airfield on a black winter's night). Having accomplished these tasks I knew that my name would be appearing on the Battle Order very shortly and in anticipation I drank my fill around the pubs of Lincoln. The favourite with the NCOs was the 'Crown', whilst the officers usually repaired to the 'Saracen's Head', more commonly known amongst the crews as the 'Snake Pit'. It was rumoured that one of the barmaids here was in the pay of the Third Reich: careless talk was not encouraged! The most popular topic of conversation was how many ops various people had done, who had got the chop on the last raid and who, if anyone, had amassed the seemingly impossible total of thirty trips and become 'tour expired'. At this stage of the bomber war, very few did.

Our normal routine on the squadron was, if not flying the night before, to report to the crew room at 9.30 in the morning. At ten o'clock the phone in the ops room would ring and the station would be connected to Bomber Command ops room on a command hook-up. The message would be either 'Stand-Down,' in which case the crews could bank on another twenty-four hours respite, or 'Ops on tonight,' usually accompanied by 'Maximum effort'; in which case everything and everybody would be airborne. The message would also give two pieces of vital information. Although the target for the night would not be revealed to the crews until briefing, the bomb load and fuel load for the aircraft would be given, so that the ground crews could start preparing the aircraft. Old hands at the game could then make a shrewd guess. A bomb load of 10,000lb mixed HE and incendiary plus 1850 gallons of fuel usually spelt the 'Big City'. And so it was at 10 o'clock on the morning of 16 December 1943. An hour later the Battle Order was published. My name was on it.

As it was once again a maximum effort, all eighteen of 61 Squadron's crews were detailed. Under the list appeared the words: 'Sergeant Parry to report to Squadron Leader Moss at Main Briefing.' It also gave the time of the pre-flight meal, referred to by some as the Last Supper. This was at 1300 hours and the Main Briefing as at 1430. As I read these words I feel my heartbeat quicken and was aware of a small cold lump forming in the pit of my stomach. It was like a leaden golf ball and was a sensation with which I was to become familiar over the coming months. It would last until I climbed into the aircraft and then - as I became absorbed in the routine of pre-start drill and checks and the Merlins coughed and spluttered into life - it would disappear, to be replaced by a feeling of cautious optimism. It was always the other blokes who got the chop: we were going to be all right.

I went to the locker room to check my flying kit. I cleaned my goggles, checked my helmet and intercom on the test rig; drew my harness and chest-type parachute from the safety section, checked my Mae West, emptied my pockets of everything except my penknife and signed for my escape kit and emergency rations. I took off my collar and tie and knotted my lucky silk scarf around my neck. I wore this scarf on every one of the 57 ops I eventually flew and still have it to this day. I was organised and, leaving my kit ready in my locker, walked to the mess for the meal. I can't remember what it consisted of, but I do remember marvelling at the nonchalant good humour and relaxed manner of my fellow airmen. If they had lumps in their stomachs, they certainly didn't show it. The meal over, we enjoyed a quick smoke and then - off to briefing. The briefing room at Skelly was a large Nissen-type building with a trestle table for each of the thirty-six crews and seven chairs at each table - one for each crew member. A raised platform at the end accommodated the briefing team and on the wall was a large map which covered the whole of the United Kingdom, the North Sea and Channel and the continent from northern Denmark to the Pyrenees and as far east as the Polish border. Before the briefing commenced it was obscured from our view by curtains.

Most of the crews were already there and the air was thick with cigarette smoke, I found Jimmy Moss and reported to him, 'Ah! Parry,' he said. 'Come with me and I'll introduce you to Flight Lieutenant George Harvey. You're flying with him tonight.' Harvey was an Australian with an all-Australian crew and on the squadron they had the reputation of being a bunch of tough nuts. They were seated at one of the front tables, as Harvey was one of the more experienced pilots and was about half way through his tour. Their dark blue battle dress contrasted with the light blue around them. They were engrossed in the maps and charts on the table in front of them. We approached the table and Jimmy Moss said: 'This is Sergeant Parry - he will be flying with you tonight.' Seven pair of eyes looked up at me. Nobody spoke or smiled, except someone who muttered: 'Jeez - not another Pommy sprog!' Eventually Harvey said: 'Get a chair and sit down.' I did as I was bid and had to sit on the outside of the tightly knit group, as no-one moved to make room for me. I felt my lump get bigger and colder. I realised afterwards that their apparent animosity was not directed at me personally, but at the fact that I should be occupying the seat in the cockpit normally taken by their engineer. Squadron Lancasters were all solo aircraft: there was only one pilot and one set of flying controls. Next to the pilot, on his right, was a small collapsible seat known as the Rumbold seat after its inventor and usually referred to as the Rumble seat. From this position the engineer started the engines, supervised the fuel flow, kept the tanks balanced, monitored the engine temperatures and pressures and, in an emergency, would feather and shut down a failed engine, possibly having to deal with a fire into the bargain. To have these tasks carried out by a greenhorn only added to the hazards they would soon be facing. Sprog second dickies were not welcome in any crew!

Cigarettes were doused in anticipation of the arrival of the Station Commander, the briefing team took their positions on the platform and the Met man arrived - to be greeted with loud cheers and some quite original catcalls mostly advising him what to do with his charts. The Station Commander arrived, gave permission to smoke and we all lit up again. The Station Navigation Officer drew back the curtains and the target was revealed. Those who had bet on the 'Big City' were in the money. The red tape marking the route stretched across the North Sea, crossing the enemy coast near the Friesian Island of Texel and then crossed Holland and Germany straight to Berlin. This was known as the 'Straight' route. On leaving the target the tape turned northwards, crossed the Baltic coast between Lübeck and Rostock, then turned westward across Denmark towards he comparative safety of the North Sea on its way back to England. Some thirteen hundred miles in all; most of it over enemy territory and through one of the most efficient and determined air defence systems the world has ever seen.

There would be a total of 700 aircraft participating, we were told - a mixed bag of Lancasters and Halifaxes with a few Stirlings thrown in. [72] The attack would be in four waves and the whole force would pass over the target in twenty-five minutes. We were to be in the fourth and last wave. The weather for the trip would be fine, clear over the target. It was to be a cold night with a temperature of minus 50°C at 20,000 feet. On our return the UK would be misty, with frost on the ground, but the visibility was not expected to fall below three miles. Take-off time was 1630 and complete radio silence was in force. Finally we were wished good luck and I left the briefing room with Harvey and his crew feeling that we probably need it. Back at the Squadron we donned our flying kit, had another smoke and then waited outside for the crew bus to take us out to the aircraft. I don't remember a letter of the aircraft [QR-R], but my log book tells me its airframe number was DV399 and that it was a Mark I Lancaster with Merlin 22 engines.

Twenty minutes before take-off time the rear gunner peed on the tail wheel for luck and we climbed aboard. The crew were more friendly now, as I scrambled up through the fuselage, over the main spar and into the cockpit. We took our seats and started up. As the Merlins came to life I realised that the lump in my stomach had disappeared. I became absorbed in the routine and began to feel one of the team. Once the Merlins were warm enough we checked the magnetos, propellers and generators: they were all as sweet as a nut. Harvey checked each member of the crew on the intercom and received a reassuring response from each. The navigator checked the Gee and we were ready to taxi out. Harvey waved away the chocks and I reported: 'All clear starboard.' On the pan opposite to us another Lancaster was also ready to taxi. I looked at Harvey and he obviously read my mind. He said: 'We'll let him go first and then we can close up behind him and his slipstream will keep our motors cool.' Taxiing to the take-off point we would obviously be going down-wind and Merlins were notorious for running hot on the ground. If they did so it would mean pulling off onto the grass, turning into the wind and running them at fast idle to cool them off. I was in the hands of an expert and would do well to keep my eyes and ears open. There was much to learn. We pulled out behind the other aircraft and joined the long queue wending its way down to the take-off runway. We passed the hangers: all the airmen and WAAFs were outside and they waved and gave us the thumbs up. Some of the girls blew kisses, but I hadn't been there long enough to qualify. Slowly the long snake of aircraft inched forward as one by one they were given the green light by the runway controller and turned into wind on the runway. Down each side of the runway were most of the station personnel, waving and cheering as each aircraft started its take-off run. It was nice to know that somebody cared.

The aircraft in front of us moved onto the runway and started his take-off run. As soon as he did so the controller flashed us a green and we took up our position. Harvey said: 'Zero boost.' I opened the throttles. Harvey released the brakes and we started to roll. He took the throttles and opened them steadily, leading with the port outer to check the swing and, as the tail came up, said: 'Your throttles, full power!' As I opened up to full power with the boost override pulled -3,000 rpm and +14lb - the engine note became a deafening roar. My love affair with the Merlin had begun and I can still hear them sing to this very day. The airspeed mounted steadily and at 110 mph Harvey eased the Lancaster off the ground. The wings took the weight and we were away: wheels up, 2,850 rpm + 9lb boost and climbing away into the twilight.

At about 1640 BST (one hour ahead of Greenwich) we passed through a layer of stratus at 3,000 feet and broke into the brightness, lit by the rays of the setting sun. We continued on a westerly heading, gaining precious altitude before turning east towards the Lincolnshire coast. Around us, from various 5 Group bases in Lincolnshire, dozens of other aircraft were doing the same thing. We were certainly not alone. At 6,000 feet we turned on our easterly heading, which we would follow for the next four hours or so. The light was fading now and I sensed that it was going to be a long and eventful night.

We passed out over the coast, unseen to those below the layer of stratus. Further east the cloud was breaking, giving credence to the forecast that it would be clear over the other side. At 10,000 feet Harvey ordered: 'Oxygen on.' I opened the flow valves. We put on our masks and were to wear them for the next six hours. The gunners requested permission to fire a test burst and, on receiving it, fired a short burst from each turret. The aircraft shivered as the turrets went into action. Acrid cordite fumes from the front turret, manned by the bomb aimer, drifted back into the cockpit. It was darker now and the dozens of aircraft we had seen previously disappeared one by one into the gloom. They were still there, of course, but unseen. At 18,000 feet we levelled off, set 2,400 rpm with throttles at the gate and settled down to cruise at a steady 164 mph. The navigator said: Ten minutes to the Dutch coast.

Ahead now tiny pinpricks of light at about our level showed where people in the first wave were running the gauntlet of the outer defences, known to the Germans as the West Wall. Texel was reputed to have more than its fair share of 88mm flak guns. Harvey told the gunners: 'Wakey-Wakey and start searching!' I doubted if they needed prompting. They were all too aware of the danger of night fighters and also of the fairly high risk of collision with one of our own aircraft. In a closely packed bomber stream it was by no means unusual to be bucking around in the slipstream of some unseen aircraft a few hundred yards ahead.

But night fighters were our real worry. By this stage of the war the German air force had developed a sophisticated system. Ground controllers directed the fighter force in the general direction of the bomber stream. One of these night fighters, equipped with efficient AI (airborne interception) radar, could home in on a bomber from twenty miles' range. It could then close up to it from astern and shoot it down without the bomber crew being aware that it was there. The enemy aircraft were mostly Ju 88s and Me 110s. They had a good speed advantage over us, were heavily armed with 20 or 30mm cannon and were flown by skillful, brave and determined men. It didn't do to sit back and relax!

The pinpricks had by now become flashes. Harvey said: 'Hang on to your hats,' and quite suddenly we were in the barrage. Searchlights appeared and lit up the sky around us. In the light I could see the black puffs of the shell burst. Harvey said reassuringly: 'Don't worry unless you can hear it.' I was somewhat disconcerted when I realised that I could, in fact, hear the crump-crump above the din of the engines. Something rattled on the side of the cockpit and a voice muttered 'Bastards!' on the intercom. Then as quickly as it had begun the barrage faded away and, apart from the occasional distant burst, we were in the clear. We flew on over Holland. There was a long way to go.

As soon as we were clear of the flak, Harvey checked each crew member in turn on the intercom. They were all OK. He warned the gunners again about the need for vigilance: we were, he said, approaching 'bandit country'. Some fifteen minutes later, we crossed the border from Holland into Germany proper. With 700 RAF aircraft over Germany I wondered if Goering was rehearsing another speech to explain his statement made a few years earlier: 'No enemy aircraft will ever fly over the Third Reich.' Things had changed since 1940!

The night enfolded us in blackness now, giving us an entirely false sense of security. We were of course surrounded by dozens of other aircraft - all more or less at the same height and all on the same course, heading for the same release point over the target. Hundreds of eyes searched the darkness, seeking that glimpse of a fleeting shadow that could mean the difference between disaster and survival. More than once the aircraft rocked and bucked as we hit the slipstream of an unseen aircraft in front, prompting the navigator to say on one occasion: 'Wacko! We must be on track!'

The cockpit was blacked out and we relied entirely on the luminous dials of the instruments - the glow of a well lit cockpit would have been seen from some distance on a dark night. Each bank of exhaust stubs on the Merlins had a muffler to conceal the blue glow of the exhausts. The only people in the aircraft allowed the luxury of a light were the navigator and the wireless operator and they were concealed behind blackout curtains. Harvey, a few feet from me, was a black, rock-like figure framed dimly against the stars.

As we flew on, I was becoming increasingly aware of a problem which, so far, I had kept to myself. It was my job to monitor the engine dials and gauges on a panel on the cockpit wall, just about level with my right knee. It was the cylinder-head temperature of the starboard outer engine which concerned me. It had been rising steadily for five minutes or so and was now approaching the red line at 125°C. The oil temperature was now also rising and, worst of all; the pressure was fluctuating and dropping. I decided to share my worries with Harvey and said: 'Skipper, the starboard outer is running hot.'

'How bad?' he asked and when I told him what was happening he said: 'It must have collected a lump of flak.' Even as we spoke, it was getting worse: the oil pressure had fallen below the acceptable minimum and the cylinder head needle had passed the red line and was hard over against the right hand side of the gauge. A slight vibration was running through the aircraft and we both knew what would happen next - it would go on fire. Harvey said: 'Blast! You'd better shut it down before it brews up.' I pulled my torch from the top of my flying boot and prepared to do so. I was acutely aware that the safety of the aircraft and its crew was now in the hands of a Pommie sprog. The crew were quiet. Nobody said anything. I switched my torch on, shielding the light as best I could. Frankie Fall's advice on feathering a propeller sounded in my ears. 'Do it slowly and get it RIGHT,' he had said in what now seemed a different age. I closed the right hand throttle slowly, giving Harvey a chance to take up the yaw on the rudders and get some trim on. Pitch lever fully down. Press in the feathering button and hold it in. Engine master cock off. There were four of everything and to get it wrong would mean disaster. The propeller ran down and stopped, one blade pointing vertically upwards against the dim horizon, like an admonitory finger. I said to Harvey: 'Do you want the switches off, or shall I leave them caged on?' 'Leave them caged on,' he replied. The reason for this was that the magneto switches were caged in pairs and to switch off the starboard outer would mean uncaging the switches on the inner engine. Not a good thing if we were going to be involved in any hectic manoeuvres later on. I reported to Harvey: 'Starboard outer ... shut down and feathered.'

'Good show, sport,' he said. My confidence zoomed up. 'Put 2,650 and +4 on the other three,' said Harvey and I did as I was bid. This was the maximum weak-mixture power setting: the Merlins would run at this for as long as there was fuel in the tanks. There now followed a debate on tactics between Harvey and the navigator. The navigator pointed out that if we turned around and went back we would cross the coast in about thirty-five minutes. On our own, we would be easy meat for a night fighter or the flak gunners. Harvey's reply to this suggestion was emphatic: 'Turn round my arse. We've never aborted yet and we shan't now.' Someone said on the intercom: 'Here we go again. Shit or bust.' Someone else replied: 'Bust most likely.' 'Belt up,' said Harvey, 'we're going on.'

He was now faced with two choices. With the bomb load on board he could either reduce speed and try to conserve as much height as possible, or he could start a drift down and sacrifice height in order to maintain speed. Maintaining the speed would keep us up with the fourth wave - if we dropped behind would again be easy meat for the defences. But if we drifted down we knew than we would eventually level off at about 9,000 feet, some 10,000 feet below the rest of the force. Our situation over the target would then be unenviable - there would be just as much ironmongery coming down on top of us as there would be coming up. Harvey decided to drift down, maintain speed and keep up with the rest. As he did so, the bomb-aimer pointed out that if we jettisoned the 4,000lb cookie we would be better able to maintain height, but Harvey would have none of it. The cookie was going to Berlin along with everybody else. This last exchange was greeted with silence by the crew. The silence was broken by a voice - I thought at the time it might be the rear gunner - with a broad Aussie twang: 'Hey Skipper, you don't need to jettison the cookie. Jettison that bloody Pom - he's a Jonah! My heart skipped a beat and I held my breath. To my relief they all laughed and Harvey leaned across the cockpit and punched me on the shoulder. 'Can't do that,' he said. 'We might need him.'

We flew on, slowly losing height and penetrating deeper and deeper into hostile territory, maintaining the incessant search for other aircraft. The mid-upper gunner was gravely disadvantaged in this respect, as the hydraulic power to his turret had died when we shut down the starboard outer engine. He was having to traverse the turret by hand - a slow and laborious business. We were passing through 12,000 feet when the cosy darkness was shattered by a bright blue searchlight a few miles to starboard. Immediately another six or seven lights came on and homed on it, forming a cone of light. At the top of the cone a tiny speck, like a small moth, could be seen twisting and turning in a desperate attempt to escape. Flak streamed up the centre of the cone and the apex became a spatter of exploding shells. A red glow appeared, followed by a blinding red and orange flash. Flaming debris dribbled down the cone like melting red sealing wax. It happened in about two minutes. Seven men had died. The mid-upper gunner said laconically: 'There's a flamer going down on the starboard.' The navigator said: 'OK. I'll log it.' Nobody else spoke and we flew on.

So far there had been no sign of fighter activity, but we knew that by now the German fighter controller would have plotted our track, had probably decided that Berlin was the target and had vectored his fighter force in our direction.[73] It wouldn't be long now before they caught up with or intercepted us. Sure enough, a few minutes later tracer slashed across the sky in front and above us. 'Fighters about,' said Harvey to the gunners. 'With any luck they'll be above us. Keep searching!' Almost immediately both gunners reported: 'Fighter flare behind.' I twisted round in my seat and looked through the back of the canopy. A bright flare hung in the night sky above and behind us.

We were now passing through 10,000 feet and Harvey started a slow continuous weaving motion known as a corkscrew. 'Twenty-eight fifty,' he said and I put the revs up. He was taking no chances. If there was going to be a combat, he was ready. Another flare appeared, still above us but on the port side, followed immediately by a flashing exchange of tracer. Whoever the bomber was, he was fighting back. 'Good on yer, Blue,' the rear gunner said. It went quiet and black again and we put the revs back to 2,650, nursing our three engines as though they were made of flesh and blood. We were now down to 9,000 feet and she was holding the height and still maintaining 160 mph. The navigator said: 'Thirty minutes to the target.' The Path Finders and the leading wave would be there in a few minutes.

As we neared the target the bomber stream gradually converged towards the release point. The Lancasters and Halifaxes would be anywhere between 15,000 and 20,000 feet, with the Lancasters on top - a good position to be in! The risk of collision at our basement level was small: our main problem would be light flak and searchlights. We were well within the range of 40mm flak guns, in addition to which all the bombs and incendiaries released by the aircraft above us would pass through our level on their way to the ground. Our first sight of the target was distant searchlights and the tiny pinpricks of light which I now knew were flak bursts a long way off. More fighter flares burst in the sky above us and in their light we saw several of our own aircraft gradually getting closer together. Tracer cut through the sky again; followed by the orange flames I had seen before. This time we could see a Halifax on fire down the starboard side with little ant-like figures tumbling out of the nose hatch. 'He's a gonner,' someone said.

We could see the target markers now - reds and greens cascading down onto the aiming point. Incendiaries from the leading wave followed them and soon a pool of fire developed on the ground, speckled with the bright flashes of exploding HE. A few miles in front of us and above an aircraft blew up with a brilliant red and orange flash. Harvey gave no sign that he had seen these things: he was concentrating on the instrument panel and holding the aircraft rock-steady as the target came into the range of the bomb sight. 'Steady, steady,' said the bomb-aimer. Searchlights flicked onto us and a light flak battery opened up. The red balls of the tracer shells rose slowly and gracefully from the ground, gathering speed as they got nearer. They flashed past, just to our starboard. Above us the defences had established a box barrage over the approach and the sky was thick with the black puffs of bursting shells, easily visible in the light from the target. 'Left, left,' said the bomb-aimer and Harvey jinked the aircraft accordingly. 'Steadeee, steadeee.' If twenty-four hours was a long time in Bomber Command, I now realised that a minute was forever on the bombing run. There were still some seven or eight minutes to the release point. We lost the searchlights, but more light flak whizzed past us, not so close this time: they were firing at random.

'Twenty-eight fifty' said Harvey and I put the revs up. The target inched its way down the bomb sight. The bomb-aimer's voice became more strident as we neared the release point. Under Harvey's hands the aircraft flew as though it were on rails: the air speed, height and heading were all dead steady; he had shut his mind to what was going on around us. 'Bomb doors open!' said the bomb-aimer. 'We're nearly there. Steady - steady - steady -' his voice was rising to a crescendo - 'BOMBS GONE!' The release arm, known as the 'Mickey Mouse', started its semi-circular journey round the contact points, one for each bomb station. The bombs were thus released in a predetermined order, so that the trim of the aircraft was preserved. The Lancaster soared and shook itself, like a big black Labrador coming out of the water.

With the aircraft 10,000lb lighter we all knew we now had a fighting chance. Harvey still held the aircraft steady, waiting twenty more seconds for the photo-flash to go off. This ensured that we took back a photograph of the target at our release point. I looked over my side of the aircraft at the sea of fire underneath us. The long straight black line running through the middle of it was the Unter den Linden. I thought of the burning streets of East London in 1940, of the carnage I had seen outside Liverpool Street station when a bomb had dropped on a rush-hour queue. There was no compassion in my heart for those on the ground below. Rather, I heard Churchill's voice: 'You have sown the wind, but you will reap the whirlwind. For every bomb you drop on London, we shall repay you ten-fold.' We were the whirlwind, riding high above them, over Hitler's Chancellery at the heart of the Third Reich. I wondered if he was getting the message.[74]

We left the revs at 2,850 and cleared the target, climbing slowly. We would be able to maintain at least 12,000 feet now, which would keep us clear of the light flak defences. We turned to a north-westerly heading and started off across the north German plain towards the Baltic coast, which we would cross between Rostock and Lübeck. The light from the target faded astern of us and we were soon concealed again in the false security of the velvety blackness. The stars were more easily visible now and we could clearly see the Great Bear. Harvey reminded me how, by using it as a guide, the Pole Star could be found and identified. 'That little joker is the best compass there is,' he said. Months later this advice was to save the lives of myself and my crew on a particularly fraught occasion off the Danish coast. But it was quiet now. We had been able to reduce the power setting on our three Merlins to 2,500 rpm and they were singing along beautifully. As we neared the coast we could see that the defences of both Rostock and Lübeck were active, indicating that stragglers in the first waves had strayed over them. Harvey aimed at the black gap between them and we passed serenely out into the Baltic, soon turning onto a westerly heading which would take us north of Kiel on our way to the North Sea. Harvey put 'George' in - the automatic pilot. I found my thermos flask and we had a cup of coffee. It tasted like nectar. We put the thermos away and concentrated on the next task, which was to cross the Danish-German border. The navigator said: 'Ten minutes to the coast.'

We were flying over an area notorious for night fighters - there were several airfields in the vicinity. To our left, searchlights and flak shattered the blackness. 'That's Kiel' said Harvey. Our track would take us over the island of Sylt, on which there were at least two night-fighter airfields. I began to wonder if it was going to be as difficult to get out of Germany as it had been to get in. We flew on unmolested and soon crossed the coast out into the comparative safety of the North Sea. We now had 200 miles of water to cross before we would see the Lincolnshire coast. We eased the revs back to 2,350 and started a slow descent. After half an hour or so we passed through 10,000 feet and were able to take our oxygen masks off. The coffee went round again and the tension subsided. There was no need now to maintain radio silence and the wireless operator was busy trying to contact HQ 5 Group to get a met forecast for landing at Skelly. We still searched and quartered the sky, but with any luck all aircraft would be friendly. Someone sang *The Wild Colonial Boy* and they all joined in the chorus. Ned Kelly, I thought, would be proud of them.

We were down to our last 300 gallons of fuel and the met reports were not good. Several bases in north Lincolnshire were closed, as were some of the fields in Yorkshire, the home of the Halifax force. We still hadn't got a forecast for Skelly. Finally it came through: it said clear sky, visibility 3,000 yards and frost on the runway. We were flying level at 4,000 feet with the Merlins still at 2,350, trying to save as much fuel as possible. No wife or lover was ever handled with as much care and consideration as those three engines.

Our first sight of the coast was a searchlight battery, friendly of course, waving from side to side to show the returning bomber fleet the way home. It was a pleasant sight. Harvey put the navigation lights on and soon we could see the lights of other aircraft appearing out of the darkness. He contacted Skelly on the VHF and, because we were on three engines, we were given a priority landing. This meant that we could join the circuit straight away without having to descend through the stack. The fuel was down to less than eighty gallons each side. We were at 2,000 feet now and could not see the ground: it was hidden beneath a bluish haze, with white patches here and there. 'Blast,' said Harvey. 'It's fogging in.' We saw an airfield beacon; it was Fiskerton: we would soon be home.

We were over the top of Skelly before we saw the red ident beacon. The tower gave the visibility as 2,500 yards. We found the Drem and from a downwind position the flare path was barely visible. Harvey called for 15° of flap, wheels down and 2850 rpm. We followed the Drem and it led us to the funnel. Left into the funnel, 30° of flap and the flare path came into view. We were in a double green, just right for a three-engined landing. In the threshold

Harvey said, 'Your throttles - slow cut' and I eased them back. The Merlins coughed and spluttered as the power came off. The big smooth Palmer tyres kissed the runway and we were down. It was perfect. We had been airborne for eight hours and ten minutes. We turned off at the end of the runway and came to a halt. I shut down the port outer and we taxied slowly back to dispersal on the inboards. Harvey swung the aircraft round onto our pan, the marshaller held his wand across his throat and we shut down the two remaining engines. As the propellers came to a standstill, the silence was shattering. We sat there for a few seconds trying to adjust to it and then climbed slowly and stiffly from our seats, made our way down along the fuselage and out onto the concrete of the pan. It felt firm and good beneath my feet.

The crew had moved away from the aircraft and stood in a group, waiting for the crew bus. I joined them and was included in the banter and the cigarettes, conscious of the fact that I was now a fully paid-up member of this strange fraternity whose life expectancy revolved around a ten o'clock phone call. The bus pulled into the pan and we climbed aboard. It was a Dodge, dimly lit inside with three small blue lights. The air was thick with cigarette smoke, the tips glowing in the gloom, in which the faces were barely recognisable. We were greeted with a great deal of ribaldry, mostly to do with the lengths some people would go to get a priority landing. We drove off to de-briefing. Just inside the door of the de-briefing room were two or three large urns of tea and coffee and the rum bottle - or rather, several rum bottles. Every British serviceman is, b) tradition, entitled to a rum issue before going into action. In the RAF the rum ration is issued after the action, when the crews are safely on the ground. There were ten or so de-briefing tables, their number limited by the number of de-briefing teams available. We stood around, drinking our rum and coffee and exhilarating in our safe return and the thought of a probable day off. The noise in the room was considerable, everyone talking at once, the aircrew talking at the top of their voices, their hearing deadened by eight hours of engine roar.

And so to the Sergeants' Mess for egg and bacon and there to bed. I went to sleep feeling that I had earned my day's pay of thirteen shillings and sixpence (67½ pence). The next day we learned that 54 aircraft had been lost on the operation, more than half of them over the UK owing to fog and shortage of fuel.[75]

I was now fully qualified and my crew and I were allocated our own aircraft, DV401, which carried the squadron letter 'Z'. It was known as *Zeke*, after a cartoon character popular at the time. We flew *Zeke* to Frankfurt on 20 December and to the 'Big City' on the twenty-third. Apart from the barrage over the target, both trips were uneventful and we returned unscathed. A total of 57 aircraft were lost on these two operations.[76]

We were now stood down for Christmas. There was a dance in the Sergeants' Mess on Christmas Eve, well attended by all the WAAFs and local ladies and what with one thing and another it turned out to be one of the best Christmases I can remember. The stand down lasted until 29 December, when it was the 'Big City' again.[77] This time the route home was north of the Ruhr and the flight time was seven hours and five minutes Again, apart from the target, we had an easy ride. Not so for Harvey, for this was the night his luck ran out. On my return I stood in the ops room and stared at the blank space on the ops board where his landing time should have been. I couldn't believe it. I hung around until his endurance had expired and I knew he must be down somewhere. There was no news of him diverting and MISSING was chalked up on the board opposite his name. I went back to the Mess with a heavy heart. Twenty-six aircraft were lost on the raid and he and his crew were amongst them. I never did hear what happened to them: they just disappeared, with all the others, into that black void on the other side of the North Sea, which was gobbling up men and machines with increasing ferocity. The next day, Harvey's name had been erased from the board in Jimmy Moss's office. [78]

On New Year's Eve my crew and I went on seven days' leave. While we were away, on 2 January 1944, *Zeke*, flown by another crew, failed to return from the 'Big City'. The average life of a squadron Lancaster at this stage of the war was thirty-six flying hours. [79]

Fifty years have passed since these events took place. Sometimes when I stand outside the house on a black, starlit winter's night and see Orion climb above the south-eastern horizon, or trace along the line of the Great Bear to find the Pole Star, my imagination plays tricks with me. I hear again the snarling roar of the Merlins; the crump, crump of bursting shells; and above all the voices and one in particular pontificating on the rival merits of 4,000lb cookies and sprog Pommie pilots. I have never forgotten Harvey and his crew. If the unofficial motto of wartime Bomber Command was 'Press on regardless', nobody did so better than they.' [80]

Footnotes Chapter 11

71 The 'Gen Men' or 'Old Sweats' on 'P-Peter' flown by Squadron Leader Edward Henry Moss DFC and whose crew were on their 20th operation on the night of 30/31 March, were all killed when shortly before midnight, Hauptmann Fritz Rudusch of 6./NJG6 flying a Bf 110 shot them down near Rimbach, north-west of Fulda. It was his first victory.
72 Some 483 Lancasters and ten Mosquitoes were detailed to attack Berlin. The bomber route again led directly to Berlin across Holland and Northern Germany and there were no major diversions. Another formation, consisting of 26 Stirlings, 12 Mosquitoes and 9 Lancasters were to carry out raids on two flying-bomb sites near Abbeville.
73 The German controllers planned the course of the bombers with great accuracy; many fighters were met at the coast of Holland and further fighters were guided in to the bomber stream throughout the approach to the target. More fighters were waiting at Berlin and there were many combats. Widespread mist and fog at 150-300 feet in the North German plains reduced the overall effectiveness of the fighter defence and 23 aircraft, mostly Bf 110s had to abandon their sorties prematurely yet 25 Lancasters were shot down.
74 Berlin was cloud covered but the Path Finder sky-marking was reasonably accurate and much of the bombing fell in the city.
75 All told, 29 Lancasters (and two Stirlings returning from mine-laying operations) either crashed or were abandoned when their crews bailed out.
76 After a lull in operations, on Monday night, 20/21 December 650 bomber crews were detailed to attack Frankfurt. Little went to plan. A diversion operation to Mannheim by 44 Lancasters and ten Mosquitoes did not draw fighters away from the route to the target until after the raid was over. The German control rooms were able to plot the bomber force as soon as it left the English coast and they were able to continue plotting it all the way to Frankfurt so that there were many combats on the route to the target. Altogether, 41 aircraft failed to return from the raid on Frankfurt.

In the early hours of Christmas Eve 364 Lancasters, 8 Mosquitoes and 7 Halifaxes were detailed for Berlin. This raid was originally planned for a late afternoon take-off but a forecast of worsening weather over the bomber stations caused the raid to be put back by seven hours to allow the bombers a return in daylight. German night-fighters encountered difficulty with the weather and the German controller was temporarily deceived by the Mosquito diversion at Leipzig. At the target there were no fighters and few searchlights because of scattered cloud but only eleven of the 39 Blind Markers released their markers mainly because of H_2S failures. Just one other aircraft was able to drop its 11 Green TIs and these landed six miles away. Most of the Main Force had bombed by the time the PFF Backers-Up could get their markers away and mainly the bombing was in the suburbs of the German capital. The main force of fighters only appeared in the target area at the end of the raid and could not catch the main bomber stream. Fifteen Lancasters were shot down.

77   This raid, the final one to the 'Big City', was a maximum effort involving 712 aircraft, 457 of them Lancasters and the remainder, 252 Halifaxes and three Mosquitoes.

78   Flight Lieutenant George Henry Harvey RAAF was piloting DV399 QR-R (the same Lancaster that Keith Parry flew as a second dickie on the night of 16/17 December). It was hit by flak and exploded, killing Harvey and five other crewmembers. Only Pilot Officer D. F. Thomas RCAF survived and he was taken into captivity. In total, twenty aircraft - 11 Lancasters, 9 Halifaxes - were lost.

79   *Zeke*, flown by Flying Officer George Arthur Tull, crashed at Mirns in Friesland. There were no survivors. Altogether, 29 Lancasters were lost on Berlin.

80   Keith Parry went on to complete 57 'Ops'. He was awarded the DSO in 1944 and stayed on in the RAF and retired with the rank of Squadron Leader in 1965. He carried on flying up to the age of 73. See *Memorial Flight 2000; Journal of Lincolnshire's Lancaster Association, No.33*, spring 2000 and No. 34, autumn 2000.

Chapter 12

'V for Victor'

Sergeant Ben Frazier

Every squadron had a bulletin board. Orders, news, bits of this and that. You looked at it every day. What used to get me was if you saw that a new crew came in and they'd come in together. So there would be seven new names and they'd be under the title 'Arrivals' and then you'd see, sometimes, those seven names, bing, bing, bing, bing, all seven and they'd be posted under the title 'Missing In Action.' Same board, same day, you understand. In other words, one operational flight, one kick at the cat and that was it. They never had a chance to learn what it was all about. Just one flight and down. Maybe safe, Holland, Germany, in a camp somewhere, but more likely a million-and-one pieces mixed with the ship.
You never got to know them.
You never got to know them[81]

On the night of 29/30 December 1943 Berlin was again the target for RAF Bomber Command and 712 aircraft including 457 Lancasters were dispatched. At the 1 Group aerodrome at Elsham Wolds, Sergeant Ben Frazier, *Yank* Staff Correspondent boarded 'V-Victor' on 576 Squadron for the operation to the 'Big City' with Flying Officer Gomer S. 'Taff' Morgan and his crew. This famous Lancaster III had originally served on 103 Squadron, as had Morgan (576 was formed from 'C' Flight of 103 Squadron on 25 November) and the Berlin op would be ED888's 58th sortie.

'England. A small village lay tucked away in the fold of a valley just below the high, windswept, bleak plateau where a Lancaster bomber station was situated. Housewives were busy in the kitchen preparing food and the men had left their ploughing to come in for the noon-day meal. In the lichen covered Gothic Church, the minister's wife was arranging decorations and placing on the altar freshly cut chrysanthemums that had managed to escape the north winds and were still blooming in December. The placidness of the village life was in sharp contrast to the bustling activity at the airfield. It seemed as remote from war as any hamlet could possibly be, although the provident farmers, living so close to an obvious military target had wisely provided themselves with shelter trenches at the edge of each ploughed field. Nevertheless, the name of this quiet, lovely village had spread far. By borrowing it, the bomber station had made it one to strike terror into the heart of the Nazi High Command.

'At the airfield, 'V for Victor's crew lounged around 'B' Flight's Office waiting to see if operations were on. They kept looking up into the sky as if trying to guess what the weather was going to be like. Some of the men chuckled. 'Papa Harris is so set on writing off the Big City that he hardly even notices the weather,' one of them said. 'The last time, there were kites stooging around all over the place. The met boobed that one.'

'It was a strange new language. What the airmen were saying was that the last time out the meteorological men had given a wrong steer on the weather and the planes had been flying all over looking for the field on the return trip. 'Papa' Harris was Air Chief Marshal Harris, chief of Bomber Command.

'V for Victor's captain came back from the operations room with the news that there would be ops. That settled the discussion. You seemed to be aware, without noticing anything in particular, of a kind of tension that gripped the men; like they were pulling in their belts a notch or two to get set for the job ahead.

'And with the news, everybody got busy - the aircrews, the ground crews, the mechanics, the WAAFs, the cooks. The ships already had a basic bomb and fuel load on board and the additional loads were sent out in ammunition trailers and fuel trucks. The perimeter track lost its usually deserted appearance and looked like a well travelled highway, with trucks and trailers, buses and bicycles hurrying out to the dispersal points. It was just like the preparation at any bomber base before taking off for enemy territory - but going over the Big City was something different. These men had been there before. They knew what to expect.

'In the equipment room, June, the pint-size WAAF in battledress, was an incongruous note. Over a counter as high as her chin, she flung parachutes, harnesses and Mae Wests. The crew grabbed them and lugged them out to the ships. You kept thinking they ought to be able to get somebody a little bigger for the job she was handling.

'In the briefing room, the met officer gave the weather report and the forecast over enemy territory. There would be considerable cloud over the target. The men grinned. An operations officer gave a talk on the trip. The route was outlined on a large map of Germany on the front wall. It looked ominously long on the large scale map. He pointed out where the ground defences were supposed to be strong and where fighter opposition might be expected. He gave the time when the various phases should be over the target. He explained where the 'spoof' attacks were to be made and the time. He told the men what kinds of flares and other markers the Path Finders would drop. There was the usual business of routine instructions, statistics and tactics to be used. The Group Captain gave a pep talk on the progress of the Battle of Berlin. And all the while, that tape marking the route stared you in the face and seemed to grow longer and longer.

'Outside it was hazy and growing more so. But this was nothing new. The men were convinced that the weather was always at its most variable and it's dampest and it's haziest over their field. What could you expect? Ops would probably be scrubbed after all. Hell of a note.

'In the fading light the planes were silhouetted against the sky. They looked, on the ground, slightly hunched and menacing like hawks. Seeing them there, in the half-light you would never guess how easy and graceful they are in flight. Nor would you realise when you see them soaring off the runway, what an immense load they take up with them. It is only when you see the open bomb bay on the ground, that you get some idea of a Lancaster's destructive power. The open bomb bay seems like a small hangar. The 4,000lb-block buster in place looks like a kitten curled up in a large bed. It is a sobering sight.

'In the evening some of the men tried to catch a few winks; most of them just sat around talking. The operational meal followed. It was only a snack, but it was the last solid food any one would get until the fresh egg and bacon breakfast which has become a ritual for the proper ending of a successful mission.

'As there was still some time to wait before take-off 'V for Victor's crew sat around the ground crew's hut near the dispersal point, warming themselves by the stove or chewing the rag with the ground crew. The Wingco came around to make a last minute check-up. The medical officer looked everyone over. The engineer officer checked the engines.

'The minutes crept by until at last the time came to get into the planes. The deep stillness of the night was awakened by the motors revving up; one after another until each one was lost in the general roar. The crews scrambled into the planes and took their places. The great ships were guided out of their dispersal areas by the ground crews who gave a final wave as the Lancs moved off slowly down the perimeter track. They appeared more menacing than ever creeping along in the dark with their motors roaring. One by one they turned onto the runway and noisily vanished into the night.

'From now on, until they would return, the members of 'V for Victor's crew were a little world in themselves, alone and yet not alone. For all around them were other similar little worlds, hundreds of them with a population of seven, hurtling through space, lightlessly - huge animated ammunition dumps. For its safety, each little world depended utterly and completely on its members - and a large dash of luck.

'There was not much conversation over the intercom. When you're flying without running lights on a definite course and surrounded by several hundred other bombers, you have not time for any pleasantries. The navigator was busy checking the air speed and any possible drift. Almost everyone else kept a look out for other aircraft, both friend and foe. A friendly aircraft is almost as dangerous as an enemy plane, for if two blockbusters meet in mid-air, the pieces that are left are very small indeed.

'Occasionally the ship jolted from the slipstream of some unseen aircraft ahead and frequently others overhauled V for Victor, passing by to port and starboard, above and below. V for Victor gained altitude very easily for maximum ceiling. She was a veteran of over 50 ops and had the DFC painted on her port bow to celebrate the fiftieth, but she had the vitality of a youngster. Blondy [Sergeant J. R. O'Hanlon], the wireless-operator, broke the silence. 'Taff, the W/T has gone u/s.'

'The wireless is not used except in an emergency such as ditching, but it is nice to know it's there. We went on. Occasionally Taff, the pilot, would call into the intercom, 'Bob, [Sergeant C. E. 'Bob' Shilling] are you OK?' There would be a silence for a moment while the rear-gunner fumbled to turn on his intercom, until you wondered if he had frozen back there. Then he'd sing out, 'OK, Taff.' He and the mid-upper gunner [Sergeant A. Newman] were the only two outside the heated cabin. Inside the cabin it was warm and snug. You didn't even need gloves. Jock [Sergeant J. R. 'Jock' Mearns], the navigator, wore no flying gear, just the Air Force battledress.

'Up ahead the Path Finder boys dropped the first route markers, flak shot up into the air and the men knew that V for Victor was approaching the Dutch coast. An enormous burst of flame lit up the night off to port. 'Scarecrow to starboard,' the mid-upper reported on the intercom. Jerry intended the 'scarecrow' to look like a burning plane but it did not take long to see that it was not. [82]

'Jock's Scots accent came over the intercom: 'Taff, we're eleven minutes late.' 'OK, we'll increase speed.' The engineer pushed up the throttles. Everything was black again below. Occasionally there was a small burst of flak here and there.

'Plane to starboard below!'

'OK, it's a Lanc.' As 'V for Victor' passed it you could seen the bluish flame from the exhausts lighting the aircraft below in a weird ghostly manner. It was unpleasant to realise that our own exhausts made 'V for Victor' just as obvious as the other plane.

'Away off the port bow, a glow became visible. It looked like the moon but it was the first big German searchlight belt, encompassing many cities. The beams were imprisoned under cloud. [83]

'That will be Happy Valley,' Jock said. Another route marker appeared ahead.

'Tell me when we're over it,' the navigator replied. Shortly the bomb-aimer [Flight Sergeant N. A. 'Digger' Lambrell RAAF] said, 'We're bang over it now.'

'OK, Digger.'

'Taff, we're nine minutes late.' The navigator took a couple of astro sights to get a fix. From this he could determine the wind and the drift of the plane.

'Another searchlight belt show up to starboard. It was enormous, running for miles and miles. It was all imprisoned under the cloud but it was an evil looking sight just the same.[84] The top of the clouds shone with millions of moving spots, like so many restless glow worms, but the impression was much more sinister - like some kind of luminous octopus. The tentacle-like beams groped about seeking some hole in the cloud, some way of clutching at you as you passed by protected by the darkness. The continuous motion of the searchlights caused a ripple effect on the clouds, giving them an agitated, angry, frustrated appearance. Once in a while one found a rift and shot its light high into the sky. Flak came up sparkling and twinkling through this luminous blanket. 'V for Victor' jolted violently from close bursts, but was untouched. It passed another Lanc, which was clearly silhouetted against the floodlit clouds.

Another leg of the trip was completed. The navigator gave the new course over the intercom and added, 'Seven minutes late.'

'OK, Jock. Mac, [Pilot Officer E. M. Graham, flight engineer] make it 165.'

'V for Victor' passed plane after plane and occasionally jolted in the slipstream of others. A third searchlight belt showed up, this one free of cloud. It was a huge wall of light and looked far more impenetrable than a mountain. It seemed inconceivable than any plane could pass through and reach the opposite side. You thanked your lucky stars that this was not the target. To fly out of the protecting darkness into the blaze of light would be a test of courage you would rather not have to face.

'Nevertheless, there were some facing it right now. The flak opened up and the searchlights waved madly about. It was a diversionary attack, the 'spoof'. You watched in a detached, remote sort of way. It seemed very far away and did not seem to concern you at all. Until suddenly, one beam which had been vertical, slanted down and started to pursue 'V for Victor' and you realised that it did concern you very intimately. The seconds ticked by as the beam overtook the plane. But it passed harmlessly overhead and groped impotently in the darkness beyond.

'Four minutes late,' Jock called over the intercom.

'The target itself, the Big City, came into view like a luminous patch dead ahead. It was largely hidden by cloud and showed few searchlights. It seemed so much less formidable than the mountain of light just behind, that it came as a sort of anticlimax. Surely, you felt, this cannot be the Big City, the nerve-centre of Europe's evil genius.

'It was quiet. There was no flak as yet, no flares and just the handful of searchlights. You tried to imagine what it was like on the ground there. The sirens would be about to sound; the ack-ack batteries would be standing ready, the searchlights already manned. You wondered if the people were in shelters.

'But it was too much of an effort. It was too remote. Your problems were flak, fighters, searchlights and whether you were on the course and on time. What happened below was an entirely different problem, which had nothing to do with you. What happened below might just as well be happening on Mars. 'V for Victor's own little world simply hovering off this planet and leading a life of its own.

'Ever so slowly 'V for Victor' crept up on the target. The two worlds were coming inevitably together. But it still had the quality of unreality. It was like a dream where you were hurrying somewhere and yet cannot move at all. Nevertheless, 'Victor' was passing plane after plane and jolted in somebody's slipstream now and again. The other Lancs looked ominous bearing down on the target, breathing out blue flame as they approached.

'The minute of the attack and still the target was quiet. One more minute ticked by - still quiet. The engineer opened up the throttles to maximum speed and increased the oxygen supply. Still quiet. The whole attack was a minute or two late. Winds, probably. Suddenly the whole city opened up.

The flak poured up through the clouds. It came in a myriad of little lights. It poured up in a stream of red, as if shaken from a hose. It would be impossible to miss such a brilliantly marked objective. Bright flashes started going off under the clouds. That would be the cookies from the planes ahead. V for Victor started the bombing run. The bomb-aimer called the course now.

'Left, left...Steady now...Right a bit...Steady...steady...Cookie gone!' 'V for Victor' shot upward slightly. 'Steady...Incendiaries gone...' V for Victor surged again ever so slightly.

'Stand-by, Taff,' it was the voice of Bob, the tail-gunner. 'Fighter.'

'Instantly the pilot sent V for Victor over to starboard and rushed headlong downward. A stream of red tracer whipped out of the dark, past the rear turret and on past the wing-tip, missing by what seemed inches. A second later the fighter itself shot past after the tracer, a vague dark blur against the night sky.

'Me 109,' Bob said calmly.

'V for Victor' squirmed and corkscrewed over the sky of Berlin. You wondered how it could be possible to avoid all the other planes that were over the city. But the fighter was shaken off and 'V for Victor' came back to a normal course again.

'Down below through rifts in the cloud, you could see that Berlin was burning. The bright, white flame of the incendiaries showed up as a carpet of light, always growing. And flash after flash went off as the blockbusters fell. The dark, black shapes of many Lancasters could be seen all over the sky, against the brilliant clouds below. They were like small insects crawling over a great glass window. It did not seem possible that these tiny black dots could be the cause of the destruction, which was going on below. The insects crawled to the edge of the light and disappeared into the darkness beyond. They had passed safely through the target, V for Victor close behind.

'Shortly the course was set for the return and Berlin was visible for many miles on the port quarter. The attack was over now. It took only fifteen minutes. The ack-ack was silent. There was no flak flashing over the city, but the city was brighter than ever. The clouds were getting a reddish tinge, which showed that the fires had caught hold below.

'And so the capital of Nazism dropped astern, obscuring the rising moon by its flames. The Government which came into power by deliberately setting fire to its chamber of representatives, the Government which first used wholesale bombing and boasted of it, was now perishing in fires far more devastating than any it ever devised. It was perishing to a fire music never dreamed of by Wagner.

'But it was impossible to connect 'V for Victor' with the death struggles of Berlin. There was no time for contemplation.

'Stand-by, Ju 88 starboard - corkscrew,' came Bob's voice. Again with lightning speed, the pilot put 'V for Victor' over and dived out of the way. The Ju 88's tracers missed us and shot down another Lanc which had not been so fortunate.

'After that the route home was uneventful. Crossing the North Sea, 'V for Victor' went into a gentle incline towards home base, as if by a sort of homing instinct. The searchlights of England sent out a greeting of welcome. For miles along the coast they stood almost evenly spaced, vertical sentries guarding the island. Then they started waving downwards in the direction of the nearest airfield. No doubt they were helping home a damaged bomber. How different they were from the menacing tentacles over the German cities. 'V for Victor' arrived over the home field. The wireless-operator called base over his repaired equipment. He said simply. 'V for Victor'.

'The clear voice of a girl came pleasantly over the intercom, 'V for Victor', prepare to pancake'. The short business-like message in service slang was a wonderful welcome home. V for Victor circled the field, losing altitude.

'V-Victor in funnels.'

'V-Victor, pancake,' the girl's voice said. 'V for Victor' touched down, ran down the flarepath and turned off on the perimeter track.

'V-Victor clear of flarepath.' The ground crew met 'V for Victor' and acted as a guide back into the dispersal area.

'How was it?'

'Piece of cake,' someone said. The crew got out, collected their gear, the parachutes, Mae Wests, the navigator's bag, the guns, etc and then, as one man, lit up cigarettes. The pilot walked around the plane looking for any damage. There was one small hole through the aileron but it was too dark to see it then. The bus arrived and the crew clambered in with all the gear and were taken back to the locker room. June was there and gathered all the stuff over the counter and staggered away, lost from sight under a mound of yellow suits and Mae Wests. Then back to the briefing room where a cup of hot tea with rum in it was waiting. Each captain signed his name on the board as he came in. Crew by crew, the men went into the Intelligence room, carrying their spiked tea with them. There were packages of cigarettes on the table and everyone chain-smoked, lighting up from the butt of the previous one. The Intelligence Officer asked brief questions and the replies were brief such as 'The heavy flak was light and the light flak heavy'. It was over in a very few minutes and you went back to the briefing room and bantered over the trip with the other crews. No trouble, any of them, but there were gaps in the list of captains chalked on the board.

'It's like that,' the Wingco remarked. 'In night flying, you usually get back intact, or you don't get back at all. If you get coned, or a fighter sees you before you see it, then very often you've had it, but if somebody else gets coned then its that much easier for you.'

'You thought of the other Lancaster the Ju 88 got with the same burst that missed 'V for Victor'. And you lit another cigarette. The first signs of dawn were coming over the field now and off in the distance, on the bleak, windswept, little knoll, 'V for Victor' stood guard over the empty dispersal points from which other men and ships had gone out a short while before.

'…If somebody else gets coned then it's that much easier for you.'

Footnotes Chapter 12

81 *Six War Years 1939-1945, Memories of Canadians at Home and Abroad* by Barry Broadfoot (Paperjacks Ltd, 1985).

82 It was only after the war that it was discovered that the Germans did not use an explosive device to simulate an exploding bomber. What the men saw, in fact, was a fully loaded bomber exploding, having either been hit by flak or night fighter attack.

83 A Spoof raid was in progress.

84 Leipzig, where the bomber stream appeared to be heading before turning north-east for Berlin.

85 In all, 20 aircraft (11 Lancasters and 9 Halifaxes) failed to return. A long approach route from the south, passing south of the Ruhr and then within 20 miles of Leipzig together with Mosquito diversions at Düsseldorf, Leipzig and Magdeburg, caused the German controller great difficulties and there were few fighters over Berlin. Bad weather on the outward route also kept down the number of German fighters finding the bomber stream. 182 people were killed; more than 600 were injured and over 10,000 were bombed out. Despite atrocious winter weather Nachtjagd claimed 169 victories during the final month of 1943 against 28 lost.

Chapter 13

Yanks and Lancs

I always had just one bad moment, just at that time we're on the line and getting the go-ahead and those four Merlins are roaring away and the full power is on against the brakes and all I do is let go with the brake and we're heading down the runway, building up to 90 knots and there's a six-ton cookie in the belly and enough incendiaries to burn up Dortmund or Essen and over the fence, over the valley and we're on our way. From then on, it's okay. I can get along. But just back before the brakes come off, that short time and my guts turn to mush. Every time. Fifty-two missions and 52 times I get stomachy mush.

We had this American kid at Tail-end Charlie and he was a cocky little bastard and just at that time, every time he'd turn on his intercom and he'd crack: 'Nobody can kill us. One day the crew of old 'G for George' will rule the world.' Always that and the mid-upper would say, 'Fucking right, Barney' and that would kind of ease the tension. I never loaded it on those two, because gunners don't have a very happy life and especially Barney out there in the tail - that's the end of the world as far as I'm concerned. Bloody cold and bloody lonely out there in the tail section, with the glass out and dark all round. It got to be a thing, those two guys, Barney and the mid-upper and if they hadn't given their bit of repartee just before take-off I think the rest of us would have felt, 'Oh oh, bad luck. Breaking it off. Bad luck.' But they kept on and we started as a crew and we finished as a crew and kept lucky. But there wasn't a day, not a night, when I didn't get those goose pimples in my gut for those few minutes. And let me tell you, the last operation, into Bremen, that was the worst. The very worst. The last, always the worst.

Goose Pimples in My Gut by a Canadian airman in RAF Bomber Command.[86]

Hubert C. 'Nick' Knilans had left Delavan High School in Wisconsin in 1935 and in the summer months he milked cows and worked the horses on the family farm in Walworth County. Delavan was a thriving manufacturing town about half way between Milwaukee and Chicago where Knilans looked for jobs when winter came. But Knilans' ambitions lay elsewhere. In October 1941 when his call-up papers had run out, the 24-year old had driven up to Canada to join the RCAF with the intention to become a 'Yank' in Canadian clothing in Bomber Command. At that time the United States was still neutral but many adventurous young Americans who were not prepared to wait for the call to arms. They 'defected' to Canada and 'signed on' to join the RAF with the intention of becoming a fully fledged pilot on fighter or bomber aircraft; men like Pilot Officer Hubert Clarence 'Nick' Knilans, who became a Lancaster pilot on 619 Squadron at Woodhall Spa, one and a half miles from the Victorian spa town. At the time most Americans wished to remain neutral, millions choosing to follow the progress of the Blitz and the war in Europe by tuning in to Edward R Murrow, head of CBS European Bureau in London for his penetrating radio broadcasts, *This Is London*. Millions more digested the column inches graphically written by reporters who were syndicated in many hundreds of newspapers throughout the USA but not all columnists were as enthusiastic as Murrow when it came to championing the British cause. Boake Carter, who was syndicated in 83 newspapers with a combined circulation of more than seven million readers asked, 'Where does the Roosevelt Administration drive the idea that Americans want to go gallivanting forth to play Sir Galahad again?' Walter Winchell, syndicated in 150 newspapers, 8½ million-circulation, struck home; saying, 'The future of American youth is on top of American soil not underneath European dirt.' [87]

American observers in Germany and career officers such as General Raymond Lee, the US Military Attaché in London, too, remained sceptical about Britain's massive industrial commitment to heavy bombers. During a lunch at the Dorchester Lee told the assembled British officials and four Air Marshals that 'the British had no proof yet that their bombing had been any more effective than the German bombing of England'. He added, 'I thought they were asking the United States for a good deal when they wanted it to divest itself of all its bombers and devote a lot of production capacity to the construction of more bombers, thereby committing the US to the policy of reducing Germany by bombing, without affording sufficient proof that this was possible.' Attitudes had changed little after America entered the war. In April 1942 the American air attaché in London reported to Washington that, 'The British public have an erroneous belief, which has been fostered by effective RAF publicity, that the German war machine can be destroyed and the nation defeated by intensive bombing.' While General Lee never flew an 'op' in a Lancaster as Murrow would, he did at least venture northeast to see what Bomber Command was capable of and he observed RAF bomber crews at a station somewhere in England.

'They were a queer conglomeration, these men - some educated and sensitive, some rough-haired and burly and drawn from all parts the Empire, Great Britain, Canada, New Zealand and Australia ...Some, of them were humming, some were singing, some were laughing and others were standing serious and thoughtful. It looked like the dressing room where the jockeys sit waiting before a great steeplechase... [At take-off] the control officer flashed a green ray for a split second, which was the signal that this plane was designated for take-off. Its roaring grew louder and louder as it dragged its heavy tail towards the starting point like a slow, nearly helpless monster. About twenty yards away we could just discern a vast dinosaurish shape; after a moment, as if stopping to make up its mind ..; it lumbered forward, raising its tail just as it passed us and turning from something very heavy and clumsy into a lightly poised shape, rushing through the night like a pterodactyl. At this instant, a white light was flashed upon it and a Canadian boy from Vancouver who was standing beside me, put down its number and the moment of departure. It vanished from sight at once and we stood, staring down the field, where in a few seconds a flashing green light announced that it had left the ground ...A great calm settled over the place as the last droning motors faded out in the distance and we all drove back to the control room where a staff hang onto the instruments on a long night vigil...I went to sleep thinking of the youngsters I had seen, all now 150 miles away; straining their eyes through a blackness relieved only by the star-spangled vault above them.'[88]

On the night of 13/14 January 1943 66 Lancasters raided Essen. Two 'Oboe' Mosquitoes had to return without marking and the sky markers of the third Mossie failed to ignite above the cloud but the city was bathed in light. German aircraft even dropped decoy flares to try to distract the Lancaster crews. The sky was steel blue and everywhere below there was the restless crisscross pattern of long white beams. Sergeant Robert S. Raymond had never seen so many searchlights or so great a barrage, as over the Ruhr before. Raymond was an American volunteer who originally served in an American Ambulance Unit in France in 1940, before travelling via Spain and Portugal to England. His second pilot, a new boy on 44 Squadron, who was there to get some experience, was on his first operational flight. The neophyte could not stop shaking but Raymond's boys, having made a few trips by now, were 'absolutely steady and normal under fire'. Raymond even found time to study the scene which to him represented a 'marvellously beautiful picture' especially on such a night with a few scattered clouds and the moon in its second quarter.

In the bomb bay Raymond's crew carried a 4,000-pounder and more than a thousand incendiaries. Down they went, the Cookie adding to the great red mushroom explosions of the other 4,000-pounders and the fire bombs stoking up the long strings of incendiaries being laid out in geometrical patterns among the buildings. It was destruction on a colossal scale and terrifying in its concentration and intensity.

Four Lancasters failed to make it back to their bases. Usually Raymond's Lancaster was among the last to return to Waddington because he and Griffiths his flight engineer believed in saving their engines. He was a 'miser with petrol', Raymond thought 'quite rightly' and the engineer's most famous remark was in crossing the Alps when the pilot asked for more power to gain height. Griffiths opened the throttles about half an inch and said, 'There, that's all you can have.' His knowledge of the Merlin engines, due to long experience, was amazing for a young man of 19 years. One of the Lancaster's engines overheated badly at more than half-throttle, so that it was not much help. Griffiths and his pilot talked over the possibilities and procedures in such cases by cutting other crew members off the intercom; otherwise they would have too much to think about. The air temperature was -30°C and the North Sea is pretty cold at this season. But this was the shortest trip they had ever made, a fact which would have been lost on the 'new boy' on the squadron who was still shaking after they landed back at Waddington. Interrogation after the trip was always a pleasant time for Raymond and the crew. It was carried out in the warm, brightly-lighted mess while they were eating. WAAFs moved about serving food. All of Raymond's own officers were around and usually a number from the Air Ministry looked on. There was much laughter and many enquires among the crews about incidents en route. There was much kidding if a pilot did not land promptly when it was his turn. The whole scene was a complete contrast to that of half an hour earlier when most of them were stacked on the circuit listening to the others and the WAAF in the control tower 'cursing like troopers if any stooge didn't land on first try.' [89]

On the night of 16/17 January 1943 Sir Arthur Harris sent 190 Lancasters and 11 Halifaxes on their way to Berlin - the first attack on the German capital in 14 months - with the words, 'Tonight you are going to the Big City. You will have the opportunity to light a fire in the belly of the enemy that will burn his black heart out.'

Sergeant pilot Robert Raymond wrote: 'We all knew that sooner or later during this winter we should go there. Any raid on that city has tremendous propaganda value and is good for morale. Nevertheless, although it was not entirely unexpected and everyone wanted to have it on a line in his Log Book, I felt rather weak in the knees when I walked into the Briefing Room and saw that name on the big board. Price, my wireless operator; said, 'I'd rather go to Essen than Berlin and I hate Essen as a target.'

'We took off about dusk and never saw the ground after leaving Base until we were over Berlin, which fortunately was in a clear area. Just heavy flak and lots of it over the target; no tracers from light guns, which only reach up to about 8,000 feet, no balloons, no searchlights or night fighters, etc. They knew what height we were and put up a box barrage all around us. We were straight and level for two minutes for the bombing run and every second seemed like a year. The whole of northern Europe is covered with snow and the moon being nearly full, the ground detail was clearly visible. The only colourful parts of the target were half a dozen flares and the great glowing mushrooms from our four thousand pounders. We carried one 4,000lb bomb and nearly a thousand incendiaries and got a fairly good photo of our results. Since Carter has been AWOL [Absent Without Leave] for three weeks, we took another rear gunner. It was his first Operational flight and he was so excited before, during and after the trip that he wasn't worth much. Much of our report on the trip depends on his accurate observations over the target where he has a better view than anyone else. Before take-off he looked up into the bomb bay and asked if that big cylindrical object was a spare petrol tank. It was the 4,000lb 'cookie' [blockbuster bomb] and he had never seen one before.

'Cloud over base when we returned was less than 1,000 feet and I did a short cross-country flight until most of the others had landed. I don't like being stacked up on a circuit in cloud at 500 feet intervals with a dozen other tired pilots.'

This raid saw the first use of varicoloured markers, or Target Indicators (TIs), dropped on the aiming point by selected crews. The operation, however, was a disappointment. Thick cloud en route and haze over the target caused problems and the bombing was scattered. The Berlin flak had proved light and ineffective and it was assumed that the greater altitude of the attacking force had surprised the German gunners. Only one Lancaster was lost.

Harris repeated the raid on the 'Big City' the following night when the weather was better. Robert Raymond wrote.

'Had eight hours sleep and all crews that had serviceable planes were briefed for Berlin again. Over the North Sea climbed up through layers of cloud tinted with the red glow of the setting sun. In the clear air between them it looked like some of those dreamy cloudland shots in Lost Horizon. Just a space without a horizon except for the banded cloud of soft greys, mauve, purple and grey blues and with 'George' flying I had plenty of time to think - odd thoughts as mine always are - how scared I had been in a nearby town two nights ago when sitting in a cafe during an Air Raid Alert. Several enemy planes bombed from low level and one bomb demolished the building across the street. The blast effect even from that small effort was considerable and made me appreciate what we were doing to the enemy targets with our forces and weight-carrying capacity. Verily it is better to send than to receive in this racket. Then I thought about the message from the Chief of Bomber Command which had been addressed to us tonight and read out at Briefing, 'Go to it, Chaps and show them the red rose of Lancaster in full bloom.' Someone behind a desk had given an order to a great organization and here we were a few hours later, one of the pawns in the game, sitting up over the North Sea with the temperature at minus 30° Centigrade, wondering if we would ever see England again.

'Vapour condensation trails were plainly visible in the clear moonlight above cloud, showing that many other planes were a few minutes ahead on the same track. They are always a curious phenomenon and form at the trailing edge of your wings, due to the decrease in pressure there. Out over the sea we pay no attention to them, but over enemy territory they always result in attacks by night fighters. Conditions over the target were about the same as the previous night, except the visibility was even better. Several members of the crew heard shrapnel from spent bursts bounce off our fuselage and the rear gunner saw five members of a crew bail out and go down on their white silk umbrellas. We passed quite close to them. Flak was more accurate than the previous night and several times I saw the black smoke puffs indicating shell bursts right in front of us as we were leaving the target area.

'Collected some ice on the return trip, but I have no fear of that now, having studied diligently and knowing why, when and how it occurs. It is only necessary to be able to recognise the type of cloud, the frontal weather conditions and have an accurate thermometer to avoid its cumulative effects. Each time I climbed to lower temperatures or descended to clearer areas and we went through it confidently although I have reason to believe that it accounted for some that are missing.

'Impossible to land at base and we were diverted nearly 200 miles, by which time we were running on the fumes that came from the last drops of petrol that Griffiths was squeezing out of the tanks.

'Came back to base today and found many missing and the rest scattered over England in various ways. More and more I find that knowledge is a more valued asset than courage. Each member of the Crew is still learning. Griffiths has found the best speeds to fly and rates of climb for most economical fuel consumption. We keep our own charts and are improving steadily.

'Two consecutive nights to Berlin leaves me with but one thought when I have finished this letter. To sleep for at least 12 hours. And my stomach reminds me that I haven't seen an egg for nearly a month and our food is very poor.'

The month of May 1943 opened on the 4/5th with the first major attack on Dortmund, by nearly 600 aircraft - the largest 'non-1,000' raid of the war to date. The largest mining town of the Westphalia coalfield and the southern terminus of the Dortmund-Ems Canal, Dortmund's industries included iron, steel, engineering and brewing. One of the 97 Squadron crews that took part was skippered by Squadron Leader Kenneth Holstead 'Bobby' Burns DFC, an American from Oregon, who had received the award of the DFC in February while on 61 Squadron. He lost the use of one engine on the outward flight. To continue offered the prospect of having to jink from night-fighters and flak with a lagging aircraft that might at any moment become completely unmanageable. Burns continued, got to the target, 'pranged' it and returned to Bourn, that dead engine still giving no sign of life. [90]

A few nights afterwards, on 13/14 May, 156 Lancasters and twelve Halifaxes set off on a long eight hour round trip to bomb the Skoda armaments factory at Pilzen in Czechoslovakia again. When all of two hundred miles distant from his target Burns ran into a thick curtain of flak. His aircraft was hit and the air-speed indicator rendered unserviceable. Burns again went on, knowing he would have to come back over territory where gunners would be waiting for him. He again bombed his target 'vigorously' and got home. His actions earned him the award of a bar to his DFC.

On the last night of August 1943 622 bombers of the Main Force assembled in a giant stream and headed for the 'Big City' once more. One of the ten Lancasters that failed to return was 'L-London' on 97 Squadron at Bourn flown by Wing Commander 'Bobby' Burns DFC* which was the victim of a head-on attack by a FW 190 a few minutes short of the target. Burns called to his crew: 'This is it. Out you go blokes.'

Pilot Officer Earle Dolby DFC the Canadian bomb aimer had asked if he should let the bombs go but Burns had said 'No - leave 'em be and I'll aim the kite where they'll do some good.' He trimmed the aircraft to head down for the already burning centre of Berlin ahead. Then he unclipped his seat harness and was just raising his hand to take off his helmet when there was a huge flash as the bombs exploded. Burns woke up lying on soft ground under some pine trees on the outskirts of Berlin. His right hand and half the forearm were missing. Strangely, as the numbness wore off, the worst pain came from his right ankle and foot. He looked at his watch. It was still ticking and he saw by the luminous hands that it was 3.30 - he had been there three-and-a-half hours.

Shakily he got to his feet. He found he could walk. Concerned that if he didn't get help quickly he would bleed to death, he looked around for a sign of habitation. It was then, for the first time, that he became aware of his seat-type parachute still dangling behind his thighs. Of course he must have come down by parachute - how otherwise could he be alive? But when he released the harness and the parachute fell to the ground he saw that the ripcord was still in position, that only one of the four flaps had burst open and that so little silk had been dragged out, it could only have cut his falling speed to a trifle below terminal velocity. When he crashed through the pine trees, however, it had undoubtedly played a decisive part in slowing him down before he hit the ground. For a moment he stood there while his mind tried to comprehend how he had achieved the apparently impossible, but he was in no condition for rational thought and presently, having dismissed it all from his mind, he staggered away from the spot. A signalman found the American wing commander near his signal box beside the tracks of a Berlin suburban railway. Still unconscious Burns was taken to the sick quarters at Tempelhof where he was given an immediate blood transfusion. Then he was rushed to hospital in north-west Berlin where doctors cleaned up the stump of his arm and drained one of his lungs which had been collapsed by the explosion and had filled with blood. Some weeks later when he had been moved to prison camp, it was found that Burns had yet another injury; his back was broken. In 1944 Burns was repatriated to England via Sweden. He recovered and after being fitted with a false hand, resumed his flying career. [91]

On 11 March 1943 Flying Officer Joseph Charles 'Big Joe' McCarthy DFC RCAF, a burly 23-year-old, 6-foot 3-inch Irish-American from New York City, had just beaten the odds by completing his first tour with 97 Squadron at Woodhall Spa. A few days later he received a telephone call from Guy Gibson. The 24 year old Wing Commander told him, 'I'm forming a new squadron. I can't tell you much about it except to say that we may only be doing one trip. I'd like you and your crew to join us.'

It was on 17 March that 'Squadron X' was formed, at Scampton in Lincolnshire. McCarthy, who was fascinated by all things aeronautical was a favourite of his fellow pilots and was known on the squadrons as 'the big blonde American'. On his uniform he wore dual shoulder flashes 'USA' and 'Canada'. Born in St. James, Long Island, on 31 August 1919 Joe McCarthy was raised in Brooklyn. His family had a summer home on Long Island where one of his summer jobs was as a life guard at Coney Island, the money helping to pay for private flying lessons at Roosevelt Field where, in 1927, Charles Lindbergh had taken off on his epic solo New York-to-Paris flight. In 1940-1941 McCarthy tried three times to join the US Army Air Corps but he never heard back from them! One of his neighbourhood lifelong friends was Donald Joseph Curtin who suggested that they enlist in the Royal Canadian Air Force. Because of the war, Curtin had been laid off from his job as a cruise director with the Holland America Steamship Company. McCarthy and Curtin boarded a bus and headed north for Ontario. They crossed the St. Lawrence River by ferry and the Canadian Customs helped them get a connecting bus to Ottawa. They spent the night at the YMCA and the following morning, 5 May 1941, they proceeded to the Recruiting Office. However, they were told to come back in six weeks! The two Yanks told the officials that they did not have the money to return again so if the RCAF wanted them they had better decide that day!' The Warrant Officer in charge took a second look at the two American volunteers, changed his mind and had them sign enlistment papers!

Pilot Officer Curtin went on to fly Lancasters at Syerston with 106 Squadron and he was awarded the DFC after his first sortie in July 1942 and a further award of a bar to his DFC was approved in January 1943. During the period Curtin was with 106 Squadron Guy Gibson was his commanding officer. It was during a visit to see Curtin at Syerston that McCarthy first met Gibson. He remembered him as one of those men to whom leadership came as naturally as breathing; autocratic and impatient at times, yet commanding instant respect. It was a foregone certainly that Curtin would have been invited to join 'Squadron X' if he and his crew had not been lost in a Lancaster over Nuremberg on the night of 25/26 February. Don and his crew were buried in the war Graves Cemetery in Dumbach, Germany.

All but one of Joe McCarthy's crew of six eventually decided to follow their aircraft captain to Squadron 'X'. Sergeant George L. Johnson his bomb aimer, almost did not make it, as he was due to get married on 3 April and his bride to be had warned him that if he was not there on that date then he needn't 'bother to come at all.' McCarthy with his customary directness told Gibson that they had finished their tour and were entitled to leave. They got four days leave and Johnson made it to the church on time.

Of the 133 men who would crew the Lancasters on the secret operation only twenty of them were decorated. Gibson selected many of these such as McCarthy, Hopgood, Burpee and Shannon, personally. He chose Squadron Leader Henry Melvin 'Dinghy' Young DFC* who came from 57 Squadron at Scampton, as his 'A' Flight Commander. Young's father Henry was a solicitor and a second lieutenant in the Queen's Royal West Surrey Regiment and his mother, Fannie Forrester Young, formerly Rowan, was an American from a socially prominent Los Angeles family. Sister of a well-known architect and used to moving in glossy social circles, she was a graduate of the Marlborough School for Girls in Los Angeles and of the Mount Vernon Seminary in Washington DC. She married Henry Young in California in 1913 and moved to London with him. Their son was born in Belgravia on 20 May 1915. The family split up briefly in 1928, Fannie moving back to Los Angeles with young Henry and putting him in the Webb School and later the Kent School in Connecticut and Pomona College, Claremont, California. Father Henry came out to join them but by 1933 his career in American law had not prospered, so he took the boy away to London again. By 1938 that boy was a student of Trinity College, Oxford where he studied law and was an Oxford rowing Blue, rowing at number two in the University Boat Race, rowing weight 12 stone 12lbs. After four miles and 374 yards, or 20 minutes and 3 seconds of supreme physical effort the Oxford crew crossed the finishing line two lengths ahead of Cambridge and a thousand hats were thrown into the air, seen for the first time on television by the very few people who had them. Pilot Officer Henry Young, down from the varsity with his pal Leonard Cheshire, turned up at RAF Driffield in the East Riding of Yorkshire, home of 102 Squadron, in June 1940. Cheshire would become legendary in RAF Bomber Command, finishing the war with the VC, a bar to his DSO and the DFC.

In 1940 102 Squadron were equipped with the Whitley. Earlier versions of this aircraft had been barely able to reach 200 mph in level flight unladen and carrying their 7,000lb bomb load they cruised more around the 130mph mark. By this time they had Rolls-Royce Merlin engines and could make a better effort, although were still very slow and cumbersome compared to the German fighters. Relatively the opposite on the road was Leonard Cheshire's car, a Bentley Speed Six, top speed 84mph, one of the marque that, according to Ian Fleming, a certain Mr. Bond, James Bond, had put in store for the duration. As Cheshire and Young disembarked, among the small crowd of admiring officers around them that afternoon was Pilot Officer Geoff Womersley (later Group Captain DSO DFC) who, as well as flying regular ops, was responsible for getting the squadron's new boys' flying up to scratch. Later in the war, pilots would arrive on squadron with 450 hours in their log books flying single-, twin- and four-engined aircraft, plus another 50 or so, on the Link flight simulation trainer. RAF Bomber Command in 1940 was not quite so fussy, especially if the chaps were the right sort. Womersley commented: 'Young and Cheshire arrived with about 50 hours each on Tiger Moths. I was the squadron instructor and these were the first pilots sent to us from the university air squadron. They'd had no twin-engined training at all, so I took them up in our Whitleys for day and night flying.'

The first of Young's ditchings which earned him his nickname was in a Whitley on 7 October 1940 when he and his crew spent 22 hours in a dinghy in the Atlantic before being rescued. Henry Young's flight commander on operations was Squadron Leader O. A. Morris. Who recalls:

'We were attached to Coastal Command for a while in September and October 1940, hunting for U-boats and protecting convoys, operating out of tents at Prestwick with packing cases for furniture. It was not a popular posting. We had no training for a maritime role and no instructions about what we were supposed to be doing. Our Whitleys were not suited to the job either. For a start they wouldn't take the standard depth charge so had to be modified and we soon found out that low flying over the sea made the engines liable to fail. One chap who could certainly vouch for that was Flying Officer Young, who was well out in the Atlantic when his engines stopped. After a considerable time in the little dinghy they issued you with, the crew were picked up by an American destroyer, one crossing the ocean on the lend/lease scheme. Anyway, it had a photographer on board from Life magazine and this was just the ticket for him and a well illustrated feature subsequently appeared. It happened on 7 October and they had been in that little dinghy for 22 hours before Town Class destroyer HMS *St Mary*, ex-US Navy, picked them up.'

'Many people have said what a welcome addition the American destroyers would be to our fleet' wrote Young. 'I am sure that no one is likely to give them a more hearty and grateful welcome than that given by my crew and myself one afternoon a couple of weeks ago, when, after drifting aimlessly about in a rubber dinghy off the coast of Ireland for a very long time we suddenly saw on the crest of a wave the funnels of a destroyer. It happened like this: We had been detailed to escort a convoy and had met it inward bound at about midday. Several hours later while we were still on patrol, the rear-gunner reported a trace of smoke from the starboard engine. I could see very little myself; the oil and radiator temperatures were quite normal and I was not unduly worried. I decided, however, to return to base at once and the wireless operator reported to base that we were doing so. But almost immediately our trouble increased, the engine got very hot - and so did I - and it was only a matter of a very few minutes before we found ourselves cooling rather rapidly in the Atlantic.

'I saw clouds of smoke pouring from the engine, the temperatures shot right up and 1 had to throttle the engine back to prevent it catching fire. We were only at about 500 feet at the time and the aircraft would not maintain height on the other engine. I told the crew to stand by for a landing on the sea and out dinghy drill had to be carried out pretty rapidly. The tail-gunner came forward to the dinghy, the second pilot and the navigator went aft, followed by the wireless operator after he had finished sending his SOS. They all braced themselves for the shock of hitting the water, This we must have done with quite a crack, in spite of my efforts to hold off as long as possible and reduce speed, as the fuselage broke nearly in two just forward of the leading edge of the wings. The cockpit immediately began to fill with water and I thought it was time for me to be moving. I climbed out through the escape hatch in the roof and found the rest of the crew in the sea with the dinghy which was just opening.

'I scrambled across the gap in the fuselage and walked aft. The dinghy was fully open and the rope tying it to the aircraft had been cut but it was still caught in the angle between the fuselage and tailplane so I was able to step straight into it. This was a great stroke of luck as the hardest job is usually to get the first man into the boat. We pushed ourselves clear of the aircraft and then I helped the crew in. The wireless operator was the most urgent case as he had hit himself jumping in and had swallowed a lot of salt water when he went under; he was very nearly unconscious. We got him in after quite a struggle and the rest of the crew came aboard in turn. The aircraft had sunk by the time the last had got in. This happened at about four o'clock in the afternoon; there were about three hours of daylight remaining and of course we hoped very much that our SOS would have been received and that we should be picked up or at least sighted that afternoon. We were at the time within sight of land, but a strong south-westerly wind was carrying us away out to sea. Darkness fell without a sight of ships or aircraft and we resigned ourselves to at least another fourteen hours afloat. At first we could see the beam from a lighthouse, but that disappeared by midnight, as the wind which was increasing nearly to gale force blew us farther from land.

'There were only three things to do all night, to keep awake, to keep warm and to try and keep the boat as dry as possible. We had all, except the rear gunner, swallowed some salt water and were seasick. I was lucky and was not very bad, but some felt most unhappy inside all night and wanted very much to go to sleep. However we all kept awake and found three exercises which seemed the most practicable for keeping warm. First we would pat our hands briskly on our thighs; that warmed both hands and thighs and was our commonest exercise, which later in the night we did about every ten minutes.

Then we did the 'cabman's swing' swinging our arms across our chests as taxi-drivers do on cold days and we found that good for keeping the circulation going. Finally we smacked each other on the back. I must have been somewhat vigorous in this last exercise as my neighbour said it was too much like being hit by a pile-driver. We did our best to keep cheerful and as my watch was watertight and working I reported the time every half-hour and the number of hours to daylight. It was a great landmark at one in the morning when the night was half over and then six hours only to go.

'I found also that I kept warm by baling out the water, which we did with my shoes. At first we shipped water quite often as the tops of the waves broke over us. Later, though the seas were steadily rising with the wind increasing through the night, we became quite expert at riding the huge Atlantic rollers and found that if we kept two of us facing into the wind and two with their backs to it we could watch the waves and by leaning away from the bad ones ease ourselves over the top of them without shipping water very often.

'The night passed very slowly indeed. I had decided not to open the rations till morning as I knew we should be much hungrier then. I am afraid I adopted rather a Captain Bligh of the Bounty line over the rations as I wanted to make them last for three days. Dawn crept upon us at about six-thirty after an apparently interminable night of back-slapping and wave-climbing. It was quite light by seven-thirty and we were out of sight of land, but suddenly to our joy we saw a ship in the west. It got larger and was heading almost in our direction; then it altered course and came straight for us. We stood up in turn and waved and we all shouted, but she was to windward and neither saw nor heard us. We could see her quite clearly and she passed within two or three hundred yards and was, I think, a small armed merchantman. That was a dreadful disappointment as we had practically decided what we would have for breakfast; biscuits and brackish water were a very poor substitute for bacon and eggs. However as some slight consolation and to warm us I allowed us each a very small swallow from our rum flask, which I was saving for emergencies.

'We saw several aircraft during the morning, but even those fairly near did not spot us because the sea was a mass of white horses. About ten o'clock the rear gunner was washed overboard by a wave breaking crossways over us, although he was sitting on his hands holding the rope as we all did. However, he kept his hold and we got him aboard again and did our best to warm him up with rum and exercise.

'At midday there were more biscuits and Horlicks tablets for lunch, but I don't think we were really hungry yet as some of the crew wouldn't eat their biscuits. I told the crew that we should probably have to spend another night in the dinghy and they stayed remarkably cheerful in spite of this dreary prospect. Suddenly about 2 pm we thought we saw some ships in the distance. All the morning, however, we had been seeing low islands and lighthouses which proved to be merely the crests of waves breaking in the distance, so I didn't have much faith in any of these ships. Then we started looking round again and to our joy saw from the crest of a wave a flotilla of destroyers steaming towards us in line abreast. The second pilot recognised the four funnels and flush deck of the American destroyers and we thought that they would pass on either side of us. Then as they drew near, they altered course away from us so that we passed to port of the port ship of the line. We held the rear-gunner up and he waved our green canvas paddle. Just as we had about given up hope again we saw people waving from the decks and she turned in a circle round us. Soon after she came alongside and threw us a line, at first shouting directions in German, as they had mistaken our uniforms.

'The ship was rolling heavily and when our navigator caught hold of the rope ladder he could not get a foothold and as his hands were too cold to keep a grip he fell into the sea. A sailor at once jumped in, put a line round him and he was lifted out. The rest of the crew and myself were able to climb aboard. We were taken below and had our skin practically rubbed off us before we were wrapped in blankets and put in officers' cabins, with tea and rum and hot food, all extremely welcome.

'As soon as I was warm I borrowed some clothes and went on the bridge to thank the captain. I learned that it was he who had first spotted us when he saw through his glass our yellow skull-caps and life-saving jackets and dinghy, which he thought was some wreckage as we appeared and disappeared on the distant waves.

'We were all made most abundantly welcome by the Navy and went ashore that night very happy men indeed.'

After the maritime interlude, the squadron moved back to bombing duties at RAF Topcliffe, north Yorkshire, a new station but still a grass field where bad weather caused many problems with boggy take-offs and landings.

Young and his crew were rescued again, on 23/24 November when, following the raid on Turin, he was forced to ditch in the sea off Torcross, Devon. Again he and his crew were rescued. In May 1941 'Dinghy' Young was awarded the DFC for his service on 102 Squadron and a bar followed in September 1942 when he completed a tour on 104 Squadron.[92]

The following summer he married his 33-year old American fiancée, Priscilla Lawson, a graduate of Brearley School, New York and Bryn Mawr College. Young has been described as, 'a large, calm man' and 'a very efficient organizer'. 'His favourite trick was to swallow a pint of beer without drawing breath.' By mid 1943 he had completed 65 ops, the most famous raid by 617 Squadron, on the Ruhr dams, still to come.

Before take off the crews went through a variety of rituals. 'Dinghy' Young tidied his room, several played cards, rolled dice and or dozed, many wrote letters home.

Joe McCarthy, commander of the second wave assigned to attack the Sorpe dam and his crew climbed into 'Q for Queenie'. A bouncing bomb attack would be ineffective against this target because an earthen wall surrounded the dam's concrete core so McCarthy would have to make a conventional bomb drop. However, during the pre-flight check 'Q for Queenie' was found to have a coolant leak in the starboard outer engine and the aircraft had to go unserviceable. Then only reserve Lancaster was ED825 AJ-T which had been flown from Boscombe Down that afternoon by a ferry pilot. Although 'T-Tommy' was bombed up there had been no time to fit a VHF radio or Aldis lamps. McCarthy and his crew jumped out of 'Q-Queenie', the big American snagging his parachute on a hook in the process and finally they got all moveable equipment out of the aircraft and rushed over to 'T-Tommy'. There they found that the compass deviation card vital for accurately flying the carefully charted route was not in the cockpit. The chances of flying the Lancaster at low level (between 75- and 120-feet) through the myriad of flak emplacements and around night fighter bases, which lay between them and their target, were zero without it. Joe McCarthy climbed down from the cockpit for the second time that evening and with his 'Irish Temper' near boiling point, jumped into a truck and headed for the hangar where he ran into Flight Sergeant G. E. 'Chiefy' Powell, 617's Senior NCO. After a very short, expletive-filled, one-sided conversation, Powell took off at the double to the squadron's instrument section. He was unsure of what exactly he was looking for but he managed somehow to locate a blank card. He thrust another parachute into the impatient pilot's lap and McCarthy headed off to the hard stand where the compass was swung with 'Upkeep;' in position. He finally got airborne at 2201, thirty-four minutes behind his section. By the time 'T-Tommy' reached Vlieland, at 2313, McCarthy had reduced the deficit to 21½ minutes. He received a 'hot reception from the natives' when 'T-Tommy' crossed the coastline. 'They knew the track we were coming in on, so their guns were pretty well trained when they heard my motors. But, thank God, there were two large sand dunes right on the coast which I sank in between.'

The Lancasters took off in three waves. The first nine aircraft were to target the Möhne and then carry on to the Eder dam followed by other targets as directed by wireless from 5 Group Headquarters. The second wave of five was to act as a diversionary force and to attack the Sorpe and the final five were detailed as back-up aircraft with alternative targets at Achwelm, Ennerpe and Dieml dams if they were not needed in the main attacks. The first wave would fly in three sections of three aircraft about ten minutes apart. After crossing the north-west coast of The Wash about five miles north-east of Boston, their route was across Norfolk past East Dereham and Wymondham near Norwich to Bungay in Suffolk and on to Southwold before heading out across the North Sea to Holland to the Möhne. The second wave would fly a different route to confuse enemy defences, to the Sorpe dam. This route was slightly further via the Friesians Islands so the second wave actually took off first. The third wave of five Lancasters was to set off later and act as a mobile reserve to be used against such dams as were still unbroken.

The fourth and fifth hits on the Möhne dam by Squadron Leader 'Dinghy' Young DFC* and Squadron Leader David J. H. Maltby finally breached the structure at 0056 hours. Melvin Young's nickname 'Dinghy' was transmitted back to 5 Group Headquarters to be received with yet more celebration but his Lancaster was hit by flak at Castricum-aan-Zee, Holland and crashed into the sea with the loss of all the crew. Melvin Young was 27 years old.

The Lancasters flown by Flight Sergeant Ken Brown and Flight Lieutenant Joe McCarthy headed for the 226 feet high Sorpe dam at the northern end of the Sorpe River. It had been realised quite late in the day that this was effective if the dam was built of concrete but no good for an earth dam, as the Sorpe was. Their instructions therefore, were to fly over and along the line of the dam at 60 feet, releasing the bomb as near the centre of the dam as they could.

Arriving over the valley at fifteen minutes after midnight, Joe McCarthy initiated a diving attack on the dam nestled at the bottom of two steep hills. As the Lancaster circled over Langscheid, McCarthy exploded; 'Jeez! How do we get down there?' He decided that he must go round the church steeple of the village to line up his run. Coming over the top of one hill, using full flaps to keep the speed of his 30-ton Lancaster under control, McCarthy dived down the slope toward the 765-yard long dam. To escape, he had to apply full power to his four Packard-built Rolls-Royce Merlins and climb at a steep angle up the side of the second hill. And if that wasn't difficult enough, a thick mist was filling the valley as he arrived. The blinding moonlight turned the mist into a writhing phosphorescent pall, which made it extremely difficult to judge the bomber's height above the lake. On the third attempt to locate the target, McCarthy almost flew 'T-For-Tommy' into the water. It was not until the tenth run that bomb-aimer, Sergeant George 'Johnny' Johnson, was satisfied and released the bomb from a height of just 90-feet. The weapon exploded squarely on top of the parapet, damaging and crumbling for more than 50-yards the crown of the earthen wall.

Shortly thereafter Flight Sergeant Ken Brown attacked the dam and then they transmitted 'Goner', indicating that they had attacked but not breached the dam.

The 'last resort' targets, the Lister (Schweim) and Dieml dams were not attacked. However, the damage inflicted in the first two attacks proved the operation's success. The surge of water from the Möhne and Eder dams knocked out power stations and damaged factories and cut water, gas and electricity supplies. As many as 1,300 civilians, including about 500 Ukrainian women slave labourers, died. Eight Lancasters were lost, 53 men were killed and three were captured. Joe McCarthy, David Maltby, Mick Martin, Dave Shannon and Les Knight were awarded the DSO.

It was decided to keep the Dam Busters in being as an 'old lags' squadron (Harris' affectionate and respectful name for experienced men who only wanted to fly ops) and to use it for independent precision raids on small targets. These would be carried out using the Stabilising Automatic Bomb Sight (SABS), which had been invented at Farnbrough in 1941 and incorporated a bulky gyro. In perfect conditions SABS could aim a bomb very accurately but a bomber using it had to run perfectly straight and level up to the target for ten miles. Harris said this would result in too many bomber losses but the argument was that SABS could be used economically by a small force operating at a fraction under 20,000 feet over a well marked target. At 5 Group the Air Officer Commanding (AOC), Air Vice Marshal The Honourable Sir Ralph A. Cochrane KBE CB AFC intended that 617 be trained to use SABS and deliver Barnes Wallis' new ten-ton bombs coming off the drawing board. In the meantime, the targets on the night of 15/16 July were two power and transformer stations in Northern Italy. The intention was to disrupt the supply of electricity to the railways carrying German troops and supplies to the battle front in Sicily using twelve Lancasters of 617 Squadron a dozen more from 5 Group. Six of the Dam Busters were led by Holden to Aquata Scrivia near Genoa and the other six to San Pola D'Enza near Bologna were led by Dams' veteran Squadron Leader David J. H. Maltby DSO DFC. The raids were not successful. No flares or markers were carried and the targets were partially hidden by haze. After bombing the Lancasters flew on to Blida in North Africa. There was little opposition and two Lancasters of the supporting force were lost.

All the Dam Busters landed safely at Blida where Flight Lieutenant Joe McCarthy DSO DFC threw his parachute down digustedly and said, 'If we'd only carried flares we could've seen what we were doing.' In North Africa bad weather grounded the Lancasters for ten days and they finally flew home via Leghorn where bombs were dropped through the persistant haze into the harbour below. Back at Scampton the crews unloaded the Lancasters. In spite of everything they could hardly regard it as a fruitless trip as they struggled to the mess with crates of figs, dates oranges, bottles of red wine and Benedictine.

In September 1943 when 617 Squadron were tasked with bombing the Dortmund-Ems Canal at Ladbergen Squadron Leader Harold Lisson, a Canadian Mosquito pilot from Edmonton was sent to Coningsby to help 617 Squadron on a special job. 'We had about two weeks training with them in preparation for the forthcoming moon period - low level (150 feet) - formation flying with the Lancasters at night without lights of any sort. We got in a good deal of practice before our first attempt. The Lancasters carried 12,000lb of bombs with 90-second delays. This allowed them to drop their bombs one at a time and get far enough away so that the blast would not affect them. The Mossies' job was to beat up searchlights and gun positions and deal with any night fighters. Our force was to consist of eight Lancs and six Mossies and our target was the Dortmund-Ems canal, just on the edge of the Ruhr Valley. On the night of our first attempt the weather was a bit doubtful inland so we sent a Mosquito on ahead to recce. He contacted us with a duff report just before we reached the Dutch coast, so we turned back. One of the Lancs struck the water during the turn and blew up, but the rest of us got back safely. The following night we again set out. This time we were blessed by good weather until we were about two minutes from the target, when we ran into heavy industrial haze from the Ruhr. On the way in, the leading Lanc was shot down over a small German town and his 12,000 pounder blew up and flames shot 2,000 feet into the air. I'm sure the entire town must have been destroyed. Over the target the flak was heavy and searchlights seemed everywhere. As a result we were kept extremely busy. Four of the eight Lancs were shot down in the area but the remaining fellows had a lot of guts and carried on. One Australian, Flight Lieutenant Mickey Martin, spent 84 minutes in the target area before he found the spot and dropped his bombs. We figure that about lour bombs were dropped in the canal and it was definitely breached and draining when I left.'

It was exactly four months after the famous Ruhr dams' raid, on the night of 15/16 September, when 617 Squadron were tasked to carry out a raid on the banks of the Dortmund-Ems Canal at Ladbergen. The first attempt the night before had been aborted. [93] Squadron Leader David Maltby DSO DFC and crew, all of whom had flown on the dam's raid, were lost on the way home eight miles north-east of Cromer when their Lancaster hit someone's slipstream and cart-wheeled into the North Sea. [94] With little sleep, eight of the crews were ordered back into the air the very next night to try again with the 12,000lb light-case bombs. Ray Grayston, the recently commissioned flight engineer on 'N-Nan' captained by Pilot Officer Les Knight DSO RAAF, says, 'We didn't think it was a very good idea and we were right'. This time the delayed-fuse mines were even bigger.

In the control tower at Coningsby Joe McCarthy, now a Squadron Leader with a DSO for the Dams raid and a bar to his DFC added at the beginning of his third tour, watched as the eight Lancasters took off and headed east for the Dortmund-Ems Canal at around midnight. Outwardly McCarthy had a personality that matched his physique. His colourful American expletives were freely lavished on all who crossed his path. This was in marked contrast to the more austere profanity of the British pilots. Also watching was a 'languid' WAAF who said, as the Lancasters merged with the darkness, 'My God, I only hope they get there tonight! The trouble the AOC's gone to over this...' McCarthy turned on her and snarled, 'The hell with you and all the AOCs. What about the seven lives in every kite!' The building vibrated as the door slammed behind him. [95]

The attack on the Dortmund-Ems Canal was led by Squadron Leader George Holden DSO DFC* MiD in 'S-Sugar'. 'We didn't think it was a very good idea,' says Dams veteran, Pilot Officer Ray Grayston, flight engineer on 'N for Nan'. 'And we were right. The new CO took us across the Dutch coast and over an industrial area with no shortage of anti-aircraft batteries. Bang, bang, bang and all of his fuel tanks were hit. There was a mile of burning fuel flying out behind him and we were panicking to get out of the way before his mine went off. We just made it clear of him as he dropped out of the sky.'[96] At the target area there was fog and we couldn't even see the ground. We circled at low level and saw a couple of guys fly into the deck. Then we did too. I jumped out at about 800 feet and the chute opened. The Lanc flew straight into a tree, caught fire and Les was killed.' Flight Lieutenant Les Knight DSO RAAF was later Mentioned In Dispatches for holding his Lancaster steady so that all his crew could bail out. What Ray Grayston did not know until after the war was that he was one of the lucky ones. Out of the eight Lancasters on the canal raid, only three returned.

One of the growing band of 'star-spangled' pilots who flew a Lancaster on the night of 23/24 September 1943 when 627 bombers set out for Mannheim, was Pilot Officer 'Nick' Knilans. He already knew the odds. Bomber Command was in the midst of an offensive against German cities with four raids on Hannover in September-October. Hannover had been the target for 711 bombers the night before. The Main Force had arrived over the city in good weather but there was a stronger wind than forecast and most of the attack fell up to five miles from the aiming point and at the end as far as nine miles from the AP. It did not help when the backers up aimed their TI greens at reds instead of yellows. Some 2,500 tons of bombs were dropped mainly in suburban areas and open country. At least 20 out of the 26 bombers lost were shot down over the target by both single-engined and twin-engined night fighters that engaged the bomber stream en masse and in Wild Boar fashion over the burning city under attack. Flak too was 'intense'. There was no reason to think that Mannheim's defences would be any different.

On the outward flight Knilans experienced divine intervention. 'The upper sky before me was still somewhat lighted. A figure of a woman, several thousand feet above slowly emerged into my startled view. I recognized this vision as that of a girl I had loved very much. She had died six years before at the age of 19. I had kissed her goodbye one evening and a short while later her feather had telephoned me to say that she was dead from pneumonia, unsuspected until it was too late. I had been one of the pall bearers. Now, she had a slight smile on her lips as I flew towards her… The vision soon vanished into the darkening sky. I said nothing to the crew then or later. I did not know whether she had appeared to reassure me that she would keep me from harm, or that she was welcoming me into her world of the hereafter. I certainly hoped it wouldn't be the latter…Maybe, I thought, someone was trying to point, for me, a way…' [97]

Knilans would remain at Woodhall Spa for eighteen months of operations on 619 Squadron and in that time 42 Lancasters with 294 men aboard were lost and most of them killed. In the first six months, no crew was able to complete its first tour. One Canadian pilot's hair turned from brown to grey before he was shot down. The strain of continuous operations began to affect Knilans' 22-year old rear gunner, Sergeant Gordon Hunter 'Gerry' Jackson, a Scot from Dumfries. When he received a telegram from his wife Phoebe in Scotland that he had a new-born son, Jackson rushed over to see Acting Wing Commander William 'Jock' Abercromby and he asked to be taken off flying duties. Abercromby was thirty-three years old and from Inverness-shire. The 'Wingco' told Jackson that he was due for leave in a week's time and that he could see the baby then. In the meantime the rear gunner had to remain on flying status.

On 4/5 October 1943 the target was Frankfurt. Pilot Officer 'Nick' Knilans' crew on 619 Squadron At Woodhall Spa were 'on' also. Wing Commander 'Jock' Abercromby had told the American Skipper that Gerry Jackson was deeply troubled but Knilans said nothing to his rear gunner. He did not need to know that his Skipper knew. As they assembled around the Lancaster before take-off they congratulated Jackson on the birth of his son. 'He was a chain smoker anyway,' recalled Knilans 'so no one thought of his nervousness as anything out of the ordinary. He seemed less despondent as we took our stations. At 21.21 hours we were at 19,000 feet over Germany and turning for our target when 'Monica', the fighter-detection device, indicated an aircraft within 300 yards, which we believed to be another Lancaster - until a stream of tracer cannon and machine gun bullets came through the port wing and thudded into the fuselage. I dived to starboard and yelled down the intercom to Gerry; 'Can you see him?'

There was no reply. Roy, the mid-upper gunner, noticed tracer entering the rear turret and causing an explosion and he was temporarily blinded by Perspex, which hit him in the eyes. We had to feather the port inner engine but we went on to bomb and stayed with the stream.'

Heading for home Nick Knilans had dropped to 12,000 feet and he sent the flight engineer aft to check on Gerry Jackson. He found him slumped over his guns. 'When we landed,' recalls Knilans, 'I told the crew they need not stay on to see Jerry taken from his turret. The ground crew were unable to open the turret doors, as the force of the cannon shells had driven Jerry against them and I had to use a screwdriver to prise them apart. Then I got hold of Jerry's collar and pulled him backwards, free of the turret. His body was stiff as I lowered it to the ground and took off his goggles, oxygen mask and helmet. His still features were unmarked. I brushed back a fallen lock of hair. His forehead was icy cold. The middle of his flying suit was badly torn and bloodstained. After examining him, one of the ambulance helpers suddenly became ill and had to walk away. The cannon shells had cut Jerry in half.

'I stayed behind in the darkness, depressed at losing my friend. When I got to the briefing room the Squadron doctor told me that Jerry must have died instantaneously. He gave me two sleeping pills but I gave them to a WAAF who was overcome with grief. She was a good friend of Jerry's and he had given her his personal effects to send to his parents if he failed to return. Before drifting off to sleep, I prayed that God would see Jerry into heaven.'[98]

In his office on the same airfield Abercromby tore up the pass for Jerry Jackson. A telegram would be going out to the gunner's next-of-kin. At Bardney a similarly worded telegram was being sent to Kathleen Leslie in Romford telling her that her husband Angus was dead.[99]

By 26 November 'Nick' Knilans on 619 Squadron was no longer a Pilot Officer, having been promoted to Lieutenant USAAF. That night he would pilot a Lancaster on the raid on Berlin A rear gunner who had already flown a tour replaced Jerry Jackson who had been killed over Kassel in October but he failed to show up to fly the NFT that afternoon. He did however show up in time for the take off. The Berlin force totalled over 440 Lancasters and seven Mosquitoes, the procession taking 45 minutes to cross the coast. Another 157 Halifaxes and 21 Lancasters flew a diversion on Stuttgart. Both forces flew a common route over Northern France and nearing Frankfurt they split. At first the JLOs thought that Frankfurt was the intended target. The difficult weather conditions had resulted in only the most experienced German crews being ordered to take off and 84 fighters engaged the RAF formations. I Jagdivision downed most of the 27 bombers that were shot down on the raid on the 'Big City' while from the smaller force seven Halifaxes were shot down by flak and fighters and a Halifax crashed on take-off at the start of the operation. Just two German night fighter aircraft were lost.

The weather was clear over Berlin but, after their long approach flight from the south, the Path Finders marked an area 6-7 miles north-west of the city centre and most aircraft bombed there. Damage was considerable and civilian casualties were high. Thirty-eight war industry factories were destroyed and many more damaged. Combined casualties for the three raids late that month had resulted in the deaths of 4,330 people killed and over 417,000 people were rendered homeless for more than a month and over 36,300 up to a month [100] Goebbels wrote 'the English [sic] aimed so accurately that one might think spies had pointed the way.'

Nick Knilans' Lancaster was attacked three times by enemy fighters. One of his engines was damaged and the American pilot feathered the propeller. The replacement rear gunner who had missed the NFT earlier in the day said that his guns were U/S and returned no fire on their attackers. Knilans lost height but continued to the target. He approached Berlin out of the darkness and the streets and the buildings began to take shape. Crossing the city amidst heavy flak bursts the rear gunner twice yelled 'we're not going to make it'. Knilans 'shut him up'. Later he would have the Gunnery Leader replace him. For the moment Knilans had other things to think about. 'From our height, with the flares above and hundreds of searchlights below, the scene became increasingly clear. It was a vivid and dramatic moment. Blockbusters, looking like 50-gallon oil drums, were tumbling down past us from the bombers above. Amid all the buffeting and noise of the light and heavy ack-ack, Ken Ryall my 18-year old flight engineer spoke up. 'Should we pray, Skipper?'

'No' I replied, 'not while we are about to kill more old men, women and children down there.'

At Woodhall Spa on 5 June 1944 everyone on 617 Dam Busters Squadron was confined to camp. One of the pilots was Flight Lieutenant Hubert C. 'Nick' Knilans. The American, who had flown a first tour on 619 and who would finish the war with both the DSO and DFC, had joined 617 Squadron at Woodhall on 14 January. On 1 June, when Avro experts had installed new automatic pilots in sixteen Lancasters for the D-Day operation, Knilans at last found out why his much-cursed 'R-Roger' flew like a lump of lead and had so often frightened his crew. The elevators had been put on upside down at the factory and 'Roger' needed longer elevator cables than the other Lancasters on the station. Knilans had been flying the aircraft for months like that and, as Wing Commander Leonard Cheshire VC DSO** DFC said 'only you and God, Nicky, know how you stayed up.'

'Not me, sirrrr,' Knilans drawled ... 'Only God. I didn't know.'[101]

On 6/7 June Argentan, Conde and Lisieux were next. 5 Group's Lancasters attacked Argentan with more than 100 aircraft and everything appeared to go well. But at 02.28 hours, 'A-Apple' and 23-year old Flight Sergeant Cliff King's crew on 9 Squadron at Bardney contacted Waddington direction finding (DF) believed asking for a weather report. Due to the weak signal, Waddington reported back the message and at 02.42 hours sent a weather report. Neither message was acknowledged. Later it was learned that 'A-Apple' had collided with trees and crashed near Belvoir Castle in the Leicestershire Wolds not far from Grantham. Only the rear gunner survived. King, whose commission had come through the day before and who had a wife in Boscombe, died at the controls of the Lancaster. The other five men on his crew, which included the navigator, 20-year old Flight Sergeant James Morton Stevenson RCAF were killed. Stevenson's parents had emigrated from Scotland to the USA and had gone to live in Parkchester in the Bronx district of New York. Their son had completed his first trip on 28 May when the squadron flew a feint towards the German battery at Ste-Martin-de-Varreville at Cherbourg. He too would not get to wear his Pilot Officer rings on his sleeves or enjoy the modest increase in pay, still way short by USAAF standards.

On the morning of 12 June 1944 Sergeant (later Flying Officer) Clayton Moore, a farm boy from Saskatchewan, Canada, rear gunner on the crew of William E. 'Bill' Siddle on 9 Squadron, got 'nobbled' by Group Captain 'Tiny' Evans-Evans, the Coningsby Station commander, for a daylight outing in ND966 (OU-C). 'Known to most of us as 'Evans Squared', the Group Captain was a typical RAF 'old boy' of enormous proportions, complete with the traditional ginger handlebar moustache. Although it was not unknown for him to be found on the battle order with a scratch crew, [102] he usually went about his business in a Spitfire which he had somehow acquired for his personal use, having first had the cockpit modified so that it could accommodate his ample frame. He was nonetheless anxious to keep his hand in as a Lancaster pilot and it was for this reason that I had been selected to make up a crew for him that day.

'After a short gunnery exercise over the wash, we headed south, to an American bomber base at Alconbury, near Huntingdon. It appeared that the Group Captain had some business or other to conduct there, so we landed and parked our Lancaster outside the control tower. The engines were switched off and we all piled out, to be met by a group of American airmen intent on having a good look over our aircraft. I engaged in conversation with an air gunner and learned from him that they were all waiting for the return of the station's aircraft from a raid on Germany. He wanted to know what it was like to fly alone over enemy territory in darkness without an escort. I replied that I preferred this to their method of attacking a target in daylight, flying in formation and thus being prevented from dodging at attacker as we cold. The debate continued, during which he pointed out our inferior fire power and our lack of a system of collective defence, plus the danger of collision in the dark.

'The American and I had agreed to differ on the friendliest of terms by the time the expected appearance of the returning Fortresses took place. As they joined the circuit for landing, my friend grew silent, anxiously counting their number, it was obvious to me that they had been subjected to a severe trouncing. More than one had a prop feathered and as each touched down on the nearby runway, the amount of damage that it had suffered could be clearly seen. Personnel carriers were by now making their way out to the dispersals, together with a couple of ambulances. One of the latter was already removing casualties from a Fortress that had not yet reached its pan, but had stopped just off the runway to effect the transfer.

'As the crew transports began to unload their cargoes of weary airmen near to where I was standing, I was struck by the look of fatigue, fear and relief on the battle beg rimed faces of the men as they passed on their way to debriefing. Silently they walked, unsmiling and grim faced; each registering shock at the significance of his recent experience. It occurred to me that they had probably witnessed in the cold light of day the killing of men who were known to them personally. Friends and mess mates whose identity would have been evident from the markings on the aircraft as it went down. Maybe it had been alongside in the formation when it was cut from the section by cannon shells. In my mind's eye I pictured the big silver plane dropping slowly out of the formation with smoke and flames streaming out behind it, setting fire to the clothing of those who had managed to bail out. Or maybe the bomb load had been detonated by a flak strike, causing the doomed aircraft to bring one or more of the others down with it. I had heard that the Luftwaffe fighters were now experimenting with the dropping of small bombs amongst the tightly-packed formations from above with some degree of success and that a new tactic involving a concerted head on attack by cannon-firing fighters was also showing some promise.

'As I continued to observe the passing procession, my American friend pointed to one of the men approaching us and asked if I recognised him. My first impression was that the man was older than most of the others - probably in his mid thirties. He was carrying a bulky parachute and his flying helmet dangled from its lead at his side. His battle beg rimed face bore the same tired and frightened look as the others around him, one of which I noted was carrying a large cine camera. The subject of my scrutiny sported a well groomed black moustache, but his equally dark hair had been flattened and disarranged by the wearing of the flying helmet. As I continued to study his features, a flicker of recognition at last came over me 'It can't be him, but by God, he sure looks like Clarke Gable' I retorted. 'Right first time Buddy! He got caught in the draft, so he's over here doing his share with the rest of us'.

'It was lunchtime, so I was treated to a slap-up meal, together with Gerry Parker our American mid-upper gunner (who had also been detailed by the Group Captain for the flight), after which Gerry and I shot a game of pool and I bought some Sweet Caporals for Rosanna and me. Meanwhile, the Group Captain had gone for a local flip in a Fortress, so it was late afternoon before we boarded our Lanc for the return flight to Coningsby.

'I had thoroughly enjoyed my brief visit to Alconbury and was particularly impressed by the free and easy attitude displayed by the many Yankee airmen I had met. Although life on a Path Finder squadron was a big improvement on that which I had experienced at Bardney, there remained a trace of class distinction which I found difficulty in accepting because it precluded the degree of co-operation between ranks that I considered to be important to the job we had to do. As was to be expected, Gerry Parker, being a native of the USA, was equally impressed by what he had witnessed during the visit and told me that while at Alconbury he had made tentative enquiries concerning a possible transfer. Gerry was attending an English university when war was declared and he had enlisted in the RAF. Because Gerry had already completed twenty-two trips with us and had proved himself a worthy member of our crew, I was concerned at the possibility of losing him and asked him to consider carefully before making such a move. He completed one more operational flight with the crew before transferring to the 8th Air Force later that same month.'[103]

On 14 June more than 220 Lancasters and thirteen Mosquitoes of 1, 3, 5 and 8 Groups carried out two separate raids on Le Havre where fifteen E-boats and light naval forces were a threat to Allied shipping off the Normandy beach heads just thirty miles away. The raid took place in two waves, one during the evening and the second at dusk. Most of the aircraft in the first wave were from 1 Group and the second from 3 Group, both waves being escorted by 123 Spitfires of 11 Group. In all, 1,230 tons of bombs were dropped on the pens. Just before the first wave bombed, twenty-two Lancasters of 617 Squadron released their 'Tallboys' on red spot fires dropped by three Mosquitoes, including one flown by Wing Commander Cheshire. They marked the E-boat pens in the eastern area of the port and eleven Lancasters attacked this aiming point. The attack was timed for 22.30 hours to catch the E-boat fleet fully armed and manned for the night sortie, just before they put to sea. The concrete-covered E-boat pens suffered hits and several near misses. One 'Tallboy' blasted a 16 feet diameter hole in the north-west corner of the blast pens. The total shipping destroyed was 53 boats of various kinds.[104] When Barnes Wallis saw the PR photos that confirmed that the pens had collapsed along much of their length he commented that the best use of 'Tallboys' against such structures was a deliberate near miss. 'Their earthquake effect undermines the foundations and thus their massive roof weight then becomes a tremendous liability!' The light flak was 'tremendous' but only the one Lancaster failed to return and a 617 Squadron Lancaster had to be written off after returning. Sergeant Alf 'Bing' Crosby, 'Nicky' Knilans' mid-upper gunner suffered a leg wound. The Nôtre-Dame district near the port was devastated but fortunately the inhabitants had been long before the raid. Other districts were also hit and 700 houses were destroyed, 76 civilians were killed and 150 injured. [105]

At Dunholme Lodge on 21/22 June 1944 one by one the various specialists gave their talks with 27-year old Wing Commander Malcolm Crocker DFC* the American CO of 49 Squadron concluding the briefing by stating that he too would be operating and would be taking along Mr. Kent Stevenson, on 'T-Tommy'. Also flying this night would be 49's two flight commanders. The CO's second tour crew would be flying their eighth operation. More than fifty Abschüsse were claimed by Nachtjagd as the result of an effective Tame Boar operation against the Wesseling force, I./NJG1 being credited with 16 victories by eight He 219 Uhu ('Owl') crews. In fact 37 Lancasters were lost on the Wesseling operation. At 03.32 hours combat exhausted 49 Squadron crews began landing back at Fiskerton. Their opening remarks gave the first hints of the disaster that had befallen the aircrew of 5 Group. Meanwhile, outside the intensity of the operations block, in another world, dawn was just breaking over the Lincolnshire Wolds, heralding the start of a fine new day. A corporal removed the blackouts from the windows, letting shafts of bright sunlight penetrate the stuffy smoke-filled room, the sun's rays played upon the operations board, where, written in large chalk white capital letters against the names of six aircraft captains were those three impassive words...'MISSING WITHOUT TRACE'. The Station Commander, having just returned from his long vigil at the Watch Office, scanned the ops board in silence, still numbed by the realisation that in just one very short evening,

49 Squadron had lost 42 good men, including its Commanding Officer, Wing Commander Malcolm Crocker. He and his second tour crew were blown out of the sky outbound near Jülich-Mersch by a night-fighter. The intrepid Kent Stevenson's broadcast now would never be heard.

Telegrams were sent to the next of kin of all those lost on Scholven/Buer and Wesseling, informing loved ones that their sons were 'missing, presumed killed' or when Red Cross confirmation was received that that they were prisoners of war. The letter announcing Wing Commander Crocker's death arrived at his parent's house in Boston, Massachusetts. The parents of Technical Sergeant Albert E Martin USAAF, one of four men killed on 'S-Sugar' on 44 Squadron flown by Pilot Officer Russell Wood RNZAF, received word that he had been killed in action. Three of the crew were taken prisoner. In Calgary, Canada Lucy McMurchy received a letter informing her that her husband Flying Officer Lorne Sinclair McMurchy, pilot of Lancaster 'B-Baker' on 9 Squadron that was lost on Scholven/Buer was dead. It must have been equally heart-breaking for relatives in Lethbridge, Alberta when they were notified that Sergeant Donald A. H. Redshaw RCAF the 18-year old rear gunner had been killed.

Near the end of the war, Big Joe McCarthy adapted to the British way, being seen with a pipe, a walking stick and a dog on a lead. 'If I'm going to be an officer and a gentleman, I'm going to have a crack at looking the part,' he said. It went without saying that few if any of the American volunteer airmen in the RAF were in it for pounds, shillings and pence.

Footnotes Chapter 13

86   *Six War Years 1939-1945, Memories of Canadians at Home and Abroad* by Barry Broadfoot (Paperjacks Ltd, 1985).

87   *See No Need To Die: American Flyers in RAF Bomber Command* by Gordon Thorburn (Haynes Publishing 2009).

88   *The London Observer* by Raymond Lee (Hutchinson, 1972).

89   Robert S. Raymond, *A Yank in Bomber Command*. (Pacifica Press1998).

90   See *Bombers Fly East*.

91   *Into the Silk* by Ian Mackersey (Granada, 1978). Four other members of his crew survived and they were taken into captivity. Pilot Officer Earle George Dolby DFC RCAF and Warrant Officer Oliver Lambert DFM the rear gunner were killed

92   *The Dambuster Who Cracked the Dam: The Story of Melvin 'Dinghy' Young* by Arthur G. Thorning (Pen & Sword 2008)

93   Eight Lancasters had set out with the new 12,000lb light-case bomb (not the 12,000lb Tallboy earthquake bomb developed later). While over the North Sea a weather reconnaissance Mosquito reported that there was fog in the target area and the Lancasters were recalled. (Martin Middlebrook & Chris Everitt, *The Bomber Command War Diaries*. An operational reference book, 1939-1945 (Midland 1985).

94   The body of David Maltby, who was 21 years old, was picked up by the Cromer lifeboat and taken to the morgue at RAF Coltishall. He was buried later at Wickhambreux near Canterbury in Kent where he had been married.

95   *The Dam Busters* by Paul Brickhill (Evans Bros London 1951).

96   South Australian Flying Officer Frederick Michael 'Spam' Spafford DFC DFM RAAF, Flight Lieutenants Torger Harlo 'Terry' Taerum DFC RCAF and Robert E. G. Hutchison DFC* and Flying Officer George A. Deering DFC RCAF on Guy Gibson's crew were KIA along with Squadron Leader Holden.

97   Forty-two bombers were lost; 21 of them to twin-engined night fighters and 11 to Wilde Sau single-engined fighters of all three Wild Boar Geschwader that operated in force over Mannheim.

98   *Private memoir, Major Hubert Knilans, A Yank in the RCAF*, RAF Museum, Hendon, archive B2455. In June 1944 Knilans, now a pilot on 617 Dam Busters Squadron, was interviewed by Edward R

Murrow for his *This Is London* radio programme.

99 Wing Commander William Abercromby DFC* and his crew on Lancaster III ND354 OL-A of 83 Squadron, 8 (Path Finder Force) Group was one of 28 aircraft lost from a force of 421 Lancasters sent to bomb Berlin on the night of 1/2 January 1944. Sergeant L. H. Lewis, flight engineer, was the only survivor.

100 *The Bomber Command War Diaries*: An Operational reference book 1939-1945 by Martin Middlebrook and Chris Everitt (Midland 1985).

101 *The Dam Busters* by Paul Brickhill. On 4/5 June 259 aircraft of all groups bombed four of the gun batteries, three of which were deception targets in the Pas de Calais. But the fourth battery at Maissy, which was covered by cloud and could only be marked by Oboe sky-markers before being bombed by 52 Lancasters of 5 Group, was in Normandy between what would soon be known as *Omaha* and *Utah* beaches.

102 43-year old Group Captain Anthony Caron 'Tiny' Evans-Evans and his crew were KIA on 21/22 February 1945 flying a Lancaster he had borrowed from 83 Squadron for the raid on Gravenhorst.

103 *Lancaster Valour; The Valour and the Truth* by Clayton Moore (Compaid Graphics 1995). Clayton Moore flew two tours and was discharged from the RCAF in April 1945.

104 *Cheshire VC* by Russell Braddon (Arrow Books 1966).

105 The following evening a similar operation was mounted against the E-boat pens in Boulogne harbour when 297 aircraft of 1, 4, 5, 6 and 8 Groups were dispatched. 1 Group Lancasters bombed their targets but cloud over the assembly area of the port prevented ten of 617 Squadron's 22 Lancasters from bombing. Even so, according to one account over 130 E-boats were sunk along with 13 other vessels wrecked or badly damaged, as at Le Havre by a tidal wave. One Halifax FTR. This and the operation to Le Havre forced the remnants of the E-boat flotillas to a new base at Ijmuiden in Holland, which was bombed by 617 Squadron on 24 August.

Chapter 14

The Nuremburg Raid

'When joining 50 Squadron, 5 Group in late January 1944 we were still unaware of the history of that squadron, or of the famous personalities who had been and were to become fellow members. At this time the squadron was based at RAF Skellingthorpe, within the boundary of the City of Lincoln and commanded by Wing Commander A. W. Howard DFC AFC (later Air Chief Marshal Sir Anthony Howard, KCB OBE DFC AFC). We were later to learn that among the squadron's previous commanders was the much respected Sir Arthur (Bomber) Harris, commanding the whole of Bomber Command; and the respected 'Gus' Walker (later Air Chief Marshal Sir Augustus Walker GCB CBE DSO DFC AFC MA). Also that Flying Officer Leslie Manser had been flying with the squadron when he was posthumously awarded the Victoria Cross. There were many more but we were yet to learn these details.

Our crew was placed in 'A' (Dingo) Flight, the deputy flight commander being Flight Lieutenant 'Mike' Beetham (later to become Marshal of the Royal Air Force Sir Michael Beetham GCB CBE DFC AFC) whose signature appeared in our flying logs during the period we were to remain on the squadron. The crew were: pilot - Flight Sergeant Garth Alec (Jimmy) Waugh from New Zealand; Sergeant Dennis Alfred (Chas) Chaston from Coventry, navigator; Sergeant Denis C. 'Jerry' Lynch, bomb aimer; Sergeant George Prince from Surrey, flight engineer; myself, Sergeant R. J. 'Jack' Dunn from Cornwall, WOp/AG; Sergeant Donald Leslie Sehlin from Alberta, Canada, mid-upper gunner; and Sergeant Roy Frederick Thibedeau from Ontario, rear gunner. The period in which we were operating was fairly intense and losses were generally high. On our first operation to Leipzig on the night of 19/20 February there were 79 aircraft lost (8.6%) and on our ninth operation to Berlin (the Big City) on the night of 24/25 March the loss was 73 aircraft (7.1%). We had trips to 'Happy Valley'. Essen, Frankfurt, Augsburg, Stuttgart and Schweinfurt; some more than once, in between time and were soon aware of our chances of surviving a tour. Training was also very intensive over this period and 50 Squadron losses were not heavy when compared to other squadrons. According to the CO this was due to the training programme. On the night of 30/31March we were briefed for an operation on Nuremburg. Take off was at 21.15 hours and we were a little surprised at the fact that a moon was a possibility, being a change in the normal moonless raids.'

A Lucky Break by Sergeant R. J. 'Jack' Dunn.

The Briefing 30/31 March 1944.[106]
'Very shortly Bomber Command will be called upon to support the invasion of Europe and Sir Arthur Harris is anxious to strike at one last major target before

this happens. It is a target he knows is very dear to Churchill's heart. All this morning there has been intense activity at High Wycombe, the Command's underground headquarters and at midday the teleprinter there began clacking out messages. The code name of the target, 'Grayling', was sent to all group commanders and in turn to stations and squadron commanders. Security was immediately put into force. All out-going phone calls were blocked and those incoming were intercepted, cutting stations off from the outside world as preparations for the raid began. The route and other details have been argued and settled. The aircraft outside and on other stations are being bombed-up, serviced and fuelled. And you are now about to learn where you are destined to go.

Officer i/c Flying. 'The target tonight is Nuremberg on the river Pegnitz 90 miles to the north of Munich. As a military target, Nuremberg is an important industrial city with a population of 350,000 (a little larger than Leeds) and a centre for general and electrical engineering. The famous M.A.N. works produce armaments of all kinds there and, since their large factory in Berlin was bombed, Siemens plant in Nuremberg has stepped up production of its electric motors, searchlights and firing devices for mines.

'You've already disproved, on many occasions, Goering's earlier boast that no bombs would ever fall on the Fatherland. Now you'll have an opportunity to dissuade the Nazis from holding further mass rallies in the city most favoured for these.

'Nuremberg deserves a maximum effort and that is what it will now get. Ten squadrons in No. 1 Group, eight squadrons from No. 3 Group, seven squadrons from No. 4, twelve from No. 5, nine from No. 6 and 12 squadrons from No. 8 Path Finder Force Group will participate - altogether 820 Lancasters and Halifaxes will take part. In addition 15 Mosquitoes will adopt an Intruder role to seek out night fighters and destroy them. So you'll have plenty of company and it behoves every one to keep a good look-out at the turning points to avoid collisions.

'H-hour is 0105 through to 0122 (17 minutes). After the PFF have marked the target, the main force will bomb from H-hour + 5 for the remaining 12 minutes.

'Our time on target is set for H-hour + 9 between the band of 20 000 to 20 500 feet. Take-off time is 22.00 hrs. Good luck; have a good trip!'

Navigation Leader: 'Navigators have already been briefed and have prepared their charts and their captains' maps. 'To minimize enemy radar detection, the main force will maintain a height of no more than 2,000 feet across country and the coast, with navigation lights on to the first turning point at 51° 50' North 2° 30' East. Please keep a very sharp lookout at this point, captains and gunners.

'At this point you will start a steady climb, switching off all lights when the turn is completed on to your south-easterly course of 130°. The Belgian Coast will be crossed at 8,000 feet just to the east of Binges to the next turning point at 50° 30' North 4°36' East, just short of Charleroi; there you will alter course to port, gradually climb to your bombing height and reach your last turning point before the target, at Fulda 50° 32' North 10° 36' East and then on to the target.

'After leaving the target continue for a short distance to 49° North 11° 5' East; then to 48° 30' North 9° 20' East and on to 50° North 3° East to cross the French coast at 50° 40' North 2° East, at a height of 4,000 feet.

'Indicated air speeds will be 172 mph to the first turning point. Then climbing at 150 across the coast to the next turning point where airspeed will be increased to 162 mph and held to the target. If it is necessary to make a second run on the target, orbit left to avoid others in the main force coming up behind you.

'On leaving the target, increase speed to 182 and hold this, gradually losing height to cross the coast at 4,000 feet.

'Corrected winds will be broadcast to the main force every half hour between 23.40 and 03.40.'

Bombing Leader: 'Your all-up weight tonight is just short of 65,000lbs. Bomb load is just over 7,000lbs with 4 x 1,000lb HEs and 3,000lb of incendiaries. You have six tanks of petrol - altogether 2200 gallons - more than sufficient for the trip tonight.

'Including this squadron's contribution, altogether 3,000 tons of bombs will fall on the target tonight. There are three main concentrations for your attack - here and here - (pointing on map) and depending on what cloud cover there may be, Path Finder Force will employ either Wanganui sky flares if the target is completely obscured by cloud, Parramata markers, dropped on H_2S, if there is broken cloud partially obscuring the target, or Newhaven ground markers dropped on visual identification, aided by H_2S. [107]

'Night maps should be marked accordingly.

'Initially red markers and incendiaries will be dropped, then green markers turning yellow; then these will be further fed by red markers, with target illuminators, from 01.09 to 01.22.

'Met. (Meteorological Officer) will tell you that a fairly stiff crosswind can be expected on target, so bomb-aimers will need to be pretty snappy with their bombing. On the other hand, they must be careful to avoid the tendency to 'creep-back' with their bombs and miss the vital areas. Make a good job of it, chaps. We don't want to go back again.

Window': one parcel a minute over the coast and up to the first turning point, over Charleroi in Belgium. At your next turning-point (Fulda) release 'window' at the rate of two parcels a minute for five minutes and at the rate of one a minute at subsequent points after leaving the target, as specified.'

Meteorological Officer: 'At the line LW, (pointed out on chart) warm air is overtaking the cold air forming a warm front which is moving northward over NE Yorkshire and SW Scotland. The line LC marks a cold front now over Ireland and approaching the western side of England. It may lead to cu-nim cloud (cumulo-nimbus), although we do not expect this to be continuous. 'What is forecast is broken but fairly good cloud cover for you all the way to the target and back, with some low cloud and precipitation in coastal areas. Winds over the Continent moderate 40/50 mph at 18,000 feet and generally blowing from SW or W. There may be some low cloud and poor visibility down to 2000 yards at base on return.

'To sum up then: for the outward flight, broken cloud can be expected everywhere except Southern Germany where it is expected to be layered. Winds WSW 40/50, veering WNW 50/60 mph over target. Local industrial smog in Groups 4 and 6 areas, with valley fog towards dawn.'

Intelligence Officer: 'The very direct nature of the route to the target tonight has been the subject of weighty discussion between Bomber Command and Group

Commanders. In particular Air Vice-Marshal Bennett, head of 8 PFF Group strongly advocated a far more indirect approach. His views, however, were opposed by other Air Officers commanding, including the Hon. Ralph Cochrane, head of 5 Group. They supported the Commander-in-Chief's plan on these grounds:- that the distance involved precludes wasting time and fuel on too many doglegs, that the present route suggests a number of perhaps more vulnerable targets to the German defences, thus persuading them to disperse and thin-out fighter concentrations, that the sheer simplicity of this route will surprise the Germans and keep them off-balance sufficiently long for you to complete the operation without too much trouble. I think you deserve this explanation and it may help to dispel any misgivings you have about the direct route as laid down.

'As a further encouragement, I can tell you that just ahead of you when you cross the coast, Mosquitoes will open the night's proceedings with low-level attacks on the known night-fighter fields in Holland at Leeuwarden, Twente, Deelen and Venlo in a bid to keep them on the ground until you're well past. At the same time off Texel and the Heligoland Bight, a force of 50 Halifaxes will start dropping mines as a diversionary move to keep German ground controllers confused. Additional to this and a while before the main force reaches the target, Mosquitoes will make a feint attack on Cologne between 23.55 and 7 minutes after midnight. A further force of twenty Mosquitoes will also drop fighter flares, markers and 'window' on Kassel between 26 and 28 minutes after midnight in an attempt to 'spoof' the German controllers into believing the main attack is to be the Ruhr and thus lead them to send the bulk of the fighters there. So far as ground defences are concerned, we've tried to route you over the coast both going and coming back where flak and searchlights are believed to be thin and the use of 'Window' here will help to blur the picture from the ground. Again, the route takes you across the southerly end of the heavy Ruhr defensive area. Obviously much depends on the accuracy of your course-keeping and your ability to maintain a well bunched-together pattern and no straying away from the main stream.

'Night-fighters can as usual be expected, but with cloud-cover and the Mosquito attacks to keep them grounded, the danger from these, we believe, will be minimized. Keep a sharp lookout for them, however and wireless operators, make sure your 'fishpond' is working at all times'.

Postscript to Briefing

'You have now been briefed on one of the thirty operational flights you will have to survive to complete your first heavy bomber tour. Some of you will be flying on ops for the very first time, others have only one trip to go; a few of you will be on your second tour of twenty trips. Several crews are due for a week's leave as from tomorrow.

'Following this main briefing, you'll more than likely go to your messes for a meal, including bacon and egg: the traditional 'fringe benefit' for aircrew on ops that night. Then you'll stroll across to the crew rooms to put on your flying kit, gather up your 'chute and bits and pieces and climb aboard one of the crew buses for your particular flight at dispersal.

The captains will issue the flying rations/escape kits to their crews, run up the engines for a final check and sign the Forms 700. You'll all have to wait around then for a Very light from the control tower, most of you inwardly hoping that it will be a red one indicating a last-minute cancellation!'

On this occasion, though, it was green at all stations and the first Lancaster off rolled down the runway at Elsham Wolds near Hull precisely on 21.16. The raid was on!

'Although we encountered a lot of flak and saw a number of aircraft go down in flames' recalled Jack Dunn, 'there was nothing close enough to us for alarm. I kept a listening-out watch and noted the Group broadcasts each half hour, plus the usual attempts at jamming the radio signals from the enemy ground stations vectoring the fighters into the bomber stream. I was off the intercom taking a group broadcast at about 0115 hours, when suddenly, out of the corner of my eye, I saw the navigator standing at my side facing the main spar. He was wearing his parachute and gesticulating to me. As my attention was drawn to him I became aware of flames leaping past the starboard porthole and sparks of electricity flashing around inside the aircraft. I switched back into the intercom system in time to hear the bomb aimer shouting 'I can't get this bloody hatch open' and the skipper ordering the crew to bail out. The navigator was climbing the main spar as I tore off my helmet and microphone and. grabbing my parachute which was stored behind me. I hastily clipped the chest 'chute and followed 'Chas' to the rear of the aircraft. I had cleared the main spar and was standing more or less upright and could see both gunners at the rear door - they were struggling and appeared unable to open the door. Almost immediately there was an explosion and I was thrown off my feet and seemed to be pinned to the side of the fuselage, unable to move - the aircraft was gyrating madly, obviously in a dive. I was unable to move a finger and my life was re-enacted by my mind. The mid-upper gun turret was just ahead of me.

'Suddenly, I was aware of being in the cool outside air, I realised I had been thrown clear of the aircraft and pulled the rip cord. It was moonlight and I could see the ground below, but I appeared to be drifting into the middle of what seemed to be a large lake. Being a non-swimmer I began frantically pulling on the lines to alter my drift and after what seemed like only a few minutes. I landed on mother earth - so easily that I was able to keep on my feet. I was on the edge of a pine forest and what I had thought to be a lake was a moonlit clearing. On my descent I wasn't sure if I had seen any other parachutes, but because of the bomb aimer's call prior to baling out, plus the obvious difficulties being experienced by the two gunners, I concluded that I had been the only survivor.

'I hastily hid my parachute and realised the aircraft had crashed only a short distance from me, having heard the explosion and been showered with debris just as I had landed. I had lost my wrist watch and also the knife which was normally kept in the small pocket of my flying boots and was aware of cuts to my hands, face and scalp, but these did not seem serious. My escape map and compass gave me some idea of where I should aim for but I knew that Switzerland, which seemed the best bet, would be 250 miles to the South-West and it was unlikely that I should get that far without some assistance. We had been in sight of the fires burning in Nuremburg to the South as I was taking the Group broadcast and I knew that I was well and truly inside enemy territory and on my own.

'Using the stars to give me some guidance I began to make my way in a general

South Westerly direction, hearing the last of the bomber stream droning away above me, I knew I was going to miss my breakfast this time. Suddenly there was a burst of what sounded like machine gun fire, but I later realised that it was probably the ammunition in the burning aircraft and not someone pursuing me.

'It was bitterly cold and on some slopes there was an accumulation of snow and the water in the ditches had ice over it. I tried to fill my water bottle with water, adding the tablets from my escape kit to make it safe to drink, but although I tied the bottle to my belt, the contents soon turned to slush. I was without my Irvin jacket - being near the main heat source of the aircraft I had been sitting on the jacket instead of wearing it and I soon became aware of the intense cold.

'Keeping to the fields and away from paths, roads or signs of any habitation, I kept on the move. I noted the absence of hedges or field fences but found, to my dismay that the field boundaries consisted of water filled ditches which had a light film of ice over them. Having fallen into these on more than one occasion, I decided to gain some sleep until there was some light to enable me to avoid them but the cold prevented this, although I tried to gain some shelter under bushes. I continued my walk and eventually, as the light was breaking, I found myself walking down a small valley which eventually met up with a road and a hamlet. Having been discouraged by constant falls into water filled ditches, I decided to keep to the road and commenced to walk between the houses down the village street. On passing a row of cottages, some men emerged dressed in a uniform type cap, obviously leaving for their employment. I kept on the opposite side of the road, but the womenfolk appeared a bit suspicious as they watched the men go off.

'The only words of German I knew were 'Guten Morgan', so I muttered this as I passed and received a reply, to my surprise. I had gashed the little finger of my left hand which was bleeding badly and I had used the tail of my vest as a bandage, so I kept this hand in my pocket. On leaving the village, I discovered the road ran parallel to a railway line, beyond which was a wide, fast flowing river, which I surmised was the River Main. Although I wanted to continue in a South Westerly direction, I decided to continue on a more easterly course to see where it was possible to cross and resume the direction I wanted.

'Leaving the road and crossing the railway line, I continued along the river bank until I saw signs of a town on the opposite bank and in a short while I came to a bridge. As I started across towards the town, a young lad on a pedal cycle overtook me and continued to look over his shoulder at me in a suspicious manner. I had removed all insignia from my battle dress, but was obviously looking very disreputable. On the far side of the bridge I noticed a group of men lounging against the parapet and the lad on his cycle stopped to speak to them, at the same time glancing in my direction. I was committed and put both hands in my pocket - to hide both my water bottle which had frozen to my belt and the bandage on my little finger, I slouched past them and to my surprise they made no comment. I turned immediately to my right and to my consternation a squad of soldiers were being marched towards me but again they too ignored me.

'Still suffering from the shock of seeing the marching German soldiers, immediately I was out of sight of any buildings, I left the road and climbed up the steep side of the valley, regaining my general south-westerly route. After avoiding a gun emplacement which I almost stumbled on and hiding from a group of children playing in the woods. I was descending into a valley following a path when I became aware of a group of people at the top of the path. At least one seemed to be carrying a rifle or shot gun and not wishing to encounter anyone at close quarters I changed direction on a branch path which led me further away from them, but not too abruptly. As I continued up the side of the valley, a voice shouted to me and I looked across and decided that discretion was the better part of valour.

'As they approached me I realised that what I had thought to be a rifle was, in fact, a felling axe. Feeling the game was up, I said to him 'RAF'. I think he was more scared than I was as he stuck his axe into my chest and insisted I put my hands over my head. The group, which included two or three women, shepherded me to their village, some distance away and 1 was placed into the custody of the local schoolmaster who seemed to be a sort of deputy mayor. Followed by most of the inhabitants of this small hamlet, the schoolmaster took me to the next village which had a burgomaster. The womenfolk were very wary of me en route and ensured their children didn't get too close to me. He contacted the military who sent an escort. Whilst I was waiting, a nun in the mayor's household made me a cup of coffee and cut me a slice of 'seed' cake which I did not like.

'An SS Feldwebel came for me in a Volkswagen with a civilian driver and took me back to the town I had passed through earlier, to an official looking building at the end of the bridge. He was surprised when I told him that I had crossed the bridge early that morning, saying it was always under military guard. I was cursorily searched, but none of my maps, compasses were found and eventually a lorry with a number of RAF, RAAF and RCAF aircrew in the back collected me and conveyed us all to an aerodrome at Schweinfurt. We were taken to a large room and, to my joy, I saw among the aircrew kept to one end away from us, were three of my crew; the skipper, bomb-aimer and engineer. I had never expected to see them again. We were searched but again I managed to keep my compass and map, placing them on a ledge in the room during the searching and retrieving them after we were locked up for the night.

'I learned that Jerry had at last managed to open the front hatch and all three had bailed out. Jimmy had landed on a cottage roof and was captured right away. Jerry was hooked up in a pine tree, but later had been seen by schoolchildren who had given him away. George, with a damaged 'chute had made a heavy landing and had been caught almost at once. They had seen only their own parachutes coming down after they left the aircraft and had thought the remaining four had perished. They had seen the starboard wing break off prior to the aircraft diving into a spin, followed by the aircraft breaking in two, just aft of the mid-upper turret, before plunging to earth. This was when I was catapulted out into the night air.

'After two or three days we were taken to Schweinfurt railway station by 'bus, from which we could see the damage inflicted by earlier raids and from there by train to Frankfurt-on-Main. A tram took us to Dulag Luft, the interrogation centre for aircrew. We were put into solitary cells for several days, only coming out to be interrogated. I was eventually released into the compound where aircrew were kept pending transport to a PoW camp and there met Flight Sergeant 'Jock' McPhee, a fair haired Scotsman who had been on the same raid as myself. [108] We spent a part of Easter period waiting for our move and eventually spent several days in a cattle truck on a journey to Heydekrug in Lithuania. We spent one night in the Berlin goods yard listening to the RAF bomb the area and trusting that we weren't going to receive any bombs ourselves. I spent the next 13 months in captivity, in Lithuania, Poland and Germany.' [109]

De-briefing
This was the interrogation of returning aircrew by Squadron Intelligence Officers, who then had to write-up Forms 540, the Operations Record Books and get these to Group HQ as quickly as possible for inclusion in a consolidated report to Bomber Command HQ. Casualties and general comments on the action had to be teleprinted or telephoned through, in time for C-in-C Harris's 'morning prayers' at 0900 the same morning.

The following is a selection of typical accounts taken down by the intelligence officers early on the morning of 31 March 1944:

Flight Lieutenant Neville Sparks DFC AFC, captain of a Path Finder Lancaster on 83 Squadron: 'We were flying at 19,000 feet overtaking the main force 3,000 to 4,000 feet above. Contrary to the forecasts, there was no layer cloud in which they could hide from enemy fighters. They were clearly visible, glinting in the moon light.

'It was on the long leg between Charleroi and Fulda when the slaughter began. We saw sparkles of cannon fire, some distant and some almost directly above us, followed by explosions, fires, plunging planes and a scattering of fires on the ground as far as the eye could see. My navigator, 'Doc' Watson, marked no less than 57 ticks in his log on the way to the target. Each tick was a four-engined bomber we'd seen shot down by German fighters. It looked like an ambush from where we were watching. It was the most terrible thing I have ever seen. The forecast was for the moon to be at about half its full strength; in fact it was about as bright as it could be. The night, too, was clear as a bell; no clouds, fantastic visibility. I'm pretty certain we brought back a good photo of the target. My bomb-aimer, 'Strobe' Foley, is wizard at operating the H_2S set. I know he identified Nuremberg correctly.

'On the way back, a powerful head-wind blew up, unpredicted at briefing, but, by getting down to 10 000 ft we got home before the CO. We flew straight across and saw nothing but a row of six flares several thousand feet above, which indicated that enemy fighters were still searching for the survivors from the main attacks.'

F/L D. F. Gillam on 100 Squadron reported an unexpected hazard caused by freak weather: 'We started leaving contrails at our allotted height of 19,000 feet. I decided to 'misinterpret' orders and get as much height as possible. We got up to about 22,000 feet which was as high as we could get fully loaded. From there I could see a mass of contrails below us; they looked like a formation of American daylight bombers.'

Sgt R. C. Corker, a flight engineer in a Halifax on 578 Squadron described a fighter attack: 'Without any warning at all, we were attacked from underneath; there was an enormous bang as a cannon shell exploded in the starboard-inner and four or five pieces caught me in the fleshy part of the bottom. The fighter shot across our nose and attacked another Halifax about 11 o'clock high from us. It blew up. He had made the two attacks in about 20 seconds.'

P/O O.V. Brooks on 15 Squadron: 'The target, if in fact it was the target, was not well marked at all. We bombed on a marker that appeared at our approx. ETA (estimated time of arrival), but we did not see much in the way of fires. It was clear from the way the bombs were falling all over the place that few people really knew where they were.'

F/L W. D. Marshall on 467 Squadron: 'We were late getting to the target and I don't think we've got a good bombing photo because we were chased by a German fighter and then a very twitchy Lancaster gunner tried hard to shoot us down.

P/O Cotter flew a Halifax that night on his 30th op; his navigator was only on his first or second trip: 'With the heavy fighter attacks, the navigator could not have had a more unfortunate introduction and eventually he was unsure of his position. Before we were due at Nuremberg, we saw Path Finder markers going down just off our track. We had not been briefed on any diversionary target here and I just thought we were lucky that we'd got to Nuremberg and so we bombed. Not one of us queried the target.'

Flight Sergeant Brian Soper DFM on 12 Squadron: 'The weather was clear and bright all the way, with just a faint haze of cloud over the target which was brightly lit when we made our bombing run. We have never seen so many exploding and burning aircraft or been close enough to see parachutes going down from crippled Lancs. I shall never forget the searchlight cones on the way back and particularly a Mossie which was caught by the master searchlight and then coned, very near us. While those unlucky blokes were getting the attention we managed to clear the area, a searchlight just crossing us a few times and with a constant barrage of flak.' W/O Jim McNab RAAF, who was in a Lancaster on 467 Squadron that reached Nuremberg that night: 'I don't think there was any question of a leakage of information. As far as we could make out, it was the bright moon which was the death-blow for our planes. It was so light that I could clearly read the squadron letters and identification numbers on a Lanc flying next to us. One of our chaps had said we were for it that night and was he right! Nuremberg was the only place covered by cloud. I saw Lancasters being shot down by anti-aircraft guns as well as fighters.'

Another Australian from the same squadron: 'The section of the route from Aachen to the target was reminiscent of a battlefield of burning aircraft.., very noticeable in the last half-dozen trips is the fact that so many aircraft were seen going down in flames from operational height I would suggest that the enemy is using a new type of ammunition.'

P/O J. D. Whiteman of 10 Squadron told his Group Commander Air Vice-Marshal Carr: 'I did not think we were going to reach the bloody target, let alone return to base.'

What went wrong?

From even that small collection of aircrew comments at just a few of the de-briefing sessions, it will be clear that a major disaster for the RAF had occurred. In fact, the hours between midnight and 07.25 on the 31st March 1944 became known as Bomber Command's 'Black Friday.'

Our dead and wounded aircrew for the night's operations totalled 745. The 545 dead included 150 Officers, 24 Warrant Officers and 371 NCOs. A further 159 aircrew were taken prisoner, some of them badly injured. Loss of aircraft amounted to 108: 94 were shot down by night fighters and flak over enemy territory.

Because the success of every Bomber Command raid depended on the weather over the routes and the targets, it is only reasonable that we should first look at the meteorological counterpoint that was being dished out at that time.

At 15.25 on the afternoon of the 30th, a weather Mosquito confirmed to Bomber Command that the outward flight in the moonlight had little chance of cloud cover and if the cloud seen over Nuremberg persisted it would rob the Path Finders of the ability to mark visually by moonlight. A further forecast was handed to the Deputy Commander Sir Robert Saundby at 16.40. It read: 'Nuremberg: Large amount of strato-cumulus with tops to about 8000 ft and risk of some thin patchy cloud at about 15 to 16 000 ft.'

Many years after the war, Sir Robert recalled: 'I can say that, in view of the met report and other conditions, everyone, including myself, expected the C-in-C to cancel the raid. We were most surprised when he did not. I thought perhaps there was some top-secret political reason for the raid, something too top-secret for even me to know.' The conditions reported by the Mosquito were not passed down to the stations. Every effort was made to keep from crews the unpleasant fact that they were to fly a constant course through a well-defended part of Germany for 265 miles in bright moonlight with little chance of cloud cover. At a dozen stations, met officers forecast that there would be cloud cover at operational height. No one, not even the Path Finder squadrons, was told of the 'large amounts of strato-cumulus' now forecast for Nuremberg.

From the original force of 782 heavy bombers that had taken off for Nuremberg, 725 crossed the Belgian coast. The others had aborted for various reasons: engine failure, oxygen supply problems, unserviceable radar sets and so on.

As the bombers flew due east from the Charleroi turning-point, they began to drift north of the correct track and to fall behind time. The wind had veered due west and had decreased and the Windfinder system had already broken down. The leading Path Finders were detailed to transmit the 'found' winds back to their Group HQ who would in turn broadcast these to all the bombers on the half-hour. That night, the few reports that did get through were so conflicting that it was impossible to send out common forecasts.

Just after midnight, the first bomber was shot down by flak over Liège; at the same time, over 200 night-fighters were on their way to the 'Ida' and 'Otto' beacons, straddling the course of the Long Leg. The diversionary feints had failed to fool the Luftwaffe generals.

The 45-mile section of the route between the German frontier and the Rhine cost the RAF ten Lancasters and two Halifaxes and two more bombers had been damaged.

The Germans circling at the 'Ida' beacon were listening out to the running commentary from the Deelen underground ops room and were justifiably amazed to be told that the main bomber-stream was heading straight for them in the clearest weather conditions possible, under a brilliant half-moon.

The bomber crews were deeply shocked to meet night-fighters in such strength so early in their flight, waiting dead on track in every semblance of an ambush laid with advance information. And as if this wasn't enough, a completely unforeseeable weather phenomenon occurred at this point. Vapour or condensation trails, rarely found below 25,000 feet started to appear behind each bomber flying at 19 to 20 000 feet. The dead-straight streams of pure white cloud in the bright moonlight were welcomed enthusiastically by the waiting Germans.

Unbeknown to Bomber Command, many of the German night-fighters were equipped with a newly-developed and deadly form of armament the Luftwaffe had named *Schräge Musik;* literally translated, it means 'slanting music', more colloquially, 'jazz'. Two 20mm cannons were mounted in the fuselage at an angle of 800, firing forwards and upwards. The pilot would approach the bomber from below, unseen by both gunners and line up an aiming point on either side of an inner engine; both wings at this point carried the fuel tanks. Because they attacked from the very close range of 70 to 80 metres, it was considered too risky to aim at the unprotected belly of the bomber and possibly to detonate the bomb-load.

The crews of two Me 110 fighters that night each destroyed no less than four bombers in one flight. Oberleutnant Helmut Schulte landed and was amazed to find that his two *'Schräge Musik'* guns had used only 56 cannon shells; when Leutnant Wilhelm Seuss fired at his fourth Lancaster he hit the bomb bay in error and had to dive violently to escape the massive explosion as the bomber blew up. It is almost certain that at no time had any crew seen either Messerschmitt.

The biggest score of bombers destroyed during the night was achieved, however, by Oberleutnant Martin Becker using the conventional technique von unten hinten, from below and behind. In half-an-hour between the Rhine and the end of the Long Leg he found and destroyed three Lancasters and three Halifaxes. Only eight nights earlier, on a Frankfurt raid, he had shot down six of the 33 aircraft lost by Bomber Command.

At a quarter to one, the leading bombers reached the end of the Long Leg and started to turn south to Nuremberg. German fighters and unreported wind changes had caused further dispersal. The 220 miles from Liege to the turning-point was by now clearly marked by the blazing remains of 41 Lancasters and 18 Halifaxes. It is unlikely that a single hour, before or since, has seen a greater rate of aerial destruction.

The target was now 75 miles to the south; without the tail wind, this would be a 20-minute flight. The turning-point was a tricky one, above the forests of Thuringia with no recognizable feature or nearby town. Most of the aircraft turned well to the north of the right place and slightly short of it.

The Luftwaffe fighters kept attacking. The first half of that short leg to Nuremberg claimed ten more bombers; and as the leading Path Finders flew past the searchlights of Bamberg, only 30 miles from the target. They suffered yet another critical setback in the shape of a thick blanket of cloud, less than 2,000 feet at base and extending up to 11,500 feet. Not only was Nuremberg covered by cloud but the winds from the west had suddenly increased in velocity and were blowing the big bombers sideways to the east. So, instead of flying over Erlangen and on to Nuremberg, some of the Path Finders had crossed another small town, Forchheim and then approached Lauf, much smaller than the real target but with similar characteristics on the H2S radar screens, being situated on a river and surrounded by woods.

Thirty-nine bombers were shot down on the final approach and over the target area. The force had by now lost 79 aircraft, exceeding the Leipzig total of six weeks earlier. Of all the aircraft shot down on the outward flight, there was only one from which the entire crew survived; from one crew in every three there were no survivors at all.

Mosquitoes of 627 Squadron opened the activities of the Primary Marking Force at two minutes to one, offloading 500-pounders and 'Window' at the rate of four bundles a minute to disrupt the 100-odd radar-predicted flak guns known to be defending the city. Ten minutes later, 65 Path Finders and Supporters had done their best, but the conditions were hopeless. Instead of a clear and vividly marked target for the Main Force bomb-aimers due to arrive at 01.10, there was one group of skymarkers over Nuremberg and another group ten miles to the north-east near Lauf, both being blown eastwards and falling towards the clouds.

It was Zero Hour by now and 559 Main Force bombers should have started to arrive. During the first five minutes only 33 aircraft bombed. The majority of the force had turned from the Long Leg well north of the right track and were, therefore, some minutes flying time further from the target than planned.

Seeing two groups of markers, the Main Force crews were understandably confused; so were the Backers-up among them whose duty it was to renew the skymarkers. They managed to re-mark the group over Lauf which now gave off the most light and attracted by far the greater number of bombs. Some of the later Path Finders placed their markers accurately over Nuremberg but the damage had been done and soon there was a ragged line of skymarkers more than ten miles wide. The wrecks of nine aircraft shot down on their bombing runs formed a long straight line from Bamberg to Lauf. The creep-back started early and soon measured 15 miles.

Altogether, 512 aircraft bombed in the Nuremberg area; what had happened to the other 119 bombers that should have done so?
A chapter of accidents misled at least a hundred of them. Both radar sets in a Mosquito had failed and the dead-reckoning navigation had been adversely affected by the changing winds. Just before Zero Hour the crew found a well-defended industrial area they presumed was Nuremberg, especially as they had been briefed to expect clear weather there. The bombs and markers were accordingly released, amid within a few minutes the indicator flare had attracted seven Lancaster Supporters and their bomb loads. Another Lancaster in the area was shot down and the blazing wreckage was the final signal for many bomb-aimers to assume they'd arrived on target and 48 crews took back

clear bombing photographs - of Schweinfurt! Damage was done to all three of the ball-bearing plants.

Thirteen other bombers released their loads when they realized they were lost; these fell on unspecified targets, including Bamberg, 30 miles north of Nuremberg and a small town 60 miles north.

When the bombers flew away from Nuremberg and Schweinfurt they were pursued for a short way by the German fighters and several more combats took place; it would be wrong at this stage to talk of a 'stream' for the bombers were spread over a huge frontage. The tail wind which had helped them along from the Belgian coast to the target in just over 100 minutes was now a heavy head wind and the flight back would be for most a long, boring drag of three hours or more. The force lost three more aircraft before leaving Germany, all near Stuttgart.

Just over an hour after leaving Nuremberg, those aircraft that were following the planned route flew over the Rhine north of Strasbourg and on into France. A sense of anti-climax, boredom and increasing fatigue set in with most crews, but the bombers were still not out of danger. New combats occurred including Martin Becker's seventh victory of the night - another Halifax. Night-fighters were responsible for the destruction of five or six bombers between the German border and the Channel coast. Two more were shot down by flak and there was a tragic collision north of Metz. Both aircraft were at least 40 miles off course.

It was almost 06.00 before the last stragglers reached the coast and flew out over the English Channel. Ninety-four bombers and their crews were missing. Fourteen more bombers crashed in England, among them the Halifax Excalibur on 578 Squadron captained by P/O Cyril Barton who was later awarded a posthumous VC for 'gallantly completing his last mission in the face of almost impossible odds'.

Ten Luftwaffe night-fighters were shot down by RAF air gunners, Four Ju88s, three Me 109s, two FW 190s and one Me 110; eleven crew members were killed.

Official summary of the Raid:
'In their Würzburg sets, the Germans detected intense air activity as far away as the Norfolk area before Bomber Command crossed the English coast and began to put the night-fighters in a state of readiness. German ground controllers, under General Schmidt, were not fooled by the British diversionary attacks and by the time that Bomber Command's main force crossed the coast they had their night-fighters circling their beacons and ready for interception. Contrary to met expectations, there was no cloud cover at all so that, in bright moonlight, Bomber Command flew into an ambush as soon as the 725 Lancasters and Halifaxes crossed the enemy coast and were involved in a running fight over the next 750 miles with a force of 246 night-fighter aircraft.

'Higher velocity than forecast winds (80 to 90 mph) also upset navigation and heavy cloud disturbed the accuracy of the bombers that managed to reach the target. Loss of life and aircraft were heavy.'

German assessment of damage at Nuremberg: '133 killed (75 in city itself),

412 injured; 198 homes destroyed, 3,804 damaged, 11,000 homeless. Fires started: 120 large, 485 medium/small. Industrial damage: railway lines cut and major damage to three large factories; 96 industrial buildings destroyed or seriously damaged. Bombs dropped (target area). 30 'mines', 145 HE (11 duds), 60,000 incendiaries. Bombs dropped (decoy sites): 6 'mines', 110 HE and numerous incendiaries.'

Although this provided confirmation of the determination of many crews to press home the attack, Nuremberg citizens had good reason to be grateful to their night-fighters whose activities spared them the full force of a saturation attack such as those suffered by Berlin, Cologne, Dresden and Essen and several other centres pounded to rubble by area bombing.

'It was not a unique disaster but a night on which an unhappy coincidence of clear skies to guide the fighters and bad tactical planning gave the German controllers an uncommonly easy task, leading to losses that were statistically a little worse than those at Leipzig and Berlin in previous weeks.'
Sir Arthur Harris.

Footnotes Chapter 14

106 Wing Commander F. Lord DFC and Flight Lieutenant P. Fox delivered to the Johannesburg Branch of the South African Military History Society on 9 June, 1977. Both authors flew in Bomber Command during World War II.

107 These code names were so-named by Donald C. T. Bennett, the founder of the Pathfinder Force. 'Newhaven' was for ground target indicators on the ground; 'Parramatta' was when the target was ground marked using H2S only, owing to bad visibility or broken cloud; and finally 'Wanganui,' which was pure sky-marking, when Main Force crews were required to bomb through these sky-markers on a required course detailed by 8 Group. These three code names continued in use for the rest of the war in all the tactical instructions sent out by Path Finder HQ each day. The names for these three methods were chosen very simply. Bennett asked one of his air staff officers, Squadron Leader Ashworth, 'Pedro, where do you come from?' And he replied, 'From Wanganui.' Bennett then said, 'Just to keep the balance with New Zealand, we will call the blind ground marking by the name of Parramatta.' Then looking for a third name for visual ground marking, Bennett summoned Corporal Ralph, his confidential WAAF clerk and said, 'Sunshine, where do you live?' And she replied, 'Newhaven.' Thus it was that these famous code names were born. In cloud conditions the target was located by Pathfinders using H2S and then flares would be dropped on parachutes set to ignite above the clouds and so indicate the target to the incoming Main Force.

108 McPhee was the navigator on Pilot Officer Donald Charles Cameron Crombie RAAF's Lancaster crew on 514 Squadron and one of only two who survived (the other was Pilot Officer H. G. Darby the bomb aimer) when the aircraft was shot down by a night-fighter while outbound at 22,000 feet and drawing close to the final turning point. Crombie's Lancaster was one of six lost on the Squadron this night. *RAF Bomber Command Losses of the Second World War, Vol.4 1943* by W. R. Chorley (Midland 1996).

109 'Eighteen years later, on an isolated farm at Constantine in Cornwall, I again met 'Jock' McPhee, then a Detective Sergeant in the Metropolitan Police Murder Squad, who was assisting me in the investigation of a murder in my area where I was an Inspector at Helston. Many years later, I established that our aircraft crashed about 1 km southwest of the village of Mauschendorf at about 0100 hrs (German time) on 31 March 1944. The three of our crew who were killed were found in or near the wreckage of the aircraft, and were originally buried in the nearby village of Gerach on the morning of 1st April 1944 by the inhabitants led by the then Burgomaster of Gerach. After the war their bodies were moved, being exhumed and re-interred at the British War Cemetery at Bad Tolz/Durnbach in February 1949. The town I walked through after crossing the River Main was Eltmann, the whole area being close to the present borders of West and East Germany. The two Canadian gunners - Don Sehlin and Roy Thibedeau - were commissioned posthumously'. *A Lucky Break* by R. J. Dunn, writing in Intercom; the official quarterly magazine of the Aircrew Association.

Chapter 15

Mailly-le-Camp;
Memories of a Bomber Raid

Geoff Gilbert was born at Burythorpe, a village near Malton in North Yorkshire. He was a rear gunner. He had never wanted to be anything else except a rear gunner. His father worked for the hunt. He moved about a lot in his job and Geoff was educated in Northumberland and Gloucestershire before the family moved to Cambridgeshire in 1936. When Geoff left school, he went to work with his father looking after the foxhounds. That was the custom of the day, following the same line of work as your father. When war broke out, Geoff worked at a large Army Food Supply Unit near his home. He grew up knowing how to ride a horse and how to shoot. Shooting was his strength and he fancied manning those four guns in a rear turret. So he applied to join the RAF.

'I completed my training on Ansons. We crewed up at the Operational Training Unit at Silverstone. We all collected in a hangar and the pilots selected their crews and Don Street approached me and asked me to join his. I had noticed Don. He looked reliable. He was older than most of the men in the hangar. He was 24. I've had a lucky life and I was lucky then. Don was a regular. He'd been a corporal fitter on 61 Squadron and finished up as Flying Officer DFC on the same squadron. Some men are good at flying aeroplanes and some are good at operations. Don was one of the latter. He had soon assembled his crew and we developed an understanding and camaraderie that was to stand us in good stead. Some say that the crew became your family and I suppose in a way they did but the feeling was deeper than that. We worked as a group in conditions and experiences that were unique to the times. Don was the pilot. The navigator was Dave Grant. He was Canadian. Douglas Boothby was the wireless operator and Charles Waghorn was the flight engineer. He was quiet and unflappable. Waggy had been a sergeant fitter in 1939. He was reliable and worked well with the crew but he kept himself to himself when we were on the ground. He was always smart, dressed like a new pin. We reckoned he had his eye on the CO's daughter. Then there was Jock Haddon, a Scot. He was a scruffy little devil but he finished his career in the RAF as a warrant officer and he was the smartest man in the camp by then.

'I was on my own as a rear gunner. It was lonely and it could be cold but you didn't think of that. My job was to watch out for attacking fighters and shoot them down and I didn't rest for a minute. I was looking out all the time right until we were safely back at Skellingthorpe. You never knew when fighters would appear and you had to be ready for them. They had a habit of coming up to you from below especially if there was a light sky. Then the Lancaster would make an easy target because it was silhouetted in their sights. German fighters had upward pointing guns and we had to watch out for them. I didn't lose my concentration for a second, not even to reach for a flask of coffee. I tried not to look at the explosions on the ground in case the bright lights affected my eyesight and made it difficult for me to identify approaching German fighters. Sometimes a German fighter would follow us back to base. If the call, 'Scatter bandits,' was heard, we scattered. There were cases of returning aircraft being shot down when they were almost home and dry by one of these bandits.

'50 Squadron was also stationed at Skellingthorpe and there was a lot of friendly rivalry between the two squadrons but there was no malice. We were young and high spirited and we did a lot of silly things like taking the station bell and leaving it in unusual places and borrowing underclothes from the WAAF's clothes line and hoisting them up the flag pole.

'When the corporal came round to announce that there was a war on, we knew there was to be a raid that night and we invariably asked what were the 'cookies' and 'cans'. 'Cookies' were the 4,000lb bombs we would be carrying and 'cans' were the incendiaries that would be included in the bomb loads. We would also want to know how much fuel had been put in the tanks. That would give us some idea of where we would be flying; 2,000 gallons and 1,000lb cookies invariably meant a raid on Germany, 1,500 gallons was mostly France. Maximum fuel and fewer bombs meant a long trip. The corporal would continue - 'meal 18.00 hours, briefing 19.00 hours, take off 22.00 hours.'

'We would all attend the main briefing. Our target was pointed out and red tape would mark our routes to and from it. Then we would divide into smaller groups for our own individual briefings. I joined the gunner leader. Then we would draw our kit and parachute packs. These were handed out by WAAFs. The first time I collected mine, I noticed a mug of water on the side and I asked for a drink. I took three sips of the water and put the mug down and I did that every time I went to collect my parachute, took just three sips of water. It became a ritual. The girls would have the mug of water waiting on the table for me. A lot of the men had lucky charms or performed some actions which they thought would bring them safely home again. Some crews piddled on the wheels of their aircraft but we didn't do that. The crews hated change. They would be uneasy if one of their crew was ill and they had to have a substitute in his place. They would see that as bad luck. To a certain extent, some of the men blamed the Path Finders for the problems at the raid on Mailly. We were using a different kind of marking for the target and some of the men didn't like it. 617 were low level markers. It was different to the method that had been used before and some of the crews were hesitant, almost superstitious about the change. I had a fox mascot. Mother had bought me it to remind me of home. I used to take the fox with me and put the name of our target on him. When we had completed our last tour, one of the other rear gunners asked me if he could take the fox with him and I gave it to him. He didn't come back. You can't swop your luck.'

'We would be driven out to our planes in buses. The drivers were WAAFs. We couldn't have existed without them. The WAAFs worked really hard and they virtually ran the station. Each crew would be dropped near their Lancaster, ours was 'Y for Yoke' and we would stand around waiting while the skipper completed all the checks. It would be standing on the apron ready for us, fuelled and bombed up. The ground organisation was excellent and we got to know our ground crew. Everything would have been checked, the engines, airframe, controls, radio and radar units, compasses, bombing gear, electrics and armaments. Guns were cleaned and minor defects rectified before the night's loads were hoisted into the racks and the fuel pumped in.

'We would get into the plane, find our places and prepare for the flight. The engines would start up. There is nothing like the sound of the Merlin engines and the throb of a Lancaster. Then we would be moving in a long line of bombers towards the end of the runway, ready for a signal from the runway caravan for take-off. I would close my eyes and say a little prayer as we rose higher into the air, 'Please God, don't let me be burned or branded.' I'm not a religious man but that prayer was important to me at that time.

'We flew our whole tour together. We were on one raid to Gelsenkirchen near Essen when we were coned (caught in the searchlights) for eleven minutes and we couldn't get away from them. The blue white master beam had latched on to us and, almost immediately, four or five white searchlight beams were following our flight as well. Inside the plane, everything was a blinding glare. 'Shoot down the beam' the skipper had ordered but that was easier said than done. Thankfully there weren't any German fighters in the air at that moment but there was plenty of flak and Don was twisting and turning to get out of the light. The experienced pilots kept well away when they saw another aircraft caught by a searchlight. We did. We knew how easy it was for the beam to transfer to another plane in the vicinity. We were caught in the beam for eleven minutes and eleven minutes was a long time when you're airborne.

'Hang on, everybody' Don said, 'we're going down, 'and he rammed the control column forward and dropped the port wing in a diving turn to the left.

'The altimeter unwound losing height by 500 feet-1,000-1,500-2,000. He rolled the aircraft over to a starboard turn still losing height, 2,500-3,000-3,500-3,700 feet and then they were gone as suddenly as they came and there was blackness all round. The pilot reached forward, turned on the orange shaded cockpit light and hauled the aircraft up and back on course. It took a while for my eyes to become accustomed to the change from penetrating light to dark.

'Another time we were bombing Brest. There were lots of searchlights and explosions. We had just left the target when the Lanc went into a steep dive and I found myself looking at the sky. We were going straight down and I thought we had been hit and it was the end of the road. Strangely, I felt detached from it all. I didn't feel frightened. It was almost as if it was happening to another person. Then suddenly we had straightened out. I'd been thrown about a bit and I sorted myself out and said, 'What was that for Streetie?'

'I thought we'd better get out of there quick' he replied.

'God,' Dave Argent's Canadian accent commented, 'I never knew there were so many nuts and bolts in a Church roof.'

'We had plenty of flak holes but the ground crew patched them up with biscuit tins. We were badly shot up over Stuttgart and one of our engines was shot out. We limped home and were a long way behind the rest of the flight. We didn't expect the corporal in the mess to have waited up for us with our cups of cocoa and bread and cheese. She was a right tartar. Nobody tried to argue with her. But she was waiting for us.

'I knew you'd get back' she said as we went in. She got on with our crew. We could generally get round her. Sometimes when there was no raid and we'd gone into Nottingham; we often wouldn't get back until four in the morning and we'd be hungry and make for the mess. 'Couldn't those birds you've been with give you a bite to eat?' she would say but she generally found us something.

'We had to be alert all the time we were airborne and the skipper never questioned us and reacted immediately. 'Skipper, night-fighter coming in to starboard' and Don would be diving out of its path in a second.

'We were on one raid when there was a full moon and the moonlight reflected against the haze. The light was at the brightest I could remember it and it was difficult to keep watching out for enemy fighters because the reflected light was so bright.

'Skipper, I've picked up a bandit at 1,200 yards astern and to port'. The wireless operator was watching his small radar screen.

'Thanks. Gunners, sharp look out.'

'The skipper's order wasn't necessary but it established the rapport.

'1,000 yards now, Skipper. The closing rate isn't high' and a few minutes later, '800 yards.'

'Any sign of it, rear gunner?

'Can't see a thing'.

'Mid upper?'

'Not yet, Skipper.'

'600 yards, still there' called the wireless operator.

'Gillie, Jock, any sign yet?' The pilot was getting anxious.

'500 yards, still there,' came the steady voice of the wireless operator, '400 yards, no change. Could be one of ours with his IFF (Identification Friend or Foe) not switched on.'

'Let's find out. I'm turning 90 degrees to starboard. Now.'

'Don realised he was crossing the bomber stream as he swung on to the new heading so he held the plane at a steady altitude to lessen the chance of a collision. He needed to identify the aircraft that was shadowing us. The poor visibility left no time for doubt. The gunners would shoot or be shot at the first glimpse. We were ready. We stayed on the new heading for several minutes when the wireless operator s voice broke the tense silence, 'I've still got him Skip, right behind, 400 yards.'

'OK I'm turning left back on to course now. Any sign Gill, Jock?'

'300 yards, 250.' Doug's voice was full of anxiety.

'Then: 'Got him, corkscrew port. Go, go go.' I had a clear view of him and, as the Lancaster dropped down in a turning dive, I added, 'it's a Junkers 88.'

'He hadn't fired at us. The evasive action had been too quick and he had lost us in the haze. When 950 feet had unwound on the altimeter, the pilot turned the aircraft 60 degrees to starboard and into a climbing turn.

'Where is he, Doug?'

'He's moving to rear, across to port side about 300 yards, 200...

'The fighter was changing its position rapidly as the bomber followed an evasive pattern. 'Have you got it gunners?'

'Corkscrew port' I started but Jock interrupted. 'Hold it Skipper, hold it.' The Lancaster was still climbing with a slight turn to starboard. Now the pilot held it straight and level. Then it all happened in a split second. The Browning guns rattled.

'He's breaking away to port,' the wireless operator called.

'He's going down rapidly.'

'He's on fire. We got him' shouted Jock.

'Are you sure?' queried the pilot.

'We've got him. He's on fire,' I shouted.

'He's hit the deck and there's two parachutes,' the wireless operator was standing up with his head in the astrodome and shouting excitedly.

'Where is it?'

'We were only too keen to tell him.

'Good show. Well done. Log the time and the position Dave. One Junkers 88 destroyed. Settle down now fellas and let's get home. '

'Back at base on the dispersal pan with the parking drills completed and the engines stopped, we felt quiet and drained. It was quietly suggested to the ground crew that they could add a swastika to the bomb symbols painted on the side of the fuselage. Then we made our way to the debriefing room. We grabbed a mug of tea, perhaps with a shot of rum before we sat down with the debriefing officer. The crew were weary, war weary as were so many of the other crews. It was some time after this that I heard I had been awarded the DFM (Distinguished Flying Medal) and was to go to Buckingham Palace to receive it. I think my mother was more excited than me especially about going to Buckingham Palace. The three of us, Mum Dad and me, went to Kings Cross by train. We had ordered a taxi but it failed to turn up. We waited for a while then went for a bus. I asked if it went to the Palace and the conductor told me that it did. It took us to Crystal Palace. Well we got back to Central London and we started to run down the Mall. We were late. A car pulled up and we were told to jump in by a full General with his own personal driver. We rolled up to Buckingham Palace in style.

'Then it was 3 May 1944 and the corporal came round announcing that there was a war on and we knew there was a raid that night. By this time we were more than two thirds through our tour and we were beginning to feel confident that we would complete it. The target that night was Mailly-le-Camp and there was nothing in the briefing to blunt that confidence. It was a straightforward bombing raid and no problems were expected. Targets over France were proving so much easier than those over Germany that it had been announced in April that we needed to complete three raids over France before we could claim one towards our total of completed operations.'

'As usual on the day of the raid' recalled Gordon Wallace, a rear gunner on 101 Squadron at Ludford Magna 'we went to the flight office after breakfast to see if the squadron was operating that night. It was and later on in the morning we were told that our crew was on the battle order. About 6 o 'clock we had a flying meal of egg and chips and then a briefing when we were told what the target was and our take off time. I had never heard of Mailly-le-Camp but we all gave a sigh of relief as French targets were supposed to be easy. They only counted as a third of an op. A normal tour was 30 ops.'

Sergeant Ron 'Curly' Emeny, the 20-year old mid-upper gunner on New Zealand Warrant Officer Leslie Harry 'Lizzie' Lissette's crew on 'F-Freddie', a Lancaster III on 207 Squadron at Spilsby had completed one tour (30 raids) and was on his second. The 26-year-old pilot's girlfriend had been a nurse on a hospital ship bombed off Crete and was believed lost but 'Lizzie' a tough, powerfully built New Zealander, who had been a teamster with four horses hauling logs out of the mountains near Napier, never spoke much about it. He was on his fourth operation. Emeny, who was from Bow in London, had joined up when he was seventeen and a half and volunteered for air crew. 'All air crew were volunteers. There was one thing you learned in the forces and that was to get on with all types of people but this was particularly true of the crew on a Lanc. They became your second family. There was one man who had been a gamekeeper and he lived in the woods between raids. He was a good crew member but he preferred the fresh air. He built himself a tree house and slept there even in the depths of winter. If you weren't alive in the war, I suppose you'll find it difficult to understand the atmosphere that existed or the sense of humour amongst the troops. It was forbidden to have brothers in the same squadron but the Aussies always found ways of ignoring the rules. We had two pairs of New Zealand brothers on our strength. We'd just returned from a raid one day and I was walking behind an Aussie when the CO came across and put his hand on his shoulder. 'I'm sorry, Dave' he said, 'but your brother's plane has bought it. There are witnesses who saw it explode in the air. I'm afraid there were no survivors.'

'That's all right, Sir' Dave said, 'I'll have his egg and bacon.'

'We went on some long raids. A trip to Turin, for example, was ten and a half hours in the air and we had to stay alert for every second of it. When a fighter approached, I would only have it in my sight for a matter of seconds and that was my only chance to shoot at it. There was a feeling of excitement and adventure and determination and as soon as you donned a uniform you became part of it. There was a tension at times but you learned to live with it. You had to. You got used to this constant movement of men as they were posted to other stations, except for your own crew. Once we had been formed as a crew, we stayed together. Death was part of the scene and you'd feel a sense of sorrow when a certain crew had not returned but then you got on with the job. You never thought that one day you could be the one that didn't return. It always happened to the other man.

'As soon as we were over the coast, we could expect tracer fire and flak. The experienced pilots jinxed to avoid enemy fighters and tried to use cloud cover so that they couldn't be picked up by searchlights. It was the clear, moonlight nights we feared when the planes would leave vapour trails across the sky.'

Jimmy Graham, a member of the crew of 'Q-Queenie' on 576 Squadron at Elsham Wolds had completed a dozen operations and he had awaited another routine briefing. 'Nothing special was anticipated. It never was. We were on stand-by and had lazed the morning away waiting for the afternoon briefing. Our crew had been together throughout almost all of the operations we had completed and tended to do everything together during our off duty time as well. We were a mixed bag of people but had come to rely very heavily on each other in the air and that created a bond that was last throughout our lives. I was in a reserved occupation when war broke out, working in a local iron foundry. I watched my pals go off one by one to join up and knew the excitement of the war. A close friend and myself resolved to volunteer but we were turned away because 'we are full up at the moment.' John and I then went to Glasgow and we joined up there. It seemed like a good idea at the time. John was accepted for the marines, I for the RAF. I never saw him again.

'It was late morning when the briefing was called. Security was very tight. There was the usual anticipation of the string drawing out the route to the target. It was a short string. It looked like another short, easy operation. Then the Intelligence Officer introduced the reality. Details followed of Mailly's function as a gathering and servicing centre for German Panzer Divisions. This was seen as crucial to repulse an allied invasion in Northern Europe. It had to be removed from operational use. The penny dropped. It was just another raid but this one really mattered.'

Up until 1940 Mailly had been a French Army artillery training area. The whole complex covered about 55 squaremiles but the barracks, workshops and garages were concentrated into about 400 acres at the northwest corner next to the village of Mailly. The area was known to be defended by two six-gun batteries or radar-controlled 88mm heavy anti-aircraft guns and about 28 37mm and 20mm light guns. In all, 346 Lancasters and 14 Mosquitoes of I and 5 Groups were detailed to attack a Panzer regiment HQ at Mailly-le-Camp, almost halfway between Troyes and Châlons-sur-Marne, about 50 miles south of Rheims. The camp housed three Panzer battalions belonging to regiments on the Eastern Front and elements of two more as well as the permanent training school staff. I and 5 Groups provided the Main Force and were to attack Mailly in two phases. Some 173 aircraft of 5 Group would go in first and aim their bombs at a point near the southeast end of the barracks area. This would be followed by another 173 Lancasters of 1 Group, most of which would attack the northwest end of the barracks while 30 aircraft were to concentrate on a special point near the workshops. Wing Commander Lawrence Deane or his deputy, Squadron Leader Neville Sparks, both of 83 Squadron, would orchestrate the attack.[110] The weather forecast was for mostly clear skies and good visibility in all areas and there was nearly a full moon.

Jack Spark DFM, who was from Carlisle was the 21-year old wireless operator on 'U-for Uncle' piloted by Flight Sergeant Fred Brownings on 103 Squadron at Elsham Wolds 'which overlooked the Humber, was cold with nothing between us and Russia and that was where the winds came from'. 'It was a good station' Spark recalled. 'There was a happy atmosphere at Elsham Wolds but we all knew we had a job to do and we did it. The spirit of co-operation and comradeship was terrific.'

Mailly was Jack Spark's 14th operation. Brownings' crew had been attacked by fighters on every one of their first ten operations. On the fourth, towards the end of the Battle of Berlin, the rear gunner, Sergeant Bob Thomas, had been killed in his turret while fighting off the first of three attacks from a Focke Wulf 190 and it had taken all of Fred Brownings' strength and skill to fly the crippled aircraft home.[111]

'The target and route was explained to us at the briefing together with the details of the bomb load we were carrying and the weather conditions we could expect en route. We were told that it would be 'a piece of cake'. And we believed it. There was always a sense of tension; a tightness when there was going to be a raid which was quite different to the days when no raid had been announced. Then there would be a rush to get ready for a night on the town. There wasn't the usual tension on May 3rd. We didn't expect any trouble.'

'Briefing continued' recalled Jimmy Graham. 'There were three main targets. Group Captain Cheshire's Pathfinders were to mark the target area with flares, more detailed marking than usual. Second stage briefings were for individual groups; pilots, gunners, navigators, bomb-aimers, radio operators and engineers. Then it was personal preparations, parachutes, letters and shaving and the special treat, an egg with our bacon.'

'After our operational meal' says Jack Spark 'we returned to our billets to get ready. Some of the men were superstitious and would go through a set pattern of behaviour before we went on a raid. Others would have a lucky mascot which was important to them. I just got myself ready and joined up with the rest of the crew. In a way, the crew were family. A close relationship had developed between us. We were so used to working together that we hated it if one of the crew was sick and we had someone we didn't know in his place. On this particular raid, we had a new plane and a new rear gunner, Bert Buckman'.

Gordon Wallace went to the crew room and put on his flying gear. 'I wore long Johns and vest, battle dress, kapok flying suit, gabardine outer, heated gauntlets, socks, electrically heated socks (like slippers) and sheepskin boots. On top of this I put on a parachute harness and a Mae West or life jacket. I collected a parachute from the store and the crew bus took me and the rest of my crew out to the aircraft. We all climbed on. I turned left towards the tail and slid down the ramp to the rear turret. I settled in, plugging in my suit and the intercom that connected the headset in my leather helmet. The pilot called each of us in turn to check everyone was OK.

'OK rear gunner?'

'OK'. When he got a signal from the ground he taxied the aircraft to join the queue to take off. The time was 22.00 hours. There was a caravan at the end of the runway and, as each plane took off and cleared the runway, a signaller would flash a green Aldis lamp to the pilot of the next plane. We were one of the 19 aircraft that took off from Ludford Magna that night.'

'We were driven out to the dispersal area' says Jimmy Graham 'and killed a bit of time with idle chat. Ginger ran a final engine check and we were ready for the off. It was 2300 hours; time to go. It was a clear night and visibility was superb. Charles started us rolling and the raid was on.'

The thing that really impressed one rear gunner on 103 Squadron at Elsham Wolds was the way the men gathered round their own Lancasters waiting for their captains to tell them to get on board. 'And I was one of them.' 'The captains seemed so important yet most of them almost strolled round their aircraft as they did the final checks. There was Squadron Leader Jack Swanston with his cap pushed to the back of his head and Pilot Officer Pat Furlong who always looked incredibly smart. Then there were three Flying Officers; Way, Leggett and Young who seemed to be great friends and a couple of Canadians, Pilot Officer Moore and Flight Sergeant Tate. You wouldn't have argued with those two. Pilot Officer Rowe was a typical Australian who didn't seem to have a care in the world and the others that I can't remember too clearly; Flying Officer Broadbent, Armstrong and Morrison, Pilot Officer Whitley and Flight Sergeant Brownings. The life expectancy of a wartime pilot was forty hours and that didn't do a lot for my confidence but it helped when we were airborne and I could see other Lancasters flying steadily behind us.'[112]

'There was tension as we waited on the apron to climb in to Lancaster 'Y for Yoke' continues Geoff Gilbert. 'There always was before a raid and men eased that tension in different ways, some by making jokes and others by going to one side and having a quiet moment on their own. Somehow the tension was not so high that night. There wasn't expected to be any trouble. Some even referred to it as a milk run. Both 61 and 50 Squadrons at Skellingthorpe were on the raid. As it happened we were the last to lift off. Once we were in the air, we became more relaxed. We all had work to do and we needed to concentrate. I don't know if Don was suspicious that the raid was not going to be as easy as expected but he took evading action as we crossed the Channel.'

'The route was not direct' says Jimmy Graham. 'Defence installations in North West France were well known and our route was a course avoiding them. We had 'Window' on board, silver strips which filled the enemy radar screens with snow storms and we dropped this at regular intervals. Our Canadian navigator, Tug, had a fairly straightforward bit of work ahead of him, at least on the outward run. We headed for the collection area above Châlons to wait for the order to attack when the Pathfinders had marked the target. It was all quiet as we approached Châlons. Mac had imposed R/T silence to keep the air clear so that he could receive the signal to go in and bomb. Everything was quiet. There was no ack-ack guns, no German fighters. We started to circle above Châlons. We circled again and again and again. There was no message. There was no radio silence either. There were American voices and Glenn Miller music. It was the Germans trying to jam our communications or so we thought. Whatever the reason, our contact with the Pathfinders and the Master Bomber was broken.

'Enemy coast ahead' the navigator on 'Y for Yoke' announced. 'There was no emotion in his voice' recalled Geoff Gilbert. 'We weaved our way to the target. Our golden rule was that we could expect trouble whenever we were over enemy territory and we were to be ready for it. The approach to the target was trouble free. Then I heard the navigator's voice saying that there was no need for his services. He could see the target ahead. I couldn't see a thing at the tail end of the plane but they carried on their chatter for my benefit. I was taken aback to hear that a Lancaster had exploded in the air and that there were fighters amongst the bombers. It seemed that a number of Lancasters had not yet cleared the target area and we had to wait off while they went in and bombed. There's always a danger in circumstances like that that a bomber can drop its bombs on a friendly plane beneath it or that two Lancasters can collide. We had a near miss ourselves. The navigator was the pilot's eyes. He was reliable, observant and accurate. 'Look ahead, Skipper' he said and immediately the pilot lifted the Lancaster up. We missed the plane that had been flying in front of us by a matter of yards. 'I saw the rivets on that one, Skip' came the Canadian drawl.'

'The prospect of being left behind by the main stream was unnerving' recalled the rear gunner on 103 Squadron 'but fortunately that didn't happen to us; rather the reverse. There was a build up in the numbers over the marker and I could sense the tenseness from the skipper over the intercom. The Lanc climbed steeply at one point and I heard the exclamation, 'That was close.' But I couldn't see what was happening in front. I was a rear gunner, a tail-end Charlie and I could only see what was happening to the rear of us and that was plenty. German night fighters were close and I was ready for them but they approached at such a speed that I would only see them for a matter of seconds in the target aimer before they were up and over us. I can remember a Messerschmitt coming at us with its guns firing. I fired at it as soon as I had it in my sights and it sprayed us with bullets but it didn't affect our flying luckily. I doubt if I saw the thing for more than five seconds. It all happened so quickly.

'We came up to the target at 23,000 feet. The markers were visible. 'Bomb doors open' the statement came over the intercom. Some flak was coming up at us and it was like riding a bike with flat tyres over cobble stones.

'Jack stated, 'Bombs gone.'

'Alec gave the course for out and the Skipper said, 'Let's go home.'

'There was no flak. The gunners had left it open for their night-fighters to attack. I had a different view now and I looked back on a scene of absolute carnage. There were flames and smoke from the place we had bombed but there was also the sight of fallen and falling planes.'

Gordon Wallace's pilot had followed the course he had been given at the briefing. 'We flew at 7,000 feet, the navigator checking the course and giving the pilot course corrections. On most raids I didn't hear any sounds over the RT (radio-telephone) but that night, as we got nearer the target, we could hear the Pathfinders talking to each other. We were ordered to circle some yellow flares on the ground north of the target. There were fighters active but I could only see dark shapes in the sky. I saw some aircraft explode and others go down. Because I could hear the radios, I could hear the crews. I heard one man screaming, calling out for his mother.

'We were still circling round and round. It felt as though we were circling for hours but it was probably only minutes. Over the radio I heard a voice I recognised from another aircraft asking, 'Hello Pathfinder, can we come in and bomb now?'

'A voice replied, 'No, continue circling'.

'It may have only been a few minutes but it felt like hours had passed when I heard the same voice ask the same question and get the same reply, 'No, do not bomb, continue circling.' The voice, which belonged to Kit Carson who had a distinctive Canadian accent replied '.... the RAF; we're coming in'.

'I heard one of the Pathfinders say, 'I've been hit. I've got to go down, 'in such a matter of fact way as if he was saying he was going out for a walk. (I think he later escaped from France with the help of the Resistance).

'At 12.32, after circling for what seemed like hours, we were called in to bomb. Our pilot Tom steered the aircraft straight and level over the target and the bomb aimer released the bombs as close to the target as he could. We turned back for home.'

Jack Spark heard Fred Brownings say on intercom 'To hell with this. It's like moths caught in a candle' and he flew on and started circling thirty miles away. We were called in to bomb at 1232 hours. We should have bombed at 1215. Those extra minutes were disastrous for so many crews. It gave the Germans time to muster their forces and there were four night fighter stations within reach. Their fighters were waiting for us when we returned. So were the searchlights; not that they were really needed. The moon was a better light and there was no escaping from it. I saw two Lancasters going down with smoke trails behind them. We were preparing for pour bombing run when we heard a man screaming. It's a sound I will never forget. It frightened me to death.

Then this cold, commanding voice broke in: 'If you must die, die like a man' it ordered. It was more shocking than the scream.

'After what seemed hours we heard a voice through the mush on the R/T saying 'Go in and bomb'. Needless to say we didn't waste any time. The bomb aimer took over the plane. We had hardly got into position when another Lanc, twenty feet above us pressed the bomb release. Our gunner shouted out 'For God's sake duck.' It all happened too quickly for us to realise what a lucky escape we had had. As we were leaving the target the rear gunner spotted a FW 190 coming in from dead astern and yelled 'Corkscrew starboard go!' He fired one long burst at us but missed and thankfully we lost him after that. As we turned for home, another plane exploded in the air. It was mayhem.'

'Outside, hell had broken out' continues Jimmy Graham. 'German night fighters had arrived in force and were attacking the circling bombers. Lancaster down... and another and another two fly into each other and explode in the air and others scatter so that they are not hit by the debris. And still there was no attack order. Stan, the mid upper gunner and I kept our eyes open but no fighter attacked us. There were plenty of other targets.

'Suddenly R/T was broken by a strong Aussie voice. 'The hell with this, let's go before we're picked off.' And go we did. Charles lined us up for a clear run in and Nick dropped his bombs right on target and we made a bee line for home without further incident but going like hell.[113]

'Don asked the navigator for a course away from the chaos' continues Jimmy Gilbert 'and we circled further out. When we returned to the target, the skies were not so congested but there was still plenty of activity and our crew was silenced as we saw another bomber being hit and diving towards the ground.

'We were flying towards a lot of trouble. There was no mention of that as each of us in turn reported to the skipper. The navigator announced, 'Coming to target' and the bomb aimer took over from him. The navigator gave him the most recent estimate of the prevailing wind and the bomb aimer would start to adjust the position at which the bombs were to be dropped. The wind can affect the direction at which the bomb travels as well as the aircraft. The run up to, through and out of the target area was a disciplined drill. We were ten miles out from the final run in. I was searching the skies for enemy fighters as we approached and listened through my headphones as the bomb aimer's voice gave instruction to the pilot. Then the order came for us to go in and bomb.

'Bomb doors open. Left, left steady. Right to starboard. Bombs away. OK Skipper.'

'He didn't have to say that the bombs had been dropped. The aircraft was always much lighter to fly after the release of the bomb load. We had been carrying a 4,000lb cookie and 16 x 500lb GPs (General Purpose) bombs. We felt them go. We had to wait about thirty seconds for the target photo flash. Then the announcement came, 'Bomb doors closed.' We should have bombed at 00.04 hours. We went in at 00.34. We were 30 minutes late. We were the last aircraft to bomb. The four Merlin engines were harmonised. The pressures and temperatures were as they should be. Don's voice, with as much expression as I had ever heard him use on a raid, said, 'Let's get the hell out of here.'

'Although we had been doing our own jobs, we were aware of the devastation going on around us. We could see burning aircraft on the ground, black smoke drifting like funeral pyres and, even as we turned, another Lancaster exploded to our starboard side and there were still the German fighters flying amongst us. As we turned for home, we picked up a Messerschmitt. Don dived immediately and we lost it. We didn't wait around. Don told the navigator to plot a new course. We didn't want to stay too close to the mainstream because some of the German fighters were trailing them. We were the last to bomb at Mailly and because I was rear gunner I was the last airman to leave.

'The skipper asked the navigator how far to the coast and repeated the question every few minutes. We were all relieved as we reached the Channel and realised that we were on our own. We avoided the Channel Islands. They were deadly. They were so heavily defended, particularly at Sark. We landed at Skellingthorpe, went for the debriefing and went to bed. It wasn't until the next morning that we found how many planes and men had been lost. Our Squadron was lucky. They all returned but 50 Squadron lost four of their Lancasters'.

One of the Lancasters on 50 Squadron that was lost was LM437 VN-P flown by 22-year old Pilot Officer Ronald Stanley Hanson, which crashed at Trouan-le-Petit in the Aube with six crew dead.[114] Only Sergeant W. 'Dicky' Richardson the wireless operator, severely burned on the hands and face, bailed out. He was taken prisoner but despite his terrible burns was given only cursory medical treatment. Soon after D-Day the town in which he was in hospital in Northern France was heavily bombed. The Germans evacuated the town and several days later when Allied troops arrived they found Richardson lying in a cellar blind and with a gangrenous right hand. The hand was amputated and he was brought back to England to the Queen Victoria Hospital plastic surgery centre at East Grinstead where the long slow process of his recuperation began. Plastic surgeons gave him a new nose, chin, ears, eyelids and upper lip; his sight they could not restore.[115]

In 1950 he acquired a tobacco and confectionary shop in Ronkswood,

50 Squadron formation at Skellingthorpe on 23 July 1943 led by VN-T DV197 which was SOC a week later due to damage.

Left: Crew of Lancaster ND556 on 207 Squadron flown by Flight Sergeant Lissette RNZAF (centre, holding the mascot) which were shot down on 3/4 May 1944 on Mailly. Back Row L-R: Sergeant Ron Emeny, mid-upper gunner (Evd); Sergeant Laurie Wesley, bomb aimer (PoW); Flight Sergeant Jack Pittwood, navigator (Evd); Sergeant Nick Stockford, flight engineer (Evd). Front: Sergeant Ron Ellis, rear gunner (KIA); Lissette and Sergeant Philip King, wireless operator (Evd). Lissette was critically injured and died soon after in a French Hospital. (via Phil King)

Below: Fred Brownings' crew on 103 Squadron at Elsham Wolds on 25 March 1944. That night the crew were attacked by a night fighter and the rear gunner; Sergeant Ronald Thomas (far right) was killed. The rest of the crew went on to complete a further 26 operations, with a replacement gunner, Sergeant Bert Burrill, finishing their tour on Orleans on 4 July 1944. From left are: Flight Sergeant Jack Spark DFM, wireless operator; Pilot Officer Ron Walker DFC, navigator; Pilot Officer Norman Baker DFC. Bomb aimer; Flight Sergeant (later Pilot Officer) Arthur Richardson DFC, flight engineer; Flight Sergeant (later Pilot Officer) Fred Brownings DFC, pilot and Sergeant Ken Smart, mid upper gunner.

Sergeant Norman Ellis 'Greg' Gregory, bomb aimer on 101 Squadron at Ludford Magna. (Norman Gregory)

'Kriegie' post card sent from prison camp by Norman Gregory to his parents in England. (Norman Gregory)

Above left: Flight Sergeant 'Dave' Jacobs, navigator on Les Davidson's crew.
Above right: Sergeant William Hayman, one of the gunners on Les Davidson's crew.
Below left: Sergeant Lionel Milligan, WOp/AG on Les Davidson's crew.
Below right: Sergeant (later Pilot Officer) Les Davidson RNZAF. (all Norman Gregory)

Lancaster B1 RA530 DX-Y on 57 Squadron at East Kirkby, which was destroyed in a takeoff crash in Stockney village on 20 March 1945 at the start of the operation on Bohlen. Flying Officer Charles Alan Cobern RAAF and five of the crew were killed instantly, a sixth crewmember died of his injuries on 1 April.

Lancaster cockpit.

Lancasters on 405 PFF Squadron RCAF.

Armourers haul a 'Cookie' into position.

The raid on Dresden in progress on the night of 13/14 February 1945. The city was devastated by 796 Lancasters and by 311 bombers of the 8th Air Force the following day. (IWM)

The crew of 'Q-Queenie' on 12 Squadron at Wickenby.

The debrief at Wickenby after the raid on Boulogne on 15 June 1944. Left to right: Sergeant Griggs; Flying Officer Campbell Muirhead; Sergeant Dunn; Sergeant Norman; Sergeant Cartwright; Pilot Officer Horsfall and Flying Officer Vernon. The American pilot's stock reply when asked to report on any damage by any WAAF officer who had not debriefed this crew before was: 'only to my wedding tackle'. (Muirhead via Philip Swan)

Flight Lieutenant Campbell Muirhead. (Muirhead via Philip Swan)

Lancaster PP687 G-H Leader on 149 Squadron at the American 94th Bomb Group B-17 base at Bury St. Edmunds (Rougham) in the last few months of the war.

Lancaster on 15 Squadron at Mildenhall dropping food to the Dutch during Operation 'Manna' in May 1945. From 29 April to 7 May Lancasters flew 2,835 food sorties and delivered 6,672 tons of food to the starving Dutch people during Operation 'Manna'. RAF Mildenhall's Lancasters alone dropped enough supplies for around 50,000 people. (via Harry Holmes)

Above: On VE-Day Flight Sergeant A. D. M. Anderson of Handsworth, Birmingham was flown back from a prison camp in Lancaster PB422. Anderson was the only survivor on the crew captained by Flying Officer Eric Albert Williams DFC that was shot down on the night of 11/12 April 1944 on the operation on Aachen. On 27/28 January 1944 Anderson had been one of four survivors on Pilot Officer Williams' crew on Lancaster W4315 QR-Q, which was ditched off Guernsey after being hit by flak south of Hanover while homebound from Berlin.

Lancasters on 635 Squadron start engines at Lübeck during Operation Exodus on 11 May 1945 when Bomber Command ferried newly-released prisoners of war back to Britain. Operations to Brussels and other airfields began on 26 April and continued until 1 June. Five hundred PoWs per day were repatriated from Juvincourt airfield near Rheims alone. By 1 June approximately 75,000 men had been brought home by Bomber Command. (IWM)

Lancaster B.Mk.VIIs on 617 'Dam Busters' Squadron in the white (top) and black (undersides) finish adopted for aircraft of 'Tiger Force' operating from Benares, India in early 1946.

Avro Lincolns on the line.
(Avro)

Lincoln B.2 VN-C on 50 Squadron at Waddington passing Lincoln Cathedral at extremely low altitude in 1948! (via Terry Hancock)

RAAF Lincoln MK.30s RE301 and SX983 bombing Communist positions in Malaya during the Emergency in 1954.

Worcester which his wife, Eileen, helped him to run. The wedding had been planned for August 1944 but Richardson was then on the lists of the missing. When next Eileen saw him he was blind and disfigured almost beyond recognition. But to her, her fiancée's tragedy was not half good enough reason for cancelling the wedding. And when it did take place there was a far grander reception than had been planned in 1944. It was held in Worcester's ancient Guildhall, loaned by the mayor as a civic gesture to Dicky Richardson's courage.[116]

Back in England, meanwhile, Gordon Wallace arrived back at Ludford Magna 'last of our squadron and 12 minutes after the previous aircraft.'

'We had already been chalked up as lost but the aircraft we were flying that night was slow. We disconnected ourselves and clambered out of the aircraft. The crew bus took us back to debriefing where we told an intelligence officer what we had seen and heard. The IO would have heard some of the radio exchanges during the raid from what he could pick up on the radio at the base. After debriefing, I went to the Sergeants Mess and had a meal, egg and chips again and went to bed. We found out later that the camp and 37 German tanks were destroyed but 42 out of the 350 aircraft which took part in the raid were lost. Soon after this raid, there was another, which also had heavy losses and after that, all raids on France were counted as one op.'

The rear gunner who had feared that they would be left behind by the main stream made it home to Elsham Wolds but he hardly had the strength to climb out of the Lancaster. 'I was absolutely exhausted. I hadn't done anything to make me feel so tired but I suppose reaction had set in. We looked round the Lanc. It had been knocked about and it would need to be patched up before it flew again. We were all subdued as we went to the de-briefing. We took our coffee to the de-briefing table. It had a tot of rum in it. I didn't like rum. What the hell. We had got home and I was alive. It tasted good.'[117]

'U-Uncle' on 103 Squadron and 'Q-Queenie' on 576 Squadron also landed safely at Elsham Wolds. 'We were one of the last planes to return to Elsham' said Jack Spark 'and, although our ground crew were pleased to see us, there was a subdued air in the camp.'

'Q-Queenie's' crew went straight to debriefing. 'We were safely home and glad to be so' recalled Jimmy Graham. 'Good mission, we thought, or was it? The truth of the losses was beginning to come in - 42 crews lost.[118] The radio jamming had caused the delay and the circling Lancasters had been easy prey for the German fighters.

'It was time for us to relax, time for another treat, another egg and bacon. Time to relax but never to forget.'

'Mailly' recalls Ron Emeny 'was a disaster from start to finish and anyone else who was on that raid will tell you the same. We found out afterwards that the radio had failed but we didn't know that then. We were circling round waiting for the order to go in and drop our bombs. We were like sitting ducks in full view of the enemy because it was one of those clear, moonlit nights that we dreaded. We were hit by light flak on the port wing and began to lose fuel although we weren't aware of it at the time. Then we had three attacks by Focke-Wulf 190s and a Me 110 attacked us from below, aiming at our fuel tanks. That was a favourite trick of theirs. We were well on fire. My parachute was hanging in the fuselage. There hadn't been enough room to keep it in the turret with me. I had to turn the turret round, reach for my parachute, put it on, turn the turret round again and jump for it. Only the parachute wasn't there when I reached for it. All the lights had gone out and I was crawling through thick, black, choking smoke feeling for it. I was lucky. It was one of the luckiest moments of my life. I put my hand right on it. It had broken loose and was rolling about on the floor. I put it on and made for the rear door. Just before I jumped, I picked up the intercom and told the pilot I was leaving.

'I thought you'd gone already; you curly, black headed bastard' he said but his words didn't come easily. I could hear him gasping as he fought to control the plane steady long enough for us all to escape. They were probably the last words he spoke.' Lissette, who remained at the controls to the end, was critically injured and he died later in a French hospital. [119]

'I had to jump through flames' continues Emeny. 'The engines were well alight and there was no way I could avoid them. I didn't open my parachute until I had cleared it. Within seconds of my leaving the plane, one of the wings broke off and went over my head. It was so close that I could see every detail on it. I can remember looking up at the plane and noting that the propellers were still going round. It was as I looked up that I realised two panels of my parachute were on fire and the flames were spreading rapidly. I was falling faster and faster. I fell rather than floated and landed in a ploughed field. I was dropping so fast that I went into the earth up to my knees. I released myself from the parachute and lay there. I knew I had been burned, mostly on my head and across my shoulders. But it was my eyes that were the problem. I lay there and didn't know what to do. I heard someone coming towards me.

'Kamarad' I said.

'You silly bastard' a voice answered with a broad Yorkshire accent. 'It's me, Jack.' Jack Pittwood was the navigator. 'Come on, we've got to get moving.'

'We gathered up our parachutes so that if the Germans came they wouldn't know that there had been any survivors. Then we started walking. I had both hands on Jack's shoulders and he was telling me where we were going. We found a derelict cottage and stuffed the parachutes up the chimney. Then we crossed a road. We were half way across it when we heard trucks coming towards us. Jack pulled me after him and we made for the other side of the road and tumbled into a ditch. It was deeper than we thought with a foot of water in the bottom. The trucks pulled up right alongside us. We hardly dared breathe let alone move. Orders were given to the German troops from the trucks. They spread out along the road and started walking towards the burning plane. They obviously thought there were no survivors because they came back to the trucks quite quickly and drove off. We waited for a few minutes and then climbed out of the ditch and started walking down the road. I relied on Jack to lead me and explain where we were going. We had our uniforms on and our flying boots so there was no denying who we were. We reached a village and walked right along the main road. It was about six o 'clock by this time and people were beginning to move. The baker was standing in front of his shop. A couple of other people stood and stared at us. Nobody said anything or tried to stop us. We went into a cemetery and found shelter in a big, old family tomb and we settled down there. That was when the pain hit me and it got worse and worse until I became delirious. The vault in which we were hiding was against a wall and an elderly couple were tending their garden on the other side of the wall. They must have realised we were there but they carried on gardening as if there was nothing amiss. As evening fell, two French men came to our hiding place. Jack was fit and they told me that they were going to take him with them and that they would be back to see to me later. I know now that they thought I would die in the night and that the old couple on the other side of the wall dug a hole beneath their vines because they thought that they would have to bury me.

'Two men from the underground came back early the next morning and, when they saw I was still alive; they fetched a doctor to look at me. He said that I needed specialist treatment and they should take me to the next village where there was a surgeon [Dr. Robert Salmon] who specialised in burns and had recently returned from Paris to take over his father s practice. The men contacted him and he came and fetched me and took me to his own home and looked after me for six weeks. It is impossible for me to put into words the feelings I have for these brave people. I wouldn't be here today if it hadn't been for them.

'I couldn't have been in better care than I was in the doctor's home. As I got better I began to worry about the risk my presence there was imposing on him and his family. The problem was that medicine was difficult to obtain. He needed sulphanilamide to treat me. The local Maquis sent a message to London asking for the drug and explaining why it was needed. Two days later, there was a knock on the door and a parcel addressed to Flight Sergeant Emeny was handed over. It contained not sulphanilamide but penicillin. I found out later that Squadron Leader Hugh Verity DSO DFC [the Special Duties Lysander Flight Commander] had flown over in a Lysander to deliver it. I had never heard of penicillin, neither had the doctor. He did not know what the dosage was or how much to give me. It was a hit and miss affair but it did the trick. I started to improve straight away.

'I stayed with the doctor for six weeks until I was considered fit enough to move to Paris. I was given French clothes that fitted me as if they had been made for me. My head was still bandaged but I could see again. The doctor had been bathing my eyes each day and it was a wonderful moment when he told me that my eyes had not been burned.

'Etienne, a fifteen year old boy took me to Paris. When we reached the station he told me that he couldn't come any further. A lady with two bikes would be waiting outside the station. One of the bikes was for me. It was important that he did not see her because, then, if he was ever caught, he would not be able to identify her. Sure enough, the lady [Virginia D'Albert-Lake, pretty American woman in her forties] was waiting. She asked me in perfect English if I could ride a bike. She had been caught in Paris when the Americans came into the war. She asked me where I came from and I told her London. 'We have another man from London' she said, 'perhaps you'll know him?'

'Oh yes' I thought.

'We reached a block of flats and, leaving our bikes in the entrance, we climbed to the top floor, the fifth. She opened the door and showed me into a small room in her flat. 'Hello Ron' a voice said and there, sitting on the floor with his feet towards the centre of the room was Len Barnes, the boy who had sat next to me at school. 'It's a pity you weren't here yesterday' he went on, 'you'd have met Reg Lewis. He was here.' Reg had been in our class as well. [120]

'There were fourteen of us in that room. There was not enough room to lie down. We had to sit with our feet towards the centre of the room and we had to keep quiet. We could not let any of the other people who lived in that block of flats have any idea that we were there. The worst thing was the toilet. We couldn't keep pulling the chain. That could have given the game away. We could only pull it five or six times.

'We had been there for a few days when Madame Virginia, as we called her, told us that arrangements had been made to get our identity cards but first of all, we had to have our photos taken. We were to leave the flat two at a time and meet outside where bikes would be waiting for us. Sure enough everything worked as she said and we set off in a long line with Madame Virginia leading us and her husband bringing up the rear. We went round the Arc de Triomphe, down La Place de la Concorde to the Boulevard Sebastopol. There we went in two at a time to have our photographs taken. That evening five of us left for Bordeaux; three Americans [Lieutenant Colonel Thomas S. 'Speedy' Hubbard, Major Donald Kenyon Willis, a former Eagle Squadron pilot and 2nd Lieutenant Jack D. Cornett] and Len and myself.[121] We made our way across Paris by Metro to the Gare d' Ouest. We got on the train without any trouble. We had the correct tickets and our papers were all in order. Mine said that I was a deaf mute. I was on my own but I knew the others weren't far away. Germans occupied all the carriages, lying along the seats so that there wasn't room for anyone else. I stood in the corridor but I was aware that Len was standing at the other end and I knew the Americans were further up the train.

'We left at six o 'clock in the morning and arrived at Bordeaux at six the following morning. The train kept stopping. There were air raids in progress throughout the night and it felt strange being on the receiving end for once. Every so often, we would pull into a siding and the engine would be changed. Allied bombers had destroyed so much that the French were having trouble keeping the trains running. We had to spend the day in Bordeaux. Our train to Biarritz was not leaving until the evening so 'Michou', the young French girl who was guiding us, took us down to a park and told us to spend the day there. It was very relaxing in the park. [122] 'Michou' returned at mid-day with sandwiches and a flask of coffee. We were happy sitting there chattering when 'Michou' returned in an agitated state and told us to get out of the park quickly. We almost ran after her. We got out of the gates and spread out along the road and started to walk away casually just as German army lorries roared up to the park gates. We carried on walking as the soldiers locked the park gates and started searching.

'I think we were all relieved when we boarded the Biarritz train. We were spread out in the same way that we had been on the train from Paris. We were travelling through a forbidden zone and I was feeling tense. We were getting close to the Spanish border and caught our first sight of the Pyrénées. We knew our passes were in order but it was still a funny feeling as we drew nearer and nearer to the mountains, part excitement but also a heightened awareness of the dangers that still surrounded us. There were two Germans in the carriage; to start with they slept peacefully. Then they woke up and started to move around. They came out into the corridor and one of them demanded a light for his cigarette. I told them 'pas de fumeur' but they wouldn't take no for an answer and started to jostle me. I didn't know what to do. I knew I mustn't do anything that would draw attention to myself. If they found out that I was a British airman, then they would catch all five of us because it was well known that people trying to escape over the Pyrénées travelled in small groups and they would also know that there was a member of the French resistance travelling with us. At that moment the train drew into a small country station and I got off. At this point the road ran along beside the railway so I simply started walking. The train pulled out of the station and I saw Len's face looking out with consternation. He hadn't seen what had been happening with the Germans.

'I left the village and carried on walking along the road. There was an old man working in his garden and he called out, 'M'sieur, m'sieur, English soldat?' I told him I was an airman. 'You walk like a soldier' he told me. He had fought alongside English troops in the First World War, so he had a little English. He stood behind me and bent my shoulders forward so that I slouched. He pushed my hands into my pockets and pulled my beret over my forehead. 'Now you walk like a Frenchman' he said.

'I carried on walking. I must have been walking for an hour when two men approached on bicycles pulling another one between them. They started riding round me in a circle when they reached me without saying anything. Then one of them asked, 'English aviator?' 'I said I was and one of them indicated the spare bike. We cycled into Biarritz and round to a cafe where the others were waiting. We stayed there until it was time for us to take a tram for Sibour, a little village at the foot of the mountains. It was more like a train than a tram. It ran on rails but it had a conductor and kept stopping like a tram. 'Michou' was still with us and explained that we would have to cross the River Bidassoa by a bridge that would be guarded. She told us to walk as normally as possible and the guards would not stop us. We did and they didn't but it was a tense moment. 'Michou' took us to a little Basque hovel with mud floors and a room in the roof. There were already donkeys, pigs and hens sheltering in the place as well as the six men that had left the flat in Paris a few days before us. We settled down with them in the hay. It was alive and it wasn't long before we were too. We had only been there a short time when 'Florentino' appeared at the door and said 'We go.' The six men who had been waiting went straight away. Two days later, it was our turn. 'Florentino' had come back for us. He was one of the most powerful and purposeful men I had ever met. He had led many allied people over the mountains. I'm not the only person who owes a lot to him. [123]

'We followed 'Florentino' up the tracks and it was strenuous. We hadn't had much exercise over the last few weeks and we found it hard going. We had been moving for ten and a half hours when he called a halt. It was cold, bitterly cold. It had been pleasantly warm in Biarritz but now we were on the snowline. 'Florentino' told us to wait there while he went for food. He didn't come back. We waited for a long time. It had started to rain and the rain grew steadily heavier. We could see the glow of lights from the Spanish town and we decided that we couldn't wait any longer. We would go on on our own. At times the rain was so heavy that it was difficult to see where we were going. We were soaked through but we were beginning to go down and we could see the lights of Spain through the curtain of rain. Then we saw some sheds and, much to our surprise, there were people living in them, two shepherds, a woman and two children. They had nothing. There was no food and they were dressed in rags. They signalled for us to shelter from the rain and we were pleased to get under cover. They started talking amongst themselves. Then one of the shepherds signalled that he was leaving. Hubbard spoke Spanish. He'd picked up a bit of the language when he had traded with Puerto Rica before the war. He said it was time for us to go as well. The man who had left had told the others to keep us there. He'd obviously gone for the Germans and was looking for a reward. The other peasants tried to keep us there but we pushed them out of the way and carried on walking.

'The rain stopped in the morning so we rested for a while and dried out. We had no food but there was plenty of water. It was ice cold and those of us that had fillings in our teeth were soon reminded of them. It was early in the morning that we caught sight of the Spanish town and we made for it. We found out later that it was Pamplona. Half way down the mountain, we came across a young man sitting on a rock. He had a hand of bananas and a skin of wine. He was 'Florentino's son and had been waiting there for us for three days. That was how we found out that 'Florentino' had been shot in the legs by some Germans. His son had come into the mountains looking for us. He had met up with the shepherds who had told him that we had passed so he thought it was best that he waited at that point We had not eaten for days and those bananas were good, so was the wine. We were in much better spirits when we made for the town. The young man explained that he was going to hand us over to the police because the Gestapo kept watch on the British consul and there had been instances where they had kidnapped some of the airmen that had been rescued so we would be kept at the Spanish police station until someone from our Consul came and collected us. It was filthy. The first thing that happened to us when we reached the police station was that we were deloused. Then we were put in a cell and locked up. The other six who had been with us in Paris were already there. There was straw on the floor but, at least, we felt cleaner until the others pointed at the ceiling. There were these bugs, fully three inches long clinging to the wall above us. 'You wait until it gets dark and they come looking for warmth' the others told us.

'We'd been in this cell for a couple of days when there was this hell of a commotion and this Spanish officer arrived. He had so much gold braid on his uniform it was a wonder he wasn't weighed down by it. He assembled the Spaniards together and spoke to them for a long time without pausing for breath. Willy translated for us. It seemed that the allies had landed in Normandy and, despite all the German talk, they were falling back and the allies were advancing steadily. The men were told that they better look after us. A few hours later, we were transferred to a hotel but, first of all, the Spanish officer asked us to write something to say that we had been well treated. One of the Americans fancied himself as a writer and took a lot of care in writing out a certificate. 'This officer is a bastard and should be shot at sight.' When he went back to Spain several years after the war, he found the officer sitting at his desk with that same certificate framed and hanging on the wall behind him.

'There were baths at the hotel and clean clothes for us. They asked if we would like an English breakfast and we said, 'Yes please.' They brought in bowls of fresh fruit and then they brought in a big bowl of eggs swimming in olive oil and lumps of bacon in another dish also swimming in olive oil. We gave it to the children that had gathered round us. We ate the fruit. We then had an escort from the Spanish air force and he took us to Irún by train. We were taken to a really smart hotel there. About mid-day the following morning, a Rolls Royce arrived at the front of the hotel. The chauffeur leapt out and opened the back door and out stepped [Sir Samuel Hoare, a former British Foreign Secretary] a man about our own age resplendent in a pin striped suit, a bowler hat and a rolled umbrella. He wandered into the foyer. 'Who are the RAF chappies?' he asked. As soon as we had identified ourselves, he told us to jump into the jolly old Rolls.

'What about us?' the Americans asked.

'Oh, I expect they'll send a jeep for you,' the young man answered.

'We went to the Embassy but the consul didn't appreciate our presence. 'I do wish you RAF chappies would stop walking over the jolly old mountains' he started when he saw us. 'It makes it so embarrassing for me. I get pin-holed by the German Ambassador about you all every time I go to a cocktail party or dinner.' He really cut us down to size. We complained about him when we got back to England and he was replaced.

'We were given money and papers and put in the care of the Spanish Air force. We travelled to Saragossa by train. This was in the middle of Franco s country and was where the Headquarters of the Condor Regiment was situated. The Spanish officers were keen to get rid of us. Spain had been a neutral country during the war but many Spaniards supported the Germans especially as they had fought alongside them during their own Civil War. The Spanish regiment that had fought with the SS in Russia had returned and there was to be a march through the streets to celebrate their return. The officers thought it would be best if we were out of the town when that took place and we were taken up into the hills, to the spa town of Alamah de Arrogon. There were two hotels there, one occupied by the Americans and the other by the British and they were luxurious. I had my own room and bathroom. When I looked in the cupboards, I found that they were packed with clothes and we were told to help ourselves to them. Well, I kitted myself out. Clothes were rationed in Britain. It would be a long time before I had an opportunity like that. I selected a suit, shirts, underclothes, socks, shoes; the lot and so did the others.

'We were picked up by the British sub consul. He was a different kind of man to the other two we had met from the Embassy. He was friendly but efficient, the sort of man that you didn't argue with. He took us to the home of Mr. Williams of the firm Williams and Humbert. He owned a sherry factory. He gave us a tour of it and presented each of us with a bottle of presentation sherry that had been bottled for the coronation of Edward in 1937. As he had never been crowned the sherry had remained on the shelf. We stayed with Mr. Williams for two days and then we were collected by army lorry and taken to Gibraltar. The first thing we did when we got there was to go and buy cheap cases to carry all the clothes we had acquired. We were kitted out with uniforms in Gibraltar and put on a Dakota for home. We opened our bottles of sherry and drank them on the return journey except for Len. He kept his and sold it at an auction a couple of years later and got £2,000 for it. That was enough to buy a house in those days. 'We landed at Bristol and were taken to the station for a train to London. It was while we were on the platform that we were mobbed. Len and I had taken a hand of bananas home for our families. People in Britain hadn't seen a banana during the war and the children didn't know what they were. They tried to eat them with the skins on when we gave them some. It was the same on the train and in London. By the time we reached Marylebone, Len and I just had the stalks. We were interrogated at the Grand Central Hotel by Airey Neave [the head of MI9] from ten o'clock in the morning until four o 'clock in the afternoon. Then he said that we might as well go home and go back in the morning. Len and I only lived a penny halfpenny tram journey away. We got off the tram outside the 'Cross Keys' and decided we would pop in for a quick pint before we went home. There was such a shout when we went in. 'What are you doing here? We thought you were dead.' We had a quick drink and went home. My mother opened the door, took one look at me and fainted. They didn't even know we were still alive. They had had a telegram saying that I was missing believed killed and that was all they had heard. We took the matter up with Airey Neave the next day. He apologized and said that he shouldn't have let us go home. They didn't inform the families until the last minute in case there was a hold up on the journey. I was posted to Coningsby, to the Path Finder force. I wasn't allowed to fly over France until the allies had reached the Rhine. The problem was that I couldn't wear a helmet. The burns on my head hadn't healed as well as I thought, so I was sent to East Grinstead and became one of Archie McIndoe's boys, the great plastic surgeon who worked such marvels on damaged and burned features.

'I stayed in the RAF and retrained as a wireless operator. I flew Valiants and Vulcans. Twenty years after the war, I visited a US Air base and one of the men mentioned the CO, Lieutenant Colonel Hubbard. 'Just get a message to him and tell him that there s someone here who wants to know how the most expensive washer upper in Paris is getting on.' He said he couldn't do that but he did get a message to him when I told him what it was all about. He was one of the senior American officers who had always done the washing up in the Paris flat. Then an announcement was made over the tannoy: 'Gentlemen, smarten yourselves up, the CO is coming over' and there was 'Speedy' at the top of the steps. 'You curly headed bastard' his voice boomed out. I met the other Paris washer upper, Colonel Don Willis at another USAF base later on. We just stood and stared at each other. I can't remember which of us spoke first. The third American, Jack Cornett, had been a man in torment in Paris. When he reached Spain, he had been sent straight back to America and spent the rest of his life in the Veterans Hospital in Washington.'

Footnotes Chapter 15

110 Nineteen 'Airborne Cigar' Lancasters on 101 Squadron at Ludford Magna would jam night-fighter communications. 100 Group would provide six 'Serrate' Mosquitoes and three ECM Halifaxes on 192 Squadron to carry out Special Duty patrols in the target area. Other operations, including a raid on Montdidier airfield by 84 Lancasters and eight Mosquitoes of 8 Group would hopefully disperse the German night fighter force in the area.

111 *Battle Under the Moon: The documented account of Mailly-le-Camp, 1944* by Jack Currie (Air Data Publications Ltd 1995).

112 103 Squadron lost three Lancasters on Mailly: ME673 piloted by 28-year old Pilot Officer Sydney Lawrence Rowe RAAF; ND411 flown by 20-year old Pilot Officer John Edgar Holden and ND905 flown by 32-year old Squadron Leader Harold Swanston. All 21 men perished aboard these aircraft. Flight Lieutenant Eric Broadbent and crew were killed on the operation on Stuttgart on 28/29 July 1944. Pilot Officer Donald Elgin Tate and his crew were KIA on 25 May 1944 on the operation on Aachen.

113 Jimmy Graham writing in *Mailly-le-Camp; Memories of a Bomber Raid*

114 The other four Lancasters on 50 Squadron that were lost were: LM480 VN-U flown by Flight Lieutenant Thomas H. Blackham DFC. Five of his crew were lost. Blackham was unable to shake off a fighter, which followed them soon after leaving the target area. Luckily he was wearing a seat type parachute when the aircraft exploded. He and Flight Sergeant Stewart James Godfrey evaded capture but Blackham was picked up and later incarcerated in Buchenwald concentration camp. Godfrey was assisted by Madame Deguilly of Romilly-sur-Seine before being passed to a Resistance group but on 24 June he was killed when the Wehrmacht attacked their camp. Godfrey has no known grave. ND953 VN-S flown by Pilot Officer W. F. Dobson was shot down with the loss of four crew KIA, one taken prisoner and two, including Dobson, escaped. ED870 VN-I flown by 28-year old Pilot Officer Albert Handley was shot down with the loss of all eight crew. See *Battle Under the Moon: The documented account of Mailly-le-Camp, 1944* by Jack Currie (Air Data Publications Ltd 1995). Geoff Gilbert concludes: 'When we finished our tour, we were posted. The crew had lived and worked together and now we were being sent to different parts of the universe. We shook hands and said goodbye and went to our new posting. That was what war was like especially in the RAF. We were constantly moving on. I didn't meet some of my crew or hear what had happened to them until thirty years later. I was still in Bomber Command but I was attached to the navy and sent to Plymouth.' *Not Just Another Milk Run...The Mailly-le-Camp Bomber Raid* by Molly Burkett and Geoff Gilbert (Barny Books 2004).

115 One of the most pitifully wounded of all the wartime 'caterpillars' he was the only member the Caterpillar Club ever formally 'adopted'. Having qualified for membership of the hospital's Guinea Pig Club, Richardson remembered that he was also eligible to join the Caterpillar Club. So the hospital's welfare secretary sent off a letter of application for him in which he said of Richardson: 'In this hospital of many grievous injuries his are by way of being the worst and yet his cheerfulness and spirit are as proportionately great as are his injuries.' This was the first letter Leslie Irvin had ever received from a blind man and it was felt that Richardson deserved more than a membership card and a gold caterpillar. It was decided to 'adopt' him. A collection was taken round the factory and Richardson got a cheque for £23. It was the first of many cheques and gifts which included parcels of cigarettes, chocolate, eggs and a radio set. For the first year of his association with the Club Richardson received a cheque every month. And every birthday and every Christmas for the five long years he spent at the Guinea Pig hospital and at St Dunstan's, where he learnt Braille and to type and how to run a shop, the people who had made the parachute that saved his life sent him a gift. Only when Richardson, equipped with a new face and an artificial hand, went out to face the world again in 1950 did the Club consider his 'adoption' had ended. *Into the Silk* by Ian Mackersey (Granada, 1978).

116 *Into the Silk* by Ian Mackersey (Granada, 1978).

117 This story, written by the rear gunner, identified only by the initials 'T.B' appeared in *Not Just Another Milk Run...The Mailly-le-Camp Bomber Raid* by Molly Burkett and Geoff Gilbert (Barny Books 2004).

118 Only 58 of the 315 men lost on 44 aircraft survived, 24 were taken prisoner of war and 34 evaded.

119 Leslie Harry Lissette and Sergeant Ronald Ellis the 25-year old tail gunner who was from

Doncaster shared a joint grave in Chaintreaux Communal Cemetery Lancaster III ND556 went down at Chaintreaux in Seine-et-Marne, 12 km SE of Nemours. Sergeant Laurie Wesley the bomb aimer who was from West Bromwich became a PoW. John Pittwood from Warley, Birmingham, evaded capture. He was taken along the 'Burgundy' Line and he reached Gibraltar via Spain. He landed at Lyneham on 24 June. Eighteen-year old Sergeant Philip N. King the WOp, who was from Birmingham also evaded. He stayed put until liberation on 22 August. Flight engineer, 20-year old Nicholas John Stockford, a former boy apprentice engine fitter at a training school in South Africa before he re-mustered as a RAF flight engineer, who was from Chipping Norton in Oxfordshire, reached England on the night of 14/15 July 1944 aboard a civilian airliner from Lisbon airport which landed at Whitchurch airport near Bristol. Sadly, Stockford died from pleurisy a week after returning home.

120 Pilot Officer Leonard Barnes was pilot of a Lancaster on 630 Squadron who was shot down on the Stuttgart raid on 15/16 March 1944. Flying Officer Reg Lewis was the navigator on a SOE Halifax on 138 Squadron that was shot down over France on the night of 7/8 February 1944.

121 All three Americans were fighter pilots. Hubbard, of the 355th Fighter Group HQ, had been flying lead in P-47D Thunderbolt 52-7944 'Lil' Jo' on 13 November 1943 when the Group provided withdrawal support to B-17s coming home from their attack on Bremen and rendezvous was made over Cloppenburg at 1206 hours. Near the Zuider Zee Hubbard's P-47 started vibrating badly and shortly after the engine broke loose from its mounts and he bailed out. Major Donald Wills in the 67th Fighter Wing was flying P-38J Lightning 42-68077 on 10 April 1944 when he crash landed on a soccer field in Holland. On 27 April 1944 2nd Lieutenant Cornett in the 375th Fighter Squadron, 361st Fighter Group was flying P-47D 42-75219 when he was downed.

122 Micheline Dumont (aka 'Michou') had replaced her younger sister Andrée, known as 'Nadine' in the Comète escape line after she was caught and ended up in Ravensbrück. Micheline, who later married Pierre Ugeux, a major in the Special Operations Executive in France, and Andrée, who survived the horrors of Ravensbrück were awarded the George Medal the highest decoration that can be awarded to a foreign civilian for bravery. Andrée was made an OBE and was awarded the King's Medal for Courage.

123 Florentino' Goïcoechea of Ciboure, a tall, sturdy Basque smuggler, knew the routes to Spain like the back of his hand. Immensely strong and agile, he would carry some of the weaker or wounded airmen on his shoulders across the often swollen, fast-running Bidassoa River which formed the frontier. He was severely wounded in the leg in July 1944 but survived the war. 'Florentine', who saw several hundred airmen over the dangerous route to Spain, received the George Medal, together with the King's Medal for Courage. He died in July 1980 and is buried at the foot of his great love, the Pyrénées.

Chapter 16

Gladiators of the Air

'I should like this letter to be forwarded on to my sister if I should not return from this operation. I have written many letters in my life, but in writing this one I find it much more difficult than any yet attempted. 'First of all let me say I don't want you to grieve over my loss. This is the life I chose myself and the job which I am very proud to undertake. In this life I have learnt how to be grateful, because the crew in which I serve are the finest bunch of young men in the world. They are all willing to give their lives for the just cause. 'It's my hope that those whom I have left behind will make good the cause for which we gave our lives. This was a poor world before the war began - a quarrelsome and selfish world. I hope the horrors of war will have taught all a lesson and give justice to all. 'I have always thought how lucky you people have been to live so far away from a battlefield and to continue the quiet life which we have now learned to cherish.
In conclusion let me say God is with me and all will be well in the end.
Goodbye, but not for ever. - Robert.
Before taking off on an operational flight over enemy territory from which he did not return 20-year old Robert M. McClure RAFVR flight engineer on 101 Squadron at Ludford Magna left this farewell letter addressed to his sister, Mrs. R. Wright, 2 Comber Road, Dundonald, Belfast.

Norman Ellis 'Greg' Gregory was born on 26 January 1922 at Isabella Colliery near Blyth in Northumberland, the first of five children. Life in Britain after World War One was grim and his childhood memories were of TB epidemics and the sight of 'Tommies' who had been blinded or who had lost limbs on the Western Front. Those who had unfortunately lost both their legs pushed themselves along in the gutters on makeshift boards. Many others tried to eke out a living by selling matches or by begging. Norman's parents soon decided that Blyth was not a fit place to bring up their children and when he was 8, the Gregory family moved to Lawshall near Sudbury in rural Suffolk. Then after three or four years, they moved to the neighbouring village of Shimpling, where his parents would live out the rest of their lives and Norman would begin his life-long love of cycling. In 1935 Gregory's mother packed him off to the grammar school in Sudbury. He would cycle the ten miles from Shimpling to Sudbury and back again; that's 100 miles a week. He was a bright lad and after passing his exams he went on to St. John's College in York to train as a teacher. It was about 200 miles to York and he would often cycle there from Suffolk, staying at Youth Hostels on the way. And during the summer he was not content to laze around in rural Suffolk but rather, he took to cycling to Land's End, John O'Groats and west Wales.

'Greg' was 17 when war broke out. In 1941 he decided that he would try to enlist in the RAF. He did not want to 'drown in the mud of Flanders' or end up disabled like the 'Tommies' in Blyth and the Royal Navy too, did not offer any inducement. One of his relations had served in submarines until he was discharged in 1937, was recalled in 1938 and killed in action in the first week of September 1939 when HMS *Oxley* was torpedoed by another British submarine with only one survivor! If the worst came to the worst Norman decided, he would join the RAF. 'I knew I would get killed' he said 'but at least it would be a quick death'.

'Greg' joined a group of students went as a body to the recruiting office in York to volunteer for aircrew with the proviso that they were allowed to remain in college to take their finals. This request was granted, provided that they volunteered for the RAF, which they did. Gregory became a qualified teacher and within a week of taking his finals, he had to report to the Aircrew Receiving Centre in Regents Park. Beginning his RAF training that same year, 'Greg' logged a dozen hours in the Tiger Moth as part of elementary flying training school at RAF Ansty near Coventry. From Ansty he went to a personnel distribution centre in Hastings. He was only there a fortnight when he was bombed out. The next morning, the trainees were taken to Harrogate and then they moved on to Heaton Park before going overseas on the Queen *Elizabeth*. 'Greg' completed a bomb aimer's course in Canada and returned to England after seven months to finish his training on Wellingtons, Halifaxes (his least favourite) and Lancasters.

At 28 OTU Wymeswold air crew personnel were told to 'crew up' in the time honoured manner by seeking out the other potential members in an empty hangar. Gregory was approached by Sergeant (later Pilot Officer) Les Davidson a New Zealander and navigator, Flight Sergeant 'Dave' Jacobs. They went up to Gregory and said, 'You're a bomb aimer; tell us about yourself.' 'In no time at all' recalls 'Greg' 'we had formed a trio. Les was a farmer's son and at the age of thirteen had never been to school. When he thought about joining the air force, he sweated blood to educate himself to pass the entrance exam. Then we found ourselves two gunners and a wireless operator. Sergeant Lionel Milligan was the WOp/AG and the two gunners were Sergeants Joe Johnson from Dagenham and William Hayman, a Londoner. Twenty year old Sergeant R. M. McClure, from Belfast later joined the crew as flight engineer at Heavy Conversion Unit at Sandtoft, a new satellite of Hemswell. We converted onto Halifax Is, doing circuits and bumps. The Halifax was a dreadful aircraft. We lost six aircraft in the first fortnight; with all the crew (seven members) and the instructor. They would enter the circuit and when they turned they just went in. They attributed it to a fault in the tail unit, so the aircraft were grounded. There was a 10 percent casualty rate for aircrew in training.'

In May 1944 the crew were posted to RAF Ludford Magna or 'Mudford Magma', as it was known because although built on one of the highest stretches of the Lincolnshire Wolds it was still marshy. The remote base was home to special Lancasters on 101 Squadron in 1 Group. Now, an eighth man - Sergeant Charlie Beauregard a Canadian - was assigned to Les Davidson's crew as a 'special operator'. 'The special operators' recalled Gregory 'were kept isolated from us in every way so we knew nothing about them. They would just appear at the aircraft. If we were shot down and taken prisoner we could not tell the Germans anything about the special operator's duties because we didn't know. We knew he had special equipment but doing what with it, we didn't know.'

101 was a three flight squadron, flying up to 24 Lancasters in the bomber stream, armed and loaded with bombs just like the other heavy bombers but with an extra crew member positioned half way down the fuselage just forward of the mid-upper turret and aft of the main spar who operated four VHF wireless sets to jam enemy radio transmissions. The operator was outside the main heated area of the aircraft and he was issued with an electrically heated suit just like the gunners. The sole object of the squadron was to carry special operators in the main bomber stream and it would be their duty to find, identify and jam enemy fighter control transmissions, causing havoc and confusion to their defences. Using 'ABC' or 'Airborne Cigar' night-fighter communications equipment, the German-speaking Special Operator scanned up and down the airwaves, seeking transmissions from enemy fighters. When a blip showed on his CRT scope he tuned one of the other sets to that frequency and listened in. If the speaker was a Jägerleitoffizier (JLO, or GCI-controller) the Special Operator would flood the enemy controller's instructions with interference. Externally, 'ABC' aircraft were easy to spot. They carried three large aerials, two on the upper fuselage and one under the bomb-aimer's position. There was also no H_2S radome.

Because of their role, 101 Squadron took part in more bombing raids than any other Lancaster squadron in 1 Group. It was the 'ABC' role which was to cost 101 Squadron so dear on the night of 30/31 March 1944 when the squadron lost seven aircraft on the Nuremburg raid. Unfortunately, any signal transmitted by the 'Airborne Cigar' Lancasters could be used by a fighter to locate it and in time losses on 101 Squadron, who flew more operations than most other squadrons, lost heavily, as the enemy sought to diminish their effectiveness.

'Arriving on the squadron it felt to me and the rest of us to be a great privilege' recalled Gregory. 'The squadron ran its own flying school to convert us to the Lancaster. The skipper allowed me to fly the Lancaster. The Avro Anson was the easiest aircraft I ever flew and the Lancaster was just as responsive to the controls. She flew like a lady. The Lancaster and Halifax were as different as chalk and cheese. I was exceptionally lucky. I did once land a Wellington and I did fly the Lancaster in the air; I could also navigate, but I was the bomb aimer. So I was a jack of all trades. My worst experience was during a night exercise, which typically lasted six hours or more. Within 20 minutes of takeoff, the skipper called out that he was sick and would I take the controls? I flew the whole bloody way. What annoyed me was the fact that the pilot strapped his chute on his backside whereas I wore mine on my chest, so when he called me up, I'm sitting in the second dickey seat and I haven't got a parachute underneath me and I'm sitting low in the bucket; the flying control panel is off to my left, so I'm looking diagonally at everything and it's dark. I didn't like that one bit. It wasn't a case of being worried about it - you were too busy - it's afterward where you think what could have gone wrong'.

'Greg's position in the nose of the Lancaster would probably save his life but after flying school the crew were given a week's leave and he went home, taking his private kit with him because the kill rate was high and he knew that he 'was going to die.' 'I didn't have any superstitions about flying, but I convinced a young lady that what I really needed to protect me from all the evils over Germany was a pair of her silk stockings and I got them! I don't know what happened to them -

whether a young Fraulein got them, I've no idea.'

Davidson's crew were on the Squadron about a month doing exercises by day and by night before they did any trips. Then on 3/4 May they did their first operation, to Mailly-Le-Camp. 'We were enthusiastic to be on ops' recalls Gregory; 'this was what we had been trained for'. Their skipper had been on a trip as a second pilot before he took them to Mailly, which they came through unscathed. 'We were left orbiting the marker for about 20 minutes; all the time being shot to pieces by night fighters on a turkey hunt from a base nearby. I was in the middle of it. You didn't see the night fighters; just their results. We were glad to finally get the signal to go in. W could see the markers from the turning point, once we knew what colour to bomb on. We went straight in. Everybody hit the target spot on; including me and no civilian in the village was killed.'

'Even if you'd been flying until 4 o'clock in the morning, everybody who was aircrew had to be up at 10 o'clock to see what the flying orders were and whether you and your crew were on operations that night. If you weren't, you had the day off. If you were and you were lucky, you'd go to breakfast. If you were too late, you had to make other arrangements. Briefing would start in the afternoon with preliminary briefings in the various sections; navigators with the Squadron Navigation Officer and so on. If take-off time was 22.00 hours, the main briefing would be at around 6 o'clock. All the crews would meet for main briefing and that was the first time we knew the target. On a big black board all the names of the crews and the aircraft would be chalked in - on our Squadron there could be up to 20 crews. A big map was covered by curtains and when the Commanding Officer said, 'Tonight your target is...' somebody would pull the curtains and we could see the map marked with ribbons indicating the route, going from Ludford Magna to the target.

'We were given information about the nature of the target and maps that covered the area. Photographs of the target area would be shown on a screen and the aiming point was described. It was all very well done. The special radio operator wasn't briefed as we were, he was briefed in private. After the main briefing we went to the Mess for our meal. If you were going on a night flight your meal was invariably eggs and bacon. When you left the Mess you picked up your flying rations, usually a sandwich, a few boiled sweets and almost always a 4oz tin of pure orange juice. Aircrew were given a thermos flask - civilians couldn't buy them - and you pleased yourself if you filled it with tea or coffee. Then we went to the parachute section: a huge Nissen hut, two thirds filled with numbered steel lockers. The numbers corresponded with keys in the keeping of the WAAFs at the far end, in the parachute section. A WAAF would issue your parachute and when you asked for number 17, she would give you the key to your locker. When you'd got dressed and left in the locker anything you didn't want to take flying, you handed your key back in. The whole area was kept warm so that all your flying kit was warm and dry to put on. In the aircraft the main cabin was heated, so the pilot, flight engineer, navigator and wireless operator could fly in just their battledress, harness and Mae West. Whereas the upper gunner, the tail gunner and me in the nose lived virtually at the same temperature as the air outside, the gunners were like roly-poly men with all the kit they wore to stop them from freezing to death!

'I had special silk and wool underwear. I usually wore two pairs of socks, over them electrically heated slippers, then flying boots: suede leather outside and at least 30 layers of silk inside to form an insulated padding. Underneath my battledress jacket I wore a Submariner's jersey; very heavy, knitted wool, quite long that covered your backside and you had to turn back your cuffs. All of the crew were issued with one. The first was probably issued at OTU. It was pure white. When I went home on leave I said to my mother that I wanted the jersey embroidered with my abbreviated name 'Greg'. This was done beautifully by an old lady who lived nearby. I was as mad as could be when they recalled all the white sweaters at HCU and reissued us with navy blue because if we were evaders white was too conspicuous!

'On top of my battledress I had an electrically heated jacket, then a quilted flying suit - an inch thick with insulating materials - from my ankles to my neck and down to my wrists. The outer flying suit was canvas. I wore white silk gloves, electrically heated gloves and leather gauntlets on top. As you put the layers on, you became bulkier and more awkward, but I was 21, young and athletic.

'Otherwise I had my flying helmet, with a face mask which supplied oxygen. The face mask also had a microphone and in the ear pieces were loud speakers for the intercom. Lastly I had my parachute harness and Mae West. Early on in Squadron, the girls in the parachute section had measured us and fitted each of us with a parachute harness, which we kept. When you went to where you were going to do your night's work you plugged in your oxygen supply, your electricity supply to heat your body warmers and plugged in your intercom. There you were, all wired up!

'Your battledress had two outside pouch pockets and two inside pockets, these held two packs of escape kit. The kits contained maps, a compass, some boiled sweets, a small bar of chocolate. What looked like a toothpaste tube held condensed milk. There was money in several different currencies, a sachet of water purifying tablets and a vulgar looking balloon to fill with any kind of water - ditch or pond water. No matter how foul the water, if you used a water purifying tablet (about the size of a saccharine tablet) and left it for an hour, the bugs would have been killed.

Davidson's crew were on the Battle Order again on 7/8 May when 55 Lancasters of 1 Group were detailed to bomb the airfield and an ammunition dump at Rennes. 'The ground staff lined up buses, jeeps or lorries to take us out to dispersal. You had to be at your dispersal point at least an hour before take-off, to check your equipment. We had been given LM395 SR-Q 'Queenie' with her attendant ground crew. Our lives were in their hands. The door was towards the tail; you went up a short ladder into the fuselage. Just inside the door was the gyroscope, which repeated all over the aircraft: the cockpit, navigator's position, in the nose for the bomb aimer. You passed the upper turret, but the big snag was the main-spar. It ran through the fuselage and you had to get over that with all your flying kit on to reach the front of the aircraft. I passed through the main cabin, down the steps into the nose.

'As soon as we were airborne, I would go down into the nose and check my equipment. The skipper made a circle round, gaining height. The flight plan gave us the point to cross the coast on the British Isles. When we'd crossed our own coast, we flew on the headings in the flight plan; the whole theory was that the aircraft would amass as closely as possible to minimise the attacks from night fighters and the risk from anti-aircraft fire. Each bomb in the bomb load had a fuse and each fuse was locked by a split-pin attached to a wire. The bomb would not go off until the pin had been extracted. I controlled those wires through selector switches and when I put the switches down I would report to the skipper, 'All bombs fused.' That meant when I pressed the bomb tit to release the bombs, the split-pin from the fuse was left attached to the wire in the aircraft so the bomb could explode. If the bomb hit the ground with the split-pin in the fuse, it wouldn't explode.

'We left base for Rennes and were going across the English Channel to the west of Beachy Head, a relatively wide part of the Channel to cross, when Dave Jacobs suddenly announced, rather unhappily, that he was 'totally lost.' The skipper said, 'take over Greg - where are we?' I said, 'we're over the sea. As soon as I see the coast, I'll tell you.'

'In training, we had to memorize the coastline of Europe and the principal rivers and be able to draw them from memory. We were below cloud level and as soon as I could see the white breakers below me, I could identify where we were. I very quickly said, 'I know where we are; we're over Brest.' That was not a healthy place to be! We were a long way off course. The skipper said, 'What do we do now, Greg?'

'On your right hand side is a magnetic compass called the P4. Ignore the gyro-compass; use the compass by your right knee and fly 090: due East.'

Flying that course we came to Rennes and I bombed the target. We bombed an hour after everyone else - at least there were plenty of fires (for sighting).There was no opposition whatsoever. I imagine they heard the last bomber depart and thought they were in the clear, until we gave them something else to think about! Then we used the P4 compass to fly due north, back to Lincolnshire. After that leg the navigator came out of his trance and said, 'I know where we are now, I'll take over!' When the navigator had boarded the aircraft he forgot to turn on the gyro-compass (which was like a dustbin) just inside the tail of the aircraft, where we climbed on board. Ten minutes after switching it on, he was supposed to go back and set it up to read true courses and not magnetic courses. That's why he got himself lost. When we got back, I got a pat on the head; the navigator got a right rollicking. The navigation leader said, 'Do another thing like that again and you'll be on the ground staff, young man.'

After a lull came the rail yards at Orléans-Les-Aubrais on the night of 19/20 May when RAF Bomber Command resumed operations with raids by 900 aircraft on five separate rail targets, all of which lay within a radius of 150 miles of Caen. By now a member of 'Queenie's ground crew had painted on the nose the words 'She Drops 'em By Night' and art work showing a scantily clad female lowering her panties. Three pairs of white knickers had been added under the cockpit to denote the number of 'ops' flown!

'Because we were so low, I could see the French targets in detail' says Gregory. 'In the nose I could see more than anybody in the crew. For example, I could see the railway lines at Orleans quite clearly. When the bombs went, the aircraft lurched upwards. It was always very noticeable when the bomb load left. You had been sitting on 10 tons of explosives; it was a nice feeling to have got rid of it! In a way, I was a bit cocky about the fact that the RAF had given me an aircraft and all these men, for me to deliver all these tons of explosives. A flash bomb was part of the load, timed to explode from between 5,000 down to 1,000 feet above the target, designed to illuminate your bomb load exploding on the ground while the cameras in the aircraft took a picture of your results. The skipper had to keep the aircraft steady to get the photograph. I would say to the skipper, 'Bomb doors open.' That's a curious thing: only the skipper could open and close the bomb doors. The bomb doors opened and I took charge of the aircraft. Having put the wind-speed, direction and magnetic heading on the bombsight, as you approached the target it should appear to be running down the parallel wires of the bombsight towards you. If not you had to give directions for the aircraft to move to the left or right until that was the case. Once the target was moving down the 'railway' lines towards you, you held that heading until it reached the cross wires. Then you pressed the tit and the bomb load left the aircraft.

'When each bomb left the aircraft it was travelling at the same speed as the aircraft, running in a forward trajectory and falling under gravity. The bomb would gain speed as it fell until it reached terminal velocity. The terminal velocity differed with the different bombs, but you wanted to ensure the bombs landed in roughly the same place. The answer was to release them at different time intervals, so they all coincide when they hit the ground. If you'd done your homework properly and set up your bombsight, you should be able to make one run and bomb your target. The whole process took five minutes, usually. Crews didn't like bomb aimers who didn't know their job, who were so fumble fingered that they missed the target and had to go round again! That could make you the enemy of the crew; they didn't want to hang around the target.

'When the bomb doors closed, the navigator gave the skipper the heading for home. In addition to pointing the nose for home, the skipper also pointed the nose slightly downwards so we steadily lost height to increase speed. You might have been struggling to get to the target at 165 mph, but going home you could always pick up extra speed. Once you'd left the target area, not only were you flying lighter but also in a nose down attitude.'

At Orléans 118 Lancasters of 1 Group dropped almost 1,500 bombs or 615 tons of HE which left 200 craters in the marshalling sidings and destroyed a large number of goods wagons on the railway yards after four 'Oboe' Mosquitoes of 8 Group dropped red and green TIs and were followed by illuminating and marking by Lancasters on 635 (PFF) Squadron at Downham Market. Wing Commander W. T. Brooks the Master Bomber and his deputy, Flight Lieutenant Smith, directed the attack. Norman Gregory says. 'That was a good prang that one; I had a good aiming point. I thought I was a very clever boy because my stick of bombs fell smack on the 'neck'. In marshalling yards all the lines have a crossing point so the trucks can switch to the different tracks; we called this the 'neck'. Subsequently I wondered if it might have been better to bomb up or down from the neck, it would have destroyed more track. On the other hand, talking to people involved on the ground, I'm told the tracks would be up and going within six hours. Once they learned the bitter lesson, they learned how to cope with it and had emergency teams ready to restore the status quo.'

'Usually it was a straight line home. I think that most people, like me, ate their flying rations on the way back. Ludford Magna was near Scunthorpe, the steel town in north Lincolnshire. Scunthorpe had blast furnaces going 24 hours a day, 7 days a week. When I could see those two blast furnaces, from miles out to sea, I knew we were home. We called Flying Control from about 20 miles away. If there was nobody on the circuit we could go straight in and land. Otherwise we joined the waiting aircraft in the circuit, circling the aerodrome another thousand feet above the last aircraft waiting to land. Control called aircraft down one by one to land. You could be at 20,000 feet and see the sunrise, land in total darkness and see the sunrise all over again.'

Davidson's crew got back safely but one Lancaster failed to return having fallen victim to a night-fighter southwest of Paris. On returning, 1 Group's squadrons found that mist was forming on the Lincolnshire Wolds and a number of Lancasters were diverted to airfields further to the south. One aircraft was so badly damaged by flak that it had to be written off. A further six aircraft received varying degrees of damage as a result of enemy action and five were damaged in minor incidents, including a collision over the target at Boulogne.

'We taxied back to our own ground crew at the dispersal point' adds Gregory.

'Transport was waiting. We piled in the crew bus and went back to the parachute section, handed our parachutes in and took our flying kit off. Then we went to interrogation. The intelligence people called us in crew by crew. The Intelligence Officer asked all sorts of questions about the trip and the target. Meanwhile you were given a cup of scolding hot cocoa and if you could persuade the padre to part with a little from his bottle into your cocoa, you were damned lucky!

'After interrogation had finished with you, you went to the Mess and had breakfast. By then, you had a shrewd idea if people weren't coming back. (Certainly we knew by the next morning who was missing). If you were lucky you would be in bed by 6 o'clock. Depending how exhausted you were, as soon as you were horizontal, you fell asleep quite quickly. We were all short of sleep. In one week on Ops I only had about 17 hours sleep. We kept different hours to the ground staff on the Squadron.'

There were no Main Force operations on the night of 20/21 May but Bomber Command directed its might against German targets once again on 21/22 May when 532 aircraft raided Duisburg. 'The route was never, never in a straight line' says 'Greg'. 'You might fly 50 miles north of the target and there would be your turning point in to the target, or you might do a couple of dog-legs. You could never be too careful on a raid. In theory, the pilot should be tilting the aircraft regularly to give the best possible view below. If anybody saw anything suspicious we could say, calmly with no shouting, 'Skipper, dive port.' Down would go the port wing, down would go the nose and we would be going down at a rate of knots. For our own safety we did corkscrewing, but you couldn't indulge in that the whole time because we had to keep to the timing in the flight plan. Normally the bomber force would be split into three sections, crossing the target on three different headings. We were given a time to bomb the target. As an individual aircraft of 101 Squadron, we were expected to be over the target within a window of plus or minus 2 minutes. Navigation had to be spot on. The whole operation would normally be expected to be completed in 20 minutes. There was always a risk of collision between aircraft, never mind orbiting around the marker point, as we did at Mailly-Le-Camp.

'Duisburg was totally obscured by 10/10ths cloud. We bombed on sky-markers up in the clouds; I saw absolutely nothing. I didn't see any aircraft blow up. I didn't see any aircraft on fire. I didn't see any aircraft crash to the ground in flames. I didn't see what was going on at the target. There was just nothing to see; it was eerie.'

The 'Oboe' sky-marking was accurate and much damage was caused in the southern areas of the city. Twenty-nine Lancasters, most of them shot down by night fighters over the southern provinces of the Netherlands, were lost on the operation and three more were lost on mine laying operations off enemy coasts. Davidson's crew made it home without incident.

'As aircrew we didn't have any duties if we weren't flying' says Gregory. 'If the pub was open that was the best place to go, but there was always the Mess. We'd go to dances in the local town, or occasionally see a film. Invariably the crew went together: we were a band of brothers.'

The day after Duisburg 'Greg' was walking along the main street in Louth when he realized that there was a young woman on the other side of the street keeping pace with him; when he turned, she turned. The woman was the wife of a sergeant on 101 Squadron who had met Gregory through a mutual friend some time earlier and she invited the young sergeant to dinner at their house the next day - an invitation which 'Greg' gratefully accepted.

Gregory never made it to dinner.

The target for 361 Lancasters and fourteen Mosquitoes of 1, 3, 5 and 8 Groups on the night of 22/23 May was Dortmund. A second stream of 225 Lancasters and ten Mosquitoes meanwhile, would head for Brunswick. 'At briefing we'd been told the take-off time' says Gregory; 'if 300 were on a target it could involve 20 squadrons from all over the country, so timing was important. We received instructions to start up the engines. When the skipper and I had checked the engines, we swung out onto the perimeter track and taxied along the peri track and waited to turn onto the runway which was in use that night for take-off.'

There was the usual gathering of airmen and WAAFs at the side of the runway to wave off the bombers. By now, 'Greg' was having a recurring dream each night where he was in a tunnel with a glass wall. He was always on his own in the tunnel and the rest of the crew were always on the other side of the glass. He also clearly remembered seeing the padre at the end of the line of spectators. He was waving. 'Greg' returned the gesture and recalled the words spoken by the gladiators in the Roman amphitheatre: Morituri te salutamus ('We who are about to die salute you').

'Once we got the green Aldis lamp from the Control caravan Les revved up the engines to screaming point with the brakes on. The Rolls-Royce Merlins developed 1,500 horsepower each, so we had 6,000 horsepower roaring - a bit noisy. When he released the brakes we surged forward, belting down the runway to reach 100 mph before he pulled the stick back to lift her off - or, as we said, to get unstuck. I'd be standing in the main cabin, beside the skipper and flight engineer. We were invariably overloaded, carrying the extra equipment and special operator.

'On the German raids we flew in excess of 20,000 feet; you couldn't see the detail of what was happening at the target, just exploding bombs and flashes. Over the Ruhr it was the biggest and best fireworks display I've ever seen in my life.

All Hell was let loose. Taking in the searchlights, flak and radar, a million men were locked up in the Ruhr on anti-aircraft duty. Coming in towards the target we were at 22,000 feet over Dortmund. It was a clear night and I could see the target markers, so we went in and we bombed. It was a straight run in. (Most of the bombs that were dropped on Dortmund fell in residential areas mainly in the south-eastern districts of the city). Then the wireless operator announced that we were on fire. Over any target, you could always feel the anti-aircraft shells exploding in the vicinity; the aircraft would shudder. Not having experienced the difference of the aircraft merely shuddering and having shrapnel actually going through the fuselage or wings, we were in blissful ignorance. The skipper, flight engineer, navigator and wireless operator were in the cabin section of the aircraft. I was down in the nose where it was pretty chilly at 20,000 feet, lying on my belly for the bomb run. I said to the wireless operator, 'How do you know we're on fire?' Milligan said, 'I thought I heard some funny noises and when I opened the cabin door, the whole bloody place was on fire.'

'I said, 'Well, use the bloody fire extinguisher!'

'Not on that fire you don't.'

'We'd been attacked by four Ju 88s [possibly Oberfeldwebel Heinrich Lonnecker of I./JG300, Hauptmann Kurt Peters of St.III./JG300, Feldwebel Kurt Landl of 2./JG300 and Oberfeldwebel Hermann Wischnewski of I./JG300; all of whom claimed a 'Viermot' over Dortmund]. Unknown to us, the Germans had fitted two 20mm cannons at a 45-degree angle [Schräge Musik] so that they flew underneath the bomber and when they got us in their sights they blew us apart. Joe Johnson the tail gunner, Bill Hayman the mid-upper gunner and Charlie Beauregard the special operator were shot out of existence. We were on fire from the main spar all the way to the rear guns; the whole lot was just an inferno and I presumed that part of my incendiary load was on fire. We dropped our bombs and then the skipper, who was still at the controls, said 'Abandon the aircraft.' I was lying on the only escape hatch, so I couldn't just open the escape hatch and jump out. I had my intercom, my heated suit and oxygen connecting me to the aircraft. As I started to disconnect everything, Bob McClure the flight engineer was immediately behind me. Over the intercom I told him, 'As soon as you see me jump, you jump at once.' I was hunkered down, ready to jump, with my hand on the rip cord. I crouched, rolled forward out of the hatch, hoping to tumble freely but I rolled over and over after jumping. Bob McClure was blown through the canopy and out of the aircraft when it exploded but he was found dead on the ground with an unopened parachute. Alan Milligan the wireless operator was killed also. Dave Jacobs the navigator was also blown out of the aircraft but he survived and landed safely by parachute.

'The skipper fought and fought trying to find a way out and found a hole but only bailed out at about 2,000 or 3,000 feet. He opened his chute and the burning aircraft went into a lake at Hagen All the petrol tanks exploded and the lake was on fire. Fortunately, he was a very good swimmer but every time he came up for air he got burned. The Germans were on the scene pretty quickly. They recovered four bodies from the wreck of the aircraft in the lake and lined them up on the shore.

'Greg's recurring dream of the tunnel with a glass wall where he was always on his own and the rest of the crew were on the other side of the glass had come true; he was the only one of the crew to bail out.

'At the instant of leaving the hatch, I had the same airspeed as the aircraft. Very quickly I slowed down, losing the forward impetus from the aircraft engines, being whipped backwards relative to the position of the aircraft. I pulled the ripcord after counting ten - to get out of the slipstream, which could throw you onto the tail-plane - as I'd been taught when I had parachute training. All that time I was falling, reaching terminal velocity. As the whole bloody parachute displayed from my chest pack, I received one vicious clout on my chin and that knocked me out. When I woke up, my boots had fallen off and I was coned by a searchlight. I was expecting a bellyful of lead before I hit the ground. The searchlight kept me coned and followed me all the way down to the ground. There was no hint of anyone firing at me.

'I landed in a little village called Herdecke outside of Dortmund and I damaged my right knee. I could stand on my left leg, but I couldn't walk. Without my boots I crawled I suppose 400 or 500 yards and knocked on the door of a house. A young lady opened the door and took me in and offered me coffee. As a bomb aimer I had a large green canvas navigation bag for all my maps. At that time I was a smoker and for some mad reason that particular night I put my cigarette case in my navigation bag, so I hadn't anything to smoke. At that moment I didn't speak any German, but I made signs to her, 'Could I have a cigarette?' She went out into the village at 1 o'clock in the morning and came back 20 minutes later with two Gold Flake cigarettes.

'A short time after that the village policeman arrived. He spoke to me in German and when I shook my head he started speaking in French - he'd been a French PoW in WWI. 'Because I couldn't walk, he put me on the crossbar of his bicycle and pushed me, but when we came to another small town he said, 'it's more than my life is worth to be seen helping you, I'm sorry, but you'll just have to manage as best you can.' And so I had to hobble along from then on.' The policeman handed Gregory over to the Gestapo and the next day he was collected by a non-commissioned officer from the Luftwaffe and taken to the aerodrome outside Dortmund where he was reunited with his skipper and navigator. 'When this Luftwaffe NCO was taking me through Dortmund, the civilians wanted to get me, so he pulled his pistol and warned them off. They wanted to string me up and I could hardly blame them of course. He didn't say anything - he just pulled his pistol.'

From Dortmund the downed fliers (eighteen Lancasters were lost) were escorted to the interrogation centre at Dulag Luft in Frankfurt where they spent a couple weeks, mostly in solitary confinement. 'There were no windows, just artificial light and you were locked in. If you wanted to go for a pee, you pulled a piece of string that pulled a semaphore in the corridor and a guard unlocked your door to take you to the latrine. Otherwise you were in solitary all the time and I was still without my boots. 'They were very clever. They would turn around and say to us that they knew who we were, because they had dredged the aircraft out of the lake. So they knew what kind of aircraft it was and because of the markings, they knew where we had come from. They were very nice - 'have a cigarette' - and they put on the charm but there was no beating. The only nasty bit was the solitary confinement.'

'Greg' spent the summer at a PoW camp at Wetzlar not far from Frankfurt. It was a mostly canvas affair that turned into a small swamp during the rain and it was another few weeks before he received his first pair of shoes. They were blood-stained so he supposed that they had come from a corpse.

'I was working cleaning dishes for two Yankee airmen, lieutenants, who did the camp's cooking and we were getting along like a house afire, when they suddenly brought in a Yankee colonel and he started bossing us all about and wanting us to parade and do all sorts of things. I disagreed with him.' Gregory believed that the colonel requested his transfer and so a few weeks later, he was on his way to Stalag Luft VII Bankau in Poland. It was here that a message, weighted with a stone, was thrown over the barbed wire. It came from Gregory's skipper telling him that he and Dave Jacobs were in the same camp!

The PoWs dug an escape tunnel but it was never finished because the camp was located directly in line with the Russian advance through Warsaw and Krakow and the prisoners could hear the advance of the Russian guns. When the Germans retreated, they took the prisoners with them.

'When we started our march from Poland there was snow on the ground and there were more than 600 of us,' says 'Greg'. 'There were 300 to 400 when we finished. People dropped out from illness and exhaustion and on 21 January six men died in the night march. When we were handed over to the mayor of the town we were going through some, including my friends, deliberately hid themselves and went off to the Russian lines. Then we were put in Luckenwalde, an enormous camp consisting of roughly 20,000 prisoners, in the vicinity of Berlin. We could hear the Russian artillery going over us to Berlin and at night we could see Mosquitoes bombing Berlin. Then, one day the Germans left and we were there to run the place on our own. On 22 April Russian tanks arrived and took away all their nationals. On 7 May we heard on the radio that it was the eve of VE (Victory in Europe) Day. We celebrated with a pipe of tobacco, a walk and an extra slice of bread and cup of coffee. A bonfire burned outside the camp and everything was thrown on it.'

On 8 May American trucks arrived at about 0800 and the RAF prisoners were driven through the flattened towns of Zeibet, Treneribrietze and Magdeburg and along the autobahn to Hanover and then to the reception centre at Hildesheim. Two days' later Dakotas loaded with former PoWs took off from Hildesheim for Le Havre. They flew low over the Ruhr and Gregory could see Düsseldorf.

'Within three days I was in England.' said 'Greg'. 'At Cosford I received medical, lots of food, new uniforms and was sent on six weeks leave. We were given a telegram to send to our folks to tell them we were OK. I approached a man on the train and asked him to call my parents when he got off at Chelmsford to tell them I was on the train and ask them to pick me up in Bury St. Edmunds.'

Norman Ellis Gregory was released from RAF service in February 1946. At the time of writing this grand old nonagenarian is still cycling along the winding lanes of his beloved west Suffolk. In 2011 at age ninety he clocked up almost 6,000 miles in the saddle and he could be found out and about on two wheels almost every day! Today, Norman Gregory is well-known to all the villagers in Cockfield who wave and hoot their horns as he sets off on one of his regular bike rides.

Chapter 17

Gelsenkirchen

Campbell Muirhead

Pilot Officer Campbell Muirhead was 20 years of age when he was shipped out to Canada. He 'washed out' of pilot training in Arizona after he had soloed and then retrained as a bomb aimer. In England he joined Pilot Officer Vernon's crew. On 9 May 1944 they left No. 1 Lancaster Flying School, Hemswell to join 12 Squadron at Wickenby, which shared the base with 626 Squadron. Muirhead was 'Glad - no, that's not the word; even grateful wouldn't do justice that we came here in May rather than mid-March. For that earlier arrival here assuredly would have seen us on the Nuremburg raid of 30/31 March when 12 Squadron put up thirteen Lancs and 626 Squadron, fifteen, out of a total force of 795 bombers... Yes, to have arrived here in the middle of March rather than early May would have seen us on that Nuremburg disaster. Of that I am certain, equally certain that, being a raw and inexperienced aircrew, we would have bought it.'

Fortunately for Pilot Officer Vernon's crew they missed the disastrous Mailly-le-Camp raid on 3/4 May. Forty-two Lancasters were lost and two returned so badly damaged that they had to be written off. And yet, Mailly-le-Camp was supposed to be an 'easy target'. H. K. Gray DFM on Bob Blackie's Lancaster crew on 576 Squadron at Elsham Wolds, whose 35th op this was, recalled: 'Mailly was our most vivid memory that none of us would ever forget. It was a lovely warm May night, plenty of moonlight and the only opposition a couple of 'trainer' aerodromes - a piece of cake according to Intelligence. But I think that the whole of the Luftwaffe must have been invited to the same party. However, we left our 'present' over the target, but got into an argument with a Ju 88 on the way out. Emerging with a large hole in the wing and an engine on fire and a little later on another engine had to be 'feathered'. Fortunately, the French coast was nearby and the sight of the English one a very welcome one. At Woodbridge, we landed (with no brakes or flaps and only a few more yards of the over-shoot left). Next morning we collected as much of our gear as we could and caught a train to London as part of our journey back to Elsham. At London it was about 5.30 so we decided to visit our navigator's pub and catch the early morning train back to camp. First of all, we dumped our gear in the RTO office and set off, dressed in battledress, flying boots, naval sweaters. What a sight for the Londoners. But around the corner at Kings Cross was the 'Comus' and the friendliest people I've ever met, the real Cockneys. Before we'd had our tea there were shoes, socks, shirts, ties - everything we needed. At night it was a grand old Knees-up Mother Brown and certainly a wonderful night to remember. We all got fixed up for the night. I travelled to Hornchurch with my rear gunner Bob Newman and even the taxi driver refused to be paid. Next morning when we left Kings Cross, we had over 50 of our 'new friends' to wave us off.' [124]

A night on the town was often as big a fill-up to morale as camaraderie among the crews was on ops - even if the crew members did not always hit the bright lights together. 'Generally, we are not a closely-knit crew' wrote Campbell Muirhead. 'We do not, for instance, go out on pub crawls together. Most of the other crews seem to do this, but not us. In fact, I think the only thing we all have in common is the constant use of the copulative adjective, even Sergeant Griggs the engineer using the word now and then. I think nearly all of us now find it hard to string a sentence together without lacing it with the adjective, often more than just once. But we fly well together and that is the main thing. Vernon, an American, came from Maine or thereabouts. A very good pilot. When we go into the bombing run he responds rather immaculately to my 'left-lefts', 'right a wee bit' and so on. Then holds her as steady as a rock. Does not comment much on the proceedings except to observe, on occasions when the flak is intense: 'Christ, look at all that shit coming our way'.

Navigator, Sergeant Norman, comes from somewhere about the Midlands, I think. Right from the beginning he maintained his firm intention of remaining behind the curtains in his little navigation compartment getting on with his work, that he didn't want to see anything that was, in his own words: 'Going to blast up my arse'. Griggs, pleasant; maybe about a couple of years younger than we are. Seems over-awed a bit by Vernon, Horsfall and myself and, sometimes, quite shocked. Mid-upper gunner, Pilot Officer Horsfall, being a regular who volunteered for aircrew, he's perhaps a couple of years older than we are. Big, a Yorkshireman with rather an abrasive personality: a health fiend; rugger and all sorts of dreadful exercises.

Wireless Operator: Sergeant Dunn. He has nothing to do for most of the time except to maintain a listening watch. During our operational flights he sits in his blacked-out compartment and reads Westerns. Someone asks him if he can't read anything better than these wretched Westerns. He says he's tried murder mysteries, but that they're not exciting enough. Imagine, all that going on and he sits there reading Westerns! Rear gunner, Sergeant Cartwright, a quiet, dependable chap who, for the most part, keeps himself to himself.' [125]

The crew's first seven operations, including the one on 6 June when the Allies invaded Normandy, were to targets in France. But when Vernon's crew went to briefing on 12 June, Campbell Muirhead noticed that an armed guard was posted at the briefing room door. He had not noticed on previous briefings the posting of an armed guard 'but there was certainly one this time' he wrote. 'As far as I could make out, once the briefing had started nobody got in, or out. We had always been well briefed for those little French affairs; by the nature of things there wasn't much to brief us on, actually.' This time it was different.

'We sat together as a crew; there would be two crews to each row. Winco Nelson, that most likeable New Zealander, popular with all, started calling the roll, asking the pilots to answer for their crews. All replied OK except one who said his bomb aimer had gone sick. The Winco was rather annoyed at this and asked why he hadn't been informed earlier. The pilot replied that all this had happened only five minutes ago. Sandy Mansfield, our Bombing Leader, looked quite delighted: here was his chance (he was on his second tour) to get in another. But no joy for Sandy, a bomb aimer who had just one to do to complete his tour was hanging around waiting for an opportunity such as this and he took the sick one's place.

Then Winco Nelson nodded in the direction of the sheet covering the Order of Battle board: it was removed to show the target: 'Gelsenkirchen'. Some groaning at this: by those who didn't know it before from the earlier navigators' and bomb aimers' pre-briefing, which produced a smile from the Winco plus the observation that some of those present had been as far as the Ruhr before. After which he indicated the Intelligence Office, at the same time asking for a bit more quiet.

The IO arose and, with a long pointer, indicated Gelsenkirchen provoking, from someone in the front, the observation that we all knew perfectly bloody well where it was. This he ignored and proceeded to tell us the importance of the German war effort of the various heavy industries located there, especially the synthetic oil factory, which was our main target. He quoted facts and figures which nobody really listened to. Then transferred the pointer to the Navigation Officer, at which the joker in the front congratulated them both on managing to effect this without dropping the thing.

The NO indicated the red-taped lines leading from Wickenby via the various turning points to Gelsenkirchen then continuing slightly beyond the target before doubling back to base. All this, of course, was well known to the navigators through their pre-briefing and his request for questions was not, as a result, taken up.

Next it was Sandy Mansfield's turn, as Briefing Leader. Again, we as bomb aimers had our pre-briefing and already knew the layout of the bomb load, distribution readings and so on. He therefore confined himself to stating time on target, the fact that the Target Indicators would be four reds surrounded by greens and to remember to bomb the centre of the reds. He repeated the old plea to have the reds dead on the cross of the bomb-sight and not to press the tit that fraction of a second too early and thus start the raid slipping back. He added that if we had to jettison the bomb load we'd have to do four hours' flying before landing. He concluded with his usual old hoary effort about not forgetting to fuse our bombs before dropping them, no laugh at this: neither did he expect it.

The Meteorology Officer then told us how much cloud he predicted along the route and over the target. I forget exactly how much, all I remember is that he received a subdued cheer when he predicted no cloud over Wickenby on our return.

The Gunnery Officer started off by saying, 'Right Gentlemen', which provoked an outburst of coughing. He then indicated on the map the various night fighter stations along the route making the obvious point that we could expect heavy attacks in the vicinity of them. And he repeated twice that the best method of defence was violent corkscrewing whenever anything at all was thought to be coming up behind us.

Last came the Engineering Officer's piece. It was so very technical, about revs, boost, etc that it conveyed nothing to me. To wind up, Winco Nelson resumed his stance; he intimated that we'd now heard all the Leaders and went on to say that engines were to be started in various sequences. 'A' Flight first, then 'B' Flight twenty minutes later. Times of take-off for 'A' and 'B' immediately after. The signal for operation cancelled would be two red Very lights. He ignored completely a plea from somewhere near the back praying for two reds, told us to obey the caravan and pointed out that we were to use runway number three. We were to climb to 19,000 feet over Wickenby (done by a completely monotonous to-and-fro-ing) and to time ourselves by reaching that height by about midnight. We were to maintain 19,000 all the way to the target, but to drop to 15,000 feet by the time we'd reached the first turning point beyond it. After hitting the English coast, we were to drop height enough to arrive back over Wickenby at 6,000 feet. He then pointed at a heavy white line across northern France and said that this represented the limit of the advance of our Armies to date: under no circumstances whatsoever were we to jettison bombs between this time and the coast: neither were we to jettison within 30 miles inland of the line (presumably to take into account possible advances of our own forces).

Winco Nelson concluded by yet again warning about the bombing slipping back along our approach route. One kite, he said, doers it, then another and, before you know it, the entire effort of the operation is nullified: the suburbs of the target area have been pranged and the principal object of the raid has escaped virtually Scot-free. I must admit that, Once or twice, I've been sorely tempted to press that button just that split second too soon; and when that happens I tell myself to count to three. Which I do, as slowly as I can manage. By the 'three' the target is exactly on the cross and my sighting is bang on. I think it is better to be a half second late in pressing the tit than being that half second early: if you over-shoot slightly others, sighting perhaps on the fires you raise, will plank their loads reasonably accurately.

We thought that was Winco Nelson finished. But he spent another minute or so to tell us that no Master of ceremonies would be attending the proceedings and that if we heard anyone claiming to be such we were to ignore him: he'd be the Hun trying to play a trick on us.

He asked for questions. There was none. Before declaring the briefing over Winco Nelson reminded us that the Pathfinders would keep reinforcing the target markers as and when necessary and that, if we saw fresh lots of reds and greens going down, we were to transfer our aiming points to them. He next gave us a sort of casual wave with his hand and wished us all the best of luck. He didn't say he wished he could come with us: he didn't have to.

Yes, a detailed, intensive briefing for Gelsenkirchen left us all somewhat subdued - especially those crews who, like ours, had only the French jobs behind them. Vernon it was who put it in a nutshell, 'No more farting about

over France this time', he murmured, 'We're in the big boys' league now'.
Flying Officer Vernon's 'K-for King', which carried a 4,000 pounder and 18 500
pounders, was one of 671 aircraft in a stream of 286 Lancasters with 17
Mosquitoes headed for Gelsenkirchen while 671 aircraft including 285
Lancasters, attacked communication targets in France. Campbell Muirhead
was as per usual, in the front turret. 'I always climb into it shortly after we're
airborne' he wrote. 'I could get out of easily, no difficulty at all there. And if I
was in my bomb aimer's compartment I could get out of that Lanc quicker than
anybody because I lay on top of the escape hatch: one pull and it's up and all
I had to do was to fall out. Out and down. Had one great fear which was that,
in the panic which would be enveloping me if we had to bail out, I'd forget to
clip on my parachute pack first. Told it had happened.

'Crossing the coast, the flak (which, I'd think, was from those extra-heavy
10.5 and 12.8cm guns we'd heard about) seemed to reach out for you alone as
if it was something personal. The searchlights too: again one received the
feeling that it was your Lanc only that they were trying to fasten onto. There
was no need to be dramatic and shout, 'Enemy coast ahead' because all could
see it, except, of course, the wireless operator and the navigator, both of whom
were in their little, blacked-out compartments. Yes, you could see it: maybe
not the actual coast, but the flak, seemingly solid walls of it hosing up into the
sky. We were in the second wave, so it was the first one which was getting it:
that's where I saw a Lanc buying it; he just seemed to explode in mid air.

'Over the coast and inland, leaving that wall of flak behind us now
occupied with the third wave of Lancs. Still some flak and searchlights, of
course and all predicted stuff. But now the flares were bursting all around us,
dropped, I should imagine, by Junkers 88s trying to illuminate us so that the
night-fighters could come in. Now and then I saw flurries of tracer as
interceptions were made. Occasionally I saw the silhouette of other Lancs:
comforting, because it confirmed that we were still in the bomber stream. Get
out of the stream and you've absolutely had it: you're a sitting duck and can
be picked off easily.

'Next, Cartwright the rear gunner, a quiet, dependable chap who, for the
most part, kept himself to himself, was yelling, 'Corkscrew, corkscrew', like a
man demented and Vernon had her in a stomach-wretching dive to port
followed by a steep climb to starboard then another almost vertical dive, but
to starboard this time. Cartwright then announced that he was certain we'd
lost whatever was after us and we levelled off. Was glad to note the odd Lanc
around us and that therefore we were still in the stream.

'Approaching Gelsenkirchen at last. More flak than ever, it seemed and
more searchlights than ever. Fires caused by first wave intensive. Green Target
Indicators for us; the second wave. I got them clearly into my sight and then
down went the 4,000 pounder and the eighteen 500 pounders. Shouted for
bomb doors to be closed: flew on to turning point. As we banked for our next
course I could not help staring at the fires burning below which, even from
19,000 feet, one could see clearly. Stupid doing that really; it must have
destroyed my night vision.

'Concentrated bombing of target: heavy and widespread fires raging. Flak,

Searchlights and fighter flares lit up the sky to such an extent that you could almost have read a newspaper in the aircraft. Flak bursting all around the aircraft. Was persuaded to put out the navigator's light and open his curtains while we were over Gelsenkirchen. He saw the wall of flak, shouted, 'Fuck me!' and has not emerged since: not during a raid that is. Says wild horses wouldn't drag him out again during an op and ignores questions as to how you could get any horse into a Lanc, far less a wild one.

'Rear gunner says he saw one of ours go down in flames just after target. Seventeen aircraft missing from this raid (one from this station: P/O Williams and crew). Luftwaffe dropped many dummy Target Indicators.

'That was really widespread bombing. What is now referred to as an 'area bash.' Some of my load must have fallen on houses; maybe even on air raid shelters as well. A faint niggling at the back of my mind; how many women and children had I killed simply by pressing that little tit? No point in deluding oneself over that one had killed people. But I suppose it's daft to permit your mind to think along these lines. Trouble is I'm too tired. It's now almost 08:00 and honestly I don't know why I stay up writing this when I could be in bed and sleeping, or trying to sleep, anyway. One more thing, I didn't feel scared during it; but after it felt something akin to a tremble coming on. And yet, surely that was easy stuff compared to what the bomber crews suffered in 1942. Even last year was worse when you look back on Bomber Command's losses over it, both in air crews and aircraft. Should consider ourselves lucky, I suppose.'

At the end of his tour in August 1944 Campbell Muirhead reflected that he and his crew had 'got off lightly'. He wrote: 'Especially compared with aircrews who embarked on their tours as little as a year ago. Then nearly every op was over Germany bringing with it, in practically all cases, heavy losses. When we arrived here at Wickenby it was those losses we had in mind. Which, really, is why I was so pessimistic when I started this diary. Didn't for a moment dream that in the event we would do only five over the Reich and the other twenty-five over Occupied Europe. True, losses there also, but on nowhere the same scale as those incurred by Bomber Command over Germany. Have the Invasion to thank for that and, of course, the run-up to it. Would think that, once the Allied Armies advance enough to be able to do without the services of the heavies, 'Butch' will get them all back again and will resume his dedicated task of flattening Germany. If he does, our tour has been just at the most opportune time - a comparatively easy one sandwiched between those earlier heavy losses and those which are certainly still to come when their nasty stuff is resumed. Hope I enjoy as much good luck for the remainder of the war.'

Footnotes Chapter 17

124 Letter by H. K. Gray DFM to Intercom; the Official Quarterly Magazine of the Aircrew Association, Christmas 1983.

125 *Diary of a Bomb Aimer: Training in America and Flying With 12 Squadron in WWII* Campbell Muirhead/Edited and Annotated by Philip Swan (Pen & Sword 2009).

Chapter 18

Stand Down

Campbell Muirhead

No account of squadron life would be complete without some reference to its songs. Airmen were great singers and they really came into their own in the mess - especially when there was a 'stand down'. 'Tanked up' with a lot of beer they would roar out the squadron songs to the accompaniment of a battered piano. Having exhausted their repertoire of squadron songs they would turn to Sylvest ('With a row of forty medals on his chest') or Salome which is unprintable! Parodies were made of popular songs of the time:
'A ride through London in a rattling taxi,
'With dirty noises from a horse's jacksie,
'A mattress without springs, those foolish things
'Remind me of you.'
Bread and Butter Bomber Boys by Arthur White, navigator, 100 Squadron.

21st June 1944

With no flying tonight, none whatsoever due to duff weather, a sort of spontaneous boozing session gets under way in the Mess. A Mess Rule, 'to be strictly observed' and never mind the split infinitive, is that no Mess member is to stand treat. Sensible enough: the Service just trying to ensure you don't fling away your 13/6d a day (if Pilot Officer) or your 15/6d a day (if Flying Officer) on buying booze for other bods. Yes, to be strictly observed and strictly we ignore it. Generally we ignore, in a cavalier fashion, most rules and most regulations. Except for flying ones, that is. After a few pints someone announces that we have approached recitation time. A WAAF officer, who has just arrived at Wickenby and who, from her accent, simply must be a product of Roedean, places her ladylike sherry on a table and starts clapping her hands and at the same time making anticipatory, gushing noises. She gets frowned at by all: and I take it upon myself to inform her that I have reason to believe that the first recitation might well be Twas on the good ship Venus and that accordingly she might prefer to take off. This thoughtful and well-meant advice she rejects somewhat haughtily. And as she does so some pilot, whose name I don't know, gets the first verse airborne:

'Twas on the good ship Venus
By Christ, you should have seen us
The figure-head was a whore in bed
The mast a rampant penis.

They breed them tough at Roedean; the lass stands her ground. Her smile, however, is not quite so toothy. And she gulps at her sherry as the second verse lurches under way.

'The cabin boy's name was Sam
He was a saucy nipper
He filled his arse with broken glass
And circumcised the skipper.

I say to the WAAF: 'It gets slightly vulgar after this'. She takes off. Quite smartly, her smile fading rapidly into the past. Eventually the good ship Venus founders. So next we start singing *The Ball O' Kirriemuir*. A tall navigator seems to know more verses than all of us put together. Vernon, being a Yank, has never even heard this subtle piece of folk-lore before and is rather bemused. I inform him that this account of a dance in Fife, Scotland, which ended up in a frantic free-for-all sexual orgy, basically is true (as it is although perhaps enlarged upon somewhat by numerous Service choirs), to which he replies shit, pull the other and whose round is it, by the way? I tell him it's Horsfall's: but that worthy is too absorbed in the intimate details of yet another incident which it is alleged took place at Kirriemuir to even think about ordering a round. We get to what must surely be around the thirtieth verse (which is the one where *Aggie McCafferty* had us all in fits, a-jumping from the mantelpiece and bouncing on her; guess whats?), when the Mess Secretary strides in and immediately closes the bar. He is awarded the Hitler salute together with cries of Mein Fuhrer from some, a two-fingered salute from a couple and, from one, the offer of a dance. This he refuses. He bestows on each of us an intense glare which suggests that he's recording mentally all our names as against any Mess damage and strides off again. We all repair slowly to our billets.

16th July 1944

Being stood-down 'they' usually have a job for you. But this time it's not in the least an enjoyable one. Together with some Flying Officer, whose name I forget, I form a Committee of Adjustment. This is an entirely ridiculous title for two of you who go through someone's personal effects. When a Lanc doesn't make it back to Wickenby, the RAF wait a few days for the gen to reach them as to its fate. If the Lanc hasn't made it to some other airfield in the UK, then the crew are either dead or are PoW. It is at this stage that the Committee of Adjustment are appointed at the Lanc's home station to deal with the effects of each of the lost 'aircrew, in my case a Pilot Officer navigator. This is the procedure: the two of you go to this Pilot Officer's room and sift through everything that's in his locker. The whole point of this exercise is that all he has is to be returned to his next-of-kin. And the exercise requires two of you so that, in the most unlikely event of that next-of-kin, on receiving these effects, claiming that some expensive item of his was not among them, the RAF can reply that two officers carefully examined all his effects and that that item simply was not there. And that they have signed accordingly. You've got to be very careful. For instance, you check for French Letters? You wouldn't return these to some fond mother who had never for a moment thought her son would indulge in that sort of thing. Same for pornographic photos. And the letters he retained, well, you had to read them to see what was in them and who they came from; after all, maybe there was a fiancée. Yes, a careful assignment it was. But this P/O was married. I'm not recording his name; despite all I say, what I'm writing now might well come into other people's hands and, if read, could cause extreme unhappiness. And there's enough of that around these days without my adding to it.

The guy, as I've noted above, was married. Extremely handsome, looked like Errol Flynn. But as randy as hell (which kind of fits, I suppose - EF is supposed to be like that). Really, any attractive girl, whether civvy or WAAF, was a challenge to him: he went all out to shag her. He used to say that he was certain that he would buy it during the tour and that accordingly, even though married, he was going to 'do' every woman he could. Someone in the Mess once said: 'God, you'll shag yourself to death'. To which he retorted, 'Isn't that a better way than being shot down?' There is, of course, no answer to such a retort. According to what we discovered, he lived up to this. There were, for instance, enough FLs to kit out the entire Squadron. And he must have had immense charm to persuade girls to fall for him as they did. As for the letters, well, they all went into the fire. We checked and double checked that nothing which was returned to his wife would give her any impression other than that of a devoted and faithful husband.

PS. Added end July. Learned he's in the bag. Ah, well, no nookie for him there. But that was a Committee of Adjustment which ended up on a comparatively light note. Most don't. And one pilot admitted to me that it was the most upsetting job he'd ever been handed since coming here to Wickenby. He knew the bod concerned had been killed, because he had been right next to him over the target, had seen the other receive a direct hit from flak, seen it explode with nobody getting out. He found going through the dead chap's effects a numbing experience: felt there was something pathetic about the trivial items which the dead man had so obviously treasured and visualised the parents when these items were returned to them. He was almost unable to read the letters from his parents and found his eyes watering to read phrases like, 'May God protect you and return you safely to us' and, 'We pray for you every night'.

While nodding my understanding, I said that Winco Nelson had an even more disturbing task: he had to write to these parents (maybe he doesn't have to, but I understand that he does) and couch his letter in such a way as to try to give them some comfort, which I'd reckon is almost impossible. Then the Padre too had to write similarly and not just now and then what with all these losses. One thing I do know about these Committees of Adjustment and that is that nobody on them would retain any item for himself no matter how trivial. Even if your uniform was on the scruffy side and the deceased's was brand new and a perfect fit you'd never think of switching. Would be ghoulish, that. Don't know what would happen if the parents wrote and said they didn't want his uniform back. Would probably be put up for sale in the Mess. But would they forward the proceeds of this sad sale to the parents? Doubt it; somehow or another it wouldn't seem right. Must find out about that sometime. Wonder if my parents would want my uniform back if I get the chop. What on earth would they do with it? Would, I think, be a constant, sad reminder to them that once I wore it.

17th July 1944

The Station cinema's a good refuge when not flying and at rather a loose end. Not very democratic, I'm afraid, in RAF cinemas the two back rows invariably being reserved for officers, the next three or four for NCOs and the remainder a free-for-all for airmen and WAAFs. Still, I suppose it's got to be that way; you couldn't have officers jostling with all and sundry for the best seats, not very conducive to good discipline.

One of the most enjoyable facets of the cinema here (and this applies more or less to all Station cinemas in the RAF) is the constant barrage of wisecracks from the audience should the film lend itself to them. It only needs someone on the screen to express surprise at a particular item and to ask what he or she should do with it. The advice, which never varies, is usually provided from all over the cinema, the WAAFs being prominent in their offering of it.

Such advice, however, varies. In one RAF cinema (at Dumfries, I think) they showed an ancient effort in which Hedy Lamarr debarked from a rowing boat at some remote island off some unspecified coast to be surrounded immediately by a mob of savages who, according to what passed for a plot, had never seen a white person before and were shrieking away in hostile gibberish. Undaunted, Hedy said: 'Take me to your leader'. This provoked much merriment among the audience. More merriment when, from the front stalls, someone advised, 'Take her to the bloody Groupie', which, in turn, was followed by, 'Who'll have them down even before she knows it'. The Group Captain was not present at the screening, which was perhaps just as well.

One film that went down well in the Station cinema was, *In Which We Serve*. No cracks at this one: it was watched and, listened to, in complete silence. About the only thing you could almost hear was the wave of sympathy for Richard Attenborough when he couldn't take any more.

20th July 1944

Feel like writing something about this room I have here at Wickenby. In a hut of course and just a few yards from the Mess. I'm lucky in that it's rather a large room and I have it all to myself. Contains a hospital-type issue RAF bed, a small chest of drawers and a bedside table; also a miniscule carpet. Managed to acquire a small table and chair from the NAAFI (No Ambition And Fuck all Interest) which I think the manager has now given up looking for; this I refer to as my 'writing desk'. It's nice being on your toddy, not having to talk when you don't feel like it, staying up writing if you do feel like it, getting into the pit whenever you feel like it and so on.

But returned from an op to find that they had shoved another two beds, two side-tables and two chests of drawers into it. I had company: two Pilot Officers. One from the Irish Free State, not unsurprisingly called Paddy; the other from Cardiff and, surprise, surprise, answers to the name of Taffy. And to them, of course, I'm Jock. They're crewed up together, Paddy being pilot and Taffy navigator: rest of crew are sergeants. [Though Campbell Muirhead was on 12 Squadron the two new arrivals - Pilot Officer George Thomas 'Paddy' Ryan and his navigator, J. E. Palmer were on 626 Squadron]. A bit nervous; understandably so, because they haven't done their first yet. How many had I done? I tell them. To their next question I say yes, shit scared, until airborne and then it's not so bad. (But when I say this, the looks on their faces reflect that they think I'm taking the Mick.) I invite them up to the ante-room where I confuse their confirmed impression of the Scots by buying them a pint. Vernon and Horsfall are there. I introduce them as the worst bloody pilot in the whole of 12 Squadron and a mid-upper gunner who couldn't hit an FW 190 if it impaled itself on his guns. They see those footprints up one wall, along the ceiling and down the other (some other crew's been at the game again) and say are we all round the bend? We reply that indeed we are and that it's high time they bought another round. Which they do. On the way back to our room Paddy asked if I had any real tips to offer. I said none, really, except that if you even thought you were being tailed to corkscrew like hell, but to get back into the middle of the stream once you'd shaken him off. So important to keep right in the middle of the stream.

Added later
Paddy and Taffy came with us [to Stuttgart on 28/29 July]. They didn't come back with us. Grim that: for your first op you get a bastard like Stuttgart where you maybe have a slight chance if you're experienced, but where you have virtually no chance if you're a sprog crew. (Yet, having said that, many an experienced crew has bought it on what looked like a simple daylight over France.) They've now removed the two beds etc. from my room and I'm on my own once more. Paddy and Taffy: I never knew their names. With a bit of luck they're maybe now in the bag. But to get it on your very first; oh, Christ! 126

Sergeant Wells, a bomb aimer on 626 Squadron, who evidently accompanied us on quite a few of the same targets, is still chuckling over an incident involving some of the Aussie sergeants who had indulged in some crafty sheep stealing. On a foggy night, when there had not been any flying, he and the other NCOs in the crew had been lying around in their hut on the outskirts of the airfield feeling bored when suddenly the door was banged open and an Aussie sergeant charged on to invite them to come for a good nosh up. They followed him through the fog to the Aussie's hut from which, as they approached, they could detect a delightful aroma of roasting meat. On entering, Wells found himself wondering why the hut hadn't gone up in flames: both the heavy cast iron stoves were red hot to half-way up the chimney pipe and joints of meat were hanging all around them being grilled, the fat dropping all over the hearths and the floor boards. About 50 airmen were jammed into the hut, all eating away with expressions of delight. He was told that some of the Aussies had been over the fence at the adjoining field, caught a couple of sheep then slaughtered and butchered them, being careful to bury all the non-edible parts so that no evidence remained. Wells joined in, eating with bare hands: said it was one of the best meals he'd ever had.

4th August 1944

Mess games under way again tonight. Kicked off with the pyramid effort in which three of four bods crouch down and press their shoulders against the wall at the same time encircling each other with their arms. Rather like one half of a rugby scrum. Then those remaining take running jumps from the far end of the ante-room and try to build on this base. Success is proclaimed if the pyramid can be added to until the last to jump on to it has his back against the ceiling. Alas, this stage was not reached tonight as some ill-mentioned individuals tickled the testicles of the centre members of the base, which caused the entire structure to collapse amid much shouting and not a little swearing. All was not lost, however, because the struggling mob on the floor involved itself into two rugger teams. It wasn't a question of pilots and navigators versus bomb aimers and gunners: it was more a question of everybody against everybody: with, it goes without saying, Horsfall playing a most prominent part. The damage was not all that extensive; just two chairs demolished. On the personal side, Vernon got his blouse ripped, Horsfall lost his tie and I got a slight tear in my trousers (not my best ones, I'm glad to record).

After a rest, three started on the old footsteps-up-the-wall-and-across-the-ceiling nonsense. Just after the ante-room had been re-decorated too; the Mess Secretary will do his flaming nut. That done, two started on 'Cats on the roof tops, cats on the tiles, cats with (a certain part of their anatomy) wreathed in smiles', but this tailed off when nobody else seemed to want to listen and either went off to play billiards, cards or dominoes. Some even returned to the bar. One sat himself in an easy chair to read The Times, but testily put it down again when he spotted a crafty and cunning advance being made on him with a lighted match. People began to drift off to their billets. When I left there was only one bod at the bar and even he said it was his last, for that evening, he was quick to add.

Footnotes Chapter 18

126 Sergeant J. E. Palmer the navigator on the crew of Pilot Officer George Ryan survived when they were shot down by a night fighter and was taken into captivity. Ryan and the other five members of his crew were killed. Lancaster I LL895 crashed at Valhingen, 8 kilometres south-west of Stuttgart.

Chapter 19

'Aircraft of Bomber Command last night raided Dresden'

I participated in the Dresden affair, which was a terrible thing. The fire raid. I understand there were about 135,000 or so people killed in that raid. We were told that the Russians were advancing and the Germans were falling back into these cities and when the Russian armour went by, the Germans would fan out and cut their supply lines up and for these reasons, certain cities had to be obliterated. This is what they told us. And then it started to filter through later that this wasn't a tactical thing. What I think really happened was that the Russians were moving very, very rapidly and the Allies decided they would show the Russians that even though we had a tremendous army, we also had a tremendous air force, so don't get too cocky, you guys, or we'll show you what we could do to Russian cities. This was Churchill and the rest. This was a calculated atrocity, no question in my mind.

We weren't in the first phase, we were in the second. Even then, the city was burning. We could see the great flare in the sky for a long way out and we knew that was Dresden burning. Burning cities is a technique, you know. You didn't need any atomic bombs; you could create what is called a fire storm. You had incendiaries and then heavy bombs and this would create an artificial wind roaring up the streets and it sucked the oxygen out and people didn't die, or die all that much, of fire; they died because the life was literally sucked right out of them.

We went there at night and the Americans went there the next day and they had the long-range fighters protecting them and strangely, the Germans had fighter protection for the area, but the order was never given and so their fighters sat on the fields. The American fighters went down and strafed the poor bastards in the streets who were picking up the corpses and this German who told me this after the war, was very bitter about that. This strafing in the streets, by the Americans. That was a beastly thing, wasn't it? Our guys didn't do that, did they? Only the beastly Huns did that, didn't they?

We carried incendiaries over Dresden and the Pathfinders were leading us into places where major fires hadn't started yet. I mean, there would be a patch over here, say some residential area and the Pathfinder pilots would scoot over there and drop their markers. It was wholesale destruction of a city, using the latest in city-burning techniques. It was indescribable! When we saw the photos two days later, it was dreadful. Dreadful. It was then that I felt we'd all been had. I thought it was a pretty...Dresden was an unarmed city. Maybe a couple of battalions of home guards or Boy Scouts or something and there was no military justification for that. As far as I've ever been able to find out later, I was right. A straight political destruction of the city. No tactical advantage. The straight politics of destruction.

A Canadian airman of RAF Bomber Command. [*127]

Stanley Harrison RAAF pedalled on his bicycle up to 460 Squadron RAAF 'B' Flight office at the front of one of the large hangars at Binbrook. It was the morning of 13 February 1945. The Australian pilot was unaware that it was the 13th of the month and would not worry about it. In any case he was not superstitious, at least about the date. He could not know that he would be part of the BBC news in the early hours of the following day. But as he rode up from the officers' mess he realised that the weather was fine and that meant that they would be operating over Germany that night. Having checked that all the crew members were fit for flying at 0915 he reported this to his 'B' Flight Commander, Squadron Leader Bob Henderson DFC. All the aircraft captains, or 'skippers', were sitting round in the Flight Office talking shop or any interesting happenings, personal or otherwise, in which Bob Henderson joined every now and then when something concerning the Flight, operations, the performance or operation of the aircraft was being discussed. At 10 o'clock Henderson went to the daily conference in the Squadron Commander's office. The three flight commanders and the navigation, bombing, wireless and gunnery leaders were all present and while they reported their state of readiness, details of the 'Operations for Tonight' came through from Bomber Command via Group and base headquarters. Harrison continues.

'At lunch in the mess Bob Henderson told me that we were flying that night in 'J-Johnny' instead of our usual kite 'T-Tommy' and that, as briefing was not until later in the afternoon, we would have time to run-up the engines and check the aircraft. I contacted the crew in the sergeants' mess and told them to be at the locker room at 2pm to take our gear out to the aircraft, to run it up and check it over. There we collected our Mae Wests. Jack Peacock, the wireless operator, took the kit bag of our leather flying helmets, Peter Squires, the flight engineer, took his bag of tools and on the way out to the aircraft we collected the eight .303 Browning machine-guns for the turrets.

'After the crew bus had taken us to our aircraft dispersal area on the perimeter of the airfield, Peter and I gave it a thorough check over externally and internally, including starting up the four engines with a complete test in all phases of operation for each. When the starboard outer engine was run up, 'Curly', officially Flight Sergeant Tony Walker, tested his mid-upper gun turret for smooth, efficient rotation, elevation and depression of the guns. He counted into his intercom microphone as he did so, to test that the intercom was OK in all positions of the turret. Maurice Bellis, the bomb-aimer, tested the H_2S radar transmitter, as Max Spence our navigator was still at Navigation Section waiting for any 'gen' that may have come through concerning times for navigators' briefing, etc. When the port outer engine was being run up, Jock Gilhooly, the rear gunner, tested his turret in the same way as the mid-upper, while Jack tested the 'Gee' radar receiver.

'After a thorough check of the cockpit controls and instruments, compasses, transmitters and intercom at all points, we left the bomb doors open ready for loading from the bomb trolleys and switched off the motors. Leaving our gear in the aircraft we returned to the Flight Office to learn that briefing was at 1800 with a meal at 1700 but the navigators' briefing was at 1645. This was unusual as the navigators were normally briefed after the meal, before the main briefing, so I thought that maybe it was a very long trip, or a very involved route. The fuel load was 2,154 gallons - maximum load.

'While sitting in the anteroom of the mess after our meal, a few whispers were going around about our target for tonight. The Russians were pushing westwards in the southern sector of the Eastern Front, so we looked at the map in the newspapers and my tip was Dresden. I mentioned this to one of the navigators and he blurted out, 'Who told you?' The cat was out of the bag now but naturally I kept it quiet, sitting there thinking of the route we might fly and the heavily defended areas along the way.

'At about 0540 I went over to the briefing room and drew the Aids Boxes, for use if we were shot down and our flying rations. There was the usual moan when we had 'Empire' chocolate, as it was the worst grade of chocolate available but it was remarkable how good it would taste after we left the target and settled down to the long tiring trip back. Then we would be trying to stay alert, when a natural winding down from the tension of the bombing run and general fatigue set in. We each received two small three-penny bars of chocolate, half a box of barley sugar sweets, or about six sweets each and two packets of chewing gum. Our Aids Boxes contained concentrated foods, a compass, rubber water bottle, some water purifying tablets and some Benzedrine tablets, which bucked you up if you needed a little extra to make a break for it, etc.

'We emptied our pockets and then put back only handkerchiefs, about £1 in money, an identity card and an Aids Box. The rest of the contents of our pockets - keys, letters, bus tickets and anything else - were placed in the bag that had contained our Aids Boxes with a label for each crewmember. Then all individual bags went into the big crew bag and the intelligence clerks locked this in a safe. This ensured that if we were shot down, there was nothing to tell the Germans where we came from, so they would be unable to identify our squadron and its location. At least this was the theory. But some of our Squadron who were shot down and interrogated and later escaped back to England, said that the first thing the German interrogator said to them, after hearing that the crashed aircraft had our Squadron letters 'AK' on it was, 'How is your commanding officer, *Hewgie* Edwards VC?' (The Germans never could get their tongues around 'Hughie'!)

'Maurie had his target map and we looked at the route on the big map at the front of the Briefing Room and the photos of the target area, its defences and known searchlight areas, as well as the heavily defended areas on or near our route. Times for sunrise, moonrise and moonset, as well as the phases of the moon, were all on the board. So were 'phase of attack' times, 'H' hour (the actual time of the start of the attack when the first phase commenced dropping their bombs), take-off time, total distance, bomb loads and ETA back at base. On another board was all the signals gen: the Master Bomber's call sign, together with those of the Deputy Master Bomber, radio link and the VHF radio channel on which to receive them. Shortly before briefing was due to start, Max came in with his navigator's bag crammed full with maps, charts and instruments. In reply to my query of, 'What do you think of it Max?' he made the dry wisecrack, 'I wish Joe Stalin would get an air force of his own or come and fight on the Western Front if he wants our help like this!'

'The corniest crack of all was overheard from behind. 'I guess there won't be many Jerries left in Dresden after tonight!' Similar wisecracks were being passed and general back-chat was being indulged in around the room while the crews all waited. Max told me that we were in the second phase 'H+2' to H+4' and that we were on the lowest bombing height again! (There were four bombing heights, each 500 feet above the next, starting from our height and going up.) Then everyone was on their feet as the Squadron Commanding Officer entered, followed by the station CO and the base commander. We waited until they were all seated then we all sat down again but there was no talking now and the room was suddenly quiet as the Squadron CO, Squadron Leader 'Mick' Cowan, walked to the front and started the briefing proper.

'Your target tonight is Dresden. [128] The attack is divided into three phases.[129]. Here are your aircraft letters, phase times and bombing heights. First phase on target from 'H' to 'H+2 minutes'. 'B-Beer', Flight Lieutenant Marks.'

Flight Lieutenant Marks stood up. 'All correct sir!' (Indicating that all his crew were present and ready to fly).

'18,000 feet.'

'This checking of the crews and allocation of the heights was repeated until all the aircraft in the first phase had been detailed.

'Second Phase on target from 'H+2' to 'H+4'.

'O-Oboe', Flying Officer Whitmarsh.'

'All correct sir!'

'19,000 feet.'

'J-Johnny', Flying Officer Harrison.'

'I was on my feet. 'All correct sir!'

'18,000 feet.'

'As I sat down there was a whispered comment from my friend Doug Creeper, who was sitting behind me.

'Can't that kite of yours get any higher than that, Stan?'

'I did not bother to reply. Our aircraft, 'J-Johnny', was certainly not new, had completed more than 30 raids on Germany and was not the fastest in the Squadron but as I had pointed out to my crew, 'Johnny' had developed a very good habit of coming back at the end of each trip.

After all the crews had been allocated their bombing heights, the CO called for the various specialist leaders to give their briefing.

'The Flying Control Officer produced his blackboard. 'The runway for take-off is '22' (i.e. the compass bearing was 220 degrees). 'A' and 'B' Flight aircraft will taxi round the perimeter track behind the control tower to this side of the runway, whilst 'C' Flight aircraft will turn left from their dispersal areas and taxi to the other side of the runway. On a 'green', taxi on to the runway and take off on the second 'green'. Watch the comer of the runway. It's soft on the grass there, so taxi slowly and keep on the asphalt!'

'We had heard most of this at every briefing since we joined the Squadron but there were some new crews and repetition did no harm considering the speed at which some clots taxied. A fully loaded Lanc had a maximum overall take-off weight of 84,000 lb, so it took some distance to stop. This could lead to trouble when 23 aircraft had to taxi to the end of the runway and even with 'C' Flight coming round from the other side, there would still be 15 of us following one another along that side.

'Foggo', as the Control Officer was affectionately known then had his little joke. 'The runway for return will be the long one (2,000 yards) but I cannot tell you at this stage from which end we will be landing you!' This raised a small laugh and we were thankful that the forecast was not for strong winds.

'The beacon will be flashing the usual 'BK'. Join the circuit at 2,000 feet and do not call up (for permission to land) until you are over the airfield! All three emergency airfields are fully serviceable.'

'This was a very comforting thought in case we lost engines; brakes or the undercarriage would not lock down.

'When coming back over the East Coast, you must be at 6,000 feet, as the Dover belt of ack-ack guns are still in operation to guard against flying bombs. Do not exceed 250 mph.' (This caused general laughter as the Lanc cruised at 180mph.)

'Burn only your navigation lights and not your downward recognition light! Any questions?'

'As there were none, the CO called the 'Met bloke' who had charts drawn showing where the weather fronts were located and another giving cloud amounts, heights of bases and tops for the whole of the route to the target and home again. He gave us the gen on the weather to be expected during the whole flight. Cloud was expected from the French coast in to the target, hopefully with some breaks near the target, to give a clear view on the bombing run.

'Weather here 'mainly clearing', with no cloud over England on return.' (I hoped he was right this time, for we did not want another cloud base of 150 feet after a long trip like this one, with everyone tired and 23 aircraft having to find their way down through it to our airfield. One of these recently was enough for a very long time to come!)

'Icing level 3,000 feet, with Icing Index 'Moderate' to 'High' in cloud. Any questions?'

'How about contrails?'

'Only above 20,000 feet, so they won't worry you! Anything else?'

'The CO called on the Bombing Leader. 'All aircraft are carrying the same load, one 2,000lb and eleven containers of incendiaries.'[130]

'Bomb-aimers select and fuse bombs when the bomb line is crossed. After bombing check immediately that all bombs have gone and if unable to get rid of any hang-ups there, do not jettison them on the track out of the target but keep them until you cross the jettison area in The Wash on your return.' (Not long back some clot jettisoned a canister of incendiaries in the first leg of the route out of the target and gave every night fighter within 50 miles a clear signal of the route being flown from the target.)

'Set target pressure (estimated atmospheric pressure) as you enter the aircraft and I use the Broadcast Bombing Wind, multiplied by 1.1.'[131]

'The Signals Officer will give the time of this broadcast. All aircraft are carrying flashes. Captains, keep your aircraft straight and level while the red light is on and let us have some really good photos tonight.'

'That sounded easy in the Briefing Room but with other aircraft, slipstream turbulence, not to mention searchlights and ack-ack, it was not quite as simple as that over the target and our camera had fogged up with condensation on our last three trips.

'Bomb-aimers obtain your pro-formas and bomb-stations for your aircraft from the Bombing Section after the briefing. Any questions?'

'The CO then called the Gunnery Leader. 'Just a word to all gunners! Enemy night fighters are particularly active in this area, so keep an even sharper watch in your search pattern than usual.' (Comforting news, I don't think but then he was not likely to tell them that there were no fighters about and that they could go to sleep was he?)

'You all know your search plans. Cover all the sky, all the time. Load your guns while you are still in your dispersal area and do not unload or leave your turret until you are back in your dispersal area. Jerry may try an intruder raid with night fighters again and it could be tonight, so stay alert even when approaching base.'

'The CO now called the Signals Leader 'R/T call signs of the Master Bomber, Deputy Master Bomber and R/T link are 'Snodgrass 1, 2 and 3'. The Main Force bomber stream is 'Press On'. Channel 'C' on VHF and '1196'. Wireless operators listen out on your Marconi set on the wavelength shown on your 'flimsies', which are available at the back of the briefing room. Remember, skippers, if you cannot get the Master Bomber on VHF, tell your WOP to select '1196' and press button 'C'. Broadcast wind velocities will be broadcast at 0015, 15 minutes before 'H' hour and will be the usual five-figure group preceded by 'X'. Aircraft on 'Darkie' watch on the return trip will be 'G-George', Flying Officer Dowling; 'J-Johnny', Flying Officer Harrison; and 'K2', Flying Officer Creeper. Do these captains know what you have to do?'

'Yes sir,' we replied.

'On the return journey listen out on Channel D for any aircraft in trouble or lost.

'Very well, that's all. Any questions?'

'Now it was the turn of the Intelligence Officer, Squadron Leader Leatherdale and a First World War pilot, who was always worth hearing. 'Your target tonight is the Old World city of Dresden. The attack is divided into two parts. 5 Group are opening the attack at 2230, two hours before your 'H' hour, with a slightly different aiming point. You should see their fires still burning when you get there. Jerry is shifting all his government offices with staffs and records for the Eastern Front to Leipzig - raided by 4 Group last night - Dresden and Chemnitz. These three cities are roughly in a triangle. Dresden has not been attacked before as there were no targets there but now, with the 'Big City' being evacuated partly to Dresden and with large concentrations of troops and equipment passing through to the Russian Front, the city is crammed full and needs disorganising. As you can see from the target map, the city is fairly easy to identify and, on your bombing run from approximately north to south, you have several good pin-points to help you check your run.

'Now for the route. Base to Reading, to Beachy Head, to the Rhine, keeping clear of Mainz to starboard and then on until you pass just slightly starboard of Frankfurt. Frankfurt has a large searchlight area and some ack-ack guns, so keep clear and stay on track. Turn slightly north and then run up as though heading for Leipzig, or when you pass to port of that, as though the 'Big City' is your target. Just north of Leipzig, you head east and across through this searchlight belt and you may have quite a few lights put up there but there should be little or no flak. North of Dresden you have a turn of nearly 90 degrees, so watch out for other aircraft and so avoid collisions. You have a reasonably long run-up and, after bombing, you hold the same course until you have completed this short leg, then turn southwest towards Stuttgart and Nuremberg. Keep on track and pass south of these two places or you may have trouble. Then you head west, cross the Rhine on the southeast corner of France and keep clear of this area, where they are still active and getting too many of our aircraft. Cross the coast at Orfordness at 6,000 feet at least and then lose height across The Wash to base.

'The defences of Dresden are not considerable but they may have brought back mobile flak guns from the Eastern Front, so the flak may be moderate but I doubt if you will find it heavy. 'Oboe' Mosquitoes are marking the target at 'H-2' with a single red TI. Then the flares will go down and Pathfinders will drop their TIs. Red and green TIs cascading together will be used only if they can positively identify the Aiming Point. If there is cloud over the target, 'blind-marker' crews will use sky-markers, which will be green flares dripping red stars. Your order of preference for bombing will be: 1. Master Bomber's instructions. 2. Red and green TIs. 3. Sky-markers on the exact heading of 175 degrees True at 165mph indicated airspeed. 4. H2S run. Any questions?'

'The CO now walked out to the map, summarised the briefing and told us the heights at which to fly on each leg of the route.

'Phase times for return: First Phase, 10 minutes before ETA. Second Phase, on ETA. Third Phase, 10 minutes after ETA. Use Aldis lamps for taxiing out and taxi slowly, even on return, when you will have some daylight! Position yourselves on the circuit on your return and we will get you down much more quickly. Any questions? Have you anything to say sir? (This was addressed to the Station CO.)

'Yes. I just want to impress on you chaps the necessity to be very careful to keep a very keen look-out at all turning points and so avoid any risk of collisions!' (Didn't he think we knew that? About 200 aircraft all heading for the same point within 6 minutes at the most, with no lights on, was enough to make anyone 'keep a very keen lookout'! We could not guess that within two weeks he would be the one who would have a mid-air collision over France when the 'Met blokes' 'boobed' and we would have to climb through 15,000 feet of cloud. After the other aircraft crossed on top of him, wiping out all four of his propellers and his canopy, he dropped back down into the cloud and was the only survivor, losing the crew he had 'borrowed' for the trip!)

'All right chaps, that is all. Have a good trip and hit it really hard.'

'We all filed out to the locker room to change into our flying clothes. Jack and Maurie collected their pro formas and flimsies on the way. Jock and Curly started their long job of getting dressed in electrically heated flying suits, socks and gloves, while Peter and I changed too. Max had gone back to the Navigation Section. It was a cold night on the ground and the 'Met bloke' said that the temperature at 20,000 feet would be -25 degrees, which would not be as bad as the -45 degrees we had had once or twice. But it would still be quite cool so I put on my long wool and rayon underpants and long-sleeved singlet. As 'J-Johnny' was not a cold kite, I did not put on my big hip-length socks but put on my usual pair of woollen socks and a pair of woollen 'knee-warmers' before getting back into my trousers, then my flying boots. My shirt collar was left undone and tie loosened but left on, in ease of diversion to another airfield on return. It would be awkward to go around without a collar and tie. I left the front collar stud in place, as there was a small compass built into the back of it, for use if I had to try to get back from Germany on the ground. I put on my 'once white' silk scarf to keep the wool of the roll-neck pullover away from my neck, as it got very irritating after a few hours rubbing on the stubble of whiskers. Then a sleeveless pullover and the big rolled-neck one that came down over my hips, eliminating any draught between trouser top and battledress when seated. Then, with my torch and small-scale map with the whole route on it stuck into the top of my right boot and my flying rations down the left one, I was ready. I put 'George', my fur dog mascot, into my battle-jacket, then went to see how the rest of the crew were getting on. I carried my three pairs of gloves (silk, chamois leather and outer leather-zippered gauntlets) and found Peter ready and waiting for me, similarly attired, except for all the gloves. John needed practically nothing extra, as he sat on top of the heater unit. Maurie had a few extras similar to Peter and also a big scarf, as it got draughty with his head down in the open-ended perspex 'bubble' while he was keeping a look-out for night fighters homing on to us from below.

'Curly and Jock were in their electrically heated suits and socks and now Curly pulled on the waterproof outer flying suit I had loaned him, as his issue buoyancy suit was too bulky to let him and it into his turret together. (No doubt it was Curly who was too bulky but this arrangement 'suited' him very well.) Jock put on his big rollneck sweater, a sheepskin vest (by courtesy of the Australian Comforts Fund through the hands of his skipper in the cause of another warm and happy gunner). Then his battledress jacket. Long knee-hip socks and heated flying boots completed their outfits, with their heated gloves. 'Max had not come in yet but would follow later so we went to get the crew bus out to the aircraft in the dispersal area. Many crews had the same idea and after finding the right bus in the darkness and telling the WAAF driver our aircraft letter, we piled into the back and waited until the thing was full to overflowing with other crews. We visited several other 'B' Flight dispersals and wished the other skippers well.

'Have a good trip. Doug!'

'Same to you, Stan. I bet I beat you home tonight!'

'So you ought to. You have a start on me. I'm in the second phase!'

'We arrived at our dispersal and again Peter and I went right around the aircraft, thoroughly checking for leaks, looking at the tyres for pressure and seeing that the aileron and rudder chocks had been removed. After checking inside again, we were ready to run-up and when everything was in order we switched off and climbed out for a final smoke, spit, swear, yarn and a 'leak' before take-off. We had about half an hour to go and the boys on the ground crew took the wheel chocks away, as I would not be running up again, while I went over to the ground crew hut to sign the aircraft maintenance Form 700. I just took a quick look to see that it had been signed up by the various maintenance types, then signed it as taking the aircraft in satisfactory condition. The main thing was that the Flight Sergeant in charge of the aircraft said it was OK. If he said it was OK, then you could bet your boots or your life that it was!

'Max arrived, got in and sorted all his gear out, with his charts, etc, in their right places. The 'Doc' came round with his 'wakey-wakey' tablets and Peter took charge of them, except for two each for Jock and Curly. We very rarely used them but it was handy to have them in ease anyone felt really tired! They had an effect for about 4 hours and I wanted to know who took them and how often. Everyone now had their Mae Wests on and the rest of the crew had on their parachute harnesses, as their parachutes were stored separately near where they were stationed, while I sat on mine and strapped the harness on when I got into my seat at the controls. It was about ten minutes before we were due to take off so we all climbed aboard, with a final 'See you in the morning about 6 o'clock' to the ground crew and their reply, 'Right - have a good trip, Skip!'

'We sorted ourselves out in our various positions and started up the engines. We confirmed with Max that the Distant Reading compass was correct. Then we tested and left the oxygen turned on. With a 'thumbs up' to the ground staff by torchlight, we were signalled out on to the perimeter track, having the radio on in ease of a change of runway, etc. Maurie shone his Aldis signalling lamp on the edge of the asphalt about 50 yards ahead. With engines just idling we taxied slowly along. Peter kept a lookout on his side (starboard) and called the distance between the starboard wheel and the edge of the track and kept an eye on the brake pressure gauge. Jock kept the lookout behind to ensure that no one taxied into us from the rear. The Lanc was heavy to taxi with a full load but answered to the brakes and motors, although you could feel the weight on the corners. At the controls you felt that the air was its natural element and it 'suffered' this crawling along the ground, only because it was necessary so that it could become airborne again.

'This taxiing took so long that we seemed to be taking an age to get to the take-off point but then everything took so long on these operations. We were about three-quarters of the way to the start of the runway and about half-way down a slight slope beside the bomb dump when I noticed a truck coming round on the track from the airfield controller's caravan and its lights suddenly disappeared behind something in front of us. I had Maurie shine his lamp directly ahead and there seemed to be a dark shape out there, probably an aircraft but no lights were visible. Then suddenly torches and lights shone from everywhere out in front, with frantic signals for me to stop. As if I needed to be signalled to stop! I had a fully loaded aircraft; some unidentified obstacle was blocking the perimeter track in front. There was grass, probably soft, to port and a drop down to the entry to the bomb dump to starboard - where did they think I was counting on going?

'I turned on the landing light (which we never used for taxiing in ease it got into the eyes of a pilot taking off and we did not use it for landing either) and it revealed two aircraft ahead in an unfriendly embrace! Just what we did not want at this stage, a taxiing accident! Peter was already worrying me about the engines overheating, as we had been taxiing downwind most of the time since leaving the dispersal. I warned the crew that there had been a taxiing accident and we might be late taking off. Max was not amused as he would have to watch all his timing calculations very carefully now to see that we set course on time or, at the worst, try to make time on the way, which was not easy with a fully loaded aircraft. Jock was now shining his torch out the back to warn any aircraft behind us not to taxi into us - I knew that there were three following us.

'After a few minutes, which seemed a very long time, we were signalled to turn off the perimeter track on to the grass in order to pass the obstruction. How I would have liked to break radio silence to warn the others of the obstruction and to get confirmation that the grass was firm enough to take our weight without getting us bogged. But we really had no alternative. I could not go forward, I could not turn to starboard and the track behind was blocked by other aircraft waiting for me to show them that it was safe to turn to port, then swing wide to starboard round the trouble ahead.

'I became reconciled to having to risk getting bogged and I was convinced that the airfield control types out there signalling to me to move did not really know if I would get bogged or not but they also had no alternative to offer. Peter reminded me again that the motors were getting 'bloody hot, Skip!' I 'bit his head off' by telling him didn't I already know that and what did he want me to do about it? I couldn't turn into wind here and we had other problems at the moment!

'Tell me when the gauges get well into the 'red' just before they blow off!'

'They are into the 'red', Skip and I thought you should know that we haven't got very long before we have real trouble with them!'

'I realised that I was getting 'edgy' and as I started to turn off the track I said, 'Sorry, Pete but I don't like this going on to the grass caper after old Foggo's warning about the soft grass up at the corner of the runway.

'I don't like it either,' he replied, 'but it seems all right so far, Stan.'

'We made our way slowly around the two aircraft to a clear section of perimeter track. I got an enthusiastic 'thumbs up' signal in the light of a torch from a very relieved airfield control chap, who had solved one of his problems and, in a few minutes, would have only the taxiing accident to sort out. We had a clear run to the ACP's caravan and now the pre-take-off drill was done, with each item repeated aloud, so that Peter could check them all. Maurice came up out of his position in the nose for the take-off and sat beside Max. I flicked my lights to the ACP to indicate that I was ready and immediately he gave me the 'green' from his signalling lamp, as all the aircraft from the other side of the perimeter track had taken off while we were sorting out our problem.

'We taxied out slowly, keeping as near to the end of the runway as possible in order to use every yard of it that we could for take-off. We rolled forward a short distance to straighten the tail wheel, then stopped again. The friction nut on the throttles was tightened firmly so that they would not work shut if my hands came off them for any reason. Gyro was set on 'zero' and 'unengaged', i.e. it was free to spin and to indicate any change in direction in the darkness up beyond the end of the two rows of runway lights.

'I opened the throttles to the gate' (normal maximum power position) for the two inboard engines as Peter reported, 'Fuel pumps on. All set for take-off!' 'The motors were not the only thing revved up, as the adrenaline was flowing and I always got a feeling of 'goose pimples' with the sound of the Merlins at full throttle. The ACP flashed another 'green' indicating that the runway was clear. I told the crew, 'Righto, here we go!'

'With the throttles for the outboard engines neatly half opened and Peter holding the inboard throttles open, I released the brakes and pushed the control column as far forward as I could to get the tail up as quickly as possible. The aircraft had been vibrating with all this power on and the wheels locked with the brakes. Now it surged forward in spite of the full load. I corrected any tendency of the aircraft to swing with the thrust of the engines by using the starboard throttles. When we had the tail up and were heading straight along the runway, I took the outboard throttles to the 'gate' also and called to Peter,

'Full power through the gate!' He pushed all four throttles past the gate to the 'Emergency' position and locked the friction as tight as he could get it so that the throttles could not creep back when he took his hands off them.

'Full power locked on!' he reported.

'I felt the extra power as a thrust in my back. A quick glance at the gauges for revs and boost confirmed that all the engines were OK and, with both hands now on the control column, I concentrated on those two rows of lights between which we now raced. I held the aircraft down so that we were not bumped prematurely into the air as we went over a slight rise about three-quarters of the way down the runway. This would have us in the air in a poor flying attitude and one in which it took longer to build up speed. As we came to the end of the runway I eased back on the control column and we climbed away.

'Undercart up!'

'Peter repeated the order and selected 'Up'. The red warning lights came on, then went out as the undercarriage became fully retracted. We had reached 135mph, which was the minimum flying speed at which you could stay in the air with three engines and a full load. I always relaxed a little and breathed more easily once we had 135 on the clock. (Fourteen trips later I was very busy for a while at this stage, as I had to shut down the port outer engine due to a coolant leak at a height of 400 feet!) Now I asked Peter for 2,850 revs and +9 boost which brought the throttles back to the normal 'full power' position, at a height of 400 feet.

'Flaps up in easy stages.'

'Peter repeated and complied, raising them five degrees at a time, while I re-trimmed the aircraft to accommodate these changes. A mistake made with this operation, with the flaps raised too quickly, would cause the aircraft to lose lift, then a stall and a crash could occur! With training and growing confidence between the two of us, I did not hesitate to call on Peter to operate the flaps on both take-off and landing. Although he had had no training as a pilot, he now had a good understanding of changes in conditions, which required slightly different operation of the flaps. A crew that understood what each had to do and co-operated so that it was done most efficiently was on its way to being a good crew and good crews had the best chance of surviving!

'With the flaps up and a climbing speed of 145-150 mph, I asked for '2,650 rpm and +7 boost'. Peter repeated the details and brought the throttles back to our 'climbing power' setting. We climbed on a heading of 270 degrees and shortly Max told me to turn back to base, then, when back over base, we set course on our first leg to Reading and we were on our way at last! Large bombing raids certainly took a long time to get under way and were not a case of 'sit in the dispersal hut and scramble when the siren sounded' as in the Battle of Britain days for fighter boys. 'Otto' and 'Kari', our two legendary German night fighter boys, who patrolled the northern and southern sectors of Germany, were probably sitting around waiting to hear where we were heading tonight!

'At 10,000 feet we lowered the engine revs to save both fuel and the engines and completed a check of the oxygen flowing to all of the crew, also checking the emergency intercom. On this run to Reading we kept a very sharp lookout for other aircraft as they climbed from the various airfields to join the main bomber stream, all heading for this first turning point. I tested the autopilot and after an initial 'kick-up' 'George' engaged, which I anticipated, settled down and functioned quite well. I then disengaged it and we continued our climb. At Reading we had the benefit of all the other aircraft still having their navigation lights on but I still had to dive a little to avoid one clot who turned without checking that we were there!

'We set course for Beachy Head and that bacon and eggs for tea seemed well down now and I nibbled some chocolate, interrupting Peter's log keeping to give him some. He answered with a 'thumbs up' 'thank you' before going back to his log and 'gallons per hour used', etc. I called to each of the crew in turn to ask how things were in each position and to see if the gunners' heated gear was working OK. All replied 'OK, no problems' and Maurie merely rolled over and went back to snoozing. His time for hi looking for fighters and later guiding us to the target had not yet arrived.

'After altering course slightly at Beachy Head we were out over the Channel. Here I got to thinking that the tension, although under control, was too high. I thought of offering a prayer for a safe return and wondered whether or not I might be a good I leader and set an example to my crew. I was having trouble maintaining our required rate of climb, so I asked Peter for a slight increase of 50 rpm, which meant that he had to re-synchronise the four engines. If this was not done correctly, the sound of the engines developed a 'beat', which seemed to go right through your head after a few minutes and the best way of doing this was to look along the line of the two propellers on each side. The 'shadows' of the props appeared to move when they were out of sync' and remained practically still when the engines were synchronised to the same rpm. A small thing really and I suppose I should not have let it get to me but in my book it was just 'tidy' flying and one less thing to get on the nerves of skipper and crew.

'I switched off the external lighting master switch and the boys checked that the lights were all out. (Some chaps went over Germany with their lights on and a few of them even returned!) We were climbing again and Jock now had on his 'village inn', the automatic gun-laying turret. After he had adjusted the settings it worked well, giving warning 'beeps' on the intercom when another aircraft came within range of its radar scanning beam. The 'beeps' got louder and more frequent as the other aircraft came closer, building up the tension until Jock identified it through the small infra-red telescope mounted near his gunsight. All our aircraft were fitted with two infra-red flashing lights in the nose and these were visible in the rear gunner's telescope. The rate of exchange in the frequency of the 'beeps' is what I listened for and when there was little or no change it usually meant that another Lanc had drifted across our track and Jock would come through with 'It's OK, Skip, it's one of ours'.

'Maurie was now lying on his stomach with his head down in the perspex bubble, keeping a look-out down below. Max gave me an ETA for the next turning point and then muttered some suitable comments about the Germans and the radar jamming in particular, as his 'Gee' set had just become unusable because of the jamming signals obscuring everything else on the screen.

'I asked him about the H_2S airborne radar 'How is your 'Y-set'?'

'OK so far,' he replied and on we flew.

'Five minutes later Max was back on the intercom and very annoyed! The 'Y-set' had packed up now and this was serious. We were over cloud, unable to see anything on the ground and had no means of establishing our exact position, with a long way to go to the target and back again, as well as keeping clear of those heavily defended areas mentioned at briefing.

'Jack had just received the first Broadcast Wind which he gave to Max, who commented, 'I hope they're accurate tonight because we haven't got anything else.'

'He was not the only one who had that hope. I quietly thought to myself what a big place Germany was to be flying over with no navigational gear, except a compass, a watch and a Broadcast Wind! It would be bad enough after the target, as I always said that we could get home by flying 'west with a bit of north in it'. But the route going in was going to be tricky, if those Broadcast Winds were not accurate or if we missed them when they were broadcast.

'Jack,' I said, 'you will be careful not to miss those Broadcast Winds won't you?'

'That's for sure, Skip, you can count on it!'

'I quietly thought to myself, 'Yes, I knew I could' and it was that feeling of complete confidence in each other, which had grown up through our training together that was so important now. As I thought about it I realised that I had the same confidence in the other crews in the Squadron and in the other squadrons, who would be sending back their calculated details of the wind, as we had done on other trips. So of course the Broadcast Winds would be accurate! That is what made Bomber Command the force that it was!

'How's the heat tonight, Stan?' Jack was doing his usual thorough check of all his responsibilities, as well as making sure of receiving the Broadcast Winds and, I suspected at the time, was just making sure the Skipper was not brooding on the loss of the 'Y-set'.

'OK, thanks, Jack!'

'All right with you, Max?' he asked but Max was not really paying attention to the heating or anything else, except his navigational problems after the failure of his equipment.

'It's fine but if you have any spare heat you could try to unfreeze that scanner,' he replied.

'No hope of that, I'm afraid,' said Jack.

'Aye, what about the poor bloody frozen gunners?' Jock had joined in the talk. 'It's all right for you lot with all your mod cons. Curly and I have got minus 23 degrees back here!'

'Isn't your electrical heating working, Jock?'

'Aye, it is. Skipper but it's still bloody cold!'

'Don't let your turret freeze up will you?' (I realised that it was quite a while since I had felt the slight swing of the nose of the aircraft caused by the rear turret being turned from one side to the other and then back again to check free movement.) Curly joined in. 'No chance of that, Stan!'

'Good, Curly,' I replied, smiling to myself at the immediate 'banding together' of the two gunners against any implied criticism. A minute or two later I felt the nose swing slightly one way then the other as Jock checked his turret and I had another quiet smile to myself.

'We were lucky as we approached ETA Frankfurt as there was a break in the cloud ahead to port and we could see the searchlights. Max was pleased, as this put us bang on track, so we turned on ETA alongside Frankfurt. So far, so good and all was well!

'Maurie said, 'I think we're going into those lights!'

'They always looked closer than they really were, particularly from his position out front. I did not know if he thought that I would fly straight into a group of searchlights, which were not defending our target, or if he was just getting a little 'on edge'. We were right on track with not too much further to go and this was the turning-point that I was worried about when we lost the 'Y-set', as being only slightly off course would have put us right over the defences of Frankfurt.

'Nice work, Max! We hit that turning point right on the nose!' it 'Good, Stan. Those winds must be spot on, thank heavens!'

'Blast the idiot!' Some clot had jettisoned his load of incendiaries. They were strung out, burning on the ground, marking our new course for every night fighter this side of Stuttgart to see! Thank heavens the clouds were moving across again so that they were being screened. Occasionally, another aircraft was seen near us and identified as friendly, either visually or by Jock through his infra-red telescope.

'Max now wanted a slight increase in our speed to make our next turning point on time, so Peter had to re-synchronise the engines, while still keeping a lookout on the starboard side. Occasionally we 'hit' the slipstream of another aircraft and this threw us around but it was a good sign as it meant that someone else was flying our course and we hoped that his navigation equipment was functioning correctly so he was right on track. It also meant that we were not the only aircraft on this area for the German radar-predicted flak guns to concentrate on, if there was a unit near here.

'Even when experienced many times, the effect of 'hitting' the slipstream of a four-engined aircraft still caused the old heart to thump a bit. It was as though some giant hand had taken hold of the aircraft and twisted it one way and up or down at the same time! There was nothing you could do about it, except to push the control column forward and apply full opposite 'bank' to avoid a possible stall and to level the wings. After a matter of a few seconds that felt like hours, the aircraft would dive through the area of affected air and return to normal 'feel' and control again.

'As we sat there flying steadily on towards the target, I did not realize that the tension was gradually mounting until something very simple annoyed me, then I had a quiet talk to myself. 'Relax, you silly goat. Things are under control!' The clip for the oxygen tube to my face mask had slipped off the strap of my parachute harness, so that the whole length of the tube was dangling from the face mask and was dragging it whenever I turned my head, which was nearly constantly at this stage of the trip. I had got annoyed at the fool of a way of securing it, as it would not stay in place but at the next try it remained fixed and all thoughts of animosity towards it and its inventor died without trace.

'I checked through the crew again with some casual remark to each of them and judged by their replies whether their oxygen supply was OK and for any signs that they were tensing up.

'Any icicles out the back, Jock?'

'No, not yet, Stan but it's none too warm, ye know!'

'He was all right and wide awake. 'How are things on top Curly? Can you see anything?'

'No. Everything is quiet up here, Stan. Where are we now?' (Evidently my turn for a test!)

'Just running north of Leipzig, Curl.'

'Leipzig. OK.'

'Anything down there Maurie?'

'Yes. A heck of a lot of cloud but nothing else!'

'What petrol are we using at this rate, Peter?'

'About 185 per hour, Stan. I'll check on my tables if you like.'

'No, that's OK, thanks. Is that a chink of light through the curtain there?'

'Whereabouts, Stan?'

'Instantly, Peter was searching the blackout curtain between us and the navigator's area for any sign of light. 'It's all right, Pete, it's only a reflection from the perspex in your bubble.' (This 'bubble' in the side window on the starboard side allowed Peter to look down and it had caught some stray light from outside and reflected it into our area.)

'What is our ETA at this last turning-point, Max?'

'After a while Max replied, 'Well, it's hard to say as I'm only running on DR (Dead Reckoning) based on Broadcast Winds. I hope they're somewhere near accurate!'

'How do you think they are?'

'Not too bad so far, I think, Stan. Our ETA is 2357.'

'How does that make us for time?'

'About a minute late, so step it up a little, if you can.

'OK, Max, I'll try 170 but this kite is getting old now.'

'Righto, Stan but we need a bit more speed.'

'2,350 revs, thanks, Peter.

'2,350. Right, Stan.'

'The revs were increased and I kept checking the airspeed to see if I could coax that extra 5 mph. In a newer aircraft I would have just put the nose down for 200 to 300 feet, then level out when we had 170 and slowly pick up the height again. 'J-Johnny' was reluctant to go much over 17,000 feet and it would be a hard job to pick up the height that we had lost. After a while, with no increase in speed visible, I asked Peter for 2,400 revs and eased the nose forward slightly to gain that extra speed. As the speed increased I carefully kept it and coaxed 'Johnny' back up again to approximately 17,500 feet. (The Lanc was very hard to accelerate by use of engines alone. Anything up to 300 revs increase had to be used to get the extra speed. But then only 50 revs over the original were needed to hold it, so the easiest way to increase revs by the amount necessary to the hold speed and actually gain that speed was by losing height gently followed by slowly regaining the lost altitude.) 'You can put the bomb sight on now, Maurie!'

'OK, Stan. Is 'George' right out?'

'Yes and has been for over an hour!' (Bombsight gyros needed time to settle and it was best to give them about half an hour.) Up ahead we could now see the bright patch on the clouds caused by a searchlight belt and we were thankful that the cloud was there shielding us. There was nothing to do but search the sky for fighters and fly on and continue to search.

'What's that over there on the port bow?'

'Yes, there was something black there!'

'I searched for it by looking slightly away from where I thought it was and then I saw that it was another aircraft, which looked like a Lanc. 'Curly, can you see that aircraft on the port bow, slightly up?'

'After a short wait: 'Yes, it's another Lanc I think, Stan.'

'The aircraft did not close in or move away and gradually I could make out the twin fins and rudders and the four Merlins. He was close enough but he was above us and headed our way! On we flew and I started to look for the time to turn at the last turning point before the target.

'There are some fighters about, Stan, I think,' said Jock. 'I've just seen two of their flares out here behind us (small flares were used by the night fighters to indicate our route). Try looking right back past the port rudder fin. I can just see the two tiny orbs of red light dropping slowly.'

'Yes, you're right, Jock. Keep your eyes open for them now, the pair of you.

'Aye, I will! Jock replied in his broad Scots accent.

'Yes, right,' said Curly and our nervous system got another notch tighter.

'How's our ETA, Max?'

'Two minutes to run but we're still a bit late, so we have to turn early and 'cut the corner', OK?'

'Yes, OK, Max. What is the next course?'

'179, Stan - I'll tell you when to turn.'

'179! Right, Max.' I resumed searching from side to side and back again and repeated this again and again and again, as there were likely to be other aircraft making good this turning-point after some slight variation from their proper track. Others might be going to 'cut the corner' earlier than we were and could be coming across us.

'All right, start turning now, Stan.'

'Turning on to 179! Thanks!' Making sure it was clear; we came round to

179. 'Steering 179 now, Max.'

'OK, Stan. I think we should just about be right on time at this speed! Twenty-one minutes to run to the target.'

'Twenty-one! OK:'

'As I looked ahead I saw a glow in the distance and realised that it was the glow of the fires started by the earlier attack by 5 Group! After all this flying we were at last getting near the target![132] OK Max, I can see it ahead and there is a break in the clouds so should get a good run.

'Rather agitated, Max asked, 'How far is it ahead?'

'Oh, quite some distance yet - about 15-20 minutes I would guess.'

'Oh, righto. I thought you meant we were nearly there and that I had boobed and got us here too early!'

'Not likely with you worrying over our times all the way, Max!'

'This course will put us bang on target too! Turn on the VHF will you, Jack?'

'She's on, Skipper.'

'OK, thanks.' I selected channel C and after a few seconds the background noise told us that the set had warmed up and I left it turned on waiting for the Master Bomber to start broadcasting. A few more fighter flares were seen, so they knew where we were and everyone was now very wide awake and searching the sky intently. Jack received the Bombing Wind and, after Max converted it, passed it to Maurie.

'3-1-5, 25. Right, thanks, Max.'

'Maurie set it into his bombsight. We were tracking nicely towards the target and suddenly a voice came on the headphones. 'Snodgrass I to Snodgrass 2. Here is a time check. In twenty seconds it will be 0015. 10... 5, 4, 3, 2, 1. Now! Over'

'Snodgrass 2 to Snodgrass 1. Loud and clear. Out!'

'It was all so very British! Here we were running into the target in the heart of Germany after 4½ hours flying with no 'navigational aids and wondering how we were going to make it. Now, when we were at last in sight of the target, we were being greeted by a couple of typically English chaps with very English call signs, quietly checking that they had got the time right, down to the last second! Our reception was all right, so we did not have to worry about the other sets. The illuminating flares were going down now and they hung in the sky in rows like gigantic yellow lanterns. More and more of them dropped and the whole sky in that area was lit up.

'Just hold it steady about there Skip and we should be right on it.'

'OK, Maurie!'

'Curly and Jack keep that search going. They're dropping more fighter flares. Are you in the astrodome Jack?'

'In the astrodome, Skipper!'

'Aye, I've got my eyes wide open, Skip'.

'She's right, mate,' replied Curly.

'The TIs were being dropped now and Maurie was satisfied with our track towards the target. 'Yes, there go the TIs, Skipper. We're right on track!'

'How are we for time, Max?'

'Three and a half minutes to run.'

'Fair enough!'

'The target was now obscured from my view, as it had passed under the line of the nose of the aircraft. Peter was busy pushing 'Window' down the 'chute to confuse the German radar operators.

'Again a voice came loudly out of nowhere. 'Snodgrass 1 to Press On. Bomb on the red and green TIs. Bomb on the red and green TIs. Out.' This was repeated by the R/T link.

'The red and greens. OK, Skip,' said Maurie. 'Left! Left! Steady!' he chanted and I repeated and executed these instructions as he alone now guided the aircraft to the bomb release point.

'Steady!'

'I replied 'Steady' as I tried to keep the aircraft straight and level while still watching out for other aircraft near us on our level, directly above and slightly ahead. The greatest danger over the target was not from searchlights, flak or fighters (who usually stayed clear of the area immediately over the target to give the flak gunners an 'open go') but collisions or being bombed by an aircraft above us. I was watching another Lanc on my side that was slowly crossing our course slightly above us, when Peter pointed out one on his side also. I watched these two as we continued our run-in.

'Left! Left! Steady!' These were repeated and executed and Maurie's chant became, 'Steady! Steady! Steady!' The aircraft on the starboard side had crossed OK and was now just clear of us but the one on the port side was going to be a nuisance! There were not many searchlights and little flak, thank goodness! A very bright searchlight came very close but at the last moment before catching us it swung away. There was no more noise than usual while the sounds of bombs exploding, as heard in Hollywood movies, proved that the producer had never been here! Exploding flak was usually seen but was only heard when it was very close and if you could smell the cordite as well it was time for a 'damage report'!

'Steady! Steady! Left! Left! Steady!' chanted Maurie and I complied. 'That aircraft is getting closer!'

'We might just make it, as the release point must be close.

'Steady! Bomb bay doors open!' I repeated and executed.

'Snodgrass 1 to Press On! Bomb the centre of the red and green TIs. Bomb the centre of the red and green TIs. Out.'

'Did you get that, Maurie?' I switched off the VHF to cut out the R/T link's voice, which might have interfered with Maurie's instructions.

'Yes. Centre of red and greens,' Maurie replied quickly.

'Steady! Steady! Steady!'

'I felt a slight bump, like someone kicking the wooden seat of a chair you are sitting in.

'Cookie gone! Incendiaries going,' reported Maurie.

'The red camera light started to blink in front of me but I was more concerned with the aircraft that was coming from the port side and was now nearly above us. As his bomb bay doors were open, I turned away to starboard.

'Sorry Maurie!' I said. 'Another photo gone west but he nearly bombed us!'

'OK, Skip, take it away.'

'We had bombed at 18,000 feet, having lost our extra 500 feet running in from the last turning point. As we straightened up again I brought the rev levers up until we had 2,500 and with nose down we headed out of the target with 220 on the clock.

'179 is the course, Skip', Max came through, as though we were just leaving a practice bombing range.

'OK, Max. Are things quiet up there with you, Curly?'

'Yes, OK, Skip but I think there are fighters about as there's a Lanc in these searchlights.'

'OK. Keep that search going well.'

'Corkscrew port, go!'

'I heard the turret machine-guns open up as Jock's call came through. With a warning of 'Down port!' I threw everything into the corner, full port bank, full port rudder and control column forward. We heeled over and dived to port and as the speed built up we came out of it as I dragged back on the control column, calling to the gunners 'Changing - up port!' With the build-up in speed we went up like a lift. Before we lost all this speed I called 'Changing - up starboard!' Then, as we lost speed, 'Changing - down starboard!' As we started to dive again, Jock called, 'Resume course, go! It's OK, Skip, he passed us by but he's disappeared up in the starboard beam so keep your eyes open for him, Curly.'

'Starboard beam up. OK, Jock.'

'We settled down again on our course, with everyone alert and searching intently.

'Next course is 2-1-5, Stan.'

'OK, turning on to 2-1-5.'

'All clear starboard, Stan,' reported Peter. Aircraft that were visible in the glare over the target could not be seen now but we did see one or two that turned close to us. We settled on to the new course and, after a few minutes, I looked back to starboard and saw Dresden burning. While I watched, I saw a fire start in the air and there, against the target, appeared the perfect miniature outline of a Lanc. The port wing burned furiously and, after flying level for a few seconds, the aircraft heeled over and dived down as the wing fell off. We were too far away to see if any 'chutes came out. 'One of our aircraft is missing.' Max logged the time, height and position.

'Are you busy Max?'

'No, not for the moment.'

'Well, you wanted to see a target.'

'Righto, Stan.'

'Max came out from behind his curtain and asked, 'Where?'

'I pointed to the rear over my left shoulder where the yellow of the flares, the white of the incendiaries burning on the ground, the searchlights and the pin-point of light in the sky (from the flak at the stragglers from 'last phase') could clearly be seen. Clouds of smoke rose thousands of feet into the air. With the last of the red and green TIs, it completed a Technicolor nightmare of Hell.

'Aagh! I never want to see that again,' said Max. 'I'll go back to my charts. You can keep that.'

'But he stayed a bit longer to look hard at the scene, before disappearing back behind his curtain. I suppose it was an awful shock to suddenly be confronted with such a sight. I realised that the rest of us had become used to this type of scene, while Max had spent his time on each trip at his charts without knowing what was actually happening outside the aircraft and what it looked like. I never did find out what his thoughts about it really were but I suspected that he actually was a very sensitive type, who disliked being suddenly confronted with such a scene of destruction. I never knew anyone who really liked the job but I suppose there were some who did.

'It looks like we've done our job,' remarked Peter.

'Yes,' I replied. 'I don't think we'll have to come back again...All right, now, let's see that none of those fighters jump us on the way home. Are you going down in your bubble, Maurie?'

'Yes Stan. I'll give you a call when I want a rest from flying upside down.' (When he did I rolled the aircraft over until Curly could see down under us and called, 'All clear, starboard', then I rolled it over on to the other wingtip and waited for his call, 'All clear, port'.)

'We're on the job too, Stan, you can count on it,' said Jock.

'That's right, Stan,' joined in Curly.

'Good, I'm glad to hear it. How long to our next turning-point, Max?'

'Not for quite a while yet, Stan. This is a long leg and I'll let you know in good time.'

'Right, Max.'

'I noted that, as usually happened, the crew tended to be informal in speaking to me, except during take-off and landing and when we were near the target area, when it became 'skipper' or 'Skip'. I assumed this was an unconscious recognition of their reliance on me but that reliance was really on each other, so perhaps it was only a matter of naturally looking for a leader in times of stress and danger.

'Can I have the '1196' in for our 'Darkie' watch please, Jack.'

'Yes. It's on now, Stan.'

'Thanks.'

'I thought back on the attack and the roles of the various participants. From the Master Bomber who often marked the Aiming Point from only 3,000 feet, to the marker crews from the Pathfinder Force, to the Flare Force aircraft and to the Main Force; a very complex machine of destruction. The Marker crews and Flare Force aircraft dropped their TIs and flares over the target, then turned away, flying around and rejoining the stream of Main Force aircraft coming into the target, then dropping their bombs on their second run through the target. Once through the target was enough for me but before not too many more trips we were selected as a Flare Force crew, finally joining the Pathfinders for the rest of the war.

'We flew on and on, making the next turning point and turning more westerly, now that we were past Nuremberg. Presently I saw a patch of light in the sky to port and wondered what searchlights they were, until it dawned on me that they were the lights on the shores of Lake Constance, Switzerland! I wondered what they thought of the war, apart from the money they were making. Being neutral certainly paid off, when you could be the world's clearing house! I told Max and he was quite satisfied. We were slightly off track to the south but we were clear of Stuttgart so we waited until we were very close to the light before altering course to nearly due west, along the Swiss border towards France.

'I was tired and hungry, which was no wonder as we had now been in the air over nine hours. My last piece of chocolate tasted very good, poor quality or not and a cup of sergeants' mess tea from Peter's thermos tasted wonderful and helped get the eyes open again. I had 'George' doing the work now but had my hand on the lever to disengage the autopilot the moment anything happened, so there was only a partial relaxation. Across the Rhine now, we altered course for England, losing height as we went so that our airspeed built up to 200 on the clock. If the Jerry fighters wanted us they would have to find us and catch us. My thoughts wandered. Dresden had certainly copped it but hang this supporting 'Joe Stalin' and his boys - it was just too damn far. Helping Monty and his merry men was much more 'the shot' that appealed now[133]

Peter broke into my wandering thoughts to ask if I had changed the supercharger control down to 'medium' as we had descended into that range. He was happy to know that I had and it was good to know that he was still right on the job, although like all of us he was now very tired.

'Halfway across France Max told me that his 'Gee' set was working again. 'We are only fifteen miles off track, Stan but you had better alter 30 degrees to starboard to avoid that possible trouble spot they mentioned at briefing.'

'Righto, Max. Altering 30 degrees to port. Now.' (Trouble spot? Briefing? That all seemed days ago. I seemed to have been sitting in this seat for a week.) Only fifteen miles off after more than 4 hours' navigating back from the target by dead reckoning and the Broadcast Winds, was a terrific effort and I congratulated Max, who merely uttered that 'George', our dog mascot, must have really been looking after us.

'The French coast was crossed, then the Channel, through the fence of lights at Orfordness, navigation lights 'on' and nose down for base. As we approached I listened out and heard the various boys calling up as they reached home and I checked out who had arrived back safely. Our beacon flashing 'BK' was a very welcome sight. There was no 'story book' or 'Yankee film' welcome, just 'Johnny', 1,500 feet' from the control tower. I knew that my call for permission to land had been heard in the debriefing room, where we would be posted up on the 'Returned' board.

'It all happened very quickly now and after more than 9½ hours in the air I shook myself wide awake to make sure that nothing could go wrong in the last few minutes. We had permission to join the circuit. Maurie was out of the nose. I called 'Downwind' and immediately Doug called me, 'Keep in close, Stan, I'm right behind you.'

'Right, Doug,' I replied in strictly non-RAF R/T procedure.

'I flew a tight circuit on the ring of lights surrounding the circuit area, cut in close at the 'funnel' leading to the start of the runway and wasted no time. Doug Creeper would have swung a little wider and turned into the funnel a little later than usual to give me time to get clear of the landing area so that he would not have to go around again. After nearly 10 hours in the air, having to waste time by flying round the circuit again was something no one wanted, particularly when we landed 23 aircraft in less than 33 minutes.

'Johnny'. Funnels!'

'Johnny'. Pancake!'

'Johnny'. Pancaking. Out. Full flaps. 2,850 revs.

'Peter complied. I managed to grease it on and Jock gave his greatest praise - complete silence! As soon as I touched down, Control called, 'Keep rolling, '

'Johnny'.'

'Johnny' rolling,' I replied, with a quiet smile to myself. I was not likely to stop in front of my mate and have him land on me, when we had just worked things so that we could both get down quickly. I suppose our talking between ourselves was not heard officially but they 'officially' warned the aircraft that had just landed that another was landing immediately behind. At that time of the morning it was all a bit much for me.

'We arrived back at our dispersal and were greeted by the ground crew who were pleased to hear that we had no trouble with the aircraft and that there was no damage to it that we knew of. In the crew bus going back to the crew room we greeted other crews, talking tiredly about the trip and any trouble they may have had. Jack dumped his gear quickly and hurried to the debriefing room to put our name on the board and so reserve our place in the queue of crews waiting to be debriefed. The rest of us arrived shortly afterwards. By way of an informal report, the Squadron Commander asked me, 'How was it, Stan? Much flak, any damage, good run to the target?'

'A pretty quiet trip, thanks, sir,' I replied. 'Only light flak and a few fighters about but I don't think we have any damage.'

'Good - it was a long one and you will be looking for bed. Tell your crew to turn in straight away too.

'Right. Thanks, sir, I will.'

'As I turned away I thought that there was something odd about that last remark but then one of the other skippers spoke to me and the thought went out of my head. As I headed for a cup of tea, the Doc was there quietly running his eye over each of us without any fuss.

'How was it?' he asked.

'Not bad, Doc but it was a long one. Nine hours 45 in the alit'

'Yes, a good night's sleep is what you need. Do you want anything?'

'No thanks, Doc. I have no trouble. I'm off to sleep as soon as my head hits the pillow. I just have to stay awake while 'Bags of Flak' rambles on over there'. I indicated a table at which one of the crews was being interrogated by the WAAF Intelligence Officer, known to all as 'Bags of Flak' due to her habit during the interview with returning crews of asking, 'How was the target area? Bags of flak?'

'The Doc smiled, as he was in on all the jokes and sayings round the Squadron and knew what ops were like, having closed the rear door of the Flight Commander's aircraft five times, from the inside. 'That's good. If there is anything when you wake up, just drop over and see me.

'The tea and biscuits tasted wonderful and Jock and Curly were arguing as usual over whose turn it was to have the tot of rum that I didn't drink, as well as the tot each had already had. Jock knew very well that it was Curly's turn but this was a harmless way to 'unwind' a bit after the trip and the rest of us joined in with suitable comments, while silently cursing 'Bags of Flak' for taking so long with each crew. At last it was our turn.

'What time did you bomb? What did you have in your bombsight?' she asked. (I would never forget her look of dismay and then disbelief when later, after a daylight raid on Cologne, with an Aiming Point near the cathedral, Maurie, who was bored stiff with this same question time after time, decided to liven things up by replying 'Two nuns and a priest!')

'Was there much flak?' (Someone must have told of her of her nickname')

'What did you think of the raid?'

'We had a quiet trip,' I replied. 'A very concentrated attack. One aircraft seen shot down shortly after we left the target.'

'Anything else?'

'No, I think that's the lot, thanks.' I signed the report and at last was on my way to breakfast. While eating my bacon and eggs I vaguely heard the CO say that he thought we might be on again that night but I was too tired to care or connect. I was only interested in a good long sleep. I said 'Cheerio, see you later' to the others in the mess. No one was missing from the trip so we were all happy. I fell into bed at 07.45 but little did I know that I would be woken at 1245 to be told that we were on the Battle Order for that night! After a late lunch, the whole routine, just complete, would be repeated. After another trip, of 9 hours 20 minutes in the air to Chemnitz, [134] I would fall into bed tomorrow morning, exhausted and with only one assurance that there was some limit to how often we were expected to be able to continue these operations. The Doc would tell me to get 'a good, long sleep'. When I replied, 'Just like yesterday Doc?' he would quietly say, 'No - if they try to put any of you who have flown these last two trips on a Battle Order for tonight, I will declare you 'medically unfit'.'

'Thank God for the Doc! [135]

Footnotes Chapter 19

127 *Six War Years 1939-1945, Memories of Canadians at Home and Abroad* by Barry Broadfoot (Paperjacks Ltd, 1985).

128 Dresden was targeted as part of a series of particularly heavy raids on German cities in Operation 'Thunderclap' with a view to causing as much destruction, confusion and mayhem as possible. The other cities were Berlin, Chemnitz and Leipzig, which like Dresden, were vital communications and supply centres for the Eastern Front. 'Thunderclap' had been under consideration for several months and was to be implemented only when the military situation in Germany was critical. The campaign was to have started with an American raid on Dresden on 13 February but bad weather over Europe prevented any US involvement until the 14th. Dresden was to be bombed in two RAF assaults three hours apart, the first by 244 Lancasters and the second by 529 more.

129 1 Group, of which 460 Squadron was one, would be in the second phase. 244 Lancasters of 5 Group were to commence the attack at 2215 hours on 13 February, using its own pathfinder technique to mark the target. This was a combination of two Lancaster Squadrons - 83 and 97 - to illuminate the target

and one Mosquito Squadron (627) to visually mark the aiming point with Target Indicators from low level. The aiming point was to be a sports stadium in the centre of the city situated near the lines of railway and river which would serve as a pointer to the Stadium for the Marker Force, especially since it was anticipated that visibility might not be too good. A second attack was timed for 0130 hours on the 14th by another 529 aircraft of 1, 3, 6 and 8 Groups with 8 Group providing standard Pathfinder marking. Calculations were that a delay of three hours would allow the fires to get a grip on the sector (provided the first attack was successful) and fire brigades from other cities would concentrate fighting the fires. In this second attack target marking was to be carried out by 8 Pathfinder Group. The bombing technique to be carried out by the main 5 Group Lancaster Force was known as the Sector type, which had been developed by 5 Group in area attacks. This meant that each aircraft headed up to the aiming point on a different heading - in the case of the Dresden attack from about due south to about due east, each with differing delays for bomb release after picking up the aiming point on the bombsight. This meant that the bombing covered a wedge-shaped sector, resulting in a great number of fires being started over the whole sector, since a great proportion of the bomb load consisted of incendiaries. Finally, 450 B-17s of the US 8th Air Force were to attack Dresden shortly after 12 noon on 14 February. To assist the night operations of Bomber Command (a force of 344 Halifaxes were to attack an oil plant at Böhlen near Leipzig at the same time as the first attack) various 'spoof' attacks were to be made by Mosquitoes on Dortmund, Magdeburg and Hanover. In addition to the above routing and feints were to be carried out by the Main Forces to reduce night fighter reaction to a minimum. In the case of the 5 Group attack our outward route consisted of no less than eight legs with feints towards the Ruhr, Kassel, Magdeburg and Berlin using 'Window' at the same time.

130 Each container held 150 4lb incendiary bombs.

131 These settings were for the bombsight, with the 'multiplied by 1.1' to prevent any German radio interception operator from making any sense of our broadcast and so be unable to substitute a false message

132 When the illuminator force of the Pathfinders arrived over Dresden cloud cover was 9 to 10/10ths up to about 9,500 feet. The Marker Force of Mosquitoes found the cloud base was at about 2,500 feet. The cloud was not too thick and the flares illuminated the city for the markers who placed their red TIs very accurately on the aiming point. At 2213 hours 244 Lancasters, controlled throughout by the Master Bomber, commenced the attack and it was completed by 2231 hours. More than 800 tons of bombs were dropped. By the time of the second attack cloud cover had cleared to 3 to 7/10ths but despite this the Master Bomber could not identify the aiming point due to the huge conflagrations and smoke and a decision was made to concentrate bombing on areas not affected. An area was marked by the Pathfinders both to the left and to the right to assist.

133 In all, during the two RAF raids 1,478 tons of HE and 1,182 tons of incendiaries were dropped. In the third attack 316 of the 450 B-17s of the 8th Air Force dispatched attacked Dresden shortly after 12 noon on 14 February, dropping 771 tons of bombs. (The Americans bombed Dresden again on 15 February and on 2 March). RAF Bomber Command casualties were six Lancasters lost with two more crashed in France and one in England. An 8000C firestorm tore through the heart of the Saxon capital, burning thousands of Dresdeners alive. In a firestorm similar to that created in Hamburg on 27/28 July 1943, an estimated 25,000 to 40,000 Germans died in Dresden. (At Böhlen the weather was bad and the bombing scattered).

134 The 14/15 February raid on Chemnitz, again in two phases, cost 8 Lancasters and 5 Halifaxes.

135 460 Squadron RAAF flew more Lancaster sorties (5,700) than any other squadron and as a consequence, suffered the highest Lancaster losses in 1 Group (140 + 31 in accidents).

Chapter 20

Easy Does It

Russell Steer DFC

Operation 'Thunderclap' was planned to cause as much destruction, confusion and mayhem in Berlin, Leipzig, Dresden and Chemnitz the Saxon metropolis west of Dresden as possible to assist the Soviet advance on the Eastern Front. Having been under consideration for several months, it was to be implemented only when the military situation in Germany was critical. The orders had been issued to Bomber Command on 27 January 1945. Stalin was informed of the plan a week later, at the Yalta Conference and he gave enthusiastic encouragement. 'Thunderclap' was to have started with an American raid on Dresden on 13 February but bad weather over Europe prevented any US involvement until the 14th. On 5/6 March a 760-strong force (498 Lancasters, 256 Halifaxes and 6 Mosquitoes) was on the Battle Order for a fire raid to destroy the built-up area, industries and railway facilities of Chemnitz.[136] The operation began badly for 6 Group RCAF, which was detailed to dispatch 98 Halifaxes and 84 Lancasters late that afternoon. Unpredictable heavy icing conditions in a very local cloud condition affected aircraft taking off and caused seven Halifax aircraft to crash near their airfields. Two more bombers crashed in England on return. Twenty-two aircraft 14 Lancasters and 8 Halifaxes - were lost in the main operation. The loss of 94 personnel killed and 21 taken into captivity was one of the heaviest blows ever suffered by the Canadian Group in a single night. But if it was a tragic night for the Canadian Group, it was no less so for Chemnitz, for despite 10/10ths cloud, necessitating the use of sky markers, the bombers left fires, which still raged 36 hours later. The old town centre was almost completely obliterated; most of the buildings were gutted and few if any factories in the area escaped. The Siegmar factory, which manufactured tank engines, was destroyed.

The crew of 'E-Easy' on 405 Squadron RCAF at Gransden Lodge, 8 miles west of Cambridge included pilot Flying Officer Percy Cormier from near Winnipeg, Manitoba), engineer Sergeant Stan Kanka, from Cornwall, Warrant Officers J. E. 'Curly' Brearly, wireless operator from Pembroke, Ontario, Jim Gray, mid-upper gunner from Edmonton, Alberta, Nick Stroich, tail gunner; W. E. 'Al' Allan, bomb aimer from Richmond, British Columbia and myself, Flying Officer Russell Steer, navigator, from Toronto, Ontario. We had come together as a crew in April 1944 at 24 OTU at Honeybourne. Our initial crew training had been on elderly Armstrong Whitworth Whitleys. When this primary training was completed we transferred to 1664 HCU at Dishforth, Yorkshire to learn operations on the Handley Page Halifax. In August 1944 we were assigned to 429 Squadron RCAF at Leeming, also in Yorkshire. On 429 Squadron we completed thirteen operations on Halifaxes.

'In September a scouting team from Path Finder HQ arrived to review the performance of the crews. This resulted in our crew being offered the opportunity to volunteer for a transfer to Path Finder Group. The 'catch' was that we had to volunteer as a complete crew and for two consecutive tours amounting to at least 50 operations. There was no hesitation on our part. Our last operation on 429 Squadron was to Kiel with Halifax 'Q' on the night of 15 September. Then we were quickly on our way to the Navigational Training Unit at Warboys near Cambridge. Here we were introduced to the basic elements of the Path Finder technique and learned the art of flying the Lancaster. Our conversion went quite smoothly, with one exception. We had completed our first flight in Lancaster 'O' on 4 October with staff instructor Squadron Leader Wiseman and, after I had found our way back home, we landed smoothly. From the navigator's station the landing roll seemed a bit longer than usual, but I did not become alarmed until it became rather bumpy and ended suddenly with a violent turn and some crunching noises. I emerged to discover the aircraft off the end of the runway, standing in the wreckage of one of the small makeshift huts used by the ground crews and with a small car tucked under the fuselage. Our brakes had failed. As the instructors had been on board and there was no damage to the Lancaster (or the car), the aircraft was towed back to its normal spot. We completed an uneventful conversion tour of five more flights.

'Our RCAF Halifaxes had been equipped with the full navigation systems, so we were familiar with the process of finding our way and needed only to practise timing our arrivals. My job was continuously to monitor the time and our position and to provide the pilot with the necessary heading to maintain our course and schedule. Accurate timing was essential, as we had only a two-minute 'window' for our arrival over the target to drop flares, to 'refresh' those placed by earlier Path Finders. As the aircraft speed and the winds at altitude were seldom exactly as predicted back at Gransden Lodge, it was necessary to keep the pilot constantly advised of course adjustments to ensure our arrival on schedule. The position calculations and logs were kept up to the minute and it was a full-time job for our bomb aimer and myself to operate all of the instruments.

'Percy seemed to enjoy flying the Lancaster. For myself and 'Al' Allan one practical difference was that our navigation instruments in the Lancaster were behind the pilot, instead of being in the nose, as they were in the Halifax. For operations with the Halifax we were required by regulations to sit on a bench behind the cockpit during take-off and landing and could only crawl to our working positions once the aircraft was safely in the air. In the Lancaster we sat (safely) at our stations behind the pilot all the time.

'Our first flight in March 1945 was a navigational training exercise on the 1st. This was followed on 2 March by an operation to Cologne. On the 3rd we had another daylight cross-country training flight. Two days later, Percy, returning from 'signing in' at the flight office, told us that we were 'on' for an operation that night with the briefing at 1600 hours.

'On the wall in the briefing hut was a large map of the British Isles and Europe. This map always made me think that Europe had the measles, for it was speckled with red and green splotches. These represented German anti-aircraft and searchlight defence areas and they were especially thick in the four vital spots of 'Festung Europa' - Berlin, Hamburg, Kiel and the Ruhr. The Ruhr was very heavily defended but its red splotch had an hourglass form and the bomber streams were sometimes routed through this mythical gap in 'Happy Valley'.

'The briefing officer arrived and began marking the map. The red ribbon for the outbound route to Chemnitz went south-west from Gransden Lodge to Reading to the west of London and then bent south-east to cross the Channel at Eastbourne and on to cross the French coast near Abbeville. It then continued east into Luxembourg, angled north-east to near Karlsruhe and then took a further turn north-east, a few more small bends and a sharp turn south toward our target. There were two good reasons for such a complicated routeing. The first was to confuse the enemy as to the ultimate target and the second was to avoid, as much as possible, the well-defended areas. A clerk marked the co-ordinates of the turning points and distances, on the blackboard and we navigators plotted and checked the courses on our charts. Given the co-ordinates of the turning points, the specified time for our marker drop on the target, the bomb load, the winds and the performance of the aircraft, we calculated the take-off time, the timing for each leg and the time for each turning point. As each Pathfinder aircraft had a different scheduled time of arrival over the target, each navigator had his own set of timings to calculate. There were 13 turning points for the operation, seven on the outbound leg and six on the return. These were assigned the letters A to K. The letter 'I' was excluded owing to possible confusion with the number 1 and the letter 'X' was used to designate the point on the outbound leg where we crossed the coast, but did not make a turn. A delta symbol designated the target. In today's world of electronic calculators such calculations would entail but a few minutes' work. In 1945 each calculation had to be done by hand with pencil, paper and assistance from a special hand-operated navigational 'calculator'. We checked our plots very carefully, for mistakes were something we would not get the chance to repeat.

'Our scheduled time over the target was 2148 hours which, allowing for the predicted winds and a margin for error, would necessitate 'E-Easy's' departure from Gransden Lodge at around 1730 hours in order to begin our first leg over Reading at 1805 hours. My calculations indicated a distance on the outbound path of 668 miles and an estimated flying time of 3 hours 24 minutes. The return path was slightly shorter at 658 miles, with a flying time of 3 hours 16 minutes. As it was expected to be cloudy over the target, our aircraft (we were designated as 'blind' markers) would carry a Wanganui sky marker in addition to the regular bomb load. This was to be 'E-Easy's' second trip to Chemnitz, as we had been there three weeks earlier, on the night of 14 February.

'The general briefing for the crews was led by the Commanding Officer, Group Captain W. E. M. 'Bill' Newson. This outlined the nature and significance of the target and the co-ordination with other squadrons. It was followed by a briefing on the predicted weather over the target and the weather expected at Gransden Lodge for our return. The predicted winds on the outbound leg were particularly important to us navigators, as they determined our planned course timing for each turning point. My notes do not record the target details (other than the marker co-ordinates), nor the other squadron participants.

'My log sheet notes that air temperature at Gransden Lodge at take-off was -3°C. The air was apparently clear in our area, for we had no trouble with icing on take-off nor in the climb. Squadrons in the north were not so lucky, however. Nine aircraft of 6 Group were lost over England due to icing and 426 Squadron lost three of its fourteen aircraft contribution owing to the weather conditions. Of the

1,223 aircraft on operations that night, 31 were lost to enemy action and ten to the weather, for an operations loss rate of 2-5 per cent (3-4 per cent total).

'After the general briefing I packed the notes and charts into my navigator's bag and joined the rest of the crew. Trucks carried us around the airfield perimeter track to our 'aircraft of the day'. Each aircraft had its own idiosyncratic handling characteristics and all the pilots had their favourite. If their particular aircraft was not serviceable, the crews had to take what was available. Our favourite was 'E-Easy' and on 5 March it was available. We had first flown in 'E' on 9 November 1944 for an operation to Wanne Eickel and made a total of 34 flights in it (combined operations and training) before the last flight of our second tour on 18 April 1945, to Heligoland. Two Lancaster IIIs carried the letter 'E' on 405 Squadron, ND982 and PB183. My logs do not show which one we used on 5 March, or whether the aircraft changed during our tours.

'While the other crew members checked over their equipment I laid out my charts, maps, calculator and pencils on the navigator's table. This was located on the port side above the wing, behind the pilot's cockpit and in front of the wireless operator's position. The work station was screened from the rest of the aircraft by blackout curtains, as there were lights over the chart table to enable us to see the maps and logs in the dark. Normally I also carried a small pocket flashlight in the top of my right flying-boot to enable me to read the maps if the lights failed.

'Our Mk III 'Pathfinder' Lancaster included the latest navigation equipment. In the regular squadrons the bomb-aimer also operated the front turret. In the Pathfinder squadrons, he worked as the assistant navigator at the navigation station and would go forward to the viewport in the nose to release the markers, or bombs, if it was to be a visual drop. On 'blind' drops the bombs could be released by the bomb aimer from the navigation position using the Ground Position Indicator (GPI) and the H2S radar display.

'At the navigator's station, on the right, was the Gee, which was a short-range navigation aid. This was accurate over England and the Channel and was most useful in finding our way home in bad weather. Also in this position was the long-range navigation aid (LORAN) and the H2S radar system which provided a radar view of the ground below. Above and in front was the Air Position Indicator (API). This was fed airspeed information, elapsed time and direction from the 'remote-reading' compass and kept track of our 'air position' - the position that the aeroplane would have been in if there had been no wind. Also, above the table, was the GPI. This, used for short distances only, could project a small arrow on to a special 'homing' chart placed on the table. Starting from a known location fix, a very-short-range bombing run could be made to the target. However, this was used only when more direct action was not possible.

'Near the centre was the clock, marked in tenths of minutes, that I would watch carefully throughout the flight to time our legs. It was a full-time job for Al and myself to operate all of these instruments, keep track of our position and ensure that we reached the target on schedule.

Footnotes Chapter 20

136 There were also 52 radio countermeasures sorties by Halifaxes and Stirlings. *The Bomber Command War Diaries: An Operational reference book 1939-1945.* Martin Middlebrook and Chris Everitt. (Midland 1985).

137 Adapted from the article by Russell Steer in *Aeroplane Monthly,* June 1997.

Chapter 21

The Woodbridge Intruder

J. J. 'Jack' Lee

How often have those of us who operated over Europe during the war years seen an aircraft in distress, either coned by searchlights, mauled by fighters, or shot up by flak, wondered if the aircraft and its crew ever made it back home?

J. J. Lee, rear gunner, Lancaster PB797 VN-Z-'Zebra' on 50 Squadron. On 22 March 1945 227 Lancasters and eight Mosquitoes of 1 and 8 Groups raided Hildesheim railway yards. Some 263 acres - 70 per cent of the town - was destroyed and 1,645 people were killed. Four Lancasters were lost. Another 130 Halifaxes, Lancasters and Mosquitoes of 4 and 8 Groups bombed Dülmen in an area attack, which was without loss and 124 Halifaxes, Lancasters and Mosquitoes of 6 and 8 Groups bombed rail and canal targets at Dorsten, which also was the location of a Luftwaffe fuel dump, again without loss. One hundred Lancasters of 3 Group carried out a 'G-H' attack on Bocholt, probably with the intention of cutting communication. All returned safely. [138] Another 102 Lancasters of 5 Group in two forces attacked bridges at Bremen and Nienburg without loss. The bridge at Nienburg was destroyed though no results were observed at Bremen.

'We were engaged on a daylight raid over Bremen on 22 March 1945. The aircraft was piloted by Pilot Officer Pat Reyre and crewed by Flight Sergeant Ken Shaw, navigator; Flying Officer Jack Andres RCAF, bomb aimer; Flight Sergeant Alan 'Shorty' Thorpe RAAF; Sergeant Gerry Jones, flight engineer; and Sergeant Alf Robinson, mid-upper-gunner. 'Z-Zebra' was at the rear end of the 'gaggle' formation and bombs had been released over the target. It was a perfect day for the operation; the sky was cloudless. Anti-aircraft fire can only be described as moderate and fighters were conspicuous in their absence. We were escorted by American air force 'Mustangs'.

'Like most crews 'flak' was not an undue hazard unless it got too close and it was only by a stroke of misfortune should an aircraft fall victim to the big guns. Having said that, as we left the immediate target area I saw bursts of flak creeping dangerously close to the Lancaster directly below and astern of me. 'Poor Blighter' I thought. No sooner had this thought passed through my mind when two almighty explosions shook our aircraft. A dark trail of smoke appeared from the starboard wing, at the same time the aircraft swung to starboard and began to descend rapidly. I watched as we descended and saw the gaggle drift further and further from our view.

'Within seconds of our being hit those dreaded words came over the intercom; 'Jump, Jump.' I swung my turret to the beam, snatched the doors open and prepared to make a hasty exit. I can't recall to this day why I hesitated but I replied to the skipper; 'Did you say jump?' Back came the reply; 'No, hang on.' In the course of further conversation it transpired that both starboard engines were damaged and the props feathered. Our descent continued and then, by some great fortune, one of the engines was restarted and our sided descent was corrected. It now became obvious that we had suffered serious damage. However, we were fortunate not to have any casualties. In a matter of minutes we were on our own at a height of about 5,000 feet on a perfectly clear day and a sitting duck for enemy fighters.

'As I surveyed the sky for fighters my attention was drawn to what appeared to be long strips of brown paper drifting from the aircraft and spiralling earthwards. I was completely puzzled at the appearance of this phenomenon. I rotated the turret and peered into the fuselage where I saw the wireless operator 'Shorty' Thorpe and the mid-upper gunner Alf Robinson engaged in stripping lengths of ammunition from the ammunition tracks situated on the starboard side of the aircraft. Both tracks had been damaged by flak which rendered my two left hand guns U/S. On reflection this course of action would have virtually no effect on lessening our overall weight. However, it did seem a good idea at the time and was good for morale. By the time we had reached Holland some considerable height had been gained. Further assessment as to the amount of damage inflicted to the aircraft drifted over the intercom to the effect that the 'George' control system had been shot away, numerous fuel lines had been severed, our starboard aileron was useless and we had no brake pressure.

'Our situation was bad, but not hopeless. However, it was decided to discharge a distress signal with a view to obtaining assistance from any of our fighter escort who may still be in the vicinity. I watched as the red flare ascended then fell gently away. It was within a matter of seconds after the flare had been discharged that three 'Mustangs' appeared on our port beam, two of the fighters peeled off whilst the third positioned himself some fifty yards to the port side of my turret. The pilot waved his hand as a gesture of encouragement and maintained his position. This 'Mustang' escorted us right across Holland and over the Dutch coast. The Frisian Islands came into view. Later as we flew over the islands our aircraft was once again subjected to heavy anti-aircraft fire. As the flak opened up the 'Mustang' pilot opened his throttle and headed out to sea. No further damage was sustained to 'Z- Zebra' and we made headway towards the English coast.

'At the main briefing prior to our take off it had been stressed that Woodbridge, one of the two emergency runways catering for aircraft in distress, was out of use for reasons which I recall were never disclosed. Only Manston was available. It was due to the set of circumstances prevailing at that time that our pilot was forced to set course for Woodbridge. We still maintained height and the weather remained nigh perfect. At this stage an intercom discussion was held during the course of which our skipper gave us an ultimatum stating there was a fifty-fifty chance of putting our aircraft down in one piece. The two options open to us were either bale out or stay with our aircraft. The response was unanimous and an instant decision was made to stay together.

'As Woodbridge came into view there were excited comments over the intercom. The emergency runway was lined virtually from end to end with 'Halifax' aircraft and various types of gliders. Here was the answer to the airfield being closed. Flying control was contacted and a request for landing made. Needless to say our request was refused and we were instructed to divert elsewhere. Owing to the state of our aircraft, plus the fact our fuel situation was becoming critical, this course of action had to be refuted. Despite an almost superhuman effort by our skipper the kite was becoming almost impossible to control and our crash landing procedure was put into operation.

'There was to be only one approach to the runway due to the fact alterations to course could not be achieved owing to the failure of our controls system. Wheels were down and the undercarriage locked. The approach was made and we touched down halfway along the runway. We had no flaps and brake pressure was nil, the result being that we careered along the runway at a fast rate of knots. The end of the runway was reached and we carried onto the overshoot area which was in a similar state to a newly ploughed field. The vibration was such that I thought we were going to break up. I had rotated the rear turret facing starboard and as we trundled on I had a shaky view of a football match which was in progress some several hundred yards away. As their attention was drawn to us, players and spectators alike stopped as though riveted to the ground and gazed in amazement as we roared past them. The aircraft finally came to rest with our undercarriage intact. I virtually fell out of my turret, whilst the rest of the crew with the exception of our skipper followed suit via the main door. On making my way to the front of the aircraft I saw our skipper still sitting in his cockpit, no doubt finding it difficult to believe we had made it down in one piece.

'As we took account of the damage sustained we noticed that the bomb doors had crept open several inches. Closer inspection revealed one of our 1,000lb bombs nestled on the bomb bay doors. It became obvious we had a hang up which had not registered on our instruments and the bomb had broken loose during our bumpy entry onto the overshoot area. Had we known the bomb was still in the aircraft I doubt very much if we would have brought 'Zebra' home. Needless to say there was much twittering at the thought of what might have happened had it exploded.

'Bladders were relieved and the crew then congregated awaiting transport to the flights and our de-briefing. Ken Shaw the navigator produced a fair sized piece of shrapnel. This had become lodged in his 'Mae West'. He then went on to explain having felt a blow in the lower part of his ribs as though he had been kicked. It transpired the shrapnel had torn through his life jacket and struck the large 'rat trap' type of buckle of his battle dress jacket. The buckle had been bent almost double by the impact but had no doubt saved him from serious injury. The emergency vehicles were on the scene very promptly and we were transported to the flights for de-briefing whilst our navigator attended the sick bay where he was given a check up. It was only at the de-briefing stage we were informed that Woodbridge was on standby for the forthcoming Rhine crossing operation. This explained the presence of the large numbers of aircraft stationed on the main runway. We were further informed that strict security was being imposed on the station and all personnel confined to base. It was also made clear no mail would be allowed to leave the base until the glider force had left for its destination. After a meal we were billeted and then we commenced to have a look around the base. There were literally thousands of aircrew and army personnel scattered around the station and we met many old friends with whom we had trained prior to our operational posting.

'The giant armada finally left; a sight we shall never forget as the aircraft set off into an almost cloudless sky. The crew went into Ipswich to celebrate our survival and on our return to the base the following day arrangements were made for our return to our Squadron at Skellingthorpe. We had been absent for several days and some of the other crews thought we had been written off.

'This brief account of the experience of a Lancaster crew carrying out its duties does not highlight any acts of heroism or brave deeds, but it does bring home the occupational hazards faced by all crews engaged on operations. It also emphasises the determination of a crew and the outstanding efforts of an exceptional pilot to survive and return with their aircraft to continue the struggle.

'We returned to Woodbridge three days after the defeat of Germany and flew 'Z-Zebra' back to Skellingthorpe. She flew for two more years before joining hundreds of other redundant Lancasters in the scrap yard'.

Footnotes Chapter 21
138 *The Bomber Command War Diaries: An Operational reference book 1939-1945.* Martin Middlebrook and Chris Everitt. (Midland 1985).

Chapter 22

Manna

And had rained down manna upon them to eat and had given them of the corn of heaven.

Psalm 78 verse 24. Between three and four million Dutch people in German occupied Holland were facing imminent starvation. The deprivation of the war years and the flooding of most of their countryside created this threat which became more real in the last few months of 1944. The timetable relating to the exhaustion of food supplies was running out at the start of 1945 and the situation was further exacerbated by Dutch railwaymen striking in protest against German demands. It was only a few months after our Dutch allies had shared with our airborne forces the agony of Arnhem; Dutch men and women had risked everything to help downed Allied airmen. By April 1945 the townspeople in the West Netherlands were foraging in the countryside, eating tulip bulbs and sugar beet and camping in the fields. Something had to be done to avert a disaster

Twenty-nine year old Squadron Leader Alan Fry on 625 Squadron was the very first pilot who entered Dutch airspace on Sunday morning 29 April 1945, without knowing if the Germans would keep their promise not to interfere with the dropping of food by the British bombers - food that was indispensable to keep the enormous hunger at bay in the completely isolated areas of the Netherlands (the provinces of North and South Holland and Utrecht) where already 22,000 people had died of starvation and where nearly 3½ million people were near to death from hunger. Days before the actual operation a mechanism had been devised for dropping food from the Lancasters. The crews of Bomber Command had practised the dropping system for some days in advance. It had been discovered that single or double sacks usually burst on impact but triple sacks would protect the costly load of flour, egg powder, margarine and other foods. Alan Fry should have gone on 28 April but the weather was too bad. 'The crews were however called to the operations room on the next day and seeing that the target was food dropping on Duindigt racecourse we were filled with vociferous enthusiasm. Instead of the horrible bomb attacks that were normally our job, we were to go to Holland and drop food to our Dutch friends. The British were at that time very well aware of the famine in the Western Netherlands, especially because of the radio speeches by Queen Wilhelmina and Prime

Minister Gerbrandy, who took every opportunity to press upon the Allied political and military leaders of the misery in occupied Holland. At that time we did not know that the code name 'Operation Manna' would be adopted and in fact used Operation 'Spam' locally.

'On 29th April the weather did not look at all good with very low clouds, but we were allowed to get airborne. A shock of disappointment went through our crew when we received a W/T message cancelling the flight. Because of the large number of aircraft airborne (some 300 I believe) we flew away from the Scampton area and I was in fact over the North Sea east of Great Yarmouth when a second message came in with the word 'Go'. I was therefore well on the way to The Hague. The Germans had agreed to the flight subject to a minimum height of 500 feet, but we had to come down almost to sea level to keep below cloud all the way to the Dutch coast. We had strict instructions not to offer any provocation and indeed not to fire even if shot at. If unable to reach our dropping zone we could jettison our load anywhere in Holland. We were sure the Dutch would find it anyway.

'The Germans had clearly expected that parachutists might be dropped under cover of the food drop and had moved up anti-aircraft guns to positions round the dropping zones (Duindigt, Ypenburg, Valkenburg and Waalhaven). The last one was a mistake as it was mined and these mines were detonated by the food dropped there.

'As we reached the Dutch Coast my navigator Pilot Officer Corrigan saw a large anti aircraft battery straight ahead. As we passed over at low level the Germans waved and some even gave the famous Churchill 'V' sign. We flew towards The Hague at 200 feet and suddenly saw everywhere people waving Dutch and even Union Jack flags - we wondered where those had come from. Even tea towels and sheets were being waved as well. My rear gunner reported that our slipstream had blown a man waving a large sheet from the flat roof of his house. He evidently landed safely as he was seen still waving from his garden. I dropped my load of 350 sacks of food on the racecourse. My crew reported other Lancasters following. I flew back to the UK as fast as possible; this was my last operation and by tradition we were allowed a little extra fuel for more speed! The BBC and Dutch radio announced the drops so people cheered and waved flags, teacloths and even sheets as we went over.

'When we crossed the Lincolnshire coast we could see no other aircraft and we realised that we were probably first home. When we landed at Scampton the Squadron Commander was waiting for us and took us straight to Operations in his car. Fortified by unusually generous tots of Navy rum we related enthusiastically our story of the mission to the BBC reporter who recorded my account and it was broadcast in the 6 o'clock news. As the other crews returned we were delighted by the happy faces of the young men who, after a bombing raid, so often returned looking gaunt and haggard, knowing that they had probably killed innocent civilians.'

Dickie Parfitt, a bomb aimer on 576 Squadron at Fiskerton, recalled: 'Now we had to help feed the Dutch. Between three and four million Dutch in German occupied Holland were facing starvation and 1,000 people were dying daily. Townspeople were foraging in the countryside, eating tulip bulbs and sugar beet and camping in the fields. Something had to be done to avert disaster. The Dutch had risked everything to help Allied airmen downed at Arnhem. Now it was our turn to help them. 'A few of us went out to the aircraft to watch food being loaded. We were to carry 5,000lbs of food crammed into the bomb bay. Five panniers had been fitted and each pannier held 70 sacks. The trip would be early the following morning so drinking was out that evening but we went into Lincoln to the pictures and had fish and chips afterwards. Back at base we were told that briefing would be at 03.30; however, nobody woke us because the operation was scrubbed due to bad weather.

'The weather forecast was good for the next day, 29 April. At the briefing we learned that our destination would be Valkenburg. The dropping zone would be marked by the Dutch and we would go in at 100 feet - very low for a four-engined aircraft. If fired on, we were not to return fire. This was still occupied territory and the Germans could get itchy fingers and I would be right in their line of fire. At least at 100 feet anybody trying to hit us would have to be very quick! The flight should take less than two hours and we would be leading our squadron. There would be a lot of aircraft on this op and some crews had little operational experience. I would need to keep my wits about me. At least it was daylight I wanted to get in and out quickly!

'We soon saw the Dutch coast. Then the 'dreaded Hun' opened up with a short burst. I was ready for the drop and asked Taffy to open the bomb doors. I could see the markers ahead and 'Thank you, boys,' in front written in tulips. I let the food go; some fell in the water but most fell near the marker. With my job done I closed the bomb doors and we headed for home. We were all quiet. It had made quite an impression upon us. Back at base we were thankful to have something nice to eat. Over the next few days we dropped food on Valkenburg again plus Ypenburg and Terbregge near Rotterdam twice.'

Operation Manna took place between 29 April 1945 and 8 May 1945. In January 1945 the Dutch Resistance having communicated the worsening food situation to London, it became apparent that the 21st Army Group could not possibly carry out the dropping of food supplies by air on the scale that would be required - there were only the relatively small aircraft of 2nd Tactical Air Force available to them. The drops would have to be carried out by bombers - with their bomb bays laden with food in place of high explosive. Five panniers were fitted into the huge bomb bay of the Lancaster, each pannier able to hold 70 sacks. In April 1945 there were about 12 million British Red Cross packages in readiness on English airfields, each containing 600g parcels set aside to be dropped on POW camps in Germany. SHAEF (Supreme Headquarters Allied Expeditionary Force) handed over three million of these parcels for dropping into the 'Hunger' provinces of West Netherlands. These packages were tested at Netheravon to check that they were suitable for dropping - and it was immediately clear that they were not, for they were not sufficiently firmly packed. The urgency of the situation, however, meant that there was not time to repack and it was also realised that they would not provide enough food anyhow to save three to four million starving people. From late March onwards, the daily death toll from starvation amounted to one thousand people and was totalling about 20,000 by the time Manna began.

It was decided instead to drop food supplies in much larger quantities from altitudes as low as 100 feet and packed differently, in tins and jute bags. It was assumed that the jute bags' contents (each weighing about 10kg) would yield if the bag was dropped on soft soil from low altitude. No 115 Squadron was involved in experiments at Witchford and Netheravon in dropping provisions and in the use of panniers in the two types of bomb bays that were fitted to Lancasters. Mr D E Murray, of the Ministry of Aircraft Production, who was responsible for the production of all types of bomb carriers has put on record that a firm contract was placed with Cope & Cope of Reading, on 19 April 1945, for the manufacture of 350,000 large steel hooks for hanging the supplies in the bomb bays of British and American bombers. The first delivery of hooks took place on 24 April 1945 - such was everyone's commitment to the task.

On Friday 27 April, two days after the Allies had completed strategic air operations, hectic preparations began for Manna to start on the following day. As might be expected, the Allies and the Germans did not wholly trust each other in the negotiations that went on to set up the relief operation. Air Commodore Andrew Geddes in charge of Operations and Plans, 2nd TAF, was responsible for organising the Dropping Zones, with HRH Prince Bernhard of the Netherlands playing a decisive role in the preparations and execution of Manna. The Reich Commissioner for the Netherlands, Arthur Seyss-Inquart sought to protect the interests and security of the Wehrmacht. Four Drop Zones were initially selected, with German artillery positioned around each. German Police (Ordnungspolizie) would check that it was, indeed, food that was dropped and not weapons.

The Dutch applied themselves with great vigour to the task of organising how the supplies were to be collected, stored and distributed. Teams had to be recruited to collect the supplies at each DZ; collected goods would then, preferably by barge, be transported to stores in Rotterdam, The Hague and Leiden. Horse-drawn wagons would move the goods to where barges could move. Special teams would be needed to sort the goods in the stores and warehouses. Policemen and officers of the 'Central Crisis Control Organisation' would guard the transport, detectives would be present at the DZs and members of the collecting teams would have to be searched on leaving the dropping sites. The local Food Commissionaries in Rotterdam, The Hague and Leiden were tasked by the Dutch authorities to arrange all these matters.

The staffs of the large agricultural products companies were invited to play a large part in the formation of these teams. All these things had been arranged by Saturday, 28 April and collection teams were in place at the four DZs - Terbregge, Ypenburg airfield, Duindigt race course and Valkenburg airfield. The weather, however, deteriorated and the drop that had been scheduled had to be postponed. Sunday, 29 April, offered much better weather conditions and that morning saw many squadrons of bombers taking off from their bases manned by enthusiastic crews delighted to have the opportunity to take part in this operation.

Emotions ran high within the aircraft as they flew low across enemy-occupied territory. As the machine-guns in their turrets were trained high in the sky, they noted that the barrels of the enemy flak emplacements were trained horizontally. Shortly after 13.05 hours local time the Bomber Command aircraft appeared low over Rotterdam, The Hague and Leiden. The people heard the roar of the engines and knew that the food drops announced by the BBC and Dutch Radio were on their way. Little wonder that they were excited - their rations were almost non-existent and they were issued with only one Red Cross piece of bread each week! People waved from flat-roofed buildings with flags, handkerchiefs, teacloths and even sheets. They gathered in the squares and at other locations that afforded a good view of the air armada. They were cheering and many were in tears as emotion overwhelmed them. Aboard the aircraft, the aircrews waved back in response to the welcome.

Those Dutch who lived near to a DZ went to it quickly. An account by one lady living in Oegstgeest described how she went with hundreds of others to the motorway west of the village. From here she had an unobstructed view of Valkenburg airfield. German AA guns had been positioned close to the motorway flyover at this point. 'Oh, my God! they are going to shoot!' she thought as the Germans began removing the camouflage from their weapons. She saw then the planes, skimming the airfield and the flares which marked the target areas for the drop. The Germans stayed with their guns, scarcely showing any reaction. The lady sighed with relief before experiencing jubilation. 'There they are!' she cried as she saw more bombers coming low over fields and rooftops, approaching her vantage point. 'We can see the pilots, waving pilots, cheering, crying, waving! I am stretching my arms out as far as I can as if I can touch them.'

Over 250 RAF bombers dropped 400 tons of food on that Sunday but although London had been informed on the previous Thursday evening that Waalhaven airfield had been replaced as a DZ by Terbregge, this news had not been passed on to Bomber Command by the Sunday. Two hundred tons of food destined for Rotterdam were dropped on Waalhaven airfield - in spite of there being no target indicators (a large cross and flares) set up. A large part of the cargo landed in the harbour and the sacks which landed on the airfield detonated a number of landmines! Sacks which fell outside the airfield were picked up by the local inhabitants. Only half of the 200 tons of food was salvaged by the food authorities. One aircraft on 186 Squadron dropped three packages, but could not drop the remainder for fear of hitting crowds which had swarmed over the Waalhaven field. Another Lancaster from the same squadron experienced slight damage from small arms fire that affected the hydraulics. The aircraft's bomb doors were inoperable and over its base (Stradishall) the undercarriage showed some reluctance to come down. Manoeuvres trying to jolt the wheels down led to a package of assorted groceries cascading over the Suffolk countryside - which in turn caused a race between the local villagers and the RAF recovery party! Another 186 Squadron Lancaster was hit two days later - by two sacks from an aircraft above - but without causing damage!

By the following day London had corrected this error but Terbregge, north east of Rotterdam, a site selected by the Germans, was not very suitable; it was a narrow field, access to it was difficult and there were many buildings around. As a result, a policeman was killed, various civilians were badly injured and several buildings were set on fire by flares and smoke canisters. The field was also badly drained, so everything had to be manhandled off the DZ to a nearby road. Every day, between 30 April and 8 May, 4,000 people were involved shifting the precious 2,600 tons of food. The Duindigt DZ near The Hague was also far from ideal - it was small, with the added complication of a minefield close to it! Transport by barge was not possible from it, although that means of transport was possible from the Ypenburg and Valkenburg airfields.

Dr Seyss-Inquart agreed on Monday, 30 April, that with effect from 2 May, six more fields could be used as DZs. (The start of the dropping of relief supplies took place two days before the truce between the Allies and the Germans regarding this operation was signed). The additional DZs were Schiphol airport (for Amsterdam) and fields close to Haarlem, Alkmaar (Bergen airfield), in 'het Gooi', close to Gouda and Utrecht. Comparatively little was dropped in these areas, except at Schiphol where over 1,000 tons was dropped. The Hague received 2,200 tons while Valkenburg airfield received 700 tons.

The British dropped 1,800 tons of flour, 50 tons of yeast, 170 tons of milk powder, 340 tons of margarine, 270 tons of cheese, 370 tons of sugar, 110 tons of salt, 500 tons of dried potatoes, 460 tons of pulse vegetables, 530 tons of dried meat, 470 tons of bacon, 310 tons of sausages, 70 tons of sausage rolls, 120 tons of dried eggs, 130 tons of chocolate, 80 tons of tea, 27 tons of mustard, five tons of pepper - but only two tons of coffee! The Americans, who joined this operation on Tuesday 1 May, dropped tens of thousands of 'Army Packages' containing various foodstuffs (i.e. rock hard army biscuits) chewing gum, cigarettes, matches, water sterilisation tablets, a tin-opener, toilet paper and a booklet with religious songs (in English)! Many air crews made their own contribution. They had seen whitewashed messages on houses saying 'Thanks RAF' and 'Good Luck Tommy' and they donated their own sweet rations and aircraft issue, throwing them out of the Lancaster attached to home-made 'parachutes' and notes that said Voor Het Kind (For The Children).

Some bags landed off target, some damaged on landing; margarine was a problem - dropped as packets but converted to flat pats on impact! The Dutch authorities organised collection, storage and distribution throughout the country. They also decided the priorities: first were the church organisations looking after the sick, the children, hospitals and orphanages. Red Cross 'shops' were used for general distribution.

It was no simple job to collect the food drops. Often objects landed off target and several members of collecting teams suffered injuries. Large areas had to be covered to collect the scattered bags. Murphy's Law also was experienced - at the first Schiphol drop on 2 May, a quarter of what was dropped suffered damage - the target cross had been marked on the concrete runway and the precision of the drops meant much was lost until the cross was relocated to a softer spot! Margarine, a product formulated first in Rotterdam, was paradoxically a problem at all the DZs. A product that sailed through the air as packets became converted into pats after hitting mud, sand, duck-weed and water! The product that fell near Rotterdam was cleaned there using the local technology, but other centres were less pleased! Witnesses report that bacon and sausages were scattered everywhere!

The Dutch food authorities decided that priorities had to be set regarding the distribution of food supplies. The first recipients were the 'Central Kitchens', the kitchens of the Church organisations looking after the sick and the children, the hospitals and the orphanages. These received the perishable goods, or those not suitable for general distribution: dried meat, dried potatoes, milk powder and pulses. 'Red Cross' shops were used for general distribution. Food delivered to the warehouses was sorted, distributed and often re-packaged, this work being done by about 6,000 people who had been mobilised for this task.

The first of the dropped food supplies was distributed on 5 May to those suffering from hunger and disease and who were being nursed at home. Only on 7 May was general distribution begun. In the first week, civilians could pick up from the 'Red Cross' shops, free bread (400g) butter/margarine (100g), cocoa (50g), plus a choice from three other articles - a tin of sausages, a packet of egg powder or half a tin of bacon or cheese. Mothers of large families were allocated an 'army package' in addition.

The Bomber Command aircraft that took part in Manna came from Nos 1, 3 and 8 Groups. They dropped nearly 7,000 tons of food with 3,181 Lancaster sorties (of which 3,151 were successful) and 160 Mosquito sorties (of which 147 were successful). RNZAF, RAAF and Polish squadrons contributed as well as RAF squadrons to Manna, the very successful outcome also being due partly to the efficient organisation of the reception teams by the Dutch on the ground. The Eighth US Air Force flew 2,200 sorties during Operation Chow Hound. The co-operation of the Germans was essential but this did not prevent Reich Commissioner Arthur Seyss-Inquart from being hanged for his war crimes later.

Baroness Adrienne Van Till lived in The Hague from January 1943 until after the war and the day of the first food drops were very emotional.

'For us, the terrorized frightened hungry and fairly desperate Dutch that was the first sign that the Germans were really giving up. The first sign that perhaps we would be free again someday soon. Because it seemed unthinkable that after accepting the food drops by their enemy, the Germans would continue to fight for long. It was the first open recognition that they were incapable of holding out much longer. It was sheer glory to see the German soldiers around us looking at you, watching us cheering and waving flags and shouting for joy and dancing in the streets and see them disappear into their quarters not quite knowing what face to keep. That first dropping-day I was lucky to be at the house of friends living near the racecourse Duindigt, next to The Hague, where food was to be dropped. We had already heard of the plan days before via the English radio and for days we had been hoping and praying and waiting and each day nothing happened. And that day we got the message that in half an hour they would be coming. We ran to the racecourse and waited.

'And there they came. Low over The Hague and lower even over the field.

We could see faces and the doors open and all those sacks falling out. We cried and danced and laughed and embraced everyone around us. When they had gone we ran out to load the stuff on the few available horse-drawn carts. The first sack I found contained, of all things, pepper. Not exactly what we needed most just then, but the rest contained solid basic food and we all were very, very happy. The first loads of food went to the hospitals, pregnant women and other extra weak people, but after two or three days the food distributed by the central kitchens began to be more nourishing; it even contained beans or peas. Those who had managed to survive until then now felt pretty certain they would really survive to see the end of the occupation and be free again.

'One cannot imagine what a load those first food drops took off our minds and feelings. Not merely because of the food, however welcome, but because they brought the message of freedom and the return of justice, the end of fear and oppression. One can bear being cold and hungry, but not to be free to speak one's mind, not to be able to fight injustice and the continuous fear to be caught in some illegal act or be taken for interrogation or as a hostage is exhausting in the long run.'

The tragedies of war were not yet over, but the success of these Dutch famine relief operations gave good reason for optimism that a ravaged continent could be restored with the arrival of peace in Europe.

Chapter 23

Exodus

Operation Exodus was the name given to the repatriation by air of ex-PoWs, mainly from German and French airfields; Operation Dodge concerned the repatriation of Eighth Army personnel and PoWs from the Italian theatre of operations.

Dickie Parfitt recalls: 'With the European war over, we were given seven days leave and I went home. The shelling had stopped and people were going about their business without fear. Ed and I did the usual things: the pictures, a dance, visited Mother, attended a few fetes and flower shows. We also bought some second hand bits of furniture. Furniture, clothing and food were still rationed, of course. Ed was still working for the Prudential and we did some collecting together. It was soon time to return to Fiskerton. I wondered what would happen. The Japanese were still at war.

Back at camp we had to report to the Flight Commander who told us to fly to Brussels to pick up some prisoners of war and bring them back. My sister Babs was in Brussels in the ATS; I thought I might meet her there. The rest of the lads were keen to see Brussels as well. I had been there as a Scout on a camping holiday. We landed near Brussels and saw these thin and ragged PoW s standing about waiting to be flown home. It was a very sad sight for us but we were a grand sight for them! We put about 20 in the fuselage with the few bits and pieces they had. There would be no time to find my sister. We made them as comfortable as we could; we weren't built to carry passengers! I pointed out the Elsan and told them to expect a lot of noise for the one and a half hour flight home. I stayed with them all the way back and didn't wear my parachute harness because there were no parachutes for them! The noise meant talk was out of the question but some played cards. From time to time I was asked how much longer it would take and I pointed to my watch face. It was an issued American watch for Ron and I. If it varied more than five seconds, we had it checked; such was the standard of navigation. As we approached base I told them to sit tight. Taffy made a good landing. Once out of the aircraft we all shook hands before transport took them off.'

The airborne repatriation of PoWs mainly from German and French airfields was called Operation Exodus and 74,000 were brought home by 28 May. Runways had to be repaired first. Another problem was how many could be safely carried in each aircraft. Unfortunately, we found out the hard way when an aircraft crashed killing all 25 passengers and 6 crew. Passengers sitting mainly in the rear upset the flying trim and caused the pilot to lose control. Thereafter, no more than 24 passengers were carried and they were carefully positioned. The PoWs were provided with newspapers, magazines, cushions, blankets and special rations to prevent air sickness. Sometimes bands played as they landed and WAAFs swamped them with tea and cakes. Transit camps were set up near airfields where they had a bath, a shave, a haircut and were kitted out. They were also given cigarettes, a railway warrant and £5 in cash before they moved on.

By the end of April 1945 Lancasters were largely redundant from their primary role - the destruction of the German war machine. They were assigned other tasks, such as the dropping of food supplies to the Dutch and giving ground personnel Cook's Tours of the damaged areas of what had been the Third Reich. A further task that many Lancaster squadrons were given and which also gave them great satisfaction, was the repatriation of former PoWs. In theory, the transporting of ex-PoWs (and returning soldiers of the Eighth Army) appeared a simple operation. In practice, it was nowhere near so simple. The airfields in France and Germany that were to be used for evacuating the men had earlier been frequent targets for Allied aircraft; they were often in a very poor state. Those airfields that Bomber Command and the US Eighth Air Force had not made inoperable were subjected to some very thorough demolitions by the retreating Germans. It was also found that even when runways were repaired, the surfaces quickly became worn out again with the traffic of heavy aircraft and there were a number of minor landing accidents. Servicing aircraft were despatched to deal with these, but there were not always adequate stocks of spare parts. At Juvincourt, a desperate shortage of wheels led to an urgent call to the UK to supply 24 of them. Within a couple of hours of the arrival of the wheels, 20 had been used!

A further problem was deciding how many men could safely be carried in each aircraft. On 9 May (the day after VE-Day) Lancaster RF230 on 514 Squadron took off from Juvincourt with 25 passengers and a crew of six; it soon radioed that an emergency landing was necessary. It seems that the passengers were mainly positioned to the rear of the aircraft, which upset the flying trim and caused the pilot to lose control. In the crash that followed at Roye-Ami all aboard lost their lives. Subsequently a strict drill was evolved ensuring that no more than 24 passengers were carried, that they were positioned most carefully and that they remained in these allotted positions. Apart from the tragic Roye-Ami crash, about 74,000 ex-PoWs were brought safely back to Blighty by 28 May when the final evacuation was carried out.

Everything was done that could be done under these circumstances for the comfort of the repatriated men. They were provided with newspapers, magazines, Mae Wests, cushions, blankets and special rations to prevent air sickness. Bands played at the English airfields as aircraft landed and volunteer WAAFs served the men with tea and cakes. It was reported that at one airfield the men consumed 15,000 cups of tea and half a ton of cake!

The transporting aircraft were not all Lancasters – many Stirlings shared in the task. A most important part was played by the Dakotas of 46 Group, which also did intermediate ferrying of personnel as well as flights to the UK. An RAF observer who made several trips with 46 Group, reported: 'The enthusiasm for the task which aircrews displayed is understandable to anyone who has seen a crowd of ex-PoWs on a German airfield waiting for a plane to take them to England. They stand in patient groups, but inwardly they are sick with excitement.

'You realise, when you talk with them, that in their hearts they have built up a picture of home that, as the months of separation have grown, has got more and more beautiful and noble and unreal. When the aircraft are sighted, the men throw off all pretence of patience. They pick up their kit, start to move forward - until the officer in charge tells them to 'take it easy'. But now their faces are wreathed in smiles and they grow voluble - but keeping one ear cocked for their name in the roll call of passengers.'

This same observer was to comment how his pilot was almost in tears when it was evident that 20-30 men were not going to be able to get on the last flight that night.

Other than those affecting safety, there were no hard and fast rules which might have delayed a PoW's return. Thousands were picked up on airfields to which they had hitchhiked and if there was an aircraft available they were flown directly home. These often arrived in England in the same sorry state in which they had left the PoW camp, but on arrival in England a well organised procedure was followed which provided for their immediate needs and which looked after them until they could go home. Transit camps were set up near airfields where men could rest, feed and receive medical attention. They could get a bath, a shave and a haircut, get an issue of kit and clothing (including a Red Cross bag that had a safety razor, shaving brush, soap, toothbrush and bars of vitamin-enriched chocolate) and most likely have the welcome help of the WVS at sewing on badges on newly issued uniform. The repatriated serviceman was also given cigarettes (there were no health warnings then on the packets!), a railway warrant home and £5 cash (or a sum as an advance against pay).

Most of the RAF former PoWs went through No 106 Personnel Receiving Centre at RAF Cosford. There were 9,374 from the European theatre of war who went through this process (3,371 were to follow from the Far East later). It was not uncommon to have a 1,000 a day arrive and 1,500 came on some peak days - this for a centre originally designed to deal with 250 arrivals per day!

The time between liberation and arrival at a UK reception centre in England varied between seven and ten days, but some made it in less than three! John Ivelaw-Chapman's book [139] about his father (who as an Air Commodore was the highest ranking RAF PoW) quotes from his father's notes:

'In April 1945 after having been a Prisoner of War for close on a year, I was liberated by American Forces who overran the particular PoW Camp near Nuremburg where I had been for the past month. I got hold of a US Major and told him that I would like to get back to England pretty quickly. 'That's OK, Buddy' he told me, 'I'll get you transportation to a repatriation unit and you'll be back home within ten days or a fortnight.' That was not my idea at all and I explained to him that despite the semi-civilian kit that I was wearing at the time, I was in fact an Air Commodore and I persuaded him to give me a Jeep to the nearest airstrip. Here I asked a US Colonel whether he had anything going to England that day. 'No,' he answered, 'but I've got a DC3 coming in this afternoon. It's not going straight to England. Would you mind going via Paris?' Would I mind a night in Paris after a year 'In the Bag', I ask you!'

The experiences of an Air Commodore being repatriated are clearly exceptional, but it is a story that in several respects conveys the atmosphere of those days.

Footnotes Chapter 23

139 *High Endeavour,* published by Leo Cooper.

Chapter 24

Lincoln Legacy

Crews had no difficulty in converting to the Lincoln because it was an aircraft that had no vices and was a pleasure to handle, but it was understandable that pilots who had extensive experience of the Lancaster were unwilling to concede it pride of place to any other aircraft, even a bigger and better Avro machine. The sincerest tribute I can pay the Lincoln, after having such a tried and tested friend in the Lancaster, is to quote the squadron motto: 'Corpus non Animum Muto' (I Change My Body Not My Spirit). The bomb aimer had the luxury of a seat in the new faceted nose compartment. The aircraft had white painted upper surfaces to act as a heat reflector when used in the tropics and underneath was painted black. Ground crews regarded the Lincoln with affection from the point of view of servicing and maintenance because the aircraft was a definite improvement on the Lancaster; the motor cooling side sections were hinged to fall down and provide servicing platforms.'

Flight Lieutenant Frank Jones, commander of the Lincoln Flight at East Kirkby and Scampton, early September 1945 to January 1946.

In 1943 future plans to bring the Pacific War to a successful conclusion rested on an Allied onslaught against the Japanese mainland by long range bombers. Britain's contribution would be 'Tiger Force' and a special long range version of the Avro Lancaster seemed the ideal weapon for its arsenal. Chief Designer Roy Chadwick and his team working to Specification on B.14/43, evolved the Avro 694, or Lancaster Mk.IV, with four 1,750hp Packard-built Merlin 68As Chadwick's improvements had resulted in a much larger aircraft than the Lancaster with span increased by 18 feet to 120 feet and a much longer fuselage, at 78 feet 3½ inches, almost 9 feet longer than the Lancaster. The bomb bay could carry a 14,000lb bomb load. Little of the original Lancaster remained and so the B.Mk.IV Lancaster became a completely new aircraft, the Lincoln Mk.I. On 9 June 1944 PW925, the Lincoln prototype, was flown by Captain H. A. Brown at Ringway. Provision was made for heavier armament on the B.Mk.I production aircraft. Boulton Paul nose and tail turrets and the Bristol Type 17 Mk.II dorsal turret each carried two .5 Browning machine guns. Another design, the Lancaster B.Mk.V, became the Lincoln B.Mk.II RE289, the Lincoln B.Mk.II prototype, had four 1,750 hp Packard-built Merlins and revised armament. A dorsal turret now contained two 20 mm Hispano cannon, while a ventral position containing a .5 Browning was added and twin .5s in the nose were controlled remotely by the bomb aimer. The Lincoln III was to have been a maritime reconnaissance version and finally emerged as the Shackleton MR.I. On 23 August 1945 57 at East Kirkby became the first RAF squadron to receive the Lincoln. Following the dropping by US B-29s of atomic bombs on Hiroshima and Nagasaki, on 3 and 6 August, Japan surrendered on 15 August and there was no need for 'Tiger Force'.

On 24 April 1946 Avro's 168th and final Lincoln rolled off the production line. Up until 1955 Lincoln squadrons made annual Exercise 'Sunray' flights to the Middle East. The major post-war communist threat manifested itself in Malaya (now Malaysia). In 1945 the defeat of Japan created a power vacuum in the Far East which the emerging communist factions were quick to exploit. When the Malayan People's Anti-Japanese Army (MPAJA) was disbanded in December 1945 and told to hand in all weapons, some 4,000 refused and took their weapons into hiding. In June 1948 emergency Regulations were passed and the guerrillas were forced into the jungle where a vicious confrontation broke out between the British and Malayan Security Forces and Chin Peng's MRLA (Malayan Races' Liberation Army).

Operation 'Firedog' - the air war against the CTS (Communist Terrorists) during the Malayan Emergency - began in earnest in July 1948 with the formation of an RAF Task Force at Kuala Lumpur. Reinforcements, notably Lincolns from the UK were sent to Malaya and Singapore on detachment. The first to arrive were Lincolns on 57 Squadron. On 15 March 1950, at a time when Chin Peng's forces were slowly winning the war against the Security Forces, eight Lincolns on 57 Squadron arrived at Tengah from Waddington for operations against terrorists in Negri Sembilan. 57's Lincolns were relieved in July by 100 Squadron. In December 1950 these were replaced by Lincolns on 61 and 148 Squadrons, the latter having converted from the Lancaster at Upwood in February 1950. The Lincoln seemed ideal for the task of bombing CT hide-outs in the jungle but while five Lincolns could effectively drop 70 1,000lb bombs on a jungle strongpoint the guerrillas had by now split into much smaller and more mobile units and were almost impossible to hit by 'conventional' bombing. One operation, in the Ipoh region between July and November 1954 involving Lincolns, 22 SAS and four infantry battalions, accounted for only 15 terrorists killed. From 1950 to 1958 eight Lincoln Mk.30s of 1 Squadron RAAF at Tengah dropped 17,500 tons of bombs but killed only 16 CTs and destroyed barely 30 camps. There were successes. On 13 May 1957 an operation by the RAAF Lincolns near Seremban killed a notorious Communist leader known as 'Ten Foot Long' and four of his followers. The Malaya Emergency officially ended in August 1960 and Operation 'Firedog' ended in October.

Meanwhile, in October 1952 Britain sent RAF squadrons and troop reinforcements from Egypt to Kenya to put down insurrection by Mau Mau terrorists. The Mau Mau were a secret society among the Kikuyu tribe. In November 1953 part of 49 Squadron was detached to Shallufa, Egypt and part to Eastleigh (Nairobi) Airport, Kenya. Both elements were reunited at Eastleigh late in November and remained there until January 1954 when a 100 Squadron detachment began three months of operations. In March 1954 a detachment of Lincolns on 61 Squadron arrived at Eastleigh and these bombers made repeated strikes on the Mau Mau until June that same year. Another Lincoln squadron which saw action in Kenya in 1954 was 214 Squadron, which had received Lincolns in 1950.

Wing Commander Alan Newitt DFC who commanded 49 Squadron from 1 April 1953 to 1 May 1956 recalled that on 26 December 1954 he had been briefed to bomb a Mau Mau hide on Mount Kenya which had been designated a prohibited area for the duration of the emergency. 'It was an unusual assignment in so far as the terrorists were operating in and around Nairobi and the surrounding British farming community, although it was known that one or more Mau Mau gangs were hidden up in the forests covered slopes of Mount Kenya. Intelligence reported that several detachments of the Royal Iniskilling Fusiliers, one of which was commanded by Major Terry Troy (subsequently Brigadier T. M. Troy CBE), a native of Jersey, were on patrol in the area. As the exact positions of the detachments were not known, we were warned not to drop any bombs above an altitude of 13,000 feet as the patrols would be above that height on surveillance missions.

The flight was a routine affair. We located the hide and dropped a string of bombs across the target where there were obvious signs of recent activity in the forest. Major Troy, from his vantage point, was able to observe the whole operations below him, little suspecting that the pilot of the aircraft was an old school pal and also a native of Jersey. The sequel to the bombing was to cause some discomfort to him and his soldiers, but that is best described by the Brigadier in his own words.

'In addition to the patrols mentioned above, a large number of ambushes had been laid astride game tracks, outside the bombing area, in the hope of catching terrorists fleeing from the bombing. In the event, the soldiers lying in wait were suddenly and frighteningly faced by very enraged wild animals charging down the game tracks as they fled from the bombing. Impressed as they were by the accuracy of the RAF bombing, the soldiers' language, as they hurled themselves off the tracks and deep into the surrounding undergrowth, was highly expressive.'

'Sadly, it has to be admitted that there were many animal casualties from the bombing but the rumour is quite unfounded that our agile Brigadier was last seen shinning up a tree faster than the first rhino which came thundering up the track.'

Apart from the 168 Lincolns built by Avros at Manchester and Yeadon, a further 281 were built by Armstrong Whitworth and another 79 by Metropolitan-Vickers, bringing total production in the UK to 528. Although few in number compared to the heady days of the Lancaster, the Lincoln equipped no less than 21 squadrons in Bomber Command, as well as three squadrons in 90 Group. On 25 May 1951 101 Squadron became the first squadron to receive the Canberra B.2 and traded in its Lincolns. In January 1952 617 also converted to the Canberra. 138 disbanded on 1 September 1950 and reformed on 1 January 1955 as the first V-bomber squadron on the Vickers Valiant. In July 1951 199 Squadron, which had played a key role in 100 (Bomber Support) Group in WW2, flying RCM operations, had reformed at the Central Signals Establishment, Watton and was equipped with Lincoln and Mosquito

NF.36 aircraft, which were operated in the RCM role until late in 1957 when the unit was re equipped with Valiants. 214 Squadron disbanded on 30 December 1954 and reformed in 1956 as part of the V-force. The last Lincolns in service were operated by 151 Squadron in Signals Command at Watton, Norfolk until they were finally withdrawn in March 1963.

The valuable role played by the Avro Lincoln in Malaya and Kenya is often overlooked. They also held the line in Bomber Command for ten years before pilots swapped the unpressurised and noisy cockpits on these piston-engined bombers for modern flight decks in the V-Force.

Index